VERNACULAR
VOICES

Studies in Rhetoric/Communication
Thomas W. Benson, Series Editor

VERNACULAR VOICES

The Rhetoric of Publics and Public Spheres

Gerard A. Hauser

New Foreword by Phaedra C. Pezzullo

THE UNIVERSITY OF
SOUTH CAROLINA PRESS

Hardcover edition published by the University of South Carolina Press, 1999
Paperback original edition published by the University of South Carolina
Press, 2008
Paperback and ebook editions published in Columbia, South Carolina,
by the University of South Carolina Press, 2022

www.uscpress.com

Manufactured in the United States of America

31 30 29 28 27 26 25 24 23 22
10 9 8 7 6 5 4 3 2 1

Library of Congress Cataloging-in-Publication Data
can be found at http://catalog.loc.gov/.

ISBN 978-1-64336-285-4 (paperback)
ISBN 978-1-64336-286-1 (ebook)

To Jean Marie

CONTENTS

Contents

TABLES

FOREWORD

During a conference on *Human Rights Rhetoric* in 2010, I met Jerry Hauser in an elevator. I was an associate professor, traveling with my partner and ten-month-old child to give an invited plenary talk. I don't remember what exactly I blurted out or who was carrying the diaper bag—or the baby. I do recall I spoke up to share how his previous work had been such a profound influence on my understanding of rhetoric when I was in graduate school. I also remember he was gracious, able to recognize me as a scholar and a parent at a time when both felt like they were incredibly awkward to balance. In retrospect, approaching him in a liminal, moving space in a time in between the officially planned events might have been the most appropriate way to meet the author of *Vernacular Voices*, a book that honors such permeable boundaries as potentially vital to public life.

For those of us who write and teach about human rights, rhetoric, publics, and public relations, *Vernacular Voices* signaled a significant set of turns when it was first published in 1999 that remain palpable to this day. Although the book won the 2000 Marie Hochmuth Nicholas Book award from the National Communication Association and received due attention in book reviews, the book was not received without controversy. Criticism was expressed by those who found the decentering of elite norms (of studying rationally framed arguments and texts of US and European elites) unnerving, as well as those that hoped such an intervention might have steered us even farther away from presidential politics and Eurocentric theory. Yet, Hauser himself never claimed *Vernacular Voices* was the final word, emphasized further in his next book, *Prisoners of Conscious: Moral Vernaculars of Political Agency* (2012), which explores linguistic and nonlinguistic acts of resistance to foster human rights for people who are incarcerated in a range of contexts in the Global North and Global South.

All the political contexts of *Vernacular Voices* have changed since the book's initial publication, which I will not attempt to recount here. Instead, I want to reflect on how *Vernacular Voices* offers a pivotal step, stretching interdisciplinary and international curiosity for those of us invested in how everyday people perform agency with the potential to move our collective lives. This work has been cited in more fields than I care to mention, from the medical humanities to public relations. Briefly, I turn to some of its most notable theoretical, methodological, and political contributions.

Vernacular Voices, as noted at the time, was written in part as a response to the growing hegemonic assumptions of public opinion polling's survey techniques and quantification as unquestioned indicators of people's political beliefs. Since the 2016 US presidential election polling failures to predict the outcome, however, perhaps more people are open to critically thinking about public opinion polling. Public opinion polls are a useful tool to measure what people are willing and able to admit; they are not as helpful at recognizing what people might be embarrassed to share or unable to acknowledge. They also miss more emergent embodied performances of public opinion and the significant role of public emotions. This argument feels less controversial to acknowledge today, though many still believe invocations of polling data are signs of taken-for-granted "facts" rather than rhetorical interpretations of public culture.

Vernacular Voices builds off Turkish-American philosopher, political scientist, and law professor Seyla Benhabib's argument that publics should be imagined not as a singular space but as a plurality of networked publics. It also is influenced by European American political theorist Nancy Fraser's argument of the importance of actually lived transnational democracies, in which counterpublics serve as subaltern theaters to rehearse public opinions to then be performed more widely. Compelled by those arguments, Hauser theorizes public spheres as engaged *pathos* (emotion), predicated on a communication ecology of a common world with a varied notion of the public good, one developed through a diverse network of associations, media platforms, and desires. European American public policy, public sphere, and rhetorical scholar Robert Asen often cites *Vernacular Voices* for its deliberate and nuanced articulation of a "reticulate structure." These multiple arenas, Hauser reminds us, exceed elite centers of power and official archives, as well as political differences and national boundaries, to include a polyphony of multiple, overlapping, contested, dynamic, and affective engagement. As such, Asen and others—perhaps most notably the collection *Rhetorical Citizenship and Public Deliberation* by University of Copenhagen rhetorical scholars Christian Kock and Lisa S. Villadsen—have since theorized the significance of imagining citizenship itself as constituted through discourse.

Since its publication, *Vernacular Voices* has catalyzed a fundamental shift in the study of the public sphere from singular to plural, from idealized to actual, and from public speeches of elites to embodied public performances of everyday people. In turn, this work has inspired and continues to provoke more accurate and more engaged approaches to studying the ways people try to shape the governing of our collective lives throughout the world. Although I have never focused on "vernacular" as a key term, its legacy remains apparent in cutting-edge research that extends Hauser's arguments about the value of everyday discourse in novel and compelling ways. Consider, for example, Indian American law and rhetorical studies professor Anjali Vats's formulation of a "decolonial vernacular" to critique Western commodification of yoga through racialized intellectual property and human rights regimes. As another exemplar among many, European American communication, rhetoric of science, and digital humanities professor Michelle Gibbons articulates a "cognitive vernacular" to refer to everyday discourse about popularized psychological and neuroscientific ideas that are mobilized to cast and mitigate blame for a teenage heroin ring in the United States.

This grounded and process-oriented approach to publics advocated for a wide range of possibilities for sites of research that direct attention to performances of political engagement. *Vernacular Voices* goads us to better understand contentious matters through lived experiences of everyday people. Rather than focusing on the primacy of texts and rational deliberation, which was the norm in rhetorical studies at the time, Hauser examines key voices involved in four controversial, transnational case studies. Throughout, he encourages us to recognize how understanding publics rhetorically means appreciating how public ideas, feelings, and communities emerge or are deterred.

Since its publication, *Vernacular Voices* has been cited in work justifying the methodological need to study a wider range of artifacts and activities that embody the art of rhetorical invention. Extending Hauser's work, examples of those embodied performances that actively raise publicity for people who are oppressed include revealing how people who are unhoused may be marginalized in democratic life (voting, planning, etc.) based on a lack of a permanent address; denaturalizing the banality workers at a US nuclear power plant felt about everyday disasters through the perspective of those who had moved out of town; challenging the toxic patterns of transnational corporations through advocacy tours; engaging multiple critiques across political perspectives of the Roman Catholic Church's lack of accountability for its sexual-abuse scandal; fostering community at South Korean candlelight vigils that critiqued the US military; negotiating Venezuelan postcolonial collective memory against a tyrant; and much, much more. In each context, as Hauser had argued, what makes certain perspectives believable or not is negotiated through communities engaging each other through shared symbols, which are contextually interpreted through a deep appreciation of local cultural values, norms, feelings, and patterns of awareness.

To consider a contemporary political insight that draws on the ones highlighted in *Vernacular Voices,* the representative democracy of Malaysia, which, like the United States, has created the conditions of possibility for multiple political controversies over human rights abuses. Universiti Putra Malaysian Modern Language and Communication professors Mei-Yuit Chan, Shameem Rafik-Galea, and Ngee-Thai Yap draw upon *Vernacular Voices* to argue that online friendship interactions among youth have enabled increased participation in what the common good of public life might become. By focusing solely on texts by elite decision makers, one might miss how public opinion is being negotiated as part of our everyday lives. Chan, Rafik-Galea, and Yap argue that these dispersed interactions are informal, interactive, and significant vernacular dialogues. They conclude that these contemporary, fragmented, digital communities are vital to navigating mechanisms of control and building consequential social networks for those who might be otherwise disenfranchised to participate in deliberating matters of public consequence, including racism, freedom of speech, children with special needs, and men's rights.

As we wrote together in the afterword to *Field Rhetoric*, Hauser's (and my own) desire to engage politics as a dynamic, embodied, and consequential process of practicing, sharing, negotiating, revising, and challenging public opinions is not, in a sense, new as much as it is a recovery of perennial ancient notions of rhetoric. These values, however, became lost in the mid–twentieth-century fetishization of Great White, Thin, Heterosexual, Rich Christian Men Making Great Speeches. *Vernacular Voices* is a testament to Hauser's long-standing commitment to the grounded, messy work of researching public opinion in democratic life; how we might improve our capacity to listen to underheard voices in often overlooked spaces; and the ways we might be moved toward greater cooperation across our differences throughout the world.

Five years after meeting, I was hired by the University of Colorado Boulder to work in the department where Hauser recently had retired. Although my work focuses on publics in relation to environmental communication (particularly environmental and climate justice), Hauser always has made time to meet me for breakfast at a local restaurant to talk, whether about professional challenges, travel stories, or our mutual research interests. Conversations with him are a gift: he is a captivating storyteller, and one of the best listeners I have ever met. He also seems to have found what his Greek ancestors might have called εὐδαιμονία (often translated as "eudaimonia"), or how to live a fulfilling and meaningful life through valuing not only the cultivation of worthwhile research but also through considering how he lives his life—with good food, wine, conversations, walks, and family—as important to his own ability to flourish. That is, he attempts to live the virtues he professes. While none of us are perfect, this path to value the life he is living feels strikingly deliberate for Hauser. As his former advisee Chris Ingraham observes in the acknowledgments of his first book, *Gestures of Concern*, Jerry is a true paragon.

Since *Vernacular Voices* was published, Hauser solidified his role as a leading figure of rhetoric, including not only his well-documented research and teaching but also his service as editor of *Rhetoric and Philosophy* (2003–2017, where his beloved wife for whom this book originally was dedicated served as managing editor for years); executive director of Rhetoric Society of America (2014–2020); chair of the Boulder Faculty Assembly (2005–2007); and teacher (including directing forty doctoral dissertations, nineteen master's theses, and thirteen undergraduate honors theses). For years past retirement, Hauser has continued to host a departmental dissertation writing group at his home, visit classrooms for guest lectures, and provide sage counsel to hundreds of faculty as a confidential conflict coach and mediator on campus. As an informal mentor within and beyond those spaces, he has spent countless hours dedicated to the underappreciated labor required to build opportunities for informal and formal academic community building.

That University of South Carolina Press approached Hauser to rerelease *Vernacular Voices* over two decades after its initial publication because it still is in demand is an indicator of its enduring impact (most academic monographs don't have sales after twenty years) and still unwritten possibilities to helping us more fully appreciate the wide range of activities that are required to shape our collective lives. For those of us that share Hauser's hope of creating more viable ways of living for all, we know democratic ideals have not ended war, violence, oppression, or our perishability. Nevertheless, as *Vernacular Voices* reminds us, striving toward freedom requires us to create opportunities for dialogue about shared interests wherever and with whomever we can.

Phaedra C. Pezzullo
Boulder, Colorado
August 4, 2021

SERIES EDITOR'S PREFACE

In this comprehensive and energetic book, Gerard Hauser argues that contemporary media have encouraged us to think of "the public" as an aggregate of polling data. Hauser offers a contrasting vision of the public, recovered from the rhetorical tradition, which conceives of public opinion as emergent in democratic discourse and properly found in that discourse. Hauser describes vernacular public discourse not only as expressing but also as constantly creating, regulating, and fine tuning public opinion through a process in which we cultivate and maintain a sense of ourselves in dialogue. Through this vernacular discourse we create public opinion about particular issues and at the same time, in a side effect not merely incidental, we create and sustain our conceptions of identity and community. Hauser serves as our critical guide through the history and theory of how discourse is related to public opinion from Athens to the present. In his early chapters, Hauser sets forth in historical context a critical examination of the theory of publics and public discourse. In these chapters, working both as a critical historian of rhetorical theory and as an original rhetorical theorist in his own right, Hauser surveys and analyzes the theory of the public and introduces his own depiction of a plurality of publics that come into being in a variety of places in what Hauser calls a reticulate public sphere, in which participants are engaged in multiple, local, interactive webs of meaning and commitment that arise through discourse. In this reticulate public sphere, competing with the powerful notions of expert knowledge and universal ideals, vernacular rhetorics engage strangers in mutual talk to develop public opinion.

In a series of case studies, Hauser tests his theory of publics against the empirical detail of complex historical events. In these chapters, we explore the contrasting rhetorical experiences of postcommunist Poland and Yugoslavia, the report of the Meese commission on pornography as both a theory of the public and an attempt to influence public opinion, the Carter administration's attempt to conceive and shape public opinion in the Iranian hostage crisis, and the public's letters to Franklin Delano Roosevelt about his speeches during his campaign for a third term in 1940.

In this lucid and comprehensive book, Jerry Hauser has written a work that fundamentally redirects our thinking about rhetoric and publics and provides a model of how to create a dialogue between rhetorical theory and rhetorical criticism. *Vernacular Voices: The Rhetoric of Publics and Public Spheres* is a welcome addition to the series in Rhetoric/Communication of the University of South Carolina Press.

Thomas W. Benson
Series Editor

PREFACE 2022

The impulse for *Vernacular Voices* arose from a failed classroom assignment. My students were to analyze Lincoln's "Cooper Union Address." Alas, they missed the tensions between Lincoln's refutation of the argument that America's founders supported slavery, his defense against Southern allegations about Republican intents, and his counsel that Republicans accept slavery where it existed but oppose its spread. By taking on the South, Lincoln made himself both a serious contender for the Republican presidential nomination and anathema to the slave states. Apparently, I looked crestfallen over my charges' lack of enthusiasm for the speech because, as they were filing out, one of them stopped to offer consolation. "It's not your fault Doc," he said, "we just aren't excited by public debates." For this teacher of rhetoric, it was a body blow. On reflection, it also brought me to awareness that the discipline of rhetoric had a significant body of scholarship on public address with an emphasis on "address" and very little on "public." *Vernacular Voices* reflects my search for the nature, function, and scope of "publicness." Specifically, I was after the place of publics, public spheres, and public opinion in a democratic republic, and the place of rhetoric—I argue it is central—in their formation.

My research was animated by the creative ways publics emerge, which are specific and concrete: form around issues, contest them, and express opinions. These expressions are seldom those of rational argument. Politics begin with desire, and desires are tied to our attachments, such as the welfare of our children, safety of our communities, opportunity to pursue our economic well-being, freedom to speak and act with integrity, need to safeguard the air we breathe and the water we drink, or protection against exploitation by elites. They are often expressed in ways other than words—by our vote, but also our purchasing power, our manner of gathering and dissenting, our displays of affiliation (such as flags, clothing, and bumper stickers), and certainly our bodies. Moreover, as vernacular expressions, they are tied to the local, such as the neighborhood, community, region, nation, or culture. They are not always understood from the outside, and frequently circulate via hidden transcripts among those possessing vernacular literacy. These are expressions by ordinary citizens that decenter the voices of power, albeit not with immunity from manipulation by powerful voices and not always enlightened or beneficent expressions. As an undergraduate student once observed during class discussion: "Sometimes people say and do ignorant or dangerous things; that's the price we pay for living in a democracy."

In the two decades since *Vernacular Voices* was published, a great deal has changed. Three are deserving of note because they bear directly on the resilience of the theory it advances. First, the United States was attacked by Al Qaeda terrorists, which not only led to the longest war in US history but also the emergence of the unitary executive theory to validate whatever President Bush ordered in its prosecution. This theory, which assigns the president unilateral power to act, has troubling implications. It undermines the checks and balances of powers imbedded in the US Constitution, as was witnessed in the United States when President Trump bypassed the congressional appropriation process to use military funds to build a wall on the southern border. It also fuels deeply partisan divides, such as the meaning of Black Lives Matter and police conduct following the murder of George Floyd. Combined, these threaten democracy by supporting autocratic tendencies by a head of state, while reducing publics to tribal demographics and thereby weakening their vibrancy.

Second, the internet and new media have blossomed. Cable television has provided a megaphone to views that, earlier, would not have been given airtime because they were considered without factual foundation. Politicians and citizens alike have mastered the use of social media to skirt the press and even political parties to speak directly to citizens, circulate misinformation, and mobilize action. Partisanship is not new to democratic politics, nor are manipulation of facts, preying on fears, nasty attacks on an opponent's character, and stoking violence through prejudice. James Madison anticipated these in *Federalist* no. 10. However, Madison thought such factions would be confined to a locality and short lived. New media deny his surmise. They afford opportunity to create a national or international following and reach it with little, if any, serious check, such as led to the storming of the US Capitol on January 6, 2021, by insurrectionists who were urged to stop Congress from certifying the presidential election of 2020. Are new media facilitating the formation of publics, sculpting pseudo publics, expanding or undermining public spheres, or energizing captive tribes both created by demagoguery and a base which, in turn, holds captive their elected representatives? Does this depend on national context? These are open questions. A rhetorically based theory of publics should give us purchase to explain how new media function and evaluate whether they advance lived democracy.

Finally, the many facets of globalization have raised challenges to the autonomy of nation states and seem to be ushering in a post-Westphalian political order. Neither electronic communication nor globalized corporate interests respects national borders. The movement of money, circulation of power, and empowerment of nonstate actors who can challenge the authority of nation states are 24/7 activities. Some may be abetted and even controlled by nation states—such as Russia or China; others may act of their own accord. Their impacts on trade, labor, economic well-being, human rights, and national security sometimes exceed the capacity of less powerful nations to control their own borders. Equally, many problems that require wise governance exceed national boundaries. The crises posed by climate change and environmental degradation; the threat of terrorists; the human tragedy of political, climate, and economic refugees; and the risk of pandemics are real, shared, and global. Is the rise of nationalistic rhetoric a diversion from seismic shifts of power and emergence of global menaces that threaten survival? Can we preserve the planet without rethinking our interconnectedness in a post-Westphalian world? And what is the place of publics, public spheres, and vernacular voices in such a reimagined order?

My hope is that the ebook reissue of *Vernacular Voices* contributes to the continuing conversation about how we understand publics, how public spheres form and function, and the possibilities for vernacular expressions of public opinion to be consequential on questions, such as the foregoing, that lie at the core of lived democracy.

GAH

ACKNOWLEDGMENTS

The inspiration for this project was born of childhood experiences in a working-class family that was short of neither opinions nor gifts of expression. My extended family taught me that you do not require a university education to be an informed citizen and that you should never forget the realities of the neighborhood in which you were raised. I thank my parents, grandparents, aunts, and uncles for including me in their spirited conversations, expecting me to think before speaking, and treating my opinions seriously.

The specific contents of this project were developed while I was at several different universities and, due to a stint in university administration, over a longer period than anticipated. I am especially indebted to the students in my graduate seminars in publics theory at Penn State University and the University of Colorado for their passion, insight, and intellectual companionship. The faculty of the speech department at Temple University, and most especially Herb Simons, offered helpful criticism and encouragement during my stay with them as a visiting professor. The Institute for the Arts and Humanistic Studies at Penn State provided support for my research at the Franklin D. Roosevelt Library; I am indebted to the archivists of the FDRL for their unfailing assistance and informed suggestions. I have been fortunate to have had deans and a department head who were sympathetic to my project and provided material support to move it forward. Greg Knight and Chuck Middleton made funds available for necessary travel and clerical support. Dennis Gouran made research assistants available to me on several occasions and offered editorial assistance on chapters 4 and 6. I am indebted to Karen Ashcraft, Carole Blair, Chris Guadagnino, Gabrielle King, Sandy Rawlins, Robbin Reese, Susie Ross, and Tom Schlimmer, who served as research assistants. Bob Craig and Susan Whalen have been my interlocutors on this project since its inception. In addition to their comments on an early version of chapter 4, their conversations have helped me to think more critically about my argument. John Bowers, Kathleen Domenig, Tom Farrell, Bruce Gronbeck, and John Nelson read the entire manuscript in draft and offered generous encouragement and tough-minded criticisms from their quite different disciplinary perspectives. Series editor Tom Benson and Rosa Eberly also read the manuscript in its entirety and, in ways that are uniquely their own and make them prized as colleagues and friends, continued our long-standing and rich conversations on rhetoric. My appreciation of these compassionate

Acknowledgments

and discerning readers is matched only by my admiration for the wisdom of their suggestions. I am grateful to Barry Blose, my editor at the University of South Carolina Press, for his sage advice on bringing this project to completion. Finally, Jean Hauser shared the adventures of chapter 4 and has been my companion in the easy conversations through which we made sense of shared public experiences. She also created emotional space in her life for my project and the priority it often took over family life. Her understanding, encouragement, and patience have meant the world to me.

VERNACULAR
VOICES

INTRODUCTION:
FORGOTTEN PUBLICS

E pluribus unum

A democracy is based on the premise that public opinion should matter in deciding the course of society. Yet what counts as such an opinion, how we learn its content, and how it gets represented are anything but certain. To illustrate my point and initiate this discussion, consider the following contrasting images of what such an opinion is and how we discover it.

As the 1992 presidential campaign entered its debate season, the American television networks were overrun by interviews and exchanges with roving pundits, spin doctors, campaign officials, pollers, intellectuals, and members of the political press corps. Press coverage of American presidential campaigns customarily borders on preoccupation with our candidates' strategies, and the networks did not break form as they warmed up for the first TV debate. Two of the more dominant prognostications concerned the traits George Bush, Bill Clinton, and Ross Perot had to project to "win" the debate and the accompanying predictions of how the voters would respond to their debating performances.

Setting aside the issues then facing the nation, which spin doctors had managed to reduce to character smears and finger-pointing, it might have been reasonable to raise questions about the candidates' virtues and how the voters received them. However, given the nebulous connection between the candidates' campaign rhetoric and their visions of where each wished to lead the nation, it was unclear what would be learned from the answers. Instead commentators, reporters, and pollers felt the successful candidate had to demonstrate something other than the political efficacy of his proposed national agenda over the next four years; he had to inspire confidence.

In an interview on the *Today* program, political poller and consultant Bert Decker informed NBC's Katie Couric what "inspiring confidence" meant. According to Decker the successful candidate had to be believed to be heard: "The whole thing is trust and credibility." For Decker, these traits were the antithesis of an Aristotelian ethos established by habits of thought and character displayed in the debate. They came from nuances of delivery, gesture, and style; humor, enthusiasm,

1

fluency, and a warm smile were more important than solid analysis for inspiring confidence in the candidate's qualifications to lead.

> DECKER: If you don't reach people emotionally so that they
> believe you, and that's done at the unconscious level, . . .
> then you're not going to get your facts and figures across.
> COURIC: So it's not so much what you say but how you say it
> and how you look when you say it.
> DECKER: That's right.

Decker was not alone in the belief that smiling and not stumbling over words are more important for impressing voters than advancing sensible proposals. Presidential historian Michael Bescheloss, a respected scholar, appearing on CNN's *Newsmaker Sunday,* instructed host Frank Sesno that modern audiences are more likely to remember "tone" and "feeling" projected by each candidate than that candidate's discussion of the issues. Topics such as the economy, the subject of 1992's first presidential debate, were too complex. Candidates could not make sense of their positions in the allotted time. Consequently, Bescheloss observed, "winning" or "losing" depended on the personal impression the candidate would make with the viewers.

Immediately following this observation Sesno introduced fellow correspondent Bill Schneider, who explained that CNN would nonetheless do its part to "tap"—literally, as it turned out—public reactions to the debate. On the night of the first debate a panel of viewers located across the country was to be connected via telephone to a computer in Omaha. As they listened to the candidates, each was to tap appropriate keys on his or her touch-tone phone to register a positive or negative reaction to what was being heard. The computer-results then would be transmitted to CNN in Atlanta where graphs would visually display the changing reception each candidate received as the debate progressed. These graphs would provide evidence of public opinion to be discussed subsequently by CNN's political experts. Highlighting the significance of (not to mention their joy over) their technological breakthrough, viewers were promised that the expert discussion of the results would be aired several times.

The image of viewers tap tap tapping their likes and dislikes offers a surreal depiction of progress. CNN's coverage raises the possibility of technology graphically tracking the postmodern condition of meaning's instability at the very instant it destabilizes! Without opportunities to discuss or even reflect on what was being heard, and without any indication of what, in particular, might have formed the basis for endorsement or rejection of what had been heard, CNN's model replaced discourse with raw response. Through the wizardry of technology responses were syn-

2

thesized as *public opinion* that was graphically and dynamically televised into viewers' homes as an instantaneous technological assemblage.

Now consider a second, alternative representation for detecting public opinion drawn from an interview of public intellectuals concerning then current political developments in Europe. This representation may be less familiar to the average person in that it is developed in the style of academe, although it should not be totally strange since it portrays a practice most of us engage in daily. In 1994 the *New York Review of Books* published a discussion between Polish activist Adam Michnik and German critical theorist Jürgen Habermas on the changes that had occurred to Europe's political map since 1989. At one point in the exchange Michnik and Habermas questioned how to interpret problematic waves of German public sentiment—for example, the fact that after initial widespread support for liberation from communist rule, a rash of right-wing attacks inflicted physical abuse and arson on nonindigenous segments of German society. Habermas allowed that under successive rallying cries of "We are the people" that led to the dismantling of the Berlin Wall, followed three weeks later by "We are one people," which led to support for the reunification of Germany, the emergence of right-wing terrorism in the former German Democratic Republic (G.D.R.) was understandable. He continued:

> What I find much harder to understand is why the arson attacks [on foreigners] should have spread so contagiously to West Germany. After all, conditions there had not changed. So what happened was that the *flood-gates of public opinion* must have opened and changed the general climate to the point where stereotypes and opinions that had lurked beneath the surface and affected, let's say, 15 percent of the public, now suddenly burst forth and acquired a completely different status (Habermas 1994, 24; emphasis added).

Habermas's reference to "the public" and "public opinion" jostles our understanding of these ideas from their now common meaning illustrated by the preceding example. Usually these terms refer to sample populations and survey research results. However, in the context of his remarks their meaning takes a different twist. Habermas uses "public opinion" to refer to significantly shared understandings that indicate and even sanction appropriate actions. It is a shared awareness by an active segment of society, a "public," sensitized to and influential on a "general climate," an aura of attitude and belief, if you will, that invites certain perceptions and expressions to the surface while offering menacing signals to keep others under wraps.

Habermas's surprise at an unexpected turn in public behavior reflects his own interpretation of his society that, undoubtedly, is conditioned by his scholarly training. However, his act is not unique to scholars nor is his surprise an indication of uncertainties unique to postunification West German politics. Rather he mirrors the average person's everyday practice to determine the tenor and direction of prevailing values and beliefs. This also is a method for inferring public opinion, although different than that used with the "tappers" since it infers public opinion from social discourse.

Perhaps it is symptomatic of how we now understand public opinion that we seldom hear of surveilling discursive modes to discover public opinion; conventional wisdom advises us, instead, to check the polls. At least that is the message promulgated by politicians and the press, whose discussions of public opinion in our public forums give scant attention to alternative means for discovering and communicating public opinion. This is not to say that polls are uninformative. When well done they tell us a great deal; interpreted with intelligence they can be an important aid for shaping policy that serves the public interest. Taken at face value they can be deceiving; weighed alone they offer a limited and sometimes superficial understanding of publics and what they believe.

The average person, on the other hand, without the assistance of a personal opinion poller, must engage in daily acts of surveillance to know where matters stand in the community. We develop our sense of whether beliefs and values are stable or shifting; what is socially safe or dangerous, expected or prohibited; and what different segments of society believe and espouse through participation in a mosaic of mundane social exchanges and observations. We rely on our "social skin" (Noelle-Neumann 1993) to detect tendencies in our daily regime of symbolic exchanges on which we base our personal inferences about public opinion.

When compared to the process of social exchange by which we form and encounter public opinion, CNN's "tappers" are more like a Baudrillardean simulacrum (Baudrillard 1994), a simulation of reality that is treated as if it were authentic. Nevertheless, as remote as these "tappers" seem from the tyranny of opinion James Madison grappled with in *Federalist Paper* number 10, or citizen involvement in the Lincoln-Douglas debates, or even the discursive practices of voters manifested as recently as the 1930s and 1940s, they are consistent with the view of public opinion that currently pervades modern politics and media coverage of it in advanced industrial societies.

A monologue of reports and discussions that derive their understanding about society's activity from opinion polls conditions our consciousness of what the press and politicians refer to as "the public." We encounter this public as a faceless, anonymous body whose members are reduced to the percentage having selected predetermined choices to a poller's questions and who enter our homes as media reports of data. The paradigm of public opinion entailed by CNN's "tappers," along with its implicit devaluing of opinion as a discursive formation, creates the impression of "the public" as an anonymous assemblage given to volatile mood swings likely to dissipate into apathy and from which we personally are disengaged.

This abstract portrayal contributes to our sense of disjunction from the public it reports. Most individuals understand their speaking and writing as personal expression. Few of us are called upon to address an audience, and even fewer do so as a spokesperson for a group or cause. Most of our communication directed at persons or groups has some immediacy, and we know them in some way. We experience our transactions with them in concrete terms as addressed discourse: our own thoughts, our intended message, a specific audience to which we have adapted, and that audience's perceived response. The public portrayed by the media, in contrast, is an abstract representation whose needs, thoughts, and responses are extrapolated from survey data. We do not experience this public; we cannot interact with it, question its reasoning, or expect it to respond to our own reasoning. This public exists as what it is at the moment it is recorded: a snapshot in time reported as accurate within a standard margin of error. Although we supposedly are included in this picture, we seldom experience it as "us" and usually narrate it as "them."

This disjunction also reflects a chronic ambivalence of democracies toward "the public." Democracy posits that broadly based participation in deliberative processes will lead to laws and policies that are more inclusive and more just than measures enacted by monarchs or powerful elites. A workable democracy requires that we trust our neighbors to be reasonable and fair when given the chance. But confrontation between competing interests makes unconditional trust at least difficult and perhaps foolish. Whether in Solon's Athens, Madison's America, or Helmut Kohl's Germany, concern for factions becoming the political majority and then acting in an unbalanced and unjust fashion has always been close to the surface. The striking difference between our age and that of our ancestors lies in our forebears' apparent awareness of participatory venues in which public matters would receive the attention of those whose interests were at stake. Even in moments of misgivings, previous ages have understood "the public" to be more than an aggregate extrapolated from responses to the interrogatory du jour of a news outlet, political party, or special interest. People in earlier eras formed their awareness of personal and group interests in shared problems through active participation in the rhetorical culture of open discussion and debate. These same processes of rhetorical give-and-take provided a basis for intelligent reflection leading to shared beliefs and opinions on matters affecting their lives.

We resemble our ancestors in this respect. Humans could not establish and sustain cultural, political, and social relations without rhetoric, so we engage in and experience rhetorical exchange as frequently as they. Yet while rhetorical exchange abounds, this age differs from previous ones in the ways reflected above by spin doctors and interpreters of CNN's "tappers." The predominance of survey data has replaced conscious attention to and reflection on rhetorical transactions as evidence of "the public's" existence, character, and opinion. The authority granted to opinion polls in discussions and reports on "the public" reflects citizens, commentators, the news media, and scholars desensitized to our own rhetorical practices and their possibilities for shaping our public lives as citizens, neighbors, and cultural agents.

Recalling Habermas's expression of surprise, we should note that he invoked alternative resources to explain what may have led to unanticipated outbursts of violence in West Germany. His explanation rests, in theory, on what lies behind polls—beliefs, values, even stereotypes on which settled conviction about the "good life" rests. These are linked to awareness of being a member of society, of possessing a history, and of a shared understanding of community norms. The *problem* of opinion, for Habermas, was not that public behavior defied polling data, but that it defied an understanding of what it means to be West German. The incidents of arson and assault were difficult to comprehend because they contained, in microcosm, a dimension of public opinion that defied the reading he and others had made of the West German public mind. This dimension suggests an expression of public opinion that requires a different mode of analysis and discussion than is currently dominant. It is a dimension expressed in the ongoing dialogue on public issues among those who belong to a community or a society. It is found by examining their discourse.

The pervasive and informative role of discourse in public life is concretely illustrated by the Habermas-Michnik exchange. Their conversation considers how discursive episodes can instigate and sustain an ongoing dialogue on social meaning while simultaneously entering that dialogue. Habermas's wonderment at arson attacks on foreigners in the Federal Republic and his subsequent conclusion that the "flood-gates of public opinion must have opened" posit a relationship between a social climate and the expression of opinion. Apparently West Germans had a broadly based but undetected subterranean vein of deeply felt bitterness against non-German "outsiders." The public violence of skinheads delivered to those who harbored these private sentiments an unmistakable message that they were not alone. The sensed change in public climate removed the threat to openly expressing these resentments and perhaps even suggested that arson was a legitimate mode for their expression. Skinhead violence was of consequence beyond its status as an act of physical intimidation. Beyond the terror they inflicted on their victims, Germans perceived and interpreted their violence as a symbolic exchange that connected with a broader segment of society and, thus, as expressing a prevailing climate of opinion.

The violent acts of skinheads were interpreted as anti-authoritative expressions that challenged the postwar German aversion to endorse anything reminiscent of the sins of the fathers. Germany, especially the Federal Republic, expended much political and social energy on expiation by renouncing traditional border claims, discrediting nationalism, ratifying a constitutional prohibition against the German army engaging in actions beyond its own borders except for self-defense, and adopting a public rhetoric of atonement for the events of the 1930s and 1940s. But in the summers of 1991 and 1992 skinheads attacked foreign workers in Hoyerswerda and Rostock, both in the former G.D.R. In between and since these attacks, similar acts of right-wing violence had occurred in the Federal Republic. Beyond their overt brutality, these attacks signaled opposition to the assumption that welcoming outsiders best served German interests and questioned the apparent new realities associated with the reunification Germany.

Habermas continues by noting: "It became possible to express views that were previously taboo. This has also affected the situation in West Germany where it created a climate in which xenophobia and anti-Semitism can make their appearance, and what is worse, young people even feel that they are expressing the opinions of a silent majority. I am firmly convinced that these are not the views of the majority but the climate has changed all the same" (1994, 24). By any objective standard, these were criminal acts. But they also were symbolic acts that entered into dialogue with the prevailing language and affirmations of German society. They were a form of persuasion that apparently called to the surface sentiments of an alternative political character and that led to public verbal discourse proclaiming that these sentiments, incredibly, were those of the majority.

Although acts like these violate the moral norms of civilized society, they are nonetheless indicative of the vast and complicated terrain across which social actors converse with assertions, challenges, and invitations to create social meaning. For example, the fact that skinheads committed these acts raises the prospect that they may be an expression of their generation. Certainly the physical appearance of skinheads— young adults with buzzcuts who are partial to wearing black flight jackets and combat boots—speaks a language to German youths that is closer to their own than that of their parents. The fact that they are a right-wing faction places their acts in opposition to the policies of a state that accommodates and even encourages foreigners to immigrate as visiting workers. The fact that there were subsequent xenophobic or anti-Semitic outbreaks indicates that the violence had symbolic value as a form of encouragement to publicly manifest otherwise taboo values and views. And the fact that these youths and their sympathizers believed they were speaking for Germany's silent majority advances the claim that their acts also were expressions of public opinion. As reprehensible and misguided as their terrorism surely was, the skinheads, attending Germans, one of this century's leading intellectuals, and his eminent Polish interlocutor understood them as an influential signal of sentiment inserted into the ongoing dialogue that shapes German society.

In *The Dialogic Imagination* Russian literary theorist Mikhail Bakhtin advances the thesis that meanings are always unfolding through *dialogizing of the word*. By that he means our use of language constantly enters into dialogue with the language used by our interlocutors. By interacting with the meanings of direct conversational partners or indirectly addressed individuals, groups, or even classes of society we also interrogate them. Contact among words, utterances, and whole discourses challenges their self-contained meanings by bringing each into the space between them. These discursive exchanges begin in the individual with a struggle between authoritative discourse and internally persuasive discourse. Authoritative discourse receives its meaning from the fathers, binding us to a meaning already fused with the past and whose authority is already acknowledged. Internally persuasive discourse, by contrast, lacks the privileges and even the acknowledgment of society. It *dialogizes* authoritative discourse to create new possibilities through the interaction and interanimation of meanings that are half ours and half others'. Bakhtin (1981, 324) tells us, "The struggle and dialogical interrelationships of these categories of ideological discourse are what usually determine the history of an individual ideological consciousness."

Working from the word and the internal struggle for meaning, Bakhtin extends his analysis outward to the myriad instabilities of social meaning. Each context provides a space in which the confluence of history, society, psychology, and culture creates a turbulence unlike any that has existed before or will follow. He calls this dialogic agitation "an intense struggle within us for hegemony among various available verbal and ideological points of view, approaches, directions and values. The semantic structure of an internally persuasive discourse is *not finite*, it is *open;* in each of the new contexts that dialogize it, this discourse is able to reveal ever newer *ways to mean*" (Bakhtin 1981, 345; emphasis his).

The reaction of German public opinion to the skinheads' ruthlessness exemplifies the larger capacity of people to read the actions of other individuals and groups as statements of affiliation, preference, rejection, and urgency. These actions by strangers, often performed at a distance, are legible *vernacular* inscriptions that engage us in the internally persuasive dialogue Bakhtin describes. And we should note that in cases such as these even the most brutal and seemingly inarticulate expression of prejudice can take on profound meaning, despite the perversity of its message, when its enactment occurs in a context that provides historical and cultural referents—including the very ethnicity of the victims themselves— as a form of persuasion.

Bakhtin's depiction of dialogizing of the word has particular relevance for deciphering the symbolic transaction embodied in skinheads' targeting of foreigners. It italicizes how they alter the ceaseless conversation of society. The friction among tradition, point of view, social class, and countless other variables that interact in every context contains a surplus of meaning that exceeds what any single speaker might express and remains open to the possibilities for new insights. Moreover, and perhaps going beyond the verbal discourses Bakhtin envisioned, these social conversations often include statements that are nonverbal but perfectly understandable to their participants as vernacular expressions of preference, concern, welcome, or warning, such as beatings and arson directed at an identifiable group, especially one defined as "the other."

The dialogical process also strips Habermas's final comment of its seeming innocence by the conversation it enters with this context and the context of Germany's past. How should we interpret his observation that he does not believe the skinheads speak for the silent majority of Germans? Perhaps it was his informed diagnosis, or his intuition as a native, of the extent of right-wing xenophobia and anti-Semitism in West Germany. Still we cannot overlook Habermas's interjection on skinheads' violence as a response to their own violent comment and subsequent interpretation in the ongoing dialogue about German identity, a dialogue that cannot find exculpation from the residue of the 1930s and 1940s. Having mentioned the skinheads' claim to speak for the silent majority, Habermas cannot then let it stand unchallenged. Conceding that point would leave history's door ajar and suggest the possibility that German atrocities were not an aberration but a deeply etched characteristic in the national spirit. So he must disclaim its validity, profess that their statement is not true, and, because of the meaning it carries, suggest that they offered it merely for political effect, not as a report of political fact.

Then there is the matter of Habermas himself, the leading intellectual of the Frankfurt school, among the leading social critics and theorists of the age. His project has been to execute the Enlightenment's epistemic ideal. Never really repudiating Kant's and Hegel's visions of moral autonomy and practical wisdom achieved through reason (Benhabib 1986, 344), Habermas's theory of communicative action is a monument to this link and forms the basis for his conflict with postmodernism. His lifetime of philosophical reflection and sociological inquiry is challenged by the skinheads' claim because it asserts that the moral features of the past were not an erratic deviation; they remain part of the German identity. The polyvocal dialectic of Habermas speaking the words of the other to establish through their inner dialogue his own self-understanding lurks behind his attempt to discount their claim to speak public opinion.

Michnik also is important here. Habermas offers his remarks in response to Michnik, who in the context of acknowledging an intellectual debt to Habermas managed to call the entire enterprise of German unification into question. Michnik's statement reads: "For many years now my ideas have been influenced by an outstanding essay by Professor Habermas on constitutional patriotism. Today I perceive a certain *ambiguity* in the current German situation. The first phase of German unification brought freedom, but the second witnessed the *pogrom* in Hoyerswerda. In Poland, incidentally, matters are much the same, or could become so" (Habermas 1994, 24; emphasis added). To this Habermas replied, "That's too harsh," followed by the statements noted above.

A rarity in Poland as a native Jew, Michnik has been one of his country's leading dissidents since his university days in the 1960s. The communist regime had incarcerated him on numerous occasions for acts of political opposition, and his writings from prison (1985) are trenchant calls to political consciousness. After playing a leading role in the formation of Solidarity in 1980 and of the new government in 1989, he turned his critical eye on his former colleagues, whom he thought were excessively influenced by the Catholic Church and out of touch with the needs of Polish society. His reference to events in Hoyerswerda as a "pogrom" is a distinctly resonant reminder of the sins of the fathers, since he is the living descendant of their victims.

Michnik reads skinheads' actions as a statement of Germany coming to terms with the crisis of multiculturalism. While he does not aggressively press this as a nationalistic matter, the "ambiguity" he perceives in the current German situation carries moral intimations. The internal context of their interview cannot escape the external historical context of this German intellectual and this dissident Polish Jew whose histories condition their intellectual conversation.

Habermas's quick reply of "That's too harsh" is richly dialogic, and this signal moment in the Michnik-Habermas exchange, when the centrifugal force of expression collides with the centripetal force of context, is of a piece with Habermas's expression of moral certainty that skinheads do not speak for the silent majority of West Germans. He must distance himself from both claims, since both suggest the possibility that the guilt borne for the past fifty years was more than symbolic. Distancing himself from the "harsh" judgment of "ambiguity" borne of "pogroms" and the extravagant claim to speak for a silent majority, Habermas identifies himself, by implication, with the majority of Germans. He speaks *as if* he knows their mind, perhaps is the embodiment of majority opinion. If the skinheads are wrong, then the opposite must be true; the majority must agree with him, and things have not gotten out of hand. The sins of the fathers remain to be confronted, even if dealing with them is to refute their resurrection as a denunciation of the inheritance that burdens him. Moreover, he must say this in the presence of two Poles, the interviewer and the Polish Jew who, by labeling the acts of skinheads a "pogrom," has not only given the sins of the fathers presence but inserted them into the contemporary German context through his very personification of their victims.

This brief portion of the dialogue between Habermas and Michnik is an illustrative microcosm of the dialogue we witness daily in society. Most are not fraught with the subterranean risk to identity in the above exchange, but each is an encounter among the diverse and often disparate levels of consciousness formed by class, religion, region, education, occupation, age, gender, race, ethnicity, physical and mental ability, family status, sexual orientation, and a list of other marks of personal and public selfhood. Our manifold ways of conversing with one another express these elements of diversity and convergence, difference and identity. Mostly these conversations are mundane transactions of words and gestures that allow us to negotiate our way through our quotidian encounters. They are not formal exchanges of the podium; they are vernacular expressions of who we are, what we need and hope for, what we are willing to accept, and our commitment to reciprocity. Yet we also direct these conversations toward our public problems, and they often are the means available to us for "reading" our neighborhood and community, the political and social climate of the polity, and for expressing our beliefs and attitudes on these matters to others. These dialogizing interactions are our continuous means to form shared meaning; discover new cultural, political, and social possibilities; and shape an understanding of our common interests. They are integral to civil society's continuous activity of self-regulation. They are the definitively rhetorical exchanges that confront us with the open possibilities Bakhtin attributes to internally persuasive speech. They are the ways by which publics make their presence known; and, if we were to listen, these are the ways by which they make their opinions felt.

My concern in this book is to explore the discursive dimensions of publics, public spheres, and public opinion. I wish to explore the prospects for recovering awareness of our own discursive practices and their possibilities for shaping our public lives as citizens, neighbors, and cultural agents. I am interested in the insights we may gain into publics, public spheres, and public opinion when we regard discourse as the predominant and authoritative data from which we infer how they form and function. Who is "the public" that ventures opinions on public matters? What are the venues where these opinions appear? How are these venues shaped by prevailing conditions for discourse? How does discourse bear on the way we experience membership in a public? What relevance does membership awareness have for a public's participation in public life? What are the discursive indicators of a public's opinions and beliefs? And what is the role of this mode of public opinion—a mode that, I will argue, is rhetorical in character—in shaping the course of society? These are not novel questions. But previous attempts to answer them, as we will see, often have run amok from overemphasizing a priori ideological and critical biases without taking sufficient account of the questions' empirical character. That is to say, these questions are inquiries into how actual members of actual publics respond to appeals, how they themselves actually engage in discourse that allows us to infer their opinion, and the rhetorical conditions that color their interactions. I hope to provide initial answers to these questions by bringing an empirical attitude to a critical framework. Further, through the observations and reflections that follow, I hope to open a dialogue on the efficacy of a rhetorical framework for critically understanding the way actually existing publics function and for reclaiming our awareness of their contribution to the course and quality of civil society.

My plan for exploring the rhetorical character of publics, the public sphere, and public opinion is to set forth initial theoretical considerations to be followed by their further exploration in critical case studies. The first four chapters explore the rhetorical character of publics, public spheres, and public opinion. They develop an argument for a *plurality of publics* located in the multiple arenas of a *reticulate public sphere* in which strangers develop and express public opinions by engaging one another through *vernacular rhetoric*. Chapter 5 discusses the role of historicity in establishing a society's model of itself. It examines the contrasting models of postcommunist Poland and Yugoslavia to illustrate the way narrative bridges historicity and cultural memory. Chapter 6 explores the way discourse within and across public spheres conditions the possibilities of those spheres for public discussion and deliberation. It considers the so-called Meese Commission as a political public sphere whose final report on the literary counterpublic sphere of pornography became a source of controversy in the larger arena of public debate over its methods and recommendations. The next two chapters are case studies concerned with ways in which we understand public opinion and how our conceptions of it influence public rhetoric. Chapter 7 explores the technologizing of public opinion that occurs in privately owned opinion polls. It examines how this technologized view influenced the Carter administration's attempts to handle the Iranian hostage-taking crisis. Chapter 8 is a case study of the public's correspondence concerning and Franklin Roosevelt's campaign speeches during the 1940 presidential election race. It investigates how vernacular rhetoric can be read and responded to as an expression of public opinion. The final chapter reconsiders the empirical attitude of the rhetorical framework I will develop and apply in this study in terms of its distinguishing characteristics and the contribution it may make to understanding the public realm of late modernity's civil society.

Chapter 1

THE PUBLIC VOICE OF VERNACULAR RHETORIC

If I, young as I am, may offer a thought, I would say it were best if men were by nature always wise; but that being seldom so, it is prudent to listen to those who offer honest counsel.

Sophocles, *Antigone*

During the last half of the twentieth century academicians have devoted increased attention to *discourse*. It is now a central concern in literary and cultural criticism, liberal democratic political theory, cultural anthropology, sociology, mass communication, philosophy, and the interpretive social sciences generally and is pivotal in debates between modernism and postmodernism. The critical inspection of discourse, especially public discourse, has reaffirmed its central place in Western culture partly through the inspiration of intellectual developments in Europe, such as in the writings of structuralists and poststructuralists, deconstructionists, and the Frankfurt school of critical theorists, but also by the work of America's neopragmatists. Discursive practices provide the evidentiary base for studying and interpreting the constitution of social will.

The term has a variety of meanings, ranging from rational communication intended to establish consensus on an abstract principle to a personal statement of thoughts and feelings. As a social practice, discourse involves symbolic transactions that affect people's shared sense of the world. Usually it takes the form of verbal statements, although its reach includes symbolic exchanges generally. Within its reference world these statements advance meaningful claims about observations, thoughts, beliefs, opinions, or attitudes. Its basic form is conversation.

Despite the relatively recent cross-disciplinary status of discourse analysis, the practice of reading society and culture from public discourse is not a new enterprise. It is arguably among the Western tradition's oldest intellectual pursuits, stemming from the fifth century b.c.e. when the Elder Sophists began to teach rhetoric in Athens. In this chapter I will consider an alternative frame of reference for thinking about our publics and how they form and communicate their opinions. I will begin by tracing the origins of rhetoric in Athenian democracy, followed by a consideration of the significant change in its role that occurred during the Enlightenment. Then I will discuss how this beginning degenerated into treating the public as an idealized fantasy grounded in shared interests and accompanied by a loss of faith that it could perform its function well. I will argue that we may redress these problems by reconceptualizing the public as a plurality of publics grounded on their capacity for rhetorical engagement. I will contend that publics are *emergences* manifested through vernacular rhetoric.

Before proceeding, I acknowledge that the term *rhetoric* may be troublesome to some readers. In many quarters it still carries the scent of manipulative discourse or flowery but empty expression. Its use here is technical. I use *rhetoric* broadly to mean *the symbolic inducement of social cooperation*. It is an inevitable consequence of language. As Kenneth Burke (1969) teaches, we cannot address others without our symbols encouraging a response. These encouragements may be as subtle as the shades of meaning suggested by intonation and of attitude conveyed by an article of clothing, or as blatant as a partisan speech by a politician seeking our vote. Although our public lives often require that we engage in intentional selection and management of language and argument to influence others—a most traditional and extremely important aspect of rhetoric—we cannot avoid the inadvertent ways in which our symbolic exchanges influence and are influenced by others, by the climate for communication, by the resources of language available to us, by the situation in which we communicate and the impulse for communication it contains, and by the myriad of conditioning factors that mark our human existence. In Burke's terms (1968, 16), humans are "the symbol-using (symbol making, symbol misusing) animal."

Rhetorical acts of the sort Burke includes within the range of human symbolic activity bear on the formation of actual publics. The shared concerns that join us as members of publics are brought to consciousness through the process by which we discover and intensify them. Publics have rhetorical antecedents (Hauser and Blair 1982). This does not mean that publics can be reduced to conditions of communication but that they cannot form without communication. The rhetorical antecedents of publics influence the manner in which communicative acts occur, the relationships among public actors including those who are disempowered by institutional authority, the relationships between and among rhetors and their audiences, and the state of being shared by social actors who are cocreating meaning, as I hope to show.

Rhetoric's Place in the Athenian Democracy

Rhetoric, understood as the art of public speaking, was introduced as a formal study in Greece during the fourth century b.c.e.[1] It was taught as a form of civic education intended to prepare Athenian and, later,

Roman boys for participation in public affairs. Under the tutelage of the Sophists and rhetoricians they learned more than the art of persuasive speaking, as Protagoras observed when he sketched his program of study in Plato's dialogue that bears his name. In response to Socrates' query about what a student might learn from him, Protagoras answered, "The proper care of his personal affairs, so that he may best manage his own household, and also of the state's affairs, so as to become a real power in the city, both as speaker and as man of action" (Plato 1961, 318e). Protagoras did not discriminate between rhetorical and political skills because he thought deftness at public argument was a prerequisite for influencing public policy. He shared the Greco-Roman understanding of political activity as joined to the state and as constitutive of public life.

Classical discussions of rhetoric, most notably Athenian ones, reflected this constitutive function. The philosophical accomplishments of Plato and Aristotle, the dramatic works of Aristophanes and Euripides, Thucydides' history, Iktinius's and Callikrates's architectural design of the Parthenon, the educational experiments of the Sophists and Plato's Academy, and the punctuating elegance of Euclid's geometry made Athens the paradigm of high culture. Each of these was a signal accomplishment of unusual talent and expertise. Yet as much as Athenians revered these individual feats, their shared experience of democracy led them to regard Athens's political character as their signature achievement. Democracy encouraged an understanding of public life as the province and concern of every citizen (Glover 1935, 25–30). By extension, politics invaded every individual's life to organize relationships and serve as the principal activity defining a citizen's meaning.

During the time of the democracy Athenian political relations were beset by class tensions and the distorting influences of power-lust. The well-born and wealthy placed considerable value on the political utility of *philoi*, or friendship bonds. Political opportunists, such as Kleon and Alcibiades, placed equal value on the power of oratory to organize the *phouloi*, or common men.[2] Their countervailing import in Athens during the fifth and fourth centuries b.c.e. produced constant tension between the right of the people to reign and the privilege of the well positioned to rule (Connor 1971; Sagan 1991). However, these strains sounded in a larger theater of political possibility. Athenians were confident that public deliberation surpassed elite dictums for steering the polis. Every citizen had an interest in determining its course. The political efficacy of private arrangements diminished as the phouloi increased their activity in the public realm. The new politics, initiated by Kleon, rested on creating public consensus through direct rhetorical appeal. It organized the common citizens into an effective majority, which meant that the political process had to respect their numbers and court their sympathies. Public deliberation became more genuinely the method by which serious decisions were made, and "universal" participation led to a new form of political power emphasizing rhetorical skill over noble birth. It valued each citizen as capable, in principle, of contributing to a solution through his participation in public deliberation (Finley 1962).

Pericles' "Funeral Oration" (Thucydides 1951) provides a clear example of rhetoric's prominence in Athenian politics. In 432 b.c.e. the Peloponesian War erupted between the city-states of ancient Greece. Early on Athens prosecuted the war against Sparta and its allies with the youthful conviction of a rising power self-confident in its superiority. But its invasion of Attica exacted a cruel price, and it fell to Pericles to make sense of this sacrifice of sons, husbands, fathers, and friends to a city stricken with grief and, thereby, to console and fortify his fellow Athenians. The oration, which was ostensibly delivered to celebrate the valor of Athenians killed in battle, eulogizes the virtues of public life. Pericles reminded his listeners that the Athenian constitution provided every citizen the opportunity to participate in its political affairs. Men earned public esteem *(aretê)* and advancement through personal attributes rather than from mere rotation of office or external factors of birth or wealth. The Athenians' deep expectation for each citizen to participate in politics led Pericles to proclaim that Athens stood alone in "regarding him who takes no part in these duties [politics] not as unambitious but as useless we Athenians are able to judge at all events if we cannot originate, and instead of looking on discussion as a stumbling-block, in the way of action, we think it an indispensable preliminary to any wise action at all" (Thucydides 1951, 103). Athenians alone subscribed to an ideal of goodness that separated friendship from personal gain and coupled it to service. "In generosity we are equally singular, acquiring our friends by conferring not by receiving favors. Yet of course, the doer of the favor is the firmer friend of the two, in order by continued kindness to keep the recipient in his debt; while the debtor feels less keenly from the very consciousness that the return he makes will be a payment, not a free gift" (Thucydides 1951, 105–6). Pericles concluded that involvement and service, open deliberation, and putting the state's welfare above personal gain made Athens "an education for Greece" (Thucydides 1951, 106).

Pericles' reflections are indicative of rhetoric's powerful role in the Athenian political experience. Nicole Loraux (1986) has observed that the concrete immediacy of the polis seemed to leave Athenians without political experience beyond the empirical. Not given to treating their politics in abstract, theoretical terms, their daily encounters were, in Hegel's words, "*this actual* Athens, this Sparta, these Temples, these Altars, this form of social life, this union of fellow citizens, these manners and customs" (qtd. in Loraux 1986, 328). But the immediacy of empirical experience lacks distance to reflect on a model beyond the community's habitual and customary political relations. Reflective distance aids creation of an image on which society may model its present practices of citizenship and its future aspirations. The epideictic genre, which included the funeral encomium, provided a rhetorical space for public reflections of this sort.

By its very nature rhetorical reflection is unlike technical reasoning or disputation of the sort that characterizes dialectical exchanges among academicians or trained specialists (Zyskind 1968). It seeks to enlarge our understanding of what Edwin Black has called our *frame of reference*, a "body of convictions, attitudes and values" (Black 1965, 29). The praise and blame of epideictic address commemorates concrete moments of communal experience and memorializes them as paradigms of shared identity. And we should note that while it often elaborates upon our shared commitments, epideictic discourse can lead its audience in new directions (Poulakos 1990). As Pericles' eulogy of Athens demonstrates, rhetoric can devise a frame of reference to address the traumatizing consequences of realities that are incommensurable with beliefs and values. Pericles' comments are valuable because they present an imaginary projection by which "the Athenians made more of Athens than Athens" (Loraux 1986, 329). When Pericles extolled the political life of Athens, which included class rivalry, slavery, and the exclusion of women, for its participatory inclusiveness, he projected an image of Athenian democracy as an achievement for others to emulate and in which citizens could take pride. Pericles' Athens was a *rhetorical invention* that transformed the divisions within the city, the problems of the empire, and the wounds inflicted by war with the encomiastic topoi of valor, virtue, prestige, and bravery deserving general admiration.

Pericles' "Funeral Oration" is paradigmatic of rhetoric's inventive power. Although it lacks the precision we associate with scientific reasoning, rhetoric's strength lies in its potential to create new political realities within the open-ended possibilities of a democracy. The group in Greek antiquity who first and most completely saw its radical productive possibilities for knowledge and for public life were the Elder Sophists.

Much like social anthropologists, the Elder Sophists held an evolutionary view of civilization that placed the individual in reciprocal relation to the city. Perhaps the clearest statement of their view is expressed in Protagoras's mythic narrative of the origins of the human race. Protagoras credited the city with saving humans from a brutish existence (Plato 1961, 320d–e; 322b). He argued that the city brought law and order to otherwise wild creatures. It offered protection and security in return for participation in the community. Within the city humans had to develop political skill based on respect for others and a sense of justice (*Protagoras* 322c). The Greeks regarded these traits so highly, he maintained, that they considered anyone whose conduct failed to meet their measure as a plague to the city (*Protagoras* 322d).

Protagoras's story emphasized the reciprocity between quality of city life and the moral development of its citizens. He portrayed the civilized city, based on political skill and respect for others, and its citizens, who acquired these skills, as moving one another ever closer to an as yet unrealized goal of perfection (*Protagoras* 322d–23a, 324a–c, 327a–28a). The city was the teacher whose mores and laws educated and civilized humans with a sense of virtue and with skill in making prudent decisions. Profiting from their inherited legacy of community, succeeding generations elevated the climate of cooperation, understanding, and civil order within the polis. The enhanced perfection of the polis, in turn, elevated the level of education and civic virtue in succeeding generations.

Protagoras's mythic narrative cast the identity of city dwellers in terms of their evolving political relations, not their geographic locale. They stood apart from barbarians because their conduct was tempered by attributes of civility and community. Like Pericles' depiction of Athens, the Protagorean portrayal of political identity offers a vision of civic virtue as a rhetorical achievement accomplished through public dialogue in the assembly, in the courts, and on civic occasions. The Elder Sophists regarded deliberative exchanges and encomiastic performances as the polity's method for clarifying vague or poorly understood problems, uncovering new ways to frame issues, resolving impasses, and discovering shared grounds for communal action. As one of Thrasymachus's fragments argued, partisan biases were resolvable in the common tradition they inherited from their fathers (Havelock 1957, 231–33). By such expressions of confidence in the prudence and efficacy of consensual decisions, the Elder Sophists propounded a program for civic life that took public opinion seriously.

When Aristotle later offered his more systematic analysis of civic life, he reiterated Protagoras's insight by situating rhetoric under the ethical branch of politics. He developed his discussion of rhetoric as a *technê* or art for finding and building arguments in deliberative, forensic, and epideictic contexts.[3] In this respect he emphasized that rhetoric is a method for constructing persuasive discourse. Aristotle's (1991) keen observations of political behavior led him to postulate the possibility of a rhetorical technê based on precepts of method abstracted from successful persuasive practices. Although every citizen was entitled to speak in civic forums, few were skilled practitioners who consistently developed reasoned appeals (Aristotle 1991, 1:1.2). Most speakers relied on emotional appeals to affect their listeners (Aristotle 1991, 1:1.3–5). He withheld his endorsement of these rhetorical practices since they were not guided by the primary political virtue of *phronêsis,* or practical wisdom. Aristotle echoed Protagoras's reciprocity argument by maintaining that the quality of public decisions rose in proportion to the quality of their supporting arguments and that the *phronêmos,* the prudentially wise rhetor, was more likely to develop convincing appeals than those whose self-interest limited their political vision.

Aristotle's argument on phronêsis firmly situated rhetoric within a politics based on the ideal of civic virtue. Participation in political choice may have been the universal franchise of Athenian citizens, but the power of rhetoric to guide those choices was not drawn from a communal ethos. It stemmed from the person of the rhetor. Public wisdom was a rhetorical enactment, which meant that the reality of phronêsis and the phronêmos were as much rhetorical inventions as was Periclean Athens.

Despite serious differences with Sophistic doctrines, Aristotle nonetheless extended their seminal insight linking rhetoric to political practice. His extension was continued through the Roman rhetorics of Cicero and Quintilian (Clark 1957; Howell 1961, 1965, 1966; McKeon 1942; Stump 1978). These Roman works, especially Cicero's, endured as the principal vehicle by which rhetorical thought was transmitted in the Western tradition and retained influence on political thinking until the Enlightenment, when a paradigm shift occurred on the relationship of discourse to public life.

Civil Society and the Appearance of Public Opinion

Ancient rhetorical theory reflected the ideal of civic virtue permeating Greek and Roman political thought. This tradition emphasized the role of the individual as a public person. A public performance whose virtuosity commanded respect was a personal accomplishment that signified aretê for the Greeks and *virtú* for the Romans and would have included the oratorical accomplishments of those in the public realm. This ancient understanding of rhetoric as a political praxis has become problematic in a way that is important for our understanding of modern publics.

Both Athens and Rome grounded individual identity in citizenship. The Athenians organized themselves in terms of polis and *oikos*, politics and economics, city-state and household. Athens's ancient city wall contained the inscription "The man with no public business has no business"; underscoring that observation, the ancient Greek word for a person mute on public affairs was *idiot*. The Athenian political experience did not require a distinction between the discursive domains of the agora and the *ekklesia* (assembly) since the men interacting on public issues in one were the same men who later came together to vote in the other. Although actions by the ekklesia were official, the ongoing negotiation of how Athenians would act and interact, or politics, fused discussions in the official assembly with those in the street. Without a buffer between social and political life—since the political organized the social—Athenians had no need to conceptualize a public sphere as a discursive arena apart from that of the legislative assembly.

Later the Roman empire exerted equal power to organize individuals' public lives. *The assertion "Civis Romanum sum"* (I am a Roman citizen) issued an individual's claim to status and right because it identified a person's place in the world. The claim to citizenship carried entitlement to respect and full protection under Roman law, but the problems of coordinating these citizens was substantial. The empire was vast, with a border that stretched six thousand miles from Euphrates to Carlisle. Within Rome the emperor's presence dictated the tone of life. But outside the city local affairs tended to be disorderly and administration was beset by confusion, as the letters between Pliny, as governor of Bithynia in northern Asia Minor, and the emperor Trajan attest (Glover 1935, 316). Since there was no structure resembling the modern state, the only way to insure orderly governance was through political arrangements. Roman law, in the form of the Justinian Code, provided the basis for uniform organization to citizens living over an immense land mass. The political apparatus to administrate the empire in ways consistent with growing imperial control came from Rome's large cadre of civil servants. Law-abiding Romans acquired a unique identity as free persons through the legal code and an administrative system that was local in neither origin nor allegiance. Backed by the unsurpassed might of the emperor's legions, Rome's legal code and civil administration extended the emperor's power to all aspects of life. Although the political fiction held the emperor to be of the people, Roman citizens lacked the means to interdict his will or prevent him from imposing his political vision on their social relations, and in reality his power was unshielded. To be in Roman society, as to be in Greek, most concretely meant to occupy a space defined by its political organization.

Athenian and Roman political experiences valorized a rhetorical ideal of eloquence in which the skillful orator persuaded the actual decision makers. This ideal also centered on individual virtuosity rather than society, facilitating the persuasive rhetor's likely ascent to leadership and power. A conception of rhetoric predicated on assumptions of civic virtues continues today in both our valorizing of rational deliberation and our scholarship centering on institutional rhetors (elected officials for the most part) and institutional discourse (messages on issues to be decided by elected representatives). It reproduces assumptions of the ancient Greco-Roman period when there was no buffer between political power to organize society and the individual. Those assumptions are inconsistent with the realities of contemporary public life. Our public deliberations occur in multiple forums not exclusive to those of the official political realm, and they lead to opinions which, when widely shared, set expectations for their consequences on official policies. We refer to this montage of discursive arenas as public spheres. But these arenas themselves are situated in the larger and not always coterminous arena of *civil society.*

The roots of European civil society lay in the removal of centralized power from Rome and its distribution among the hands of the few: the church and kings. The rise of Christianity undermined the exclusive power of the state to organize people's lives. The church was an alternative institution autonomous of the state whose dogma led the faithful to organize their individual lives around a different set of principles and ideals than political ones. Christians were members of two societies: one temporal and the other spiritual, and neither subjugated to the other. On the other hand, monarchs were constrained in their efforts at nation building by the powers of feudal lords who had firmly established property rights, as did the church. To counter this preexisting social force, kings sought power by granting autonomy to towns. These became havens from feudalism in which new ideas might develop (Hall 1995). They also became the source of another political power in the burghers. The rise of burghers, who were both feisty in their independence and too wealthy to be ignored, unsettled the monarchy's success at forging political accord with vassals and bishops. For some time monarchs had found it necessary to convene the body of estates periodically in order to raise resources necessary for governance and waging war. Now they found themselves vulnerable to the uncertainties of the estates themselves.

Both the church and the estates provided a sense of social identity apart from citizenship. They provided a mode of social organization apart from the state in which members could engage in discourse unregulated by the state. They also caused great instability to states, which eventually provided support for the doctrine of absolute monarchy as the only viable mode of governance. An absolute monarch could raise money and armies independently, thereby dispensing with the need to convene the estates in order to be militarily effective. This view was justified by influential theories, such as Thomas Hobbes's, that undermined the medieval understanding of society.

Hobbes's theory marked a return to identifying society with its political organization. It suppressed features of social contract theory positing that the existence of society was prior to the state's. In response, Enlightenment thinkers, such as Locke, Montesquieu, and Rousseau, reintroduced the idea that humankind forms a community of sorts constituted under natural law and in existence prior to society, which is itself prior to the government. Their refutation of the Hobbesean identification of society with its political organization propounded the idea of *civil society* as a third arena, independent of the family and the state, engaged in conscious acts of self-management that were integrated with the state.

The concept of *civil society* refers to *a network of associations independent of the state whose members, through social interactions that balance conflict and consensus, seek to regulate themselves in ways consistent with a valuation of difference.* The tradition of civil society arose in response to the intercourse of diverse interests and opinions that occurred when national borders were opened to trade. Its roots are different from those of community, which values common beliefs and shared social practices. At its heart civil society is concerned with relationships among diverse groups and interests. Enlightenment thinkers developed this network's accommodation of diversity in their reflections on economic, political, and moral relations.

The *economic* basis of civil society was initiated by Adam Smith's free-market theory of economic cooperation. His doctrine of laissez faire advanced a model of economic behavior in which the open marketplace, freed from control by institutions of church or state, functioned in a self-regulating manner. Since consumers established value and wealth, those who entered the marketplace sought commercial alliances and adapted to marketplace conditions to secure profits. Success required sensitivity to different interests and changing conditions. Smith saw civil society as a new arena independent of the government, existing between it and the family.

The *political* basis of civil society, more important than laissez faire[4] for this discussion, lay in the concomitant rise of an autonomous public integrated with the state through expressions of its own opinion. The Enlightenment concept of public represented a new understanding that went beyond what was objectively there and open to everyone's inspection. It designated the citizens', at least the literate ones', recognition of shared concerns. Moreover, these shared concerns were expressed in new discursive spaces—newspapers, personal exchanges in coffeehouses and salons, political clubs, and the like—that extended beyond the agora and the ekklesia. These were sites for open dialogue in which reasons for and against an idea were elaborated, tested, refuted, extended, and, ideally, resolved to the extent that everyone recognized what was held in common. This recognition represented a novel conception of public opinion as more than the sum of individual opinions. The dimension of common recognition that emerged from the conversations within civil society gave public opinion a strong sense. It also introduced the radical idea of such opinion as formed outside the channels and public spaces of the political structure, such as parliament or court. Even more fundamentally, as Charles Taylor has observed, public opinion "developed outside the channels and public spaces of any authority whatever, since it is also independent of that second focus of European societies, the church. Governments were used to facing the independent power of religious opinion, articulated by churches. What was new was opinion, presented as that of society, elaborated through no official, established hierarchical organs of definition" (Taylor 1995, 217).

The *moral* basis of civil society arose through Enlightenment concern for a virtuous society. Here we encounter a subtle shift from the tradition of civic virtue. The civic virtue tradition subordinates the private self to the public realm, as is found in the work of Hannah Arendt (1958). By contrast, the eighteenth-century Scottish moralists saw the moral basis of society as a private ideal. A *civil* society was one in which individual responsibility for actions toward others could be counted on to exceed pure exchange value because, as Smith argued, humans are naturally inclined to benevolent sentiments toward one another. In civil society you did not have to like those with whom you interacted; as long as interactions were marked by tolerance and kindness, differences could be overcome in the complex web of human dialogue (Seligman 1995, 204). Unlike the tradition of civic virtue, in which one's merit was established by public conduct, the civil society tradition founded the quality of relations with strangers in the individual self rather than the individual's public being. Individual actions were seen and judged by others in terms of *propriety* rather than *virtuosity,* as they had been in the civic virtue tradition. For Smith the principle of "approbation"—the approval bestowed by impartial spectators—provided the basis for "fellow-feeling." As impartial spectators, our "sense of propriety" elicited "sympathy" for the joys and sorrows of others (Smith 1969, 58–86) and allowed us to judge the moral quality of their acts as well as our own.

The new ideas about economy, public opinion, and moral conduct, whether considered apart or as interlocking, expressed society's identity apart from the state and, moreover, established themselves as *self-regulating* domains independent of government for social coordination. Importantly for rhetoric, the arenas for public opinion formation were different from those of the polis in which the same persons populated both the agora and the ekklesia. New conditions of social congress accompanying expanded commerce, trade, and urban growth led to an ideal of encountering diversity through tolerance and to the idea of civil society as the network of associations emerging from interactions with the other. And the discursive spaces within this network displaced the state's claim to exclusivity as the domain in which social will was articulated and executed. These new spaces afforded a public sphere in which a public could form an opinion that might challenge the state's primacy in setting social purposes and that might expect its understanding to bear weight on what the state did.

The Athenian experience that linked public decisions to rhetoric is more than a vestigial remnant of democracy's origin. Historically Western politics has sustained the connection between discourse on civic issues and setting public policy. It has regarded the people's interests as its rhetorical, if not theoretical, foundation and has narrated advancing their interests as a primary virtue of governance. The transition from civic virtue to civil society has changed the locus of rhetoric's purview from the sites of official discourse to the spheres of interaction within society where publics form and express opinions that bear on the course of society. However, this does not diminish the importance of rhetoric as an inventional social resource. Rather, this shift provides the basis for exploring the rhetorical conditions in which publics form, form opinions, and assert their authority to guide governmental actions. Whether civil society is colonized by the state and power elites, as Habermas depicts in his rendition of late capitalism, or remains open to the possibility of its own self-regulation is itself subject to the rhetorical possibilities and performances it can sustain. In less theoretical terms, and accepting the precondition of free speech, whether or not civil society embraces and lives in truth is fundamentally dependent on whether or not its members are informed and attentive to the truth.

Vox Populi and the Problem of "Public" Opinion

"Vox populi, vox dei"—the voice of the people is the voice of God—has provided rhetorical capital to monarchs and democrats alike, even though their definitions of "the people" and their interests have fluctuated to suit radically different ends and tastes (Boas 1969; McGee 1975). However, as we have just seen, during the seventeenth century the voice of the people acquired the more technical meaning of *public opinion*, and the modern democratic state transformed the legitimating invocation of vox populi from a rhetorical construct used to endorse predetermined actions to the political expression of "the public" as the basis for official action.

In this century the guiding assumptions of Athenian democracy have come unhinged from Enlightenment ideals that linked discourse to public opinion. We still outwardly acknowledge the importance of democratic processes, but the *deliberative* characteristics of public discussion, including the reflective aspect of epideictic discourse noted earlier, are under assault. To give but one example, the 1990s have witnessed a surge of "talk radio" programming. These programs ostensibly invite a dialogue across the range of opinion in the listening audience, thereby appearing to be an electronic public forum. However, most of these programs with national syndication represent a narrow band on the political spectrum. The prescreening of callers and the lag time of several seconds between real-time and air-time conversation permit the unobtrusive editing of crudeness and unwanted opinions. When opposition views are aired, the host often belittles them. The repeated ritual of the vanquished caller undermines the reflective possibilities of deliberation with a perverted form of the epideictic genre based on the spectacle of public humiliation. This ritual betrays an attitude more attuned to commercial ratings than to critical opinion.

This assault is continued when political processes pay thin lip service to the ethos of public deliberation. The widely denounced but resiliently successful technique of negative campaigning and the reliance on focus groups to discover what people are really thinking are part of the same picture. They are the products of a marketing mentality toward politics intent on packaging individuals and issues with a slant toward voter susceptibilities. They also reveal a lack of conviction that wisdom will emerge from a public airing of substantive differences and even an astonishing lack of concern that public policies be informed by the electorate's interests.

On the most generous reading, these attitudes display our politicians' and political activists' apparent lack of confidence in democratic processes to produce informed and efficacious results. Even keeping more cynical readings at bay, we can find probable cause for a crisis of confidence in the sheer complexity of the realities confronting society. This is not a new observation. Pluralism and technical knowledge pose problems that have questioned liberal democratic ideals since at least World War I.

In 1922 Walter Lippmann's *Public Opinion* lamented the impossibility of achieving informed public opinion to guide public policy. He claimed that the level of knowledge and attention required for intelligent participation in public discussion bewildered the typical layperson. His solution was to concede the impossibility of a genuinely *public* opinion. In its place he suggested an elite cadre of the press as spokespersons for the people.

Five years later John Dewey published *The Public and its Problems* as a response intended to revive the concept of "the public." Both men, however, pointed to modernity as the culprit for the public's malaise. Dewey argued that the public was the basis of the state; but technological innovation, mobility, and mass communication created a surplus of information that exceeded the capacity of people to understand how decisions by others might impact on their lives. Consequently, he thought, decisions were being made on the basis of urgencies advanced by special interests. Dewey concluded that the public of his day was in eclipse. At the end of the twentieth century, after the Great Depression, World War II, and the twin onset of the postindustrial era and the age of information, Dewey's reflections from the late 1920s remain current and suggestive.

Developed Western societies are characteristically pluralistic, with diverse and often competing interests that engender fragmentation and its accompanying dangers. Organized and well-financed special interest groups can dominate public rhetoric for or against a proposal. By contrast, the majority of relatively disinterested private citizens typically lack the organization and resources necessary for strong self-awareness as members of a public. Although as vested in the resolution of public problems as the most entrenched lobby, their inability to mount a rhetorical counteroffensive on behalf of their common interests can make average citizens appear detached from the outcome of public deliberation.[5] Consequently, the dominant voices that seem to mold public opinion are less those of citizens engaged in public deliberation than those of elites who possess access to the forums that court public support, bankroll political candidates, and decide public policy.

The pervasive role of the media in Western political processes further complicates the problematic relationship of discourse to public opinion. Newspapers, magazines, radio, television, and now the internet[6] substitute for reflective deliberation in which average people play a part. Often these substitutions are staged political exchanges that displace traditional rhetorical processes for forming public opinion and instilling a sense of community.

An increasingly pessimistic understanding of "the public" and its role in the political process accompanies this displacement. Since the presidency of Franklin Roosevelt, for example, political leaders in the United States have relied almost exclusively on mass media for disseminating information and presenting persuasive appeals. Modern political campaigners consider these media, especially television, so powerful in sculpting public opinion that their campaigns revolve around media strategies, including how to engage in political activities that will generate news stories (Ginsberg 1986, 161–62). Moreover, as rhetorical analyst Kathleen Jamieson documents, since the message citizens receive is heavily influenced by the manner in which news reports tell these stories, vested parties exert considerable effort to control the images and symbols associated with public figures and events (Jamieson 1992, 163–99).

In part this effort to control images reflects the steady erosion of conditions under which political and cultural discourse occurs. Jürgen Habermas (1989) and Jean-François Lyotard (1984), arguing from antagonistic perspectives, advance the common observation that the technical character of public policy issues excludes those people lacking technical, institutional, or financial resources from the discussions that matter while it increases the power of elites. Emphasizing the technical dimensions of public problems moves them from the public to the technical sphere (Goodnight 1982), which sets the constraints for decisions in technical language and privileges mathematical expression as coin of the policy-making realm. John Kennedy remarked on just this point at a May 1962 press conference:

> Most of us are conditioned for many years to have a political
> viewpoint—Republican or democratic, liberal, conservative,
> or moderate. The fact of the matter is that most of the prob-
> lems . . . that we now face are technical problems. They are
> very sophisticated judgments, which do not lend themselves

> to the great sort of passionate movements which have stirred this country so often in the past. [They] deal with questions which are now beyond the comprehension of most men. (qtd. in Lasch 1978, 77)

In other words, Kennedy thought commonsense language was no longer able to express a "sophisticated judgment" of public issues. When participation in these discussions requires competence in information sciences plus technical expertise, the average citizen finds herself reduced to a mute and often befuddled observer (Hauser 1987).

Unquestionably, some dimensions of public problems do present technical difficulties and do require a specialist's knowledge to resolve. Still, regardless of their intent, Kennedy's remarks provide a justification for transferring deliberation on public problems from citizen forums to Lippmann-like enclaves of technically educated elites. Whenever such a transfer occurs, it severs informed and open deliberation from the process of deciding public policy. But such public deliberative processes are the rationale for public opinion. Thus, while the historical democratic role of public opinion to legitimate public action remains, the issue for policy makers is no longer to frame policies in line with the will of the governed but to shape the will of the governed in line with the policies to be enacted (Habermas 1989).

Nowhere is the consequence of this reversal more evident than in the political uses of opinion polls, which I explore more concretely in chapter 7's discussion of administrative rhetoric on the Iranian hostage-taking affair of 1980. Here I wish to note only that the owners of opinion polls (such as a political candidate) use them to take snapshots in time, often with the end of determining what the polled would like to hear. These polls do not frame policy debates, even though they appear to measure what people think. Actually, they measure attitude, which often influences what their owners will say to satisfy their constituents' needs. As Habermas has remarked, this is not the work of genuine political discourse but of group psychology (1989, 236–44).

The genuine political discourse Habermas has in mind resonates with the ideals of public deliberation that are assumed to hold in a representative democracy. C. Wright Mills (1957, 300–301) summarizes these assumptions as including:

> that the individual conscience was the ultimate seat of judgment and hence the final court of appeal, . . . that among the individuals who composed [the public] there was a natural and peaceful harmony of interests, . . . that before public action would be taken, there would be rational discussion between individuals which would determine action, and that, accordingly the public opinion that resulted would be the

27

> infallible voice of reason, . . . [and] that after determining what
> was true and right and just, the public would act accordingly or
> see that its representatives did so. (Mills 1957, 300–301)

Certainly these are the assumptions of rationality held by such proponents of classical liberal democratic theory as A. Lawrence Lowell (1913). He argues that *the public* actually exists as a community of citizens who share common ends, values, and procedures, a community that also protects the rights of all the interested parties while discovering public opinion and translating it into practice.

Whether these assumptions ever prevailed is questionable. The dictum that the people are sovereign while the elite rule was as true under Solon as it was during periods of populism in nineteenth-century America. Political scientists Frances Piven and Richard Cloward (1988, 35–41), studying voter behavior in nineteenth- and twentieth-century America, find that nineteenth-century voter turnout was often a function of clientelism fostered by big-city party machines who preyed on the tribal loyalties of ethnic communities. Recently arrived immigrants, who had yet to experience the organizing possibilities of labor unions that spoke to their interests, were vulnerable to promises of goods and services in return for their votes. Although participating in elections, they were not part of a political dialogue. Instead, by boosting the size of the voting blocs that political operatives could deliver, they were contributors to the power of ward bosses. As long as these voters were controllable by the machine, their votes served the party's interests and the machine exerted itself to deliver their vote. This pattern of voter behavior eventually came apart when a series of legal and procedural reforms in voting coincided with in the election of 1896, in which American voters deviated from patterns of clientelism and tribalism. A new voting pattern of regionalism weakened the Democratic Party in the North and virtually destroyed the Republicans in the South. The absence of party competition led to internal oligarchy within the parties and either made large turnout nonessential to the party staying in power or posed the threat of voters who could not be controlled. Party support of residency, literacy, and property tax requirements for voter registration amounted to deliberate attempts to depress voter participation by the lower economic strata of Americans whose interests were unlikely to coincide with those of elites in power (Piven and Cloward 1988, 64–95).

Additionally, the American political vision, with its marked distrust of factions from the time of *The Federalist Papers,* has reinforced the twentieth-century trend to depress universal voter participation. America's system of governance reflects Madison's bias against trusting the beneficence of citizens to secure enlightened decisions through open deliberation. Since the power of vested interests was too strong to curtail, America's founding representatives established a state-elected senate and an indirectly elected executive from distrust of popular voices. The political experience of America confirms the distrust of factions that pervaded its constitutional conventions. Special interests have significantly affected tariffs, land and water disputes, policy decisions precipitating the Civil War, tax laws, and the host of complex civil and economic accommodations that have influenced legislation to the present day. In theory a democracy is supposed to arrive at policy decisions on the basis of egalitarian principles in which the strongest ideas carry the day. However, from its inception, democratic politics has almost always been strongly influenced by well-organized lobbies.

The realities of lobby politics today are daunting for the average citizen and discourage the level of activity Lowell and Mills describe. Lobbies, especially those in the service of capitalist enterprises and developed nations, possess resources of money, information, organization, technical knowledge, and access to those who will deliberate and decide issues in which they have an interest. Whether they or others kick the political ball into play, when policy making bears on their interests lobbyists participate in the process from its outset, and in ways that can influence the outcome. For the average citizen unable to match these resources, gaining access to the field of play may seem an exercise in futility. Nor do the patterns of voter registration laws and party behaviors disclosed by Piven and Cloward encourage those on society's margins to a spirit of political activism. Certainly viewed from the perspective of institutional discourse, there appears to be widespread adoption of what Habermas (1975) has called civic and familial privatism, with its much-discussed accompanying emphases on personal interests (Sennett 1978), a lost sense of community (Bellah et al. 1985), a search for self in others (Riesman et al. 1961), and even wholesale narcissism (Lasch 1978) as defining conditions of Western life.

Of course the ideology of liberal democracy remains steadfastly at the center of Western political rhetoric. Our traditions extol the people as the authorizing and legitimating agents of social knowledge and political action, which requires that those in positions of power court their assent. This combination of exclusion and invocation promotes a vicious cycle of flawed communication. The technical character of many problems facing public officials and private entities whose actions affect publics is undeniable. However, emphasizing the technical dimensions of public problems carries epistemological and rhetorical imperatives. Those with power to make decisions reserve policy deliberations for technically trained or officially empowered elites while excluding the more general populace, who will feel the weight of these policies, from discussions that will chart its destiny. At the same time, policy decisions require citizen support. Since the terms of technical discussions exceed the typical person's capacity to understand, much less critically evaluate what is being proposed, those who seek citizen support now must find a way to secure it. Having defined the problem and the terms for its resolution in a fashion that obviates critical deliberation in the public realm, policy makers focus their rhetorical efforts on bringing public sentiment into line. The emphasis on image control that Jamieson noted as a preoccupation of professional political communicators now acquires a perverse justification from the imperative to garner support.

Noble intentions notwithstanding, it is difficult to imagine how those who mount media campaigns informed by analysis of this type could conceive of those who must certify their policies other than in the terms of group psychology that Habermas laments. And just as certainly citizens talked to in this way have every right to express cynicism or apathy toward the political processes that they are told mind their interests. Commentators, critics, and theorists surveying this scene are thereby led to a single and compelling conclusion: "the public" is moribund.

Rhetorical Antecedents of Publics

I believe these reports of imminent demise are exaggerations. Their distortion comes from looking for "the public" in the wrong places through conceptual lenses radically out of focus. Theorists, critics, and the news media typically talk of "the public" as if they were referring to a single inclusive entity held together by shared attitudes and beliefs. They portray it as if its members manifested their corporate identity through shared interests that, as Dewey put it, arise due to the consequences they suffer from the actions of others (Dewey 1954, 15–16). To be in this public of shared attitudes and beliefs is to be part of a political state in the world. There are several problems with this view.

Perhaps the most obvious difficulty stems from grounding "the public" in *shared interests*. The utter diversity of developed societies provides us with daily reminders of our differences. An emphasis on interests necessarily accentuates these differences between peoples and groups. Except for the most transcendent causes and problems, such as natural disasters, epidemics, or national emergencies, hotly contested public issues parse along lines of age, gender, region, ethnicity, class, and a host of considerations that lead to incompatible and, perhaps, incommensurable attitudes and beliefs. Unlike social and political movements of the past that centered on class interests, today's movements are spawned by issues that reflect our ideological fragmentation. Positing shared substantive interests as "the public's" theoretical basis makes it exceedingly difficult, if not impossible, to think sensibly about actually existing publics that form through and in response to these new social movements and that are attempting to influence the course of society.

Liberal democratic thought is not alone in its bias toward shared interests as a public's defining characteristic. Most understandings of rhetorical discourse conceptualize rhetorical practices as geared toward finding common ground that will lead to consensus. The difficulty of this starting assumption for a society defined by conditions of diversity would appear to be the lack of precisely this necessary starting block for building successful rhetorical appeals.

This difficulty becomes apparent when we examine the circular reasoning invoked by situating shared substantive interests at the heart of "the public." We begin by noting that shared interests ground "the public." Then we observe that pluralism and diversity create an array of interests too abundant to share. The resulting fragmentation undermines "the public." But since it is an essential agency of social and political legitimation, we issue calls for "the public's" resuscitation. Revival, in turn, will require overcoming fragmented interests through recognition of shared concerns. The argument then extols communication as the means for reasserting commonalty. But communication depends on appeals to the common ground of shared interests, which apparently are lacking. The circularity of this exercise leads such otherwise astute analysts of civic discourse as Benjamin Barber (1984), James Fishkin (1995), Alasdair MacIntyre (1984), and Daniel Yankelovich (1991), among others, to solutions that require an entirely different set of conditions for communication than currently exist for the reanimation of public life they envision.

Treating "the public" as if it consists of an entity—an identifiable group with interests that persist across time—compounds the problem of locating its basic character. The multitude of interests that inevitably lead to pluralism and fragmentation affords citizens living in the far corners of a developed society considerable mobility in their associations with acquaintances and strangers at hand and around the globe. Average citizens who lack vested power are able to access one another's opinions and actions through the vast electronic communications network that encircles the planet. They may agree with their neighbors on some matters, disagree on others, or even exhibit complete indifference. Consequently, it is not unusual to find groups such as the radical Left of American feminists and the reactionary Right of American religious fundamentalists—normally at odds with one another on political issues—joining hands when a public problem such as regulation of pornography meshes with their respective political agendas. The model of a monolithic public based on shared interests is contrary to the actually existing coalitions of interests that can cooperate in pursuing a common end, even though for different reasons. The trite but true observation that politics makes strange bedfellows seems as applicable to disparate segments of the citizenry as to institutional actors. Making an entity of "the public" gives these interrelations the appearance of nothing more than factions that have brought "the public" itself into eclipse.

The conceptual problem of modeling "the public" is not remedied by shifting the focus to epistemological grounds. For example, Lloyd Bitzer has argued that "the public" provides the authorization for public knowledge and public action. This function, he concludes, makes "the public" the epistemological guarantor of community (Bitzer 1978). However, his line of analysis is vulnerable to the charge of hypostatizing "the public" when it is actually an ideal lacking an empirical referent. In short, Bitzer's move cannot circumvent the objection that a liberal democratic "public" as such is a myth (Hyde 1981; McGee and Martin 1983).

These criticisms of treating "the public" as an entity have encouraged another line of analysis concerned with the persuasive uses of "the public." Michael McGee's research on the ideographic character of "the people" is a notable example (McGee 1975, 1977; McGee and Martin 1983). Certainly there is considerable rhetorical cachet in appeals to "the public" for mounting the appearance of support and legitimation. However, substituting a rhetoricized understanding of "the public" for a reified one does not resolve the conceptual problem we have been considering. The efficacy of invoking "the public" as a control strategy is no substitute for a conceptual anchor that can help us better understand the discursive processes that contribute to the emergence and shape of aggregates, to activating or pacifying them, and to influencing or co-opting the legitimating activities essential to cultural, social, and political life.

Our understanding of the possibilities for and the problems of society's active members requires a framework that connects their material shape and activity to discourse. We may begin this reconceptualization by acknowledging that "*the* public" is a generic reference to a body of disinterested members of a society or polity and is no more informative to an understanding of social knowledge and social action than an undefined reference to "they." It fails to capture the activities of the working part of society engaged in creating cultural awareness, social knowledge, and public policies and in evaluating deeds. These activities are often local, are often in venues other than institutional forums, are always issue specific, and seldom involve the entire populace. Rather than searching for "*the* public," we are well advised to follow Herbert Blumer's (1966) lead and commence with an understanding of developed societies as montages of *publics*, each one, as he has argued, activated as its members feel issues intersect with the conditions of their lives in ways that require their attention. Thus, we may define *a public* as *the interdependent members of society who hold different opinions about a mutual problem and who seek to influence its resolution through discourse.*

A public has greater specificity than the populace, since the populace includes all citizens regardless of interests, level of participation, receptiveness to stimuli, and like conditions pertinent to rhetorical transactions within a public sphere. A public's members form a collectivity that may manifest their attention to issues through votes but just as often by exercising their buying power, demonstrations of sympathy or opposition, adornments of colored ribbons, debates in classrooms and on factory floors, speeches on library steps or letters to the editor, correspondence with public officials, and other expressions of stance and judgment. They are not pregiven; publics emerge as those who are actively creating and attending to these *discursive processes* for publicizing opinions, for making them felt by others. Their members are society's dynamic participants and judges who are actively engaged in evolving opinions that influence how our cultural, social, and political wheels turn.

Emphasizing the discursive process by which publics form their views shifts the focus of analysis from a specific, concrete political entity to activity in the public realm. This shift does not gainsay that public action is always political in some respect, but insists that its political meaning is a function of how this activity is experienced. Sensible thought about publics requires capturing their activity: how they construct reality by establishing and synthesizing values, forming opinions, acceding to positions, and cooperating through symbolic actions, especially discursive ones. Put differently, any given public exists in its publicness, which is to say in its rhetorical character.

And it should be noted here that *rhetoric* not only refers to suasive discourse but also to a method for thinking about communication, especially its heuristic concerns for invention. Inventional methods are used to generate possible suasive statements in the given case. Invention's animus includes taking the audience's vantage point into account. At its theoretical extreme, invention is devoid of any specific substantive assumptions and searches instead for what can be said about the matter at hand with consequence for those who are addressed (McKeon 1956). Moved to the level of performance, rhetoric opens inventional spaces: places where ideas, relationships, emotional bonds, and courses of action can be experienced in novel, sometimes transformative, ways.

Rhetoric's inventional character bears significantly on how we experience the possibilities of political, social, and cultural choice, and rhetoric's experiential nature contributes greatly to the dynamic possibilities of publics. Both in perception and fact, membership in a public requires *rhetorical competence*, or a capacity to participate in rhetorical experiences. Their members, on balance, must be receptive to alternative modes of expression, engage in active interpretation to understand what is being said and how it relates to them, and be open to change (White 1984, 9). Partners in rhetorical transactions, of necessity, must actively engage one another in attempts to understand issues, appreciate each other's views, and form their own judgments. They engage in an interpretive process in which they must consider perspectives not entirely their own. They must attend to motivations and rationales that lead to differences of opinion but that open the possibility for consensus. In short, the ability to participate in rhetorical exchanges, to have rhetorical experiences, requires a certain sort of subjectivity. It is a subjectivity unlike that found in interest groups, whose members often proceed on closed-minded assumptions of the wholly knowing. Whether attention to social exchange alters or reinforces personal views, collective participation in rhetorical processes *constitutes individuals as a public.*

Thus we arrive at a conclusion that reinforces and is reinforced by previous studies of our social and political lives: We cannot make sense of our collective selves without understanding how deeply discourse shapes us. Thomas Farrell makes a similar point when he advances the idea that the call to rhetoric is the recurring theme of public life in a democracy, and it makes the rhetorical ecology an a priori consideration for understanding publics and assessing the nature and function of their role in shaping society. Differences between advocates, messages, and audiences require the institutionalized and extemporaneous settings of *rhetorical forums* to provide "*a symbolic environment . . . within which issues, interests, positions, constituencies, and messages are advanced, shaped, and provisionally judged*" (Farrell 1993, 282; emphasis his). We need competent rhetoric whenever prudent conduct is uncertain. Competent rhetoric is a pluralistic society's best hope for accommodating multiple perspectives through resolute action that serves just ends.

Conclusion

In this chapter I have traced the origins of discourse as the method of public life. We saw how the Athenian democracy placed a premium on rhetorical competence for shaping public decisions and how two millennia later that competence changed with the rise of civil society. The emerging network of commercial, political, artistic, and even religious associations outside the state and the family spawned a discursive arena, now commonly referred to as the public sphere, apart from institutional control in which social actors could engage in self-regulating activity outside the authority of the state or other institutions. In this arena differences were encountered and had to be tolerated to insure the mutual well-being of interdependent segments of society. Moreover, in this arena public opinion took on new meaning as an expression of society, formed and presented outside institutions that might presume to speak for society's members. Public opinion was the expression of society speaking for itself. This understanding of public opinion was joined to the liberal democratic ideal of "the public" as a political concept based on interests whose opinions were to guide state action.

The complex nature of cultural, social, and political life in developed societies has posed several difficulties for this conceptualization of "the public." On one side administrative interests have defined public problems in technical terms that restrict decision-making deliberations to epistemic and class elites. On the other side, the plurality of interests in complex societies and the evident fragmentation that follows from diversity have produced a commonwealth of factions. As decisions move forward to the point where democratic ideals require public approval, administrative and special interests launch media campaigns of image management to secure public compliance. Finally, the general populace seems to respond by retreating from the public playing field, either due to obstacles to their participation as voters or in response to encouragement to pursue private gains of position, wealth, and personal enrichment. In the face of its definition as a political entity based on shared interests, we seem compelled to conclude that "the public" is moribund.

Attempts to revive "the public" have resulted in circular arguments in which its rejuvenation is predicated on an idealized form of communication becoming the norm. This line of reasoning has led to the critique of "the public" as a myth and references to it as a form of political manipulation. In both the attempted rejuvenation and the debunking critique, the rhetorical undergirding of publics as empirical phenomena has received scant attention. As a result, the discourses of the active segments of society, including average citizens as well as leaders, have been interpreted in ways that subordinate rhetorical considerations to political interests. These interpretations also fail to account for the ways in which society is awash with rhetorical exchanges that contribute to the continuing cultural, social, and political education of its members.

I have argued that we can reposition the center point of our thinking from antecedent shared interests to the sentiments emerging from public engagements of deliberation and commemoration by emphasizing discourse as a given public's constituting agency. Rather than searching for "*the* public," we should expect a developed society to be populated by a montage of *publics*. And rather than anticipating publics as already existing, we should seek them through actual discursive engagements on the issues raised in civil society as *emergences of society's active members*. Here, I should note, social *activity* has a broad meaning not restricted to organized behavior and inclusive of collective disengagement or passivity and silence as signs of possible disinterest, rejection, or mute acceptance. Our relationship as members of a public is the fruit of our own rhetorical competencies, of our capacity to experience rhetoric. For this reason, rhetoric foregrounds publics and is rudimentary to their individuating identities; publics are constituted by the character of rhetorical exchanges shared among their members. These rhetorical considerations, I believe, provide conceptual and critical purchase to better explore the ways in which the conversations within and between publics shape society.

My association of discourse with rhetoric heretofore has drawn on a body of theory that is in the tradition of public address. This theory holds that democracies most commonly enact their public business from public presentational sites, such as the podium, printed page, legislative chamber, or executive office. The voices featured are those of leaders who present formal public arguments. Publics, however, also make their concerns known through rhetorical engagements among their members, as witnessed in the Habermas-Michnik exchange. Because portions of these exchanges and the language employed are frequently disseminated by mass media, knowledgeable participation transcends local boundaries. The means by which active citizens address one another are often less formal than institutional discourse, and their sites are not limited to institutional forums. More typically, in fact, a public's members converse through the everyday dialogue of symbolic interactions by which they share and contest attitudes, beliefs, values, and opinions. These are vernacular exchanges expressed in the language and style that members of a society must share to negotiate daily life in a community of strangers.[7] In the following two chapters we will consider how inclusion of these less formal discourses is fundamental to unpacking the rhetorical character of the public spheres they form and enter.

Chapter 2

DISCOURSE, RHETORICAL DISCOURSE, AND THE PUBLIC SPHERE

Civic life requires settings in which people meet as equals, without regard to race, class, or national origins. Thanks to the decay of civic institutions ranging from political parties to public parks and informal meeting places, conversation has become almost as specialized as the production of knowledge.

Christopher Lasch, *The Revolt of the Elites*

By some accounts, it would appear that a participatory public life has declined beyond retrieval. Richard Sennett has examined the possibility of living a rich public life under conditions of late capitalism and concluded that we have regressed into ritual relations with strangers. According to Sennett, we have lost the tension between our public personae and our private identities that gives meaning to both. Instead of being self-aware, we have become self-absorbed; we focus entirely on our private lives in which "we seek out not a principle but a reflection, that of what our psyches are, what is authentic in our feelings. We have tried to make the fact of being in private, alone with ourselves and with family and intimate friends, an end in itself" (Sennett 1978, 4). Writing contemporaneously with Sennett, Christopher Lasch (1978) argues that late capitalism not only encourages an inward focus in American culture but produces rampant narcissism.

Others link our society's failure to find invigoration in public life to its general lack of linguistic and conceptual tools suited for public living. Individuals seem unable to think and talk in meaningful ways that transcend the impulses and needs within their own skins. Sociologist Robert Bellah and his associates, for example, are not sold on the thesis of a psychological cause, such as narcissism, for the malaise of public life. After conducting in-depth interviews with a large cross section of middle America, his five-member research team concluded, "If there are vast numbers of a selfish, narcissistic 'me generation' in America, we did not find them, but we certainly did find that the language of individualism, the primary American language of self-understanding, limits the ways in which people think" (Bellah et al. 1985, 290). If Americans are unable to think about common problems beyond the relevant terms for their personal needs and concerns, Bellah's dismay over a constraining language of individualism is only heightened by the analysis advanced in Alasdair MacIntyre's *After Virtue*. In his quest for a common language of value to address the dilemmas of pluralism, MacIntyre (1984, 6–34) argues that the seeping emotivism in such individualistic interpretations of public problems precludes a common set of criteria for framing and adjudicating the moral issues of our time.[1] Emotivism presupposes the authority of each person to establish personal criteria for choice. By equating moral language with self-reports of attitudes, emotivism encourages incommensurable assumptions for framing and analyzing issues and assessing possible resolutions. Moreover, by emphasizing the other's instrumental value, as a means to be influenced in order to advance personal ends, emotivism devalues her from having autonomous worth, as an end in her own right. In short, emotivist discourse leaves a residue of manipulation that defies the public life of community.

MacIntyre's goal of crafting community consensus through moral discourse is seen by some as an unattainable ideal. Sociologist Joseph Gusfield maintains that the rhetoric of public problems is not necessarily in keeping with community behaviors and norms as these are lived in everyday life. Rather it presents an *image* of personal experiences and values that is resonant with society's dominant experiences. "From this standpoint," he says, "law provides a reassurance to some that the society is indeed their society, its meanings their meanings and its morality their morality." The issue, he contends, is not primarily over the extent to which these are fictional accounts of a real world. Their reality is immaterial since "the public order has a life of its own. It states the authoritative meanings of the culture as an absolutist homogeneous culture in a homogeneous society. As such it is capable of assuring those whose values it reflects that there is a society of consistent values in a culture of logical and morally satisfying meanings. It creates the illusion of cultural dominance" (Gusfield 1981, 182). Political scientist Benjamin Ginsberg extends Gusfield's analysis through a relentless critique of the ways in which the mirror of reality Gusfield identifies is aided and abetted by the use of polling data to manipulate the electorate's involvement in political public life (Ginsberg 1986). Although Western political ideology repeats Hume's dictum that all government rests on opinion, the conditions that gave rise to his dictum, Ginsberg contends, have since passed. The window of opportunity—conditions that produced representative bodies, elections, and other public expressions of will and interest required by the state in order to maintain civic order, collect taxes, and defend against external foes—has, in many respects, closed (221). In the words of Jean-François Lyotard, "Consensus has become an outmoded and suspect value" (1984, 66).

Each of these critiques suggests that the domain of public life—civil society—is in extremis. If that is so, then presumably public discourse has become inconsequential for steering public policy decisions. The field for public decision making presumably has been abandoned to propaganda; the state's discursive practices must oscillate between riling the masses to frenzy and rage or sedating them to passivity and acquiescence, as suits the purposes of those with access to the state's steering apparatus and/or the media's agenda-setting mechanisms. Such conditions make the concept of critique hollow, since we appear to lack, perhaps irretrievably so, an environment in which critique might engage minds and move spirits toward some effective change.

The power of elites to shape and even distort public discussion and public policy is difficult to deny. At the same time, for the foregoing analysis to be true, society would have to be in a passive stupor. Such analysis rests on assumptions of exclusivity and rationalism that can be challenged. In part, the assumption of exclusivity is suggested by the cliché of ordinary speech, in which we commonly refer to *the* public sphere as if it were a single, unified, and universal domain. However, the consequence is more than merely semantic insofar as this assumed singularity encourages conceptual blindness to how the *principle* of the public sphere is manifested in a *plurality* of spheres that can be differentiated from one another, as I will show. In many of these, publics not necessarily in the mainstream of civil society nonetheless contest the consequential issues in their members' lives. Moreover, blindness to these spheres unwittingly encourages imposing generalized norms of demonstration, verification, and justification to underwrite the validity of public reasoning. This rationalistic assumption overlooks the particularity of civic conversations and the problem it poses for generalizing beyond the given case.

The most important statement embodying these assumptions, and the one on which my discussion in this chapter will focus, is Jürgen Habermas's theory of communicative action as it is merged with his analysis of the public sphere. Because Habermas's model emphasizes ideal speech, it assesses the pragmatic opinions formed in the public sphere in terms of participants' competence and the rational validity of their discourse. I will argue that his model excludes many arenas in which public dialogue occurs and, moreover, establishes criteria for communication that are insensitive to its essential rhetoricality. In the process of critiquing his assumptions about communication, I will set forth an alternative set of assumptions more in tune with the rhetorical character of political exchange. These will form the basis for a more extended development of a rhetorical model in chapter 3.

Before proceeding, I must note that the problem of ordinary language discussed in chapter 1 reappears. There I argued that a plurality of publics is misrepresented by clichéd reference to *the* public. Here, however, use of the plural form presents a somewhat different problem, since cumbersome reference to multiple spheres within the more general public sphere of civil society threatens to introduce even greater confusion.

For better or worse, I have adopted the stylistic convention of referring to these multiple spheres as *arenas,* as well as *public spheres,* while retaining *Public Sphere* to refer to the undifferentiated public domain in which civic conversation, in general, occurs; I use modified references such as *bourgeois public sphere* when a specific public sphere is being discussed.

The Bourgeois Public Sphere

The nature of our public spheres is, arguably, the central consideration that conditions the possibility of a participatory public life. Our commitment to resolving public issues through open deliberation continues to be informed by Athenian democracy and its value of citizen participation. However, as we saw in the last chapter, its ideals of civic virtue presuppose a public space that enables every citizen to speak and cast ballots in an official capacity. Its citizens were active participants in a culture that was lacking a hard and fast line between the discursive realms of the agora and the ekklesia. Athens had no need for a public sphere since deliberations in the marketplace carried over to official exchanges. They were contiguous parts of a public life—what Hannah Arendt valorizes as the *public realm*— based on the ethos of individual virtuosity. The individualism of its civic virtue model produced decisions based on the authority of the strongest appeals and the most compelling deeds.

The magnitude of urban growth, the opening of far-flung commercial markets, along with the rise of representative forms of governance and the decline of the monarchy combined to change the character of the public realm from its Athenian antecedent. The seventeenth- and eighteenth-century emergence of a social and economic network of associations and exchanges outside the official institutions of power became a self-consciously autonomous domain of self-regulation.

The autonomy of civil society from state and institutional control signals more than the newly emergent inability of the state to organize society. It also attests to the importance modernity ascribes to public knowledge and informed opinion[2] for legitimating state action and regulating social relations. Democratic forms rest on opportunities for citizens to discuss issues that concern their interests so that they may influence intelligent public opinion and make it felt. Concomitantly, people engaged in everyday congress with strangers holding diverse beliefs, traditions, and interests have a comparable need for discursive forums in which they may develop a sense of prevailing opinion and participate in charting its course. The principle of a public sphere disengaged from power raises the theoretical possibility of its being impartial, so that alternative views may be tolerated and agreements may be reached on their merits (Taylor 1995, 264).

The Enlightenment problem of a discursive domain conducive to interaction among a growing society of strangers was addressed by the development of a public sphere suited to the realities of Europe's cultural, commercial, and political situation. Beginning with London, Paris, and Vienna but extending to entire nations, discussion of common matters required viable spaces for participation without necessarily directly encountering one's conversational partners. Moreover, these conversations among distanced and anonymous interlocutors required that their discussions be a discourse of reason existing outside power yet still normative for power (Taylor 1995, 265).

This experience of modernity has been explored by Habermas in his seminal analysis of the modern public sphere published in 1962 as *Strukturwandel der Öffentlichkeit* and translated into English in 1989 as *The Structural Transformation of the Public Sphere*. His study, subtitled "An Inquiry into a Category of Bourgeois Society," explores the historical development and transformation of the public sphere as the bourgeoisie's domain of legitimation for state action. Although a precursor to his subsequent development of the theory of communicative action and its accompanying model of universal pragmatics, this early formulation foreshadows his later thought. Specifically, Habermas was concerned then, as he has been subsequently, with the mutilating influence of ideological domination on public deliberation (1970a, 1971a, 1971b, 1975, 1979, 1984–1987). This model has become the center of contemporary discussion of the public sphere and provides a point of departure for developing a rhetorical alternative.

Habermas's argument for the origins of the bourgeois public sphere is important because it stresses the noninstitutional character of public discussion that engenders reasoned consideration of issues and problems pertaining to personal interests. The bourgeois public sphere originated during the Enlightenment with the development of café society in the coffeehouses of London, the salons of Paris, and the *Tischgesellschaften* (table societies) of Germany. Around the middle of the seventeenth century coffeehouses, salons, and table societies became popular centers for news gathering and distribution, literary criticism, and eventually political debate. Café society introduced a remarkable shift from the exclusive authority of aristocrats and educated humanists over matters of culture and politics. Any patron could enter these discussions regardless of birth, rank, occupation, or formal education. The only requirement was the obvious one—that a person had read literature relevant to the discussion. The coffeehouses and salons gave the middle class a participatory life in discussions of timely issues from which a general consensus or public opinion might emerge. Early in the eighteenth century London had over two thousand coffeehouses alive with public conversations over the merits of literary works and, eventually, political policies. The luminaries of café society, who excelled in spirited conversation, and the controversial topics that occupied their attention were chronicled in Joseph Addison and Richard Steele's *Tattler*, first published in 1709; the *Spectator*; and other literary journals of the day. Similarly, by the mid eighteenth century Parisian salons governed opinions more effectively than did the royal court. As a place where talent could outshine title, the salons were an experiment in equality and emancipation that assumed paradigmatic value in a hierarchically organized society.

This public sphere was launched by middle-class literary practices of reading novels and learned criticism appearing in the press in order to participate with others in conversations. Habermas observes that the exchanges of literate society "formed the public sphere of a *rational-critical debate* in the world of letters within which the subjectivity originating in the interiority of the conjugal family, by communicating with itself, attained clarity about itself" (1989, 51; emphasis mine). This practice then became generalized as fundamental to the discursive norms he considers to be defining characteristics of the bourgeois public sphere.

According to Habermas the bourgeois public sphere originated in the middle-class concern with protecting its commercial interests through political regulation of civil society. It mustered little sympathy for proletarian or peasant issues. Nonetheless, its discursive standards were not linked to political or economic ideology but to Enlightenment ideals of reason and rational opinion from which society forged a public understanding of matters that were consequential in private relations. Habermas envisions the bourgeois public sphere, above all,

> as the sphere of private people come together as a public; they soon claimed the public sphere regulated from above against the public authorities themselves, to engage them in debate over the general rules governing relations in the basically privatized but publicly relevant sphere of commodity exchange and social labor. The medium of this political confrontation was peculiar and without historical precedent: people's public use of their reason. (Habermas 1989, 27)

Here we have a mode of public opinion distinguishable from the common or vulgar opinion of the masses because it was shaped through "the critical reflections of a public competent to form its own judgments" (Habermas 1989, 90). The rationality of public opinion, itself an essential question to be addressed on each public issue, could only be guaranteed through *critical publicity,* and the bourgeois public sphere arose as a space which served the function of providing it.

Habermas conceptualizes the public sphere as an autonomous and ideally impermeable space existing between the spheres of private interests, which range from those of the individual and family through those of private commercial entities and of the state. This discursive arena is generated whenever individuals or groups gather in a public capacity, that is when they engage in discussion of a public matter. The public sphere's participants have neither a vested interest in the matter at hand nor official authority to act on it. Habermas characterizes them as *disinterested* parties, which means they are nonpartisans who occupy an extrapolitical space and are, therefore, in principle able to reach consensus based on reason.

In order to provide a rational basis for state action, the public sphere must function as the site of critical publicity that allows ideas, conduct, and proposed policies to receive inspection from all points of view. Their validity is tested by an ability to withstand refutation, which means that *warranted assent* within the public sphere is to be achieved through generalizable arguments that adhere to the norms of ideal speech (Habermas 1970b, 1979, 1984–1987). These norms project a public sphere in which there are institutionally guaranteed rights to participate in open discussion, to access relevant information, to access the means of disseminating information, and in which interlocutors are assumed competent to redeem their claims and to have equal opportunity to refute and respond, to assess utterances in terms of their capacity to satisfy relevant validity claims, and to adjudicate claims on the basis of warranted assent. They set the conditions for public opinion as an expression of rational consensus.

Habermas summarizes his position on the defining characteristics of "the public sphere" as follows:

> By "the public sphere" we mean first of all a realm of our social life in which something approaching public opinion can be formed. Access is guaranteed to all citizens. A portion of the public sphere comes into being in every conversation in which private individuals assemble to form a public body. They then behave neither like business or professional people transacting private affairs, nor like members of a constitutional order subject to the legal constraints of a state bureaucracy. Citizens behave as a public body when they confer in an unrestricted fashion—that is, with the guarantee of freedom of assembly and association and the freedom to express and publish their opinions—about matters of general interest. In a large public body this kind of communication requires specific means for transmitting information and influencing those who receive it. Today newspapers and magazines, radio and TV are the media of the public sphere. We speak of the public sphere in contrast, for instance, to the literary one, when public discussion deals with objects connected to the activity of the state. Although state activity is so to speak the executor of the political public sphere, it is not a part of it. . . . Only when the exercise of political control is

> effectively subordinated to the democratic demand that infor-
> mation be accessible to the public, does the political public
> sphere win an institutional influence over the government
> through the instrument of law-making bodies. (1974, 49)

As a normative framework, Habermas's depiction of the bourgeois public sphere establishes a counterfactual ideal (1970a, 1974, 1975, 1989) against which to assess actual practice. Certainly the rational integrity of such a system is difficult to refute, since its standards for judgment and action emphasize criteria of reason, evidence, argument, and egalitarian procedure that appear to encompass any person with a legitimate claim to participate in public deliberative processes. For this reason, political theorist Nancy Fraser has argued that Habermas's model of the bourgeois public sphere establishes a domain indepen-dent of the state for the circulation of discourses that, in principle, are capable of achieving critical judgment of the state. "It designates a the-atre in modern societies in which political participation is enacted through the medium of talk" (Fraser 1990, 57). Such a forum is essen-tial for citizen participation in common affairs and thus, in her view, "is indispensable to critical social theory and democratic political practice" (57). Of course, as a counterfactual ideal, Habermas's model remains unfulfilled in any given historical situation. It serves as a template against which actually existing discursive conditions and practices may be measured and assessed in terms of the structural and ideological dis-tortions that define any given actually existing public sphere.

Rhetorical Counterassumptions to Habermas's Model

In an era in which special interests and the state have reduced politics to mass-media spectacle and "audience" has become an economic variable of spectators who are expected to applaud and purchase, Habermas advances a critical antidote by returning the medium of deliberative speech to political relations. By conceptualizing citizen action as the prod-uct of participatory deliberation, he reasserts their rational function to evaluate and judge. However, as a broad spectrum of critics has indicated, this is a model of a particular public sphere—the *bourgeois* public sphere.[3] As such it contains problematic assumptions that fail to account for other types of public spheres and that make its generalizability questionable. It ignores the discourse of those who are not part of the bourgeoisie, which makes its theoretical adequacy disputable. In Fraser's words, the model of the bourgeois public sphere is less than satisfactory as "a category capable of theorizing the limits of actually existing democracy" (1990, 57).

Fraser proposes that we need a model that is true to the political real-ities of modern democracies without sacrificing the conceptual distinction

Habermas has drawn between the spheres of state action and private interests and that of the public arena of citizen discourse and association. To accomplish this end, she argues that we must challenge the core assumptions of Habermas's bourgeois model.

Fraser raises four counterarguments against Habermas's model of the bourgeois public sphere. She contends:

1. Habermas assumes that it is possible for interlocutors in a public sphere to bracket status differentials and to deliberate "as if" they were social equals. Fraser denies the assumption that societal equality is not a necessary condition for political democracy. Because inequalities are real and publicly known, they defy successful bracketing.

2. Habermas assumes that a single, comprehensive public sphere is always preferable to a nexus of multiple publics. However, if the ideal is participatory parity, then, Fraser contends, arrangements that accommodate contestive relations among a plurality of competing publics better promote that end than does a single, comprehensive, overarching public.

3. Habermas assumes that a public sphere's discourse should be restricted to deliberation about the common good and that the appearance of "private interests" and "private issues" is always undesirable. But this assumes that there is one common good and overlooks that discovering and disclosing participant interests are virtues of deliberation.

4. Habermas assumes that a functioning democratic public sphere requires sharp separation between civil society and the state. Fraser argues that this separation supports weak publics, whose function consists exclusively in opinion formation but has no role in decision making and fails to provide a satisfactory treatment of parliamentary bodies as alternative, strong publics.

These objections are developed in terms of a class and gender bias she finds in Habermas's model, which led her to conclude that it is unable to satisfy Habermas's own standard of critical rationality.

Habermas has responded to such critiques as unpersuasive because they distort the essential assumptions about communication that lie at his model's core. His emphasis is on the conditions of rational discourse that have normative force for the public sphere as a category of democratic action. He repeatedly makes the point that the bourgeois public sphere presupposes open, rational deliberation leading to emancipation. Insofar as groups and classes are eliminated from or excluded from the bourgeois public sphere, their very exclusion is a defining condition of the sphere, affecting its capacity for rational legitimation of state action. But since the conditions of this sphere are predicated in critical deliberation, not structural biases, these distorting omissions are always correctable.[4]

My concern here is not to enter into the specific points of contention between Habermas and Fraser but to underscore that *the Fraser-Habermas argument centers on the centrality of communication to the public sphere.* Habermas manages to offer a satisfactory response only to the degree that one embraces the normative force of ideal speech. Insofar as his theory of communicative action makes assumptions that are *skewed with respect to "actually existing democracy," his model is heuristically defective.* I believe it *is* skewed with respect to actually existing democracy, that his assumptions are at odds with the basic rhetorical character of political discourse.

Habermas's theory of communicative action guarantees the truth of political activity insofar as all decisions are reached through the process of critical publicity. At the level of *discourse,* speech is regulated by the assumption that rational discourse should prevail in public deliberations. Despite the alluring rationality of this model, the ideal of rational consensus deflects us from seriously considering the untidy communicative practices that prevail in everyday political relations at the level of *talk.*[5] Instead, it tends to regard rhetorical discourse, which is avowedly strategic in character, as a form of ideological distortion. This antirhetorical predisposition inevitably formulates an ideal for interaction contrary to the very character of political communication.

Political communication is inherently rhetorical, and rational consensus is not always a rhetorical possibility. Political rhetoric is saturated with partisanship, which makes immunity from ideological distortion highly improbable. The political environment of a public sphere is marked by naturally occurring oppositional encounters. Its ecology encourages communicative practices guided by strategic considerations for advancing partisan interests—practices that Habermas explicitly critiques as inducing ideological distortion. Given his assumptions, Habermas's negative critique of prevailing deliberative processes in actually existing democracies has the inevitability of analytic reasoning. While such practices are neither exemplary nor beyond critique, Habermas posits norms that are contrary to the character of the empirical phenomena he theorizes. To move toward a model that theorizes the public sphere in a manner coincident with actual communicative practices in actually existing democracies, we first must specify critical points of difference between rhetorically conceived communication and the normative frame Habermas has proposed. There are at least six problems with Habermas's model that highlight these differences.

Problem 1: The idealized universal public sphere *conceals the ways in which particular, often marginalized public arenas form and function.* Further, it conceals how some of these arenas are excluded, often legally, from the domain of official public action. Historical studies of the nineteenth and early twentieth century suggest that the bourgeois public sphere was one of several that had formed as functional domains of public deliberation. For example, Fraser (1990) lists the proletarian, feminine, nationalist, popular peasant, and elite women's spheres as discursive realms that Habermas's model ignores. Terry Eagleton (1984) develops an account of the tensions within the literary public sphere that produced the literary counterpublic sphere. And Geoff Eley (1992) points to the development of reasoned exchange aimed at emancipation in the nonbourgeois public spheres of the nineteenth-century peasant and working classes. Habermas's model fails to take account of this range of differences within and between spheres. It ignores publics and public arenas in opposition to the bourgeois public sphere and misses the transformations of domination to voices of nonbourgeois publics, such as those of workers, when they enter the dialogue within the bourgeois public sphere.

Oskar Negt and Alexander Kluge's (1967) analysis of the proletarian public sphere provides a fascinating illustration of the consequences that follow from differences between a nonbourgeois sphere and its bourgeois counterpart. The proletarian public sphere has a specific interest in conditions of labor. It is organized as the workers' movement, which binds those in this sphere by their shared interests and experiences and places these shared bonds on the continuum of the movement's evolution. Proletarian interests are specific to moving society in a particular direction with respect to wages, labor conditions, relations with management, and so forth. The organizing forms of the proletarian public sphere, such as unionization, draw these interests into the "life-context of society." The interests of workers evoke a natural "resistance to their bourgeois opponent," and their self-identity is realized by "maintain[ing] themselves as something concretely separate" (Negt and Kluge 1967, 93). This organizing principle is decidedly not a universal norm intended to insure the rationality of critical publicity.

Negt and Kluge point out that once workers enter the bourgeois public sphere, they lose their identity as individuals and as the working class and become a raw material to be redistributed. Their capacity to speak in their own voice is lost under the pressure of bourgeois ideology to turn "workers into objects, politically, just as they are objects of production relations in the economic domain. The bourgeois public sphere confronts the individual worker as a relationship of capital, but confronts the whole working class above all as the State power monopoly, as an extra-economic power relationship" (93). In other words, to be heard within the bourgeois public sphere, Negt and Kluge argue, the worker's movement must sacrifice the very terms in which it constitutes its own self-consciousness and present itself instead in extraeconomic terms dictated by the state.

In fairness to Habermas, his original project was intended to theorize only the bourgeois public sphere and its structural transformation, not all public spheres, although his critics and apologists have treated his model as if it were universal (e.g., Robbins 1993). In a later writing Habermas recognizes that his "overly stylized depiction of the public sphere leads to an unjustified idealization" in which a single public is assumed to appear in a homogeneous bourgeois public sphere whose underlying shared class interest ultimately enables conflicting parties to resolve their differences (1992, 424–25).

Framing the discussion of multiple spheres in terms of a single, idealized universal domain extends beyond Habermas's project, however, to the general problem of whether the model is sensitive to empirical conditions that are influencing the phenomenon under study. By recognizing the need for greater differentiation among a plurality of public spheres, Habermas makes the point that "a different picture emerges if *from the very beginning* one admits the coexistence of competing public spheres and takes account of the dynamics of those processes of communication that are excluded from the dominant public sphere" (1992, 424). Feminist scholarship has shown that these nonbourgeois spheres often emerged in response to changing conditions. Contingencies of law, religion, revolution, economics, communication, and the like influence the types of spheres that form and the discourse they will support or repress. We also need to account for the processes that impede or facilitate border crossings between spheres. Blindness to empirical conditions of exclusion and inclusion can obscure an ideological overlay within a seemingly rational and egalitarian discursive domain.[6] An effective model requires openness to those conditions that produce a plurality of spheres within the public sphere.

Problem 2: The model of the unitary public sphere *neglects the lattice of actually existing public spheres.* Related to the problem of *concealing* discourse on the margins is the problem of accounting for the functioning domains whose exchanges seek to influence society's self-regulatory processes.

Habermas finds the size and scope of the late modern state problematic for the viability of the public sphere. In this respect he shares the tendency of modern theorists, noted in chapter 1, to mint idealized conceptions of "the public" and then not find them existing anywhere. To locate a time when theory and praxis fused, Habermas (1974) turns to the mid-nineteenth-century groundswell of locales and outlets of open deliberation aimed at public opinion formation.

Habermas's analysis of Paris during 1848 is illustrative. There, he notes, "every halfway eminent politician organized his club, every other his journal: 450 clubs and over 250 journals were established there between February and May alone. Until the permanent legalization of a politically functional public sphere, the appearance of a political newspaper meant joining the struggle for freedom and public opinion, and thus for the public sphere as a principle" (1974, 53). After a constitutional state was established in France, the press was relieved of its burden to establish freedom. At that point it could and did concentrate instead on its commercial potential (53). The consequence was a transformation of the bourgeois public sphere through an influx of private interests; the generalizable interests of the bourgeois public no longer were dominant.

Habermas is quite right to fix on the commercialization of the press and consequent loss of critical scrutiny. Nor can we dismiss attempts by the state to control the course of society through rationalization rather than allow it to evolve through open deliberation. As Habermas argues in *Legitimation Crisis*, these developments undermine the basic assumptions of a rational and legitimating consensus that is the norm for the bourgeois public sphere. As a result, however, he emphasizes the decline of the public sphere under the weight of the welfare state and instrumental rationality. Although his later work suggests the possibility of a public sphere that might produce critical-rational discourse, in general he remains pessimistic about the viability of the bourgeois public sphere under conditions of late capitalism.

John Rodger's (1985) insightful analysis of Habermas's model proposes a revision to its unitary character by distinguishing between institutional and preinstitutional public spheres. The institutional public sphere includes those domains of discourse in which opinions are directly related to official actions. Preinstitutional public spheres are discursive domains that create within themselves the conditions for argument about the validity claims of legitimacy and authority.[7] This is the realm of civil society.

Civil society cannot be equated with the state or reduced to the economy. As we saw in chapter 1, it is a web of discursive arenas in which members of society engage one another in ongoing dialogues that continually confront public problems, constitute publics, and challenge within and across domains for the formation of public opinion. Some of these are structured domains that accommodate a more or less defined body of issues, such as the proletarian public sphere, while others are more ephemeral, arising and passing with the particular issues that call for discourse. A rhetorical model of the public sphere would regard each of these engagements as part of the ensemble of discourse that constitutes civil society, examining each encounter as part of a social dialogue on appropriating historicity. *A rhetorical model reveals rather than conceals the emergence of publics as a process.*

Problem 3: The principle of disinterest *excludes those subspheres whose members are decidedly interested.* Habermas advances this principle to distinguish deliberation on public issues from the propaganda of vested interests and the private conversations of individuals on personal matters. But his distinction forms an expectation that those who participate in a public sphere are capable of listening with open minds and should be resistant to the evocative discourse that engages how their personal conditions intersect the background consensus of intersubjective interpretations, or the life-world, from which consciousness of interests arises. Arenas such as the proletarian or feminist or nationalist spheres deny this expectation. Participation in these spheres presupposes an interest in the concerns of work or gender or national identity they accommodate. Even those in Habermas's idealized bourgeois public sphere are interested in this sense, since the bourgeoisie is inherently interested in the commercial economy. Discourse intent on gaining the assent of those who share the consequences of a public problem inevitably addresses them as particular individuals and groups. We adapt our arguments to our audience's readiness to attend, understand, and respond (Arnold 1968; Johnstone 1982; Wichelns 1958) through such rhetorical concerns as *kairos* (timing) and decorum. These rhetorical characteristics of addressed discourse belie the condition of disinterest.

Equally, the conditions of communication that permit or preclude concrete adaptations shape the tangible character of actual public spheres. For example, Habermas's principle of disinterest seems to require that when we participate in social discussions intended to influence public opinion our judgments ideally should be dispassionate. This is counterintuitive to the reactions that follow from being engaged, which entails considering the human consequences that follow from public decisions. A case in point is the discussion that grew from the Reagan administration's adoption of the Herman Kahn–inspired analysis of nuclear holocaust in terms of game theory. Game theory provided a dialectical context for thinking the unthinkable, in which national defense policy for the development and deployment of nuclear weapons was based on the calculated consequences of first-strike capability, on the opposition's capacity to respond, and on levels of civilian casualties acceptable to the general public (Cooper 1983). Compelling rhetorical counters to game theory analysis occurred in popular films, such as *On the Beach* and *Dr. Strangelove,* Jonathan Schell's *The Fate of the Earth,* and the TV drama *The Day After,* which focused on catastrophic and irreversible change to human life from a nuclear holocaust. Defense planners dismissed the general public's reactions of distress as irrelevant to their ongoing discussion of first-strike capability. Their dismissive response was consistent with the logical presuppositions of game theory but violated the self-regarding concerns of individuals and groups for judgments about matters whose consequences they feel. These sorts of judgments are neither abstract nor irrational. They are *nonrational* or *arational* judgments in that they revolve around projections of a *particular* world with a *particular* outcome that will have an impact on their lives. To say that outrage, fear, love, or other emotions as judgments about a possible world are irrational and, thus, irrelevant to a decision about that world reverses the normal burden of proof. The burden should be to demonstrate why one should not engage a question of the catastrophic loss of human life in terms of a self-involving future that emotions project.[8]

People become engaged because issues touch their lives. A rhetorical understanding of communication regards life-engaging decisions as necessarily involving emotions. Emotions are essential for establishing the relationship between an attentive and empowered audience and their particular circumstances. Sound judgment on practical conduct requires a public able to experience the pleasures and pains occasioned by civic relationships. How are we to appreciate the needs of others if our discourse has no means for engaging them at the level of the contingencies that inform their civic conduct? And how are we to build and sustain a community with bonds of affiliation and commitment if we lack means for making their particular interests relevant to framing public policies? In the classical tradition's rendition of rhetoric as an architectonic productive art, engaging emotions in tandem with reason is necessary for sound public judgment; it is essential to ponder proportion between acts and consequences and for prudence to prevail. For this reason Aristotle pronounced deliberative-audience judgments as most reliable *because* their own interests were at stake. Consequently, they cannot arrive at a judgment that is "disinterested."

The conditions of communication rouse and shape our awareness of interests to the extent that they influence what may be spoken about, who may speak, and what may be said. Our discourse about political, social, cultural, and economic interests constitutes our consciousness of them, suggesting that *accommodation of conflicting interests should supplant disinterestedness as a mark of a well-functioning public sphere.*

Problem 4: The criterion of communicative rationality *contributes to the exclusionary character of the public sphere by constraining open access.* Habermas distinguishes rationality that is strategic in nature, or *purposive rationality*, from that which is emancipatory, or *communicative rationality*. The former concerns finding suitable means to preordained ends, and rationality there refers to the efficiency or consistency of choices. The latter concerns overcoming obstacles to undistorted communication, and rationality here refers to the degree to which one approaches the norm of resolving conflict by the force of the better argument. The latter is the meaning he associates with communication in the public sphere.

The norm of communicative rationality underwrites the four validity claims, which Habermas recognizes as counterfactual standards in actual practice. His position is that:

> In action oriented to reaching understanding, validity claims
> are "always already" implicitly raised. Those universal claims
> (to the comprehensibility of the symbolic expression, the truth
> of the propositional content, the truthfulness of the intention-

> al expression, and the rightness of the speech act with respect
> to existing norms and values) are set in the general structures
> of possible communication. In these validity claims commu-
> nicative theory can locate a gentle, but obstinate, a never silent
> although seldom redeemed claim to reason, a claim that must
> be recognized *de facto* whenever and wherever there is to be
> consensual action. (Habermas 1979, 97)

Communicative rationality posits that every serious discussion must assume an interlocutor who is able to redeem his claims discursively. Otherwise there is no rational defense for deliberative actions aimed at securing warranted assent on the basis of the better argument.

However, the force of the better argument is a criterion whose mean-ingfulness depends on prior standards of propriety, relevance, evidence, and good reasons. These standards may differ among individuals and groups. Claims that fail to satisfy such criteria can be dismissed as irrational because they cannot be redeemed at the level of shared rational criteria. Specifically, they cannot satisfy the aforementioned validity claims. The four validity claims themselves presuppose an audience capable of rendering judgments that guarantee the quality of decisions in terms of universalizable standards of assent. Arguments that fail this test are rejected as mere opin-ion. Thus Habermas's better argument criterion excludes arguments that insist on the legitimacy of nonbourgeois interests or seek critical publicity for concerns that bourgeois interests deem private (Landes 1992, 112). Although Habermas may claim that there is no in-principle obstacle to con-sidering the arguments for such claims, the criteria of communicative ratio-nality require that in the absence of a background consensus communica-tion moves to the level of discourse, by which he means deliberation on the rational necessity of the abstract principle behind social action. At that level communicative rationality precludes the particularistic claims of interest or the public character of private problems. It also imposes the false dichotomy between reason and feeling discussed under problem 3. Over and against its emancipatory aims, the criterion of communicative rationality actually con-tributes to the exclusionary tendency of the bourgeois public sphere.

The rhetorical character of addressed arguments suggests local norms of *reasonableness* as a more appropriate criterion than global norms of rationality for assessing appeals in a given public sphere. This standard acknowledges that there are no absolutes for assessing the force of a better argument since argu-ments have no force apart from satisfying those standards that particular publics are prepared to summon. Invoking public-specific standards that can accommodate conflicting interests suggests that good reasons *are the operative basis for the actual state of agreement forged through the polyvocality of a public sphere.*[9]

Problem 5: The norm of warranted assent to be achieved by generalizable arguments *is contrary to the particularity of public issues.* Habermas posits critical publicity as the function of the public sphere. This should produce a rational consensus of warranted assent that provides rational legitimation to public policies. The norms for judging arguments transcend any particular interest; they are generalizable conclusions that are supported by universally applicable arguments. But the language of universality is contrary to the character of issues addressed in multiple arenas. They are not general problems but particular ones that develop from what the ancient Greeks referred to as *phainomena,* or appearances. These are the confusing array of individuals and events that are subject to interpretation and must be interpreted for civic decisions to be made. As such they are specifically not amenable to resolution through dialectical argument intended to achieve universal validity. Public issues raise contingent concerns that must be resolved in their particularity, and the mode of discourse by which this is accomplished is rhetoric.[10] Consequently, Habermas denies to public problems both the language of particularity most aptly expressed in vernacular modes of conversational communication and the mode of discourse anchored in *prudentia* most appropriate for resolving them.

As a correlative problem, Habermas's criterion of generalizable arguments imposes a precondition that contains a judgment about language use or style and acceptable modes of argument or propriety. His norms of generalizable arguments treat the tumult of democracy as if partisan clash were defective when, in fact, partisan conflict is the ongoing self-producing, self-regulating alternative to ideological hegemony or force. To treat contest and partisanship as evil or inherently defective is to prejudge the terms of almost all disputes, along with their less than ideal resolutions. In short, Habermas dampens the range of appearance for controversy—an inherent feature of all public spheres—by excluding rhetorical discourse in favor of the rationalistic argumentation of philosophy.

Public issues necessarily intersect reason with commitments. They involve retreats to commitment where behaviors are less than rational and evoke a *tu quoque* response.[11] A rhetorical model would reinstate these partisan discourses without a priori assessment of their validity. It would invoke different standards such as kairos or timing, *to prepon* or propriety, immediacy, and adherence, each of which is sensitive to the specificity of audience and the situated character of addressed discourse. Its concern would be with how *the dialogue within any given public sphere mounts appeals that lead participants to understand their interests and make prudent judgments.*

Problem 6: The model of ideal speech *is at odds with conditions of diversity that define civil society.* Habermas's model of communicative action finds its telos in rational consensus produced through warranted assent. The rationality of warranted assent is guaranteed by the conditions of communication adhering to the model of ideal speech. In addition to satisfying the four validity claims, the defining conditions of the ideal speech situation include equal access to discussions by those who will feel their consequences, equal access to information and their media of dissemination, and conditions of reciprocity that permit participants equal opportunities to refute the arguments of others and defend their own. Presumably when the conditions of ideal speech are satisfied, they will produce consensus based on warranted assent. The basis for such assent will be the weight of the better argument stemming from its superior rationality.

Habermas holds that warranted assent is subverted primarily by conditions that induce distortion. Distortion occurs either through strategic communication, intended to achieve assent based on less than forthcoming representations, or through the systematic distortion of ideological assumptions that produce a state of false consciousness. His model assumes that failure to reach consensus is the result of distortion. It does not take into account that dissensus also can arise from conditions of difference. In fact, Habermas's model nowhere accounts for disagreements that arise out of difference. This omission is particularly disabling because it limits his model's efficacy with respect to conditions of actually existing democracy.

Historically, civil society has been understood as a realm in which difference was a defining condition that necessitated tolerance of diverse ideas, ends, and social practices. In an interactive state of self-regulation, interdependence with strangers does not require that you agree with those aspects of belief and conduct divergent from your own, but that you are tolerant of differences in order to sustain the range of cooperation necessary for society to function. These accommodations are not entirely the pragmatic ones of economics and politics. The basic right of individuals to their cultural traditions creates a moral necessity for tolerance. But tolerance of diversity among traditions and the belief structures they support means that there can be disagreement without distortion. Put differently, understanding does not necessarily lead to agreement.

Hudson Meadwell (1995) has pointed out that by failing to take account of difference, Habermas faces a dilemma. The model of ideal speech cannot satisfy its condition of nonexclusion without admitting difference. But admitting difference means that disagreement can arise without introducing distortion, since it is possible for us to understand the views of those whose traditions diverge from our own while not sharing their culturally based views. Consequently, it is impossible for the ideal speech situation to culminate in warranted assent without violating the condition of nonexclusion, on the one hand, or satisfying the basic requirement of tolerance by which civil society accommodates difference, without foregoing warranted assent in cases where such difference leads to disagreement.

An emphasis on consensus hearkens to premodern conditions of communication, which were weak in diversity and placed a strong emphasis on shared traditions for resolving differences. In the late-modern or postmodern context, continual encounter with difference strips the productiveness of consensus as the test of communication for the pluralistic conditions of actually existing democracy. When multiple perspectives are the norm, the realistic test of a position's strength is less that it achieves agreement than that it can be understood across perspectives and, as a result, provide a basis for cooperation among interdependent partners (McKeon 1956). Mutual dependency requires that communicative partners share a common reference world in which *common understanding supplants warranted assent as the communicative norm for achieving reasonable mutual cooperation and toleration.*

Conclusion

Jürgen Habermas's critique of the contemporary public sphere grows from locating its theoretical norms in ideal speech. His emphasis on discursive practices makes an important contribution by locating an arena for participation in public issues. Yet his idealized theory of discourse runs contrary to the lived experience of political relations. His model contains an a priori disposition to overlook both discursive milieus that fall outside the institutionally sanctioned enclaves of empowered exchange and modes of discourse that do not adhere to the norms of ideal speech. Habermas envisions a universalized public sphere populated by disinterested participants who adhere to rationalistic norms and unitary modes of expression on which they base warranted assent.

This idealized vision is at odds with the rhetorical features of discourse as it is practiced in a democracy. The addressed and particularized character of discourse on public problems suggests that rhetorical assumptions are a more consonant alternative to those of ideal speech for assessing the discursive practices of actually existing democracy. They provide the basis for a rhetorical model of the Public Sphere. A rhetorical model would require openness to those conditions that produce a plurality of spheres within the Public Sphere. It would focus on civil society's lattice of spheres as the loci of society's "multilogue" on self-organization and would conceptualize publics as processes that emerge through discourse of social actors who are attempting to appropriate their own historicity. The partisan nature of this discourse makes assumptions of disinterest counterintuitive. A rhetorical model of public spheres not only expects participants to have interests but regards them as essential for the exercise of prudent judgments on public problems. It supplants disinterestedness with accommodation of conflicting interests as a mark of a well-functioning public sphere. Rather than a universal standard of warranted assent based on the rational force of the arguments, a rhetorical model recognizes that we engage in civic conversation on particular issues with specific interlocutors and audiences. Invoking audience-specific standards that can accommodate conflicting interests suggests that good reasons are the operative basis for actual consensus forged through the heteroglossia, or myriad situated meanings, of a public sphere. Equally, a rhetorical model abandons the search for generalizable arguments. Its concern is for how the dialogue within any given public sphere mounts appeals that lead participants to understand their interests and make prudent judgments. Finally, a rhetorical model recognizes that civil society's defining conditions of interdependence and diversity require that communicative partners share a common reference world. Common understanding supplants warranted assent as the communicative norm for achieving reasonable mutual cooperation and toleration.

A rhetorical understanding of public talk advances a different orientation to "the" public sphere. In the next chapter I will pursue these differences further to develop a rhetorical model of the Public Sphere. There I will consider how the conversational character of civil society is paradigmatic for the Public Sphere as a discursive realm. This type of exchange is a public's means for negotiating its members' norms and priorities for society. I will argue for the Public Sphere as a nested domain of particularized arenas or multiple spheres populated by participants who, by adherence to standards of reasonableness reflected in the vernacular language of conversational communication, discover their interests, where they converge or differ, and how their differences might be accommodated.

Chapter 3

CIVIC CONVERSATION AND THE RETICULATE PUBLIC SPHERE

It is incontestable that the people frequently conduct public business very badly; but it is impossible that the lower orders should take part in public business without extending the circle of their ideas and quitting the ordinary routine of their thoughts.

Alexis de Tocqueville, *Democracy in America*

The Enlightenment experience of mutual dependency and difference ignited the idea of society as self-regulating, in significant measure by spreading ideas and beliefs through conversation. At least in theory democratic societies still adhere to the belief that opinions formed through give-and-take in a public sphere are more than mere opinions. They are *public* opinions and provide the template of public knowledge that makes civil society, and therefore public life, possible. They provide criteria and direction for social action and are most consequential when taken seriously by some agency with power to act. As John Dewey (1954, 27ff) observed, the potency of a political public sphere requires that legislative and administrative bodies subordinate their exercise of political control to the demand for publicity, access to information, and participation in decision-making processes. The political public sphere is undermined if citizens are guaranteed access only to find it fettered with restraints of law, economics, group psychology, information, or the like. Equally, special interests arguing for their partisan advantage can deflect the attention of a public sphere from the common interest, resulting in a steady deterioration of civil society (Habermas 1970a; Sennett 1978, 224–37).

Habermas has argued correctly that critical publicity is more likely to occur when there are constitutional guarantees to safeguard public discussion, deliberation, and commemoration. Legal protections guaranteeing rights to free speech and open debate without fear of being sued or sent to prison are more likely to foster open and frank exchange than their absence. Hence, his diagnosis of any given instance of political discourse outside the state is guided by institutional conditions controlling that specific sphere's existence, nature, and function. He reinforces his emphasis on institutional constraints with his claim that a principle of the public sphere can exist without a formal institution of the public sphere only when the functioning of public opinion is guaranteed by three guidelines:

general accessibility, elimination of all privileges, and discovery of general norms and rational legitimations (Habermas 1974, 50, trans. note 3).

Institutional features undeniably are essential components of any public sphere. Jean Cohen and Andrew Arato (1992, 187), for example, maintain that the failure of the United States to institutionalize small-scale structures of direct political participation produced a corresponding identification of freedom and state aims with the negative freedoms of private life guaranteed by constitutional rights. They contend that without small-scale public structures for political exchange, Americans lack appropriate settings to establish their capacity as citizens. Meanwhile, the bureaucratic state seeks administrative solutions to questions of collective welfare. Cohen and Arato come to the Arendtean conclusion that a bureaucracy's tendency to grant its agents discretionary power to act in invisible ways behind a facade of apparently open deliberation conceals those who should be accountable for public decision making, resulting in rule by nobody.

Institutional settings have further significance as scenes for the public discourse that does appear. In a bureaucracy charged to manage the state on the principle of collective welfare, discourse is organized along lines of *power*, as the wealthy seek to retain their economic advantage; *status*, as elites of lineage, position, and knowledge seek to retain their privilege to define issues and solutions; and *need*, as those who are economically, politically, or socially disenfranchised and those whose special interests are threatened seek protection and survival under the law. A bureaucratic environment lacks spaces where these claims to privilege or exceptional status are established through an enactment of citizenship. They are established, instead, through privileged access to the decision-making process and to decision makers themselves.

However, this lack of *official* spaces for enactment of citizenly capacity does not mean that public sites fail to emerge or that discourse on matters that transcend an individual's personal affairs ceases to exist. As I have been arguing, the multiple discursive arenas of the Public Sphere are neither exclusively formal structures nor exclusively confined within institutional structures; their significance does not stem from their institutional character but their rhetoricality. Institutional constraints are significant because they regulate the kinds of content and presentation permitted in and excluded from a public's realm of discussion and, therefore, the active consideration and role of these forms in shaping a public opinion. The absence of an institutional guarantee is relevant to the character and consequences of symbolic transactions—mostly but not exclusively discursive—by which society negotiates its way from a Hobbesean community of each against all to a rhetorical community of *common meaning* able to accommodate respectful difference.

My point is illustrated by Hannah Arendt's discussion of the French resistance. In *Between Past and Future* she considers René Char's resistance story in which he and his comrades had become "challengers" whose lives were invested with meaning through opposition to the Nazi regime. By joining the resistance they had created a "public realm where—without the paraphernalia of officialdom and hidden from the eyes of friend and foe—all relevant business in the affairs of the country was transacted in deed and word" (Arendt 1977, 3). Matters of personal interest were weightless in comparison with the circumstances they confronted together. Whereas their lives in private had been filled with the emptiness of self-centered concerns, as public actors they took on transcendent meaning. In the public realm these same men and women were able to discover their individuality and, related to this, an inner strength in the sincerity of their actions. Char concludes, "At every meal that we eat together, freedom is invited to sit down. The chair remains vacant, but the place is set." Arendt interprets him to mean:

> they had been visited for the first time in their lives by an apparition of freedom, not, to be sure, because they acted against tyranny and things worse than tyranny—this was true for every soldier in the Allied armies—but because they had become "challengers," had taken the initiative upon themselves and therefore without knowing or even noticing it, had begun to create that public space between themselves where freedom could appear. (1977, 4)

The link between the resisters' positive self-awareness and their shared experience as a public in a public realm is not incidental. Their lives were enriched through acting together on issues larger than any individual. The fact that the resisters' underground public realm lacked institutional guarantees and yet produced an opinion of genuinely public character and evoked communal conduct of harmony in the pursuit of a common interest speaks to the point that institutional guarantees are not significant in and of themselves. These guarantees have meaning insofar as they relate to discourse and the actions that result from it. Even in their absence it is possible for a public realm to form and a community to act in ways responsive to human needs, as, closer to the end of the twentieth century, events dissolving the former Communist Bloc testify.

The fact that there was a general collapse of social cooperation with the Soviet states, that it occurred through countless coordinated acts and, excepting Romania, without a gunshot being fired, suggests that there was a broadly based and deeply held public opinion that had formed outside institutional forums. Doubtless this was the product of two decades of various forms of resistance to the imposed rule by the Communist Party. The resistance of Polish workers who were part of Solidarity provides ample support for this observation. The open deliberations that appeared to characterize their mode of securing unity prior to the Polish government's imposition of martial law in December 1981 remained intact afterward. Repressive acts subsequent to martial law were unsuccessful at squelching the ongoing dialogue among Poles searching for freedom—they merely forced it underground. The union's continued ability to invoke strike action and widespread public resistance, not to mention the Polish government's fear of relaxing martial law, testifies to the public realm that Solidarity had forged and to the vibrancy of that realm as the locus where Polish public opinion was being formed in the face of oppression. The official public sphere may have been the domain of apparatchiks and party members, but that fact did not stop the active members of society from locating alternative sites, such as samizdat literature, for open discussion. The resisters' unity of interests and consensus, their trust and spirit of reciprocity, in short their community, rested on the rhetorical experience of sharing a public relationship of words and deeds.

In chapter 1 I argued that the conditions of civil society have given rise to a plurality of publics whose rhetorical characteristics condition awareness of shared political interests. Granted, an understanding of "the public" is essential to politics, and, at some level, members of a public share interests in important ways. However, a public's nature is not defined by its shared political interests but by its function: *to provide critical evaluation and direction.* In fact, its critical and guiding function explains why those who require certification from the citizenry are preoccupied with opinion polls. They have become the vehicle for making citizen judgment known. At the same time, the attempt to objectify and verify "the public" through opinion polls reveals a misunderstanding of publics as technological constructs rather than as rhetorical phenomena, as I will explore later in the case of the Carter administration's handling of the Iranian hostage affair. Judgment, after all, can only be of what a public qua public has available to it. By the same measure, an object or deed that requires judgment must appear before witnesses and must receive their collective evaluation (Arendt 1958, 1977). The appearance by and criticism of objects of interpretation are themselves acts of hermeneutical communication which simultaneously define publics (Eberly 1993, 1995; Leff 1995). Consequently, if publics do appear, appear in a distorted form, or are repressed, we must look to the conditions of communication for explanations. Humans constitute their issues through communication, and communication regulates the responses of a populace with the potential to become active as judges. Our communicative environment conditions our *publicness,* defines how we experience ourselves in a milieu of strangers, and shapes the character of those publics that actually do form. The communicative ecology shapes our *public spheres.*

I have suggested that a rhetorical understanding of public talk differs in its initial orientation to "the" public sphere. A dialogizing rhetorical alternative would assume a nested domain of particularized arenas or multiple spheres populated by participants who discover their interests, where they converge or differ, and how their differences might be accommodated through adherence to standards of reasonableness and tolerance reflected in the vernacular language of conversational communication. This type of exchange is a public's means for negotiating its members' norms and priorities for society. I now wish to consider how this conversational aspect is paradigmatic for the Public Sphere as a discursive realm.

Outline of a Rhetorical Model of the Public Sphere

A *public sphere* may be defined as *a discursive space in which individuals and groups associate to discuss matters of mutual interest and, where possible, to reach a common judgment about them. It is the locus of emergence for rhetorically salient meanings.* Often these are narrowly political meanings, though not always, as the concerns of the literary public sphere testify (Eberly 1994). In some cases these meanings may be hegemonic, though not all discourse is ideologically determined. Interrogating the process by which rhetorically salient meanings are created and embodied dialogically helps us decipher the persuasive force of identifications in the process of public opinion formation.

A rhetorical model of public spheres has several important features. First, it is discourse based. It relinquishes the class-based apparatus associated with the bourgeois public sphere. Certainly there can be public arenas or encounter domains specific to classes, but to begin with assumptions of class places all discursive realms into an a priori relation with the presumed dominance of a particular public sphere. A rhetorical model, by contrast, emphasizes the prevailing discursive features in any given body of exchanges and treats class domination as an empirical claim to be inferred from data rather than as a generating assumption.

Second, a rhetorical model's critical norms are derived from actual discursive practices. This model replaces the norm of critical rationality with the rhetorical norm of *reasonableness* (Ehninger 1968; Ehninger and Hauser 1984; Fisher 1978, 1980; Gottlieb 1968; Wallace 1963). In the course of discussing an issue, arguments and appeals will differentiate themselves in terms of their persuasiveness and success in forging identifications. Assessing the status of an appeal depends on gauging its reasonableness across multiple perspectives (McKeon 1956). Its success or failure and its consequences for the public opinion that eventually emerges are a function of its range in addressing relevant needs and commitments.

For example, during the Kennedy administration some scientists advanced claims about the degrading environmental consequences from use of chemical fertilizers. The technical accuracy of their arguments may have made them convincing to the scientific community, but they were inconsequential in urging regulatory legislation. However, when Rachel

Carson (1987) translated scientific findings into a pastoral narrative that intersected the common experiences of laypeople, they acquired a salience that spawned a global social movement. Concerted public discourse has changed public consciousness of our need to protect the environment and influenced the law.

Third, a rhetorical focus emphasizes indeterminate bracketing of discursive exchanges. As Habermas has argued (1974), a public sphere is created whenever two or more individuals converse about a public matter. Each of these individualized, local associative spaces is potentially included in larger, more polyphonous exchanges. When the outcome is public opinion, what starts as a dialogue becomes part of the multilogue of voices along the range of individuals and groups engaged by a public question. For example, the press "outing" of Arthur Ashe as suffering from AIDS triggered public criticism of the press as lacking restraint. Conversations in Boston linked with those of unknown citizens in Seattle, with Ashe's appearance at the National Press Club, and with widespread commentary on the question of how to balance the people's right to know with the individual's right to privacy. Although not all public issues are as consuming as the Ashe case was, they commonly assimilate initial, often incidental, exchanges into a body of exchanges whose temporal trajectory is more extensive.

As a site of emergence for rhetorically salient meanings, a public sphere's prevailing code acquires constitutive force. Human codes of signs and symbols have an inherent tendency toward organization into vocabularies of motives (Burke 1969). Associational clusters, the social factors attendant on their use, the institutional sites where they are generated, and the personae of their users—both those who utter and those who receive—hew interpretations of experience. As a vocabulary of motives gains salience, it provides orientation, value, and even a telos that defines the subject and the community.

Recent scholarship has explored this constitutive dimension of rhetoric. These works have followed the lead of I. A. Richards (1965) by endorsing the thesis that meanings are located in use. In this spirit, James Boyd White's study *When Words Lose their Meaning* takes its title quite literally as the basic premise that underlies the character of rhetorically negotiated reality. He claims that "language is not stable but changing and that it is perpetually remade by its speakers, who are themselves remade, both as individuals and as communities, in what they say" (White 1984, x). Steven Mailloux advances the equally strong assertion that "there is no appeal outside rhetorical exchange" (1989, 167). Mailloux argues that rhetoric is the medium by which human reality is forged because the rhetoric of human communicative exchange establishes our interpretations of experience. Even theory, according to Mailloux, cannot escape the net of its own constitutive rhetorical impulses. In a more political vein, Maurice Charland (1987) has found rhetoric's constitutive forces present in the Parti Québécois's White Paper, which calls francophone Canadians of Quebec to answer their destiny as a separate people. In effect, he maintains, the rhetoricality of the White Paper constitutes an identity transformation from *Canadien Français* to *Peuple Québecois*. These works share Kenneth Burke's insight that the participatory dynamics of rhetorical acts lead to symbolically induced relations; rhetorically constituted meanings significantly shape social will.

Rhetorical meaning production has the further characteristic of being specific to particular issues and audiences or publics. Consequently, rhetorically salient meanings are unstable, and their production is an arational process. Rhetorically salient meanings defy the rationalistic impulse to confine signification to a single category. Richard Weaver (1953) has argued, for instance, that a stable base of public understanding sustained the florid spread-eagle oratory of the early and mid nineteenth century's influential public speakers. This base encouraged an association between lofty imagery and a common national identity without requiring further explanation. By contrast, broadly shared visions of America's meaning are less available to contemporary audiences. Indeed, something as pervasive during the first three quarters of the twentieth century as constructing America through rhetorical imagery of a "melting pot" is now contested by the more segmented imagery of "quilt" and "rainbow."

Symbolic constructions lacking the permanence of shared tradition are susceptible to sudden changes of affiliation. Relationships shift among groups that, regardless of status, have a sense of investments they wish to protect while envious of the opportunities of others, as the conflicting rhetorics of identity movements testify (Cloud 1994; Laraña, Johnson, and Gusfield 1994; Hauser and Whalen 1997). Relational instability induces a multiplicity of symbolic expressions and interpretations, and inserts gaps between visions of order and reality. Efforts to snatch order from the flux of rhetorically salient meanings are frustrated by processes of signification that no one can completely control. Thus, a rhetorically modeled public sphere focuses our attention equally on what symbols mean and the process whereby they take on these meanings.

Finally, a rhetorical model values communication that is conducive, where possible, to the formation of shared judgments. It includes selective discursive conditions, as Habermas has emphasized in his idealized model: It must be accessible to all citizens; there must be access to information; specific means for transmitting information must be accessible to those who can be influenced by it. Historically, the means for transmitting information have been open, face-to-face discussions undertaken by individuals in formal and informal gatherings or by representative agencies such as newspapers. In contemporary industrial societies these means include the mass media. But a rhetorical model also recognizes that in a democracy consensus is not always possible, nor is consensus the test for whether a public sphere has functioned openly and inclusively in encouraging the judgments that actually do accrue.

A public sphere, then, is a discursive space in which strangers discuss issues they perceive to be of consequence for them and their group. Its rhetorical exchanges are the bases for shared awareness of common issues, shared interests, tendencies of extent and strength of difference and agreement, and self-constitution as a public whose opinions bear on the organization of society. A rhetorical model of the Public Sphere would adapt Habermas's (1974, 49) observation on locating such associative spaces to read: Whenever private citizens exchange views on a public concern, some portion of the Public Sphere is made manifest in their conversation.

Public Conversation and the Associations of the Reticulate Public Sphere

Emphasizing the rhetoricality of public spheres foregrounds their activity. They are the loci for discussion of the sort that seeks common judgment among an interdependent aggregate of strangers who share an interest in matters relevant, in principle, to civil society. Today this type of discussion usually is initiated by the mass media but includes the face-to-face encounters of everyday life. Even though we lack personal acquaintance with all but a few of its participants and are seldom in contexts where we and they directly interact, we join these exchanges because they are discussing the same matters. These exchanges are linked as parts of a single conversation whose contours provide the overall pattern of awareness at any given time of those with whom we are mutually engaged.

Significantly, a public's rhetoric shapes this overall pattern of awareness and presents it—in how it is communicated to and in how a public's members communicate with one another (Hauser and Blair 1982). This awareness is not restricted to any single channel. Moreover, because communication makes shared awareness possible, it serves a function for our collective awareness similar to that of perception for the individual,[1] orienting a public by, in Robert Park's memorable phrase, "giving each and all notice to what is going on" (1940, 677).

Since communication is the means by which public issues acquire publicity, there is every reason to suspect that publics exist only as they manifest their publicness. A public's essential characteristic is its shared activity of exchanging opinion. Put differently, *publics do not exist as entities but as processes; their collective reasoning is not defined by abstract reflection but by practical judgment; their awareness of issues is not philosophical but eventful.*

Mostly, the events we associate with publics are specific to issues subjected to critical publicity, such as occur in local debates over school board policies or national debates over military involvement in, say, Iraq. By examining how issues are discussed and resolved, we discover evidence of speakers, messages, responses, and outcomes that allow us to infer relationships between discourse and worldly events. Still, this oversimplifies a more complex and continuous process of public conversation that provides a backdrop of rhetorical resources for creative use by public advocates.

Quite apart from our interactions on a particular issue, our daily conversations with coworkers, neighbors, superiors, subordinates, community and church contacts, group members, friends, and family provide countless opportunities to exchange views on public matters. Each exchange opens a discursive space that exceeds the boundaries of entirely personal and private matters. Across time these multiple exchanges include us as participants in the social conversation by which we learn and also contribute to themes that inculcate shared motives.

On the broadest level, this process is a conversation that spans history. Kenneth Burke's well-known description bears repeating here:

> Imagine that you enter a parlor. You come late. When you arrive, others have long preceded you, and they are engaged in a heated discussion, a discussion too heated for them to pause and tell you exactly what it is about. In fact, the discussion had already begun long before any of them got there, so that no one present is qualified to retrace for you all the steps that had gone before. You listen for a while, until you decide that you have caught the tenor of the argument; then you put in your oar. Someone answers; you answer him; another comes to your defense; another aligns himself against you, to either the embarrassment of gratification of your opponent, depending on the quality of your ally's assistance. However the discussion is interminable. The hour grows late, you must depart. And you do depart, with the discussion still vigorously in progress. (Burke 1973, 110–11)

Burke develops this analogy to indicate that the source from which all dramatic materials derive is the unending conversation of life itself. The manifestations of public spheres are often the dialogues of everyday life, and their conversational character alerts us to the limitations of the ancient rhetorical prototype of public deliberation as the discursive model for such arenas.

Consider, for example, the dialogical web that formed around the trials of O. J. Simpson for the murder of Nicole Brown Simpson and Ronald Goldman. From June 1994 through February 1997 Americans engaged in a continuous conversation in their media, workplaces, classrooms, social gatherings, and even churches over the specifics of the case and their larger implications. The participants included attorneys and expert commentators, but average citizens also were actively engaged. The criminal trial became a media spectacle, with daily worldwide coverage. However, issues of jury composition, the Los Angeles Police Department (LAPD), attorney tactics, evidence reliability, and Simpson's prior history of spousal abuse triggered more serious discussions of racial issues, domestic violence, law enforcement biases, the power of wealthy defendants to subvert the criminal justice system, and more.

Even the reporting of the Simpson trials became a public issue, as is illustrated by the coverage of the verdict in the civil trial. By coincidence, the jury reached its verdict the very evening President Clinton was scheduled to deliver his State of the Union message to Congress and the nation. TV commentators speculated over whether the president might cancel his address. When informed that the president intended to go on, NBC anchor Tom Brokaw advised viewers that NBC would continue its O. J. coverage on MSNBC so that America might "channel surf" while the nation's chief executive spoke. For those who found the media themselves a source of controversy in the trials, the surreal image of split-screen coverage and encouragement to "channel surf" provided further evidence that the scales of news reporting were wildly out of kilter. Daily dialogues, such as those in the Simpson case, form a web of multimediated interrelated discourse dispersed across society along conversational strands of the sort that Burke envisioned for drama.

For our discourse to be mutually intelligible and sensible as a conversation, we must enter a partnership in which topic, language, and meanings are shared in some significant way. Every communication opens a space of appearance. Conversation specifically constitutes a space in which intersubjectivity may appear. To be in a conversation entails acting in ways that can sustain a *we* separate from an *I*. Charles Taylor (1991, 21) reminds us that we usually move together through this space, with mutual actions that are understandable to one another and that make it possible for the conversation to go forward. Conversation requires at least two individuals who are able to open a space of intersubjectivity from which a shared world may emerge in the course of their dialogue. Disagreement is inevitable in serious and enriching conversation, and interlocutors need not agree about a specific state of the world but rather only that they are in the same world. Their mutually opened space must be one in which the *I* can appear and make a contribution for each to continue to participate.

By implication, Taylor leads us to the principle of relativity. The metaphor of moving together through conversational space can be sustained only if that space accommodates the appearance of the individual's *I* as a source of contribution. The presence of the *I*, however, invites us to understand the space and the *we* it contains from our own stance. The conversational partners *qua* individuals, or relata, must not be subsumed by the relationship or the relationship itself is lost. Their separateness is mutually necessary for differentiation. The relata and relationship, the separate *I*'s and the *we*, are mutually constitutive of each other's identity within the space they create through conversation.[2] But the *I* must continually grasp the intersubjective meaning that is always and exclusively a part of the *we*. Although personal and intersubjective meanings are always matters of perspective, mutual understanding requires that these independent points of view be linked. The *we* perspective is jeopardized when discourse partners jointly cease to grasp their common space of norms.[3]

Burke's felicitous reference to the unending conversation of history suggests a paradigm in which the intersubjective meanings negotiated and sustained in conversation can be extrapolated to larger units of society, making conversation a paradigm for society. We belong to a community insofar as we are able to participate in its conversations. We must acquire its *vernacular language* in order to share rhetorically salient meanings.

Members of pluralistic societies belong to several, perhaps many, overlapping discursive arenas in which they experience the polyphony of concurrent conversations as vernacular languages that rub against one another, instigating dialogues, as Bakhtin would have it, on the questions raised by their intersections and leading us to consider possibilities that might encompass their political, social, cultural, and linguistic differences. Vernacular discourses are, however, more than merely polyphonous expressions of local interest and understanding. They are protean. Their coconstitution of relata and relationship brings these multiple spheres into existence and gives them definition as discursive domains.

Vernacular exchanges both lack and transcend the force of official authority. As common expressions of those who participate in their conversational space, vernacular discourses reflect their speakers' sense of *historicity,* a concept I will elaborate further in chapter 5. These discourses assert the weight, priority, and importance participants ascribe to a projected world and therefore are subject to the dominion of social powers themselves vying for hierarchical political status. These exchanges reflect the basis for the general rhetorical character of our public spheres.

Common Meaning and the Associative Networks of the Reticulate Public Sphere

A conversational model of society requires that participants share *intersubjective meanings*. These are the meanings that constitute a *we* and that, in fact, are a source of significance for our own self-awareness in addition to our purely subjective stance. They are more than communal understandings of denotation. They are public in character. Taylor has defined intersubjective meanings as "ways of experiencing action in society which are expressed in the language and descriptions constitutive of institutions and practices. . . . They are the intersubjective realities of social practices and institutions" (1971, 29).

Taylor's definition implies that intersubjective meanings refer to more than brute data and are not limited to intersection with public reality. Their intersubjective character makes them constitutive of public reality. Public reality comes into being as such precisely because its meaningfulness is shared among subjects. For example, it is a commonplace that the press plays an important role in shaping public dialogue within the community at large. But the press's role is itself shaped by how we understand and use it, or our collective experience and shared expectations, descriptions, and actions with respect to it. The press is not independent of the readers it serves; it does not shape collective understanding impervious to collective expectations of and reactions to its contents. Michael Schudson (1992) points out that at one time press contents provided the basis for public conversation, whereas today the everyday tendencies of the local newspaper are mainly to dispense information.

In the first half of the nineteenth century local newspapers were more likely to develop associations and community among their readers than they are today. In large measure their conversational orientation was fostered by the affiliation of a newspaper with a political party or prejudice (Herbst 1993). Insofar as the press encouraged discourses among its readership, it promoted stability among the intersubjective meanings they shared. The information model of the press, by contrast, treats its readers as consumers. Increasingly since the mid nineteenth century the press has had to confront the complexity of diversity and fragmentation that often make community tenuous. In this context information is less likely to offend than polemics. Today the press has been challenged by radio, TV, and even the internet as a primary provider of information for the majority of its readers. Consequently, newspapers rely increasingly on advertisement over subscription sales to remain in business, which only increases the pressure to be information oriented and wary of publishing information that promotes controversy. For example, Schudson notes that the contemporary press is relatively absent of "mobilizing information." It is less likely to publish information, say, about a forthcoming demonstration two weeks in advance than the day before. On the other hand, readers show daily interest in acquiring uncontroversial information, such as reports of news, weather, local events, entertainment, information used to schedule activities, and consumer information. The contemporary press's failure to meet idealized norms as a sphere in which to carry on informed and rich political discussion and diminished expectations that it do so are not mutually independent. Schudson's observations illustrate a reciprocity between intersubjective meanings and public reality that evades linear explanation.

The intersubjective realities of institutions and social practices are themselves interrelated to form a web of meanings. Taylor (1971; 1985) makes the point that as this web strengthens, it gives rise to common meanings of relative strength. Common meanings are those "notions" of what is significant "which are not just shared in the sense that everyone has them, but are also common in the sense of being in the common reference world" (Taylor 1971, 30) The common meaning of *Québécois* shared by francophone Canadians as their national identity exemplifies his point. The idea of *Québécois* is not just shared, or known to be shared, but is a common aspiration that serves as a common reference point for all discussion, deliberation, communication, and public life in French Canadian society. *Common meaning* refers to *a communally sustained consciousness.*

A public is possible only to the degree that a communally sustained consciousness is available to its members. In addition to sharing language and descriptions that constitute their institutions and social practices, a public's members must share a web of significant meanings that define a *reference world* of common actions, celebrations, and feelings (Taylor 1971). If those participating in a public did not share this reference world, its community status would be severed. Put differently, the telos of a public is to mold a world that is hospitable to its members' shared interests. A public whose members lived in different reference worlds would be self-contradictory, as we will see in chapter 5. This does not mean that members of a public cannot have intensely divisive differences. They often do, and the intensity of their differences is often attributable to the fact that they share the same world. A public's emergence is not dependent on consensus but on the sharing of a *common* world, even when understood and lived differently by different segments of society.

For example, in 1994 California passed a referendum, Proposition 187, prohibiting social services to the children of illegal aliens. As a result, these children, almost entirely of Latino origin, were to be denied such basic services as public education and public health care. Immediately upon passage a firestorm of national outrage was directed at the measure. Opponents brought challenges in court, and public discussions of the referendum flooded national forums. Across the United States leaders of minority constituencies deplored its predicted consequences. We might question the relevance for citizens of Connecticut or Nebraska of a referendum pertaining to illegal aliens residing in California. However, this action alarmed those outside the state because it appeared to challenge the reference world of national identity shared by the larger society. From ideological commitments to protect marginalized groups to a more widespread and fundamental commitment to protect the well-being of children within the national borders, regardless of their parents' national status, the debate centered on an alarming abridgment of the meaning of America and a shared notion of the public good.

The complex multilogue of disparate voices indigenous to complex and pluralistic societies underscores the heteroglossic nature of civil society's nested Public Sphere. It is a multidimensional dialogizing space of vernacular conversations. The aggregates we refer to as publics are susceptible to the contentious behaviors of individuals who differ in opinions and interests. It is not necessarily a group in consensus. But because the Public Sphere contains multiple sites where rhetorically salient meanings may emerge, those who enter any given arena must share a reference world for their discourse to produce awareness of shared interests and public opinions about them.

Discussion is initiated by mutual interest in a topic that has some important ambiguity. Productive exploration of shared uncertainty depends on intersubjective meanings. But productive discussion does not require that its participants reach consensus, though they may. Nor does intersubjective meaning presuppose that interlocutors share essential agreements, though they may. People may disagree and still make sense to one another, provided their differences are part of a common projection of possibilities for human relations and actions. The national controversy over Proposition 187 illustrates how a common reference world anchored in common meanings can tolerate a degree of cleavage without rending society's fabric.

At the same time, such cleavages may deepen and widen to the point where those in disagreement, as appears to be the threat of Peuple Québécois, cease to share a common reference world. At that point they are no longer capable of forming as a public. Sometimes this divide may even result in civil war. When, for example, the IRA was committed to terrorist acts, it signaled that the divide between its reference world for national identity was so at odds with the reference world projected by Great Britain that discourse no longer could contain shared meaning of political intents. On the other hand, at times a society may access or be addressed by discourse that emanates from a reference world beyond its horizon of comprehension. For example, the Ayatollah Khomeini's death sentence imposed on Salman Rushdie for writing *The Satanic Verses* and issuance of a death warrant to have him executed were difficult for westerners to comprehend, since they lacked an analogous referent in modern Western tradition. During times when alien communication is in the public domain, its status in a given public sphere is more akin to an object of discussion—a datum to be interpreted—than a dialogizing intersection; it is something interacted *about* rather than interacted *with*.

The ongoing social conversation that I have been describing introduces its participants to a *network of associations* from which and in which their common meanings are developed and enriched. Heterogeneous societies involve conversational partnerships among a broad range of individuals and groups whose interests intersect with and offer the possibility of dialogue. In this context, dialogue is more than a descriptive term referring to interaction; it refers to the *achievement* of common meaning. Common meaning is an achievement because it requires engaged individuals to connect the manifold dialogues in which social, political, and cultural interests are expressed to those whose world they share. The particular manifestations of each public sphere contribute to its dynamic network of associations formed from the manifold of conversations that intersect in society's ongoing disposition of its issues.

Our association of the public realm with the democratic heritage of Western civilization tempts us to link its rhetorical character to the Athenian archive in which formal rhetoric played a major role. Certainly the comparison bears making insofar as its current discursive arenas are agonistic spaces. However, the rhetorical characteristics applicable to contemporary public spheres differ from the Athenian model in significant ways. Citizens in ancient Athens took responsibility for the state's welfare by deciding matters of its military survival and administration of its laws through open deliberation. The Athenian assumption of civic responsibilities did not entail an expectation that the state, independent of its citizens, would take their wishes seriously since there was no effective separation of the two. Moreover, the Athenian agon occurred in a space populated by homogeneous participants: male property owners who were citizens of Athens. It excluded slaves, women, children, nonresidents, and the indigent. The conditions of public life encompassed by this space were distinctly premodern. While expressing ideals of high political involvement, the Athenian experience does not mirror the realities of civil society following the intellectual and political revolutions of the Enlightenment.

The terms of these revolutions ignited the emancipatory movements of workers, slaves, and women. These emancipations, in turn, have produced an invasion of the bourgeois public sphere by a range of issues formerly sequestered in private, such as those of property relations brought by workers, of civil rights brought by people of color, of cultural bias brought by non-Christians, and of the family and control of one's body brought by women. Each of these has made the public realm a domain of heterogeneity in which the model of *agonistic relations* tending toward the recognition of virtuosity or aretê has been superseded by *associational relations* across permeable boundaries, whose shared efforts preclude the possibility of predefining the conversational agenda. Its multiple discursive arenas give the overall Public Sphere a *reticulate* structure.[4]

The contemporary Public Sphere has become a web of discursive arenas, spread across society and even in some cases across national boundaries. Each of these arenas is itself composed of those members of society who, at the very least, are attending to a discourse on issues they share and who are able to understand and respond to the vernacular exchanges that exist outside power and yet are normative of it. Our direct daily encounters with others who share our discursive spaces may be local, but our awareness of association with others who are part of its dialogue extends to locales and participants who are strangers and yet whose participation we heed and consider. Collectively these weblike structures of a particular public sphere, such as a political party or a social movement, are joined to others in the reticulate Public Sphere, where their collective rhetorical practices produce society.

The Public Sphere's associative network includes more than discursive arenas whose boundaries touch. Its actual practices form a lattice of discursive spaces with permeable boundaries. In a pluralistic and diverse society, the ideal of civil society suggests these spheres work best when their boundaries are maximally permeable (Taylor 1995, 280), not only permitting but welcoming border crossings by interests and actors from other arenas. For example, the problem of poverty in the United States is addressed on many fronts and levels of the state and the private sector. In addition to federal and state programs, political parties, churches, service organizations, political action committees (PACs), welfare recipients, and the general electorate have played active roles. In 1996, when welfare reform was forefront on Washington's political agenda, the exemplary record of churches in generating and distributing material resources and providing programs that helped their needy members find work led political parties to suggest that churches should be entrusted with this public problem. In the context of legislating welfare reform, such proposals inspired considerable cross-talk among churches, political parties, the federal bureaucracy, and Congress, thereby helping churches to evaluate and undermine the proposal that they administer welfare relief and to urge the crafters of legislation in a new direction that retained federal administration but on criteria other than economic self-sufficiency (Thackaberry 1997).

But openness is not unconditional. Arenas may be more accommodating to some relationships than others. They may even be hostile to certain ones. Openness also raises the possibility that things can go wrong. A public sphere can be invaded by special interests or the state. Information can be withheld, dispensed selectively, or falsified. Media of dissemination can have limited access to relevant data and sources. Distortions are as much a possibility when its boundaries exclude all but voices from a single perspective as when vulnerable to invasion by alien interests intent on manipulation and control. In the case of welfare reform, the government ignored the churches' advice and passed a bill that based federal assistance on the economic criteria the churches had cautioned against (Thackaberry 1997). Significantly, as deliberation on welfare reform illustrates, both failures and successes of actually existing democracy are functions of the rhetorical practices that define the discursive character of any given public sphere at any given moment in time.

The Ground of Civil Judgment

Liberal democratic theory's conception of a theoretical, transcendent public emphasizes legitimating discourse that occurs in spaces specifically created for public exchange. It presumes that discourse in institutionally guaranteed arenas, such as the press, the legislature, and the town meeting, speaks for the silent participation of spectators. Historically, this conception has hidden differences of gender, color, religion, or other discriminators by which groups are excluded and/or subjugated by authoritarian power. The theoretical model, as it has been extended to speech acts, has ignored the performative dimensions of rhetoric present in vernacular exchanges.[5] This exclusion has been challenged as society moved from a model of public life based on civic virtue to one based on difference.

A case in point is Hannah Arendt's normative political analysis, which is the most prominent contemporary case based on ideals advanced in the Athenian conception of the *bios politikos* of public life. Drawing on the ancient linkage of public life to visible performance of words and deeds, she valorizes the public realm as the space for communal values and models of virtue to appear before an audience of peers. A range of scholars who have addressed the possibility for the Public Sphere to capture the sociopolitical dynamic and problematic at the heart of the late-modernity/postmodernity debate have acknowledged her contribution (Benhabib 1992; Bernstein 1983; Habermas 1977; Landes 1992). Typically these discussions also have emphasized Arendt's premodern insistence on a distinction between the political and the social. Her resulting exclusion from the public realm of concerns over the necessities of life and their accompanying activities of labor and work has been criticized for what it excludes from the public agenda. Her apparent blindness to the nature of the struggles that accompany both domains is captured by Seyla Benhabib when she concludes, "The distinction between the social and the political makes no sense in the modern world, not because all politics has become administration and because the economy has become the quintessential public, as Hannah Arendt thought, but primarily because the struggle to make something public is the struggle for justice" (1992, 79).

Benhabib's identification of justice as the dominant struggle of our era is borne out by developments in Western societies since World War II. The increased public presence of groups other than those defined primarily by class has made civil society increasingly a site of symbolic legitimation for the treatment of the disenfranchised and marginalized. Discussion of justice for these groups, no less than for those who suffer class oppression, requires discursive spaces that emphasize freedom of participation rather than personal virtuosity and has made tolerance, which became a public virtue with the rise of civil society, the primary rhetorical challenge of contemporary public life. Rhetorical exchanges between individuals and groups who reject the authority of the other's assumptions have an inherent dialogical character. At the same time, realities of interdependence require a mode of response with efficacy for addressing common problems. The rhetoric of common ground, on which political consensus has always rested, has been challenged by conditions in which interdependent partners joined by a common problem do not necessarily share values and ends. A rhetoric emphasizing mutually acceptable outcomes for the disparate stakeholders of public problems without seeking justification in shared a priori commitments now provides the basis for cooperation among social and political actors, as well as official action. This is another way of saying that when tradition has been shattered, we make sense of what has occurred and what we now confront by reconstructing the past in a new story that is subject to constant revision and reinterpretation as the conversational partners change. The primary concern of the Public Sphere has become the constitution of discursive spaces with the capacity to encourage and nurture a multilogue across their respective borders and from which *civil judgments* sustainable in multiple perspectives may emerge.

Civil judgment is an outcome of the vernacular exchanges dispersed across media, public meetings, face-to-face interaction, ballots, and even representative deliberation. It occurs when opinions emanating from a variety of perspectives and held for a variety of reasons nevertheless converge to form a prevailing view of preference and possibly of value. It is unlike a conviction that is handed to us by a shared set of foundational and transcendent beliefs, such as theism or a hegemonic ideology. Civil judgment expresses a common understanding among diverse social actors primarily based on formal and vernacular exchanges enacted in and across public spheres. It reflects the associational character of relationships that depend on nothing beyond the common action of discussion and debate occurring in these discursive spaces. It is an association constituted by rhetorical joining and justified exclusively by the common matters from which the agency of public conversation derives its meaning.

Civil judgment expresses a shared understanding that grounds an actually existing public. Without it references to a public would be meaningless or sterile. A *public* is, after all, a construct we employ to discuss those individuals who are actively weighing and shaping the course of society. We do not confront a public in the flesh, as we can an audience. Often its members are geographically dispersed, and always they are largely strangers. When reference to "the public" is more than an empty synonym for the general populace or an unreflective expression of liberal democratic ideology, it has specificity only because concrete expressions of civil judgment provide palpable evidence that a public has formed: outpourings of letters, debate, commentary, and conversation as occurred in the United States concerning the role of radical right-wing "talk radio" programs in encouraging acts such as the April 1995 bombing of the Federal Building in Oklahoma City, in which 167 adults and children were killed; massive demonstrations of disbelief and anger as those in Los Angeles following the jury verdict to acquit members of the LAPD of criminal assault charges resulting from the video-recorded beating of Rodney King; public displays of grief, as occurred when England's Lady Diana Spenser was killed in a high-speed flight from paparazzi, followed by the media-assembled montage of remonstrance directed at Great Britain's royal family for its seeming aloofness from the tragedy and failure to offer its subjects consolation; voluntary cooperation with economic sanctions as occurred when American consumers reduced gasoline consumption in support of the Carter administration's reprisals against Iran for holding fifty-two of its citizens hostage; or even unofficial but widespread boycotts, as occurred in the spring of 1995 when the new baseball season was played before largely empty stadiums, following a long and acrimonious strike in which millionaire owners and millionaire players appeared consumed with their own avariciousness by bickering over money. As these examples suggest, the objects of attention susceptible to vernacular exchange range from affairs of state to cultural forms and icons. Such expressions reflect a common judgment about the reality of what appears in a public sphere and constitutes an association among disparate members of society participating in a dispersed public conversation.

In cases such as these the involved members of society are attentive and active from their own perspectives. They merge as a public only insofar as they are able to create the shared space between them for talk that leads to what Arendt (1958, 57) calls their *common* sense of reality. In the health care reform debate of 1994, for instance, the Clinton administration's proposal was opposed by small business. As this opposition radiated to other arenas, such as those of health care professionals and consumer advocates, diverse points of view began to converge. Participants in these spheres were witnesses of a sort, affirming the reality of the ideas and values that define their conception of acceptable health care coverage and federal support. As ideas and values crossed the boundaries of discursive arenas, their strength expanded to the point where the official arena of Congress detected that disparate groups were forming a shared judgment opposing the administration's proposed legislation. Judgments of this sort formed through the dispersed conversation of a reticulate Public Sphere authorize actions undertaken in the name of the people (Bitzer 1978).

Since civil judgment regulates power even though it is based on a discourse outside of power, it requires that publics understand what they are doing: they are forming public judgments. Public judgments are formed through practical reasoning of the kind that has been a central theme of the rhetorical tradition. They are reached about matters of opinion, rather than truths or facts. They are always specific, reflecting agreements among dialogical partners that they certify validity in the given case; they are never universally valid for all cases nor for those who do not judge or who are not participants in the specific public sphere where it is formed. Importantly, civil judgments are the vehicle for transporting us from our private and subjective existence into the common realm of shared reality. As Arendt observed, whenever we decide on an action, we also, in some measure, choose the contours of our common world and who may appear in it (1977, 223).

Rhetorical Criteria of the Public Sphere

In chapter 2 I discussed several differences between the norms of communication advanced by Habermas's model of the bourgeois public sphere and those commonly made by a rhetorical model of communication. Although I disagree with Habermas on the rationalistic biases of his norms, I have aligned with his contention that critical inspection of a public sphere presupposes that it adheres to some set of communicative norms. Farrell (1993) has argued that the quality of our civic life depends on our ability to conduct our politics within the norms of rhetorical culture. Farrell's project explores the relationship of rhetorical norms to the political realities of the present day, as manifested primarily in the more formal discourse within institutional assemblies and on specific occasions. However, if my argument is correct that there is a direct relationship between the rhetorical character of civic conversation and the attributes of any discursive arena, then the ideals of the rhetorical tradition must apply with equal force to the dispersed conversation of a reticulate public sphere.

These norms are not Kantian in their adherence to universal maxims that test the validity of discourse against a rationalistic template. Rather, they are attuned to local conditions of reasoning applied by stakeholders. They provide participants with *good* reasons on which to base their civil judgments. At a basic level, a person cannot form a civil judgment without integrating that judgment into the community to which it applies. This does not make *good* reasons a poor cousin to a Habermasean ideal of critical rationality, but rather asserts that critical rationality is but one form of reasonableness and not necessarily the one best suited as normative for deliberative discussions.

Since civil judgment in pluralistic societies must accommodate difference, its quality is assessed less in terms of universal norms of rationality than by quality of output. Certainly these include determination of whether a given judgment is redeemable as just, procedurally fair, resonant with communal values, and practically efficacious. But civil judgments also are tied to particular issues faced by particular publics; they require discursive conditions that permit its members to gain *practical* insights applicable to the conditions of *their* interdependent lives. The character of rhetorical transactions bears directly on our consciousness of the existential conditions and commitments to actions that determine our collective future. A *well-ordered* public sphere is inherently tied to the quality of its rhetorical exchanges. The particularity of its issues and its civil judgments requires a commitment to language and thought and their limits, as these function under conditions of contingency. Its rhetorical features encourage open consideration of a question from a variety of perspectives, making the quality of our public life a rhetorical achievement. At least five rhetorical norms recommend themselves as criteria by which the defining conditions of any specific public sphere may be gauged and criticized.

1. *Permeable boundaries.* We commonly restrict access to private discursive spaces, such as our families, to their primary members and guests. A public sphere also may have a primary membership, such as often is so with a social movement or deliberative assembly. Yet the issues it considers, by their public nature, exceed its boundaries in the interests they engage and the consequences from their resolution. Civil judgment presupposes that these issues are unresolvable in an enclave of like-minded persons. It gains weight as issues are exposed to a host of diverse observers who, despite their unique perspectives, collectively assert a prevailing tendency of belief and action. The borders of these spheres are alive with tension between openness and control to the possibilities and the realities of a discursive space in which social actors meet to discover their common world. These tensions are over rules of access that maximize or minimize border crossings, of freedom or repression of speech once access is gained, and of availability or exclusion of competent participants to frame judgments indicative of shared realities. Consequently, the conditions for making a discursive appearance in the public sphere are a barometer of the extent to which a common mind is possible.

2. *Activity.* Mass societies tend to treat audiences as passive; they are asked to purchase and to applaud. Publics, on the other hand, are presumed to have a guiding interest for which they have the potential to become active; they are asked their opinions. They are active whenever they engage diverse view-

points and interests that intersect on common problems and that interact in creating policies and evaluating deeds. Put differently, an active society hears and speaks to manifold interests that converge on any issue. When individuals talk to the same enclave, they become powerless to effect change. Eventually they either buy a point of view that strips them of their autonomy or they become insulated from and insensitive to perspectives of others whose cooperation is essential for resolving problems. Social actors must hear multiple voices to realize that they can do more than respond—they can choose. A diverse and active public is more likely than its mass counterpart to differentiate between the glitz of public relations satisfied with images and competent rhetoric seeking to articulate shared reality.

3. *Contextualized language.* The specificity of issues and diversity of perspectives that enter a public sphere present significant rhetorical challenges to public conversation. They require that participants adhere to the rhetorical norm of contextualized language to render their respective experiences intelligible to one another. Institutional powers and epistemic elites within mass, technologically advanced societies frequently undermine this requirement. They often preempt the possibilities for vernacular exchange by substituting technical language as coin of the rhetorical realm. Controlling the language in which issues are discussed determines how they are expressed, relevance of experience, and expertise in adjudicating the issues they raise. Language wars are contests for authority since language conveys status on its literate users as sources of knowledge and power. Without a vernacular language to address their common problems, it is small wonder that those who should be interested and active participants in the public sphere find themselves in full retreat, filled with bewilderment at the character of public conversation and cynicism at the unresponsiveness of their institutions to the concerns of their lives.

The language that dominates a discursive arena is an index to the symbolic resources that contain the norms and values of groups and classes, their knowledge of their past and their commitments to the future. Regrettably institutional public spheres often must struggle to prevent the disappearance of contextualized language from politics. A well-functioning public sphere requires that its discursive arenas contextualize public problems in ways that foster clear apprehension of the issues. The contest over which language shall have currency in the reticulate arenas of the Public Sphere contains the struggle between dominant and dissident society to appropriate historicity.

4. *Believable appearance*. Developed societies are constantly confronted by problems that involve the whole of society. Social actors require the means to appear before strangers in a believable fashion. Believability is essential to establishing an awareness of themselves as a public and an understanding of their potential as social actors. The rhetoric of public conversation establishes a participatory framework of ideas and values for the discussions shared by whoever enters society's public spheres. This framework can be added to, distracted, redirected, repressed, or even energized by a sphere's patterns of critical publicity. A public sphere's contours at any given time provide its participants an overall pattern of awareness.

5. *Tolerance*. Because civil society is constituted by difference rather than identity, by diversity rather than unity, contact with alternative ideas and traditions is inevitable. Presupposing conformity of values and ends or imposing a preordained orientation reduces the capacity of discursive arenas to accommodate the range of opinions on an issue and the strength of judgments that emerge from civic conversation. Because divergent perspectives make consensus unlikely, meanings likely to have rhetorical salience are those which produce solutions that interdependent partners regard as acceptable for their own reasons (Hauser and Cushman 1973). A well-functioning public sphere of this sort recognizes that revolution is unfeasible and therefore embraces a course of action that secures a space of open exchange apart from system imperatives. Its tendency to understand and evaluate social action requires the type of sociopolitical hermeneutic that is dialogically enacted by rhetorical constructions of meaning. Its tendency toward community based on solidarity is always in tension with political and economic relations that emphasize instrumental values and that derive their action imperatives from strategic necessity rather than from principles. Its rhetorical prototype is the self-limiting mode of self-regulation sought by Poland's Solidarity movement, which I will consider in more detail in chapter 5. Unlike the rhetoric of rational justification, the norm of tolerance offers a world of cooperation based on judgments that, despite their suboptimality from differing partisan perspectives, are sufficiently acceptable to a coalition

of public actors who can embrace them with sufficient voice to give them weight in arenas of official action.

These rhetorical norms offer encouragement toward the achievement of a common mind rather than advancement of vested interests. This is not to say that public conversation is untethered from interests and absent of partisan appeals. Still there is a difference between partisan urgings, in which responsiveness to the other side and the possibility of being persuaded are assumed, and the manipulation of propaganda, in which those who are vested become closed to persuasion. Public opinion requires public dialogue. An exchange of views is essential to arriving at a balanced judgment on competing interests. The partisan nature of political discourse would never escape personal prejudice without open exchanges of informed and compelling expressions of preferences and reasons that could contribute to achieving a common mind. Accordingly, rhetorical norms set the defining conditions for our discursive arenas. As a public sphere becomes preoccupied with influencing others by manipulation and propaganda rather than with arriving at a balanced judgment through informed deliberation, the public sphere becomes distorted. By the same measure, when civil judgment captures the experience of a shared world, it expresses a genuinely *public* opinion: the evolving judgment of a public on issues and concerns that have been the subjects of dispersed conversations in the public sphere. Without a public sphere, we could not have social actors or society as we now know it. For this reason the Public Sphere lies at the very heart of public life.

Conclusion

The concept of the public sphere has been disputed for some time. These controversies have focused on the role the public sphere supposedly plays in the political process as this is conceived within liberal democratic theory: on its identity in terms of bourgeois interests and on the apparent dissolution of the public sphere under conditions of mass society and mass communication. Surely these are legitimate indictments. They graphically expose an idealization of the political process at odds with the realities of actually existing democracies. If my analysis has any merit, it is in shifting focus away from the political role of a unitary public sphere and toward the communicative and epistemological functions of a multiplicity of spheres, in shifting focus away from the bourgeois public sphere and toward the rhetorical conditions of "publicness" that underwrite the latticed and reticulate nature of public spheres. Publics may be repressed, distorted, or responsible, but any evaluation of their actual state requires that we inspect the rhetorical environment as well as the rhetorical acts out of which they evolved, for these are the conditions that constitute their individual character. Such analysis of publics begins with an understanding of the Public Sphere's plurality of discursive arenas in which civil judgment is formed and upon which all publics depend. The rhetorical model of multiple spheres provides a framework for examining the discursive arenas in which and its discourse by which public opinion is formed. It promises to reveal the symbolic resources that are active in shaping political and social will.

Chapter 4

READING PUBLIC OPINION FROM VERNACULAR RHETORIC

> Democracy will come into its own, for democracy is a name for a life of free and enriching communion. . . . It will have its consummation when free inquiry is indissolubly wedded to the art of full and moving communication.
>
> John Dewey, *The Public and its Problems*

The 1992 and 1994 general elections provide an object lesson in the apparent volatility of public opinion. In 1992 Bill Clinton ran for the White House on a platform of change, which appealed to an electorate apparently troubled by a stalled economy, hemorrhaging national debt, and legislative gridlock. Clinton defeated incumbent president George Bush and brought with him to Washington one of the largest freshman congressional classes ever elected. Two years later the Republicans also campaigned on a platform of change, embodied in a set of pledges called the "Contract with America." The electorate, apparently still troubled by a sluggish economy, a government unable to balance its budget, and the failure of Congress and the White House to advance legislative initiatives responsive to its wishes, answered the call for change. Those on the Left interpreted the 1994 vote as an irrational expression of voter rage, those on the Right as an ideological mandate. Together they cast the meaning of the election in terms of party positions.

These readings are consistent with a vast, rich literature that addresses the political malaise of these times (e.g., Barber 1984; Dryzek 1990; Elshtain 1995; Fishkin 1995; Ginsberg 1986; Habermas 1989; Lasch 1995; Sennett 1978; Yankelovich 1991). Democratic governance rests on the capacity of and opportunity for citizens to engage in enlightened debate. Although deciding public policy through argument has little to recommend it in terms of efficiency, the purpose of public deliberation, as Aristotle recognized in his *Rhetoric*, is not efficient government but educated judgment. A common reading of the 1994 electorate's seemingly fickle vote reflected a sense of despair over its ability to meet this challenge.

Consternation over the voters' inability to arrive at an educated public judgment is not new (Boas 1969; Sagan 1991). Walter Lippmann (1949) and John Dewey (1954) wrote in the 1920s of their fear that the volume of information was too great, the interests too diverse, and the core of values and beliefs too volatile for democracy to sustain itself. Lippmann's proposed cadre of press specialists charged to act by deputy for an ill-informed public may have failed to gain popular endorsement, but that has not stemmed the proliferation of expert elites who have arrogated this role for themselves.

John Dewey, writing in response to Lippmann, understood the need for an active public if democracy is to succeed. At the close of *The Public and its Problems* he observed, "Vision is a spectator; hearing is a participator" (Dewey 1954, 219). The "hearing" Dewey had in mind was not that of a public attending to a politician, but the sort that occurs in mouth-to-mouth exchanges of conversation. "The winged words of conversation in immediate intercourse have a vital import lacking in the fixed and frozen words of written speech" (219).

Dewey's insight into the dialogical character of public opinion formation offers a promising starting point for rethinking its rhetorical character. Focusing on the rhetoricality of dialogue promises a fresh alternative to the currently dominant views on this subject. Liberal democratic theory advances a rational deliberation model that depicts the policies of the state as legitimated by the consensus-producing deliberations of interested citizens. Objectivist theory advances an opinion poll model that discovers the will of the people in the statistical findings of survey research. In contrast, I propose that an empirical disposition toward the dialogue of informal discourse, or a vernacular rhetoric model, provides a deeper understanding of public opinion than either of these alternatives. Taking actual discourses as the prima facie evidence from which we infer public opinion elevates the ongoing concerns of social actors to a central place in detecting and deciphering its content.

The rational deliberation model views public opinion as manifest exclusively in citizen actions that reflect a rational consensus on the legitimate purview of the state. In chapter 1 we saw C. Wright Mills's (1957, 300–301) summary of these assumptions positioning individual conscience as the ultimate seat of judgment, expressed through rational discussion as public opinion, which then guides a public's actions or that of its representatives. Regardless of whether such a rationally attuned public ever existed, these are the assumptions held by such proponents of classical liberal democratic theory as A. Lawrence Lowell. Writing in 1913, Lowell points to Rousseau's distinction between the freedom of humans in a state of nature to obey only their own will and the obligation of citizens in an organized state to privilege the common will: "A body of men are politically capable of a public opinion only so far as they are agreed upon the ends and aims of government and upon the principles by which those ends shall be attained" (23).[1] The theory holds that representative democracies form this opinion through the ebb and flow of reasoned discussion within a literate and informed *public.*

The opinion poll model, on the other hand, depicts public opinion as an objective datum that may be detected without attention to the processes of personal interactions producing it. Instead, it conceptualizes public opinion in scientific terms as a naturally occurring phenomenon that can be observed and described quantitatively.[2] As opinion researcher Leo Bogart asserts, "The world of public opinion in today's sense really began with the Gallup polls of the mid-1930s, and it is impossible for us to retreat to the meaning of public opinion as it was understood by Thomas Jefferson in the eighteenth century, by Alexis de Tocqueville and Lord Bryce in the nineteenth,—or even by Walter Lippman [*sic*] in 1922" (cited in Yankelovich 1991, 39). Poller Daniel Yankelovich declares the apparent victory of survey research as the barometer of public sentiment with the terse observation, "It is a practical advantage . . . to accept the steadily growing assumption that public opinion in America is largely what public opinion polls measure" (1991, 39).

The visions of public opinion as a rational ideal or an objective datum are at once discrete, contrasting, and intertwined. The evident differences in these interpretations reflect distinct ideologies and disparate scholarly and research interests. Without gainsaying their consequences, emphasis on their differences muffles their shared understanding of public opinion as a product of discourse. Moreover, even when they have given discourse thematic priority, rhetorical norms have been lost amidst the rationalism of ideal communication or the instrumentalism of degenerate manipulation (Ginsberg 1986; Habermas 1989; Mills 1957, 1963). Neither characterization exhibits empirical fidelity to the complex process whereby a public opinion is formed and communicated.[3] Neither accounts for the dialogical engagements by which an active populace participates in an issue's development; the contours of a public sphere that color their levels of awareness, perception, and participation; the influence on opinion formation of sharing views with one another; and the terms of expression warranting the inference that a *public* has formed and has a dominant *opinion*. Both, moreover, conceptualize public opinion as the expression of an entity: *the public*. Neither conceptualizes discourse in ways that account for the rhetorical processes by which those without official status—the actual members of publics—communicate to one another and respond to the messages they receive.

A conceptual model based on actual discursive practices promises a more informative account of public opinion than models that emphasize rational deliberation or opinion polling. Such a model emphasizes a different rationality from the idealized mode of liberal democracy or the means-ends logic of instrumentalism and objectivism; it accentuates the practical reasoning endemic in the use of symbols to coordinate social action, or *rhetoric*. In addition, consonant with the analysis of a plurality of publics and public spheres, it abandons conceptualizing *the* public as an entity with continuous existence whose function is to legitimize all public matters. Instead, a rhetorical model's sensitivity to the processual character of discursive formations shifts our conceptual focus to the formation of *publics* (Hauser 1985). It stresses their organic cycles of emergence and decline mirrored in the particularized and processual developments of everyday rhetorical exchanges as circumstances and issues engage the active attention of significant segments of society (Hauser and Blair 1982) Further, it distinguishes publics from special interest groups. A rhetorical model italicizes the discursive endeavors of those whose symbolic formations authorize public acts and conduct taken in their name (Bitzer 1978). Repositioning discourse at the center of public opinion promises rich possibilities for divulging *public* opinion, understanding its formation, and interpreting its meaning. Finally, centering society's ongoing conversation within the domain of forming and expressing public opinion refocuses attention on praxis, at once more complex and more faithful to the practices of actors themselves. The rhetorical model of public opinion I am proposing allows for active analysis of this broader range of expression.

This chapter advances four claims: First, to overcome the reification of publics found in the rational deliberation model, a discourse-based theory of public opinion must *widen its scope* to include vernacular exchanges in addition to those of institutional actors.[4] Second, rhetorical dialogue reflects the *collective reasoning process* that public opinion expresses. Third, a rhetorical model locates public opinion—a civil judgment—in the manifestations of *common understanding* within a public sphere. Finally, the assent peculiar to public opinion is fashioned through the *dialogue of vernacular talk.*

My general contention, in short, is that we may gain illuminating insight into a public's opinion by taking discourse, including vernacular "talk," seriously.[5] Before developing these claims, I will present a personal experience that may serve as a paradigmatic illustration of the ways in which vernacular exchanges enter into political dialogue and how this dialogue provides rhetorical experiences of public opinion.

Witnessing Vernacular Discourse: An Outsider's Experience

In May 1985 I was traveling in Greece. This was my first visit there, and I was filled with professional and personal expectations. I anticipated exciting discoveries upon visiting the sites where figures of antiquity I had studied, taught, and written about had engaged in their intellectual and political practices. I also experienced deep emotions attached to being in physical places where my maternal ancestors had lived. As it turned out, however, current events defined important, unanticipated dimensions of my pilgrimage, since my visit coincided with the final weeks of the Greek national election.

On the afternoon of my arrival the main streets of Athens were filled with the blare of automobile horns honking partisan support. I was exhausted after an overnight flight from Belgrade and an interminable delay at the Athens airport, but the deafening racket in the street made sleep impossible. I decided to take a walk. The street scene included the cars whose incessant horn blowing was intruding on my need for rest. Closer now, I could see men leaning out their windows, waving identical banners of the favored party, and shouting slogans to pedestrian traffic and sometimes their disdain at vehicles demonstrating for the opposition. Street lamps, telephone poles, and walls were festooned with campaign posters, neatly ordered in a straight line and, oddly, for only one candidate per street, as if the neighborhood were making its statement in unison. I was struck by the orderliness, uniformity, and sheer volume of these displays of support.

Later that evening the bus returning me to my hotel became entangled in a traffic jam at Sindagma (Constitution) Square. The square was illuminated by floodlights so numerous and bright as to give it the surrealistic appearance of a Fellini set: a circle of daylight within the inkwell of night. The bus driver poked his head through his window and spoke with animation to people in the street. I asked a companion what was happening. He informed me of the Greek custom of holding mass rallies for political parties the three Fridays before a national election. Each party had its own night, with this one belonging to the New Democracy Party, whose candidate for prime minister was Konstantinos Mitsotakis. The rally had just ended, and traffic in the square was heavy from political supporters now wending their way home. Evidently our driver held different political sentiments from those partisans still reveling in the square and contributing to its snarl.

The next day my wife and I left Athens for a week of travel to other parts of the country. In smaller towns and villages campaign posters hung in a fashion similar to those in Athens. Their relatively unchallenged volume in support of New Democracy created the impression of massive popular sentiment in its favor. I thought that New Democracy was headed for a landslide victory.

The following Friday we returned to Athens. After a day in the ancient agora we started back to our hotel, which proved to be an interesting journey. Along the way we were searching for a bank to exchange currency and came upon two men who were in a heated discussion and had attracted a small group of onlookers. We paused, and from comments of onlookers we inferred their disagreement was over the election. Suddenly one of the men became so infuriated at the other that he started to kick at his shins! On the chance that a melee might ensue and that it was not in our interest to be part of a political street brawl, we continued on to tend to our banking business.

Upon leaving the bank we soon found ourselves in Sindagma Square. Preparations were under way for the rally to be held there that night in support of the Panhellenic Socialist Movement, or PASOK. The balcony above the stage where that evening's speeches would be delivered was itself a stage of feverish activity, as a man wielding a furring strip hacked at remnants of the previous week's demonstration in support of New Democracy still adorning its walls. He was securing banners of PASOK in their place to create a proper backdrop for the anticipated event. The energy with which he was dispatching his mission contributed to the aura of political passion that radiated about the city.

On our way back to our hotel my wife and I stopped in an art boutique. While browsing we struck up a conversation with the clerk. We chatted about the election and the incessant blare of automobile horns. We learned that the PASOK rally scheduled for that evening would bring the campaign to its official conclusion. Since Greeks must vote in the town of birth, the next day would find Athens vacated. The clerk informed us that Sunday was to be a day of reflection before the election on Monday and that campaigning was prohibited. She also expressed her relief that life would soon return to normal. When we asked how long it would take to clear the debris from the rally and the signs now seemingly hung from every post and pole, she reacted with surprise. "They will all be gone by Tuesday. The parties take pride in keeping the city clean." Whether her report was of reality or for tourist consumption, it suggested a local understanding of the nature and limits of Greek political campaigning and campaigners not apparent to outsiders.

The last week's rally was still fresh in our minds, so as my wife and I discussed the preparations we were observing and the attitudes Athenians were reflecting, the opportunity to be a part of that evening's spectacle was irresistible. Later we ventured to Queen Amalia Avenue to watch the event that was presently to occupy center stage.

En route to our destination and continually after we arrived, a steady flow of Athenians made their way toward Sindagma Square from which then incumbent Greek prime minister Andreas Pampandreou would later speak. Many had children in tow, dressed in festive costumes that sported the rising-sun logo of PASOK, Pampandreou's political party. The adults were carrying PASOK banners and green carnations. Judging by their dress, which ranged from shorts and T-shirts to finely tailored suits, they represented every segment of Athenian society.

My wife was taking photographs of the passing scene, and several families stopped to ask if she would take theirs. Much good-natured interaction ensued when they discovered we were Americans. Several asked us who we supported. In the spirit of the occasion, we answered "PASOK," to which the Greeks replied, "See, even the Americans know who is best." They gave us partisan banners and green carnations so we could sport our "loyalty" publicly.

The crowd was growing quite large and boisterous. To American eyes it seemed odd that children, many of them no older than five or six, were accompanying their parents to the rally. We mentioned our surprise to a woman in her late fifties who was posing for a picture. She replied with mild indignation that there was no reason for concern; Greeks were protective of their children.

Doubtless this was true, but we were less certain in our estimate of how this swarm in support of a government at odds with the United States might behave toward Americans once the rally reached full swing. Our concerns were heightened when a phalanx of partisan men and some women marched past us, shoulder to shoulder, filling the entire width of the avenue from sidewalk to sidewalk and pinning us against the wall of the Royal Gardens for several minutes as it paraded by. Clearly, we were witnessing collective behavior beyond our cultural experience of political rallies (our nearest analogue being the campus protest of the 1960s and 1970s, a distant relative at best). At dusk we returned to our hotel, where we hoped to continue watching the rally on television.

When we entered the hotel lobby laded with booty of PASOK banners and green carnations, we caused a stir. The desk clerk and bell captain were party loyalists who first reacted with surprise at our appearance of "affiliation" but then quickly seized it as an opportunity to point out to their supervisor the apparent political savvy of their American guests. The bell captain then engaged us in conversation. He was curious about how we came upon the banners and answered our questions concerning the nature of political demonstrations in Greece. We inquired about what was said during the stir when we entered the lobby. He related their surprise to see Americans sporting PASOK's colors. Then he explained that our appearance offered the lobby workers an excuse to express political views they otherwise were discouraged from expressing publicly before patrons in the hotel. He seemed quite pleased to have had an excuse to tout PASOK before his boss in that manner. Sensing our interest in the campaign, he informed us that Pampandreou's speech would be on TV and invited us to join him and his coworkers in about an hour to watch it.

Pampandreou began his speech around 9:00 p.m., with the floodlit square reenacting the surrealistic transformation we had experienced a week earlier. Although Pampandreou spoke with considerable energy, he seldom occupied the screen. Instead, the cameras panned across the street scene in which an excited mass waved partisan banners in support of PASOK and chanted while the prime minister spoke. The crowd interrupted its chanting to cheer telling points Pampandreou made against the opposition party or the United States and measures for which PASOK stood. Although these partisans were vociferous with unified and unremitting chants, their concerted cheers indicated they were attending simultaneously to Pampandreou and expressing their strongest support for sentiments they endorsed.

Several extremely broad avenues empty into Sindagma Square, and the television coverage included an overlay of the street name in which the crowd shown was assembled. At one point the hotel staff members watching the speech with us became animated. I asked the bell captain what prompted the reaction. He told me that the image then being shown was of the mass jamming Omonoia (Concord) Square, about a mile distant from the site of the speech, itself only slightly smaller than Sindagma Square and fed by eight thoroughfares. The distance and size were read by these Greek viewers as an index of the level of public support for the prime minister, sufficient to jam a full mile of the broadest streets in Athens! Two days later Mr. Pampandreou was reelected to office.

Each of these episodes in the Greek national election of 1985, admittedly partial and selective, seemed to be frenzied, chaotic at times, and even threatening to the eyes and ears of an outsider. But to those familiar with the narrative of Greek politics, they were pointed expressions of public sentiment. Moreover, each was a communicative act that entered into a national discourse on policy and direction, as occurs during national elections.

Vernacular Rhetoric: The Rhetorical Locus of Public Opinion

Although the various theories of public opinion may nod toward discourse as its cornerstone, their discussions of public opinion seldom treat discourse seriously. Typically, discourse is reduced to the rhetoric of political parties. It is portrayed either as an official stance taken to represent constituent opinion or as propaganda intended to direct group behavior. Neither of these depictions offers serious attention to street-level give-and-take of contrary viewpoints from which a widely shared strong opinion may emerge. To revive a rich sense of discourse as the basis for public opinion, the theory of public opinion itself must be informative of how rhetorically engaged actors deliberate over social, political, and cultural issues. *Such a rehabilitation must widen the discursive arena to include vernacular exchanges, in addition to those of institutional actors.*

As my narrative suggests, the citizens of Greece were engaged in a robust version of street rhetoric understood by the locals and enacted with every sign of conviction that their efforts had the potential to influence opinion. Their posters, chants, and street-corner debates opened dialogue between competing factions. Although my touristly observations provided me with no evidence that the competing factions engaged one another in a serious attempt to find a common ground for policy and action, these factions would not differ in this respect from political partisans in general. Their dialogue was rather at the level of open exchanges of partisanship and difference that are possible in a free society. These exchanges provided a broad range of contrasting messages to Greece's witnessing, evaluating, acting citizenry. These included the signalizing interpolation of honking horns, street-corner debates, the myriad of private conversations that democratic experience assures us must have occurred in which Greeks puzzled over contrasting futures under the hand of New Democracy or PASOK, the public addresses of the party leaders themselves, and the mass-media coverage of the election campaign. This discursive range surpassed both restrictions of official sites and authoritative monologia of the sort Bakhtin (1981) associates with official rhetoric.

Regardless of their theoretical stripe, all statements about public opinion refer to a construct. We do not encounter a public opinion empirically in the same way as we might, say, the personal opinions of a friend in conversation. Insofar as it refers to what an aggregate of strangers believes, public opinion is an inference drawn from concrete evidence deemed significant by the theory that governs its conceptualization. Even in the case of an election, the voting result is an empirical datum. Its electoral meaning is determined by law. In that sense, it is fact, not opinion. Its meaning as a public opinion—as when the winning candidate declares that the people have spoken and provided a mandate for his or her policies—is an interpretation of the political expression behind voters' ballots for a particular candidate. This same rubric applies to a rhetorical model of public opinion, which requires, first, that public opinion be extrapolated from actual discursive exchanges.

In the Greek election campaign these exchanges were inherently reflexive, at once interpretive readings of the political milieu and expressions to be read by others who, by choice or happenstance, were observing and interacting with a dynamic political scene. Admittedly, this engagement was, in one sense, a datum to be observed. But there is more to observe than mere acts of social cooperation. Honking horns, posting signs and banners, and gathering for a mass rally would be senseless without an opposition whom such acts might engage. These dialogic encounters were also an achievement that spoke of alternative working hypotheses for comprehending and expressing reality through the friction created by their respective interpretations of the Greek context and tradition. In addition to whatever discussion the professional politicians may have been conducting, the general populace was conducting its own public dialogue on the future of Greece. If there were a barometer of Greek public opinion, it was as much to be found in the readings and misreadings average Greek citizens made of their circumstances and of one another as in the speeches of their leaders. Further, whatever discursive evidence one might find for such opinions was more evident in the dialogue being conducted by the people than in the campaign addresses of Mitsotakis and Pampandreou.

These dialogical features underscore a fairly simple but essential point for the rhetorical rehabilitation of public opinion. *The discourses by which public opinions are expressed, experienced, and inferred include the broad range of symbolic exchanges whereby social actors seek to induce coopera-*

tion, from the formal speech to the symbolically significant nonverbal exchange, from practical arguments to aesthetic expression. These exchanges are part of an ongoing dialogue in which an active society critiques, negotiates, associates, and ultimately constitutes its interests and opinions on the issues confronting them. Each contribution speaks the claims of differences and affiliations that allow us to recognize, discriminate, and interpret meanings within the socially negotiated limits that define social membership.

Certainly this was the case in the Greek election campaign. From an outsider's perspective, it was obvious that the fortunes of PASOK depended on whether one read the political winds from within Athens. Cosmopolitan, teeming with people and traffic, reeking of pollution and the lure of the fast life, Athens contrasts starkly with the countryside and everyday experience as little as twenty kilometers beyond its city limits. There the sky clears to a brilliant blue, and the landscape of skyscrapers melts into pastoral expanses where peasants use horses, mules, and oxen to work the fields.

Rural Greece showed little visible sympathy for the policies of the incumbent prime minister. This apparent urban/rural split was rooted in political policies and practices that created jobs and advanced economic interests of different segments of the population. The enormous shipping interests based at Piraeus had often been favored over those of fishing or agriculture, which are spread across the country. The growing rift between the Pampandreou and Reagan administrations over Greece's role in NATO also insinuated itself into Greek political consciousness and, in that regard, the maintenance of an American naval base on Greek soil. Participation in NATO carried implications for Greek foreign trade, which had ties to the United States and Western Europe. Pampandreou did not consider it evident that Greece's struggling economy would suffer from a freer hand to trade with the Soviet Union or that its national security would be endangered from closer ties to the USSR, which exercised considerable influence with Greece's Balkan neighbors and would not fetter it with bonds to its regional rival Turkey. For Greeks living near the country's historically vulnerable northern border or on its islands, the defensive shield of NATO provided peace of mind against external regional conflict. Pronouncements of affiliation that appeared to pit Athens against the rest of Greece were reflective, in part, of deeper economic and defense issues being considered by a relatively poor and weak nation.

A poll could capture these differences in economic interests and tell us what percentage of the population saw this or that as a major issue and how these preferences were segmented by region or class. But a poll also would portray this public as static by fixing meaning in the frozen frame of a statistic. A poll could not capture the passion with which these views were held and were being expressed, or the spontaneity and dynamism of the public engagements in which citizens individually and collectively tried to shape Greece's political horizon, or the persuasive influence they may have had on others in the political community.

This type of engagement transcends the moment insofar as it is contextualized in cultural meanings providing shared boundaries of opportunity and limitation for political expression. The Greek cultural context, for example, was explicit and kept in view by the very names of the two major parties—New Democracy and Panhellenic Socialist Movement. Both merged political aspirations of conservatives and socialists with powerful icons of national identity; they spoke of ancient glories that had made Greece the leading edge of politics, culture, and learning in Hellas.

Vernacular political discourse such as that of the Greek election reminds us that publics deliberate in ways not confined to the orderly debates of parliamentary bodies. They take a variety of forms, suited to their time and place and within the cultural understanding of their audiences, sometimes trumpeting their affiliations as literally as the cacophony of horns that blared in the Athenian streets. They resolve issues through a variety of means that suggest and urge broad-based support, sometimes even through public responses to public arguments. Despite difficult economic times, the Greek street rhetoric suggested a people who had not succumbed to anomie. Their demonstrative exchanges evidenced their continuing commitment to deal with political issues by actively and publicly engaging one another. They were assuming and also sustaining a vibrant public sphere in which shared knowledge of cultural norms moderated behavior.

These conclusions are supported by the evidentiary base that follows from expanding the discursive framework of liberal democratic theory to include active analysis of this broader range of expression. As social actors, we are continuously "reading" public opinion and expressing our own opinions (Noelle-Neumann 1989, 1993). These two activities are interrelated since our own expressions are influenced by our reading, including its accuracy, of what others think. Because they cannot be separated from one another, observing and interpreting public opinion require attention to both of these activities, that is, *of what a public is expressing and of how and how well it reads these expressions.* For the observer and interpreter, reading public opinions from the rhetorical dialogues of society's active members may surrender the precision one can gain from controlled questions administered to a randomly chosen sample population and also may lose the structural economy of examining public deliberation by institutional representatives. The vernacular rhetoric model relies on society's active members to set the terms for public opinion through their own assertions and interpretive readings of affirmation, rejection, concern, or hope that frame the public experience of their common interests and how they should be protected. Consequently, the model gains in fidelity between opinions inferred and the sample examined, as well as in the richness of the social narratives in which opinions are embedded. Moreover, the model's sensitivity to the "reading" activity of a given public—to how well it is doing—gains the practical advantage over other models of not lapsing into theoretically imposed constructions of public opinion that can result in distorted readings.

Public Opinion and Reasoning

The interactions among this widened circle of political partisans is indicative of the collective reasoning processes autochthonous to rhetorical dialogue and which public opinion expresses. Hannah Arendt has observed that the richest private life "can offer only the prolongation or multiplication of one's own position with its attending aspects and perspectives" (1958, 57). Public life, by contrast, is alive with the spectacle of actions that claim our attention and assessment. Our public and private experiences are demarcated on our respective abilities to affirm something outside our selves. She tells us, "Only when things can be seen by many in a variety of aspects without changing their identity, so that those who are gathered around them know they see sameness in utter diversity, can worldly reality truly and reliably appear" (57). Arendt's point reminds us that opinions are not moods. They are formed through critical processes; we decipher the sense of words and actions in light of our individual and collective experiences. My second claim grows from this experience: *rhetorical dialogue reflects the collective reasoning process that is the basis for extrapolating public opinion.*

Opinion is the result of judgment. It is formed on the basis of evidence interpreted within a frame of reference. There are differences between the expert opinion that offers an appraisal based on technical considerations, such as whether this building can withstand an earthquake measuring 6.2 on the Richter scale or whether the murder suspect's DNA matches that found on evidence at the crime scene, and lay opinion that addresses life's contingencies, such as whether Proposition 187 will eventually undermine education in California. This is an ancient observation captured by Aristotle's distinctions between *theoretical, practical,* and *productive* knowledge, which serves to remind us that rhetorical knowledge is of a different order from *theoria,* such as scientific/technical knowledge. It exists in praxis. In modern vintage, the same point is captured by the distinction between ontic and ontological questions as the basis of explanation and understanding.[6] These distinctions are useful here because they help us distinguish the proper domain of public opinion.

Scientific investigation presupposes that nature is governed by laws that exist apart from the individuals who discover and make them known. Rhetoric belongs to a different order of knowledge. Its domain is the *practical reasoning* that occurs when the contingencies of human relations require thoughtful choices exceeding criteria of regularity, prediction, and control. Rhetorical reasoning is directed at solutions to what Lloyd Bitzer (1968, 6) has termed "imperfections marked by urgency," whether in fact or perception, and is, therefore, strategic.

Prudential conduct is not governed by the true/false logic of propositional statements; it is concerned with beliefs and actions that have traction on the moral and pragmatic registers of those who are being addressed and asked to judge. These are considerations of "the preferable" which, as Kenneth Burke (1969) taught us, makes rhetorical reasoning hortatory. Reasoning of this sort encourages individuals and groups to share opinions and to act on "the better" or "the worse," in which the ultimate interests are over questions of "ought." Individually we make these calibrations in light of existing contingencies. Since community preferences may change with prevailing circumstances, social and even cultural relations are open to negotiation.

The ancient Greeks considered our ability to engage in this type of public moral discussion a virtue. Aristotle referred to it as phronêsis—practical wisdom or prudence. Prudence required thoughtfully assessing the consequences of proposed actions to understand their implications for oneself and the community, plus the capacity to make this understanding known through words and deeds with sufficient power to gain assent. Whereas the philosopher's wisdom, *sophia*, offered insight into truth, the preserve of phronêsis was practical conduct: what to think and do when confronted by conflicting alternatives (Aristotle 1941, chap. 6). Its end was not theoretical knowledge but responsible action to resolve the differences of divergent perspectives that surface when we address concrete problems (Graham and Havard 1984).

Forming an opinion, as distinct from holding to blind prejudice, requires the ability to see things from the multiple perspectives of those who are present in the public realm, or what Arendt terms *representative thinking*. Although Arendt is somewhat ambiguous on the precise character of representative thinking, suggesting in one work that taking other people's opinions into account occurs in the domain of the *vita contemplativa* (1971) and in others that this occurs in the *vita activa* (1958, 1977), clearly it is neither a question of empathy nor of counting noses. In *Between Past and Future* she asserts: "The more people's standpoints I have present in my mind while I am pondering a given issue, and the better I can imagine how I would feel and think if I were in their place, the stronger will be my capacity for representational thinking and the more valid my final conclusions, my opinion" (1977, 241). Representative thinking may be internal to the subject and reflective in nature, but "thinking in the place of everybody else" so that one can project "potential agreement with others" eventuates, finally, in coming to some agreement (Beiner 1982, 104).

When tending to political relations, as in *The Human Condition* (1958), Arendt intimates that representative thinking is not the product of inner debate or the spectatorship or retrospection of storytellers or historians but is related to excellence, which requires the presence of others. Insofar as judgment refers to prudential conduct, the excellence in question is the judgment that thus and so is the proper course of action.

In one of her unpublished lectures Arendt illustrates how representative thinking functions in terms that are highly suggestive of its noncognitive, rhetorical basis:

> Suppose I look at a specific slum dwelling and I perceive in this particular building the general notion which it does not exhibit directly, the notion of poverty and misery. I arrive at this notion by representing to myself how I would feel if I had to live there, that is, I try to think in the place of the slum-dweller. The judgment I shall come up with will by no means necessarily be the same as that of the inhabitants, whom time and hopelessness may have dulled to the outrage of their condition, but it will become for my further judging of these matters an outstanding example to which I refer. . . . Furthermore, while I take into account others when judging, this does not mean that I conform my judgment to those of others, I still speak with my own voice and I do not count noses to arrive at what I think is right. But my judgment is no longer subjective either. The point of the matter is that my judgment of a particular instance does not merely depend on my representing to myself something which I do not perceive (qtd. in Beiner 1982, 107–8).

Arendt's example, which she confines to the subject's own thought process, is nonetheless mimetic of the public thought process in which we engage through intersubjective exchanges of formal and vernacular discourse. The emphasis of political judgment is on phenomena understood as appearances; its concern is with determining their facticity as phenomena rather than classifying them as objects under a universal category. Political events have the characteristic, perhaps uniquely their own, of creating their own space of appearance. But their appearance within these spaces is always marked by uncertainty and requires discrimination that relies upon impartiality in order to think about what is not there—the missing evidence and future consequences of choice and action.

Arendt's analysis, which poses a strong antidote to the cognitive basis for political judgment advanced by Habermas, stops short of acknowledging the method by which this judgment is formed. The method for using representative thinking to arrive at political choice is rhetoric. Contemplation alone is insufficient to arrive at a judgment of this sort; it requires deliberative conversations to explore the self-disclosing phenomenality of the event, to discriminate among conflicting phenomena within it, and to arrive at what Arendt herself regarded as the communal basis of the vita activa: a *common sense* of reality on which our judgment rests.[7]

A rhetorical construction of public opinion begins, then, with an understanding of opinion itself as the result of deliberation over an indeterminate matter. It becomes a *public* opinion when a pattern of *sentiment*—thoughts, beliefs, and commitments to which a significant and engaged segment of the populace holds attachments that are consequential for choices individuals are willing to make and actions they are prepared to support in shaping their collective future—emerges from deliberative exchanges among those within a public sphere.

For Athenians living in the commercial and central areas of the city, the intrusiveness of their street rhetoric may have made attending to the national election less a matter of choice than would be the case in the United States. On the other hand, there was observable evidence of active engagement across the spectrum of opinion in confrontations, as between my bus driver and the supporters of New Democracy or the two men arguing in the street, and in more considered deliberations among friends and coworkers who sometimes held different views, however ephemeral, at the same time or shopkeepers who weighed the pros and cons as they explained to their American patrons the issues being contested. Institutional discursive forms also were part of this overspanning national conversation through countless public speeches and televised partisan rallies in which candidates and party officials urged their fellow Greeks to adopt free market or socialist policies, to choose the security of standing with NATO and the West or the riskier course of political and military independence that might allow the nation to alter its alliances as circumstances dictated.

A perspective on lived experiences invariably anchored this range of exchanges. Such evidence as regional displays of different political affiliations and local readings of class tensions exhibited an alternative rationality to that of the means/ends logic that guides the reasoning of professional or technical epistemic elites. The vernacular exchanges among these citizens suggest that they were reasoning from past promises and acts and present conditions and proposals as they affected them and their group and as they visibly touched the lives of other segments of society. These exchanges are representative of how social actors reach judgments expressed in their ongoing dialogical exchanges, however stubbornly partisan they may be in their immediacy, and from which we extrapolate our sense of a public having formed and of the opinions that public holds on contested matters.

Our individual perceptions and experiences of current affairs invite personal verdicts on their meaning and significance. Public opinion reflects how these same circumstances engage the wider sphere of society in the judging process. Society is engaged most profoundly when issues are transmitted beyond the media, through formal and informal communication within our network of associations in the community, the arts, education, and work. One did not have to be a Greek citizen to detect that there were different and conflicting interests that separated large segments from the lived realities of each other's lives. The stark contrasts of living conditions and of life's rhythms for Athenians and those just twenty kilometers distant, the complexity of the city itself, and the obvious economic as well as military implications of membership in NATO surely provided an abundance of deep social, economic, and political differences.

These differences and the interests they reflected could not acquire significance for social action until someone made them relevant to people's lives through compelling narratives and arguments. The Greeks I was encountering could not have formed an opinion about their interests without a prior awareness of the problems they might or actually did encounter as a result of state policies. Their intensely demonstrative politics reflected a culture engaged by an awareness of their political circumstances and in the activities of soliciting support through their participation in the multidimensional and polyvocal dialogue—a multilogue—on Greece's future course.

We cannot begin to appreciate the importance of rhetorical expressions of public opinion if we limit ourselves to an instrumentalist rendition of communication as a variable to be manipulated or limit our discursive readings to institutional discourse at the expense of actively considering the vernacular exchanges in which we detect publics and discern their opinions. Excising communication's processual and epistemic character reduces it to a datum.[8] More importantly, it obliterates the essential evidence for determining what the *engaged* segment of society—those who in some sense are participating in the discursive space of a public sphere whose participants exceed their own group and the confident bias of vested interests—believes and why it does so.

Asking and gaining answers to opinion questions, as Bourdieu (1979) reminds us, does not provide prima facie evidence that the opinion givers are even remotely engaged by the matters in question, the sine qua non for membership in a public. Nor is a shared ideology or even shared political interest a public's essential characteristic. Collective opinion is formed by the shared activity of communication (Hauser and Blair 1982). Put differently, publics are not defined by reflective thought but by judgment, however evanescent; their awareness of issues is not philosophical but eventful. The necessity of communication on public issues to engage individuals in their collectivity as social actors gives us every reason to conclude that publics exist only as they manifest their publicness.

Public Opinion and Common Understanding

The public activity of the Greek election illustrates the web of discursive spaces that constitutes public spheres: venues to receive and discuss issues, define them in light of collective experience, and finally arrive at civil judgments with collective weight. *Civil judgments reflect a common understanding that not only expresses a rhetorically formed public opinion but is the very ground for a public.*

Aristotle's *Rhetoric* provides one of the first treatments of judgment's role in discourse. His views are relevant to this discussion insofar as they offer insight into the type of reasoning peculiar to public life. Aristotle contends that the goal of rhetoric and the function of the audience are one and the same—*krisis,* or judgment. Krisis implies more than rational assent; it is the virtue of judgment informed by a disposition to act and feel in a particular way. The rationality of krisis entails the virtue of considering the phenomena of prudential conduct in terms that exceed one's personal interests and apply to every human. Krisis is not exercised as a calculus of consequences but as thoughtful consideration of contingent affairs in order to achieve the common good of *eudaimonia,* or happiness.

Aristotle's discussion implies that we are led to the point of judgment by engaging in practical reasoning. Practical reasoning is concerned with making choices about the preferable and the good specific to their situations. There is no god's-eye view that offers a single account of what these may be (Nussbaum 1986, 290–317). We locate them through deliberation tempered by the fortunes of our particular way of life. What may be good for Macedonians is not necessarily so for Athenians. The good life cannot be achieved by technê; it is not a scientific enterprise but "a true and reasoned state of capacity to act with respect to the things that are good or bad for a man" (Aristotle 1941, 1140b1, b4–b6).

Aristotle's ethical works, including his *Rhetoric,* position eudaimonia so that it is inclusive of a variety of constituents that may coexist but are nevertheless independent of one another. Good health, respectful children, wealth, friends, love, and so forth are incommensurable and desired for themselves. They cannot be weighed against one another in terms of a foreordained understanding of the good life. We estimate their relevance and importance amidst a sea of changing circumstances since they are the elements that contribute to the good life as it is gauged by the nonscientific calculus of deliberation.

A person becomes good at deliberating by knowing how to resolve a problem in line with the views of those being addressed, and the choices of wise men and women reflect their experiences in dealing with human problems subject to deliberation. Since the elements of eudaimonia are incommensurable, their meaning and relative value depend on one's view of the good life. Even though practical reasoning is not a technê, it is more than brute impulse or caprice. Aristotle regards it as an intellectual virtue, prudence, on which practical wisdom (phronêsis) rests (1941, 1106b36–7a2, 1140b24–25). Practical reasoning involves an ability to project the consequences of actions in line with an understanding of other commitments. Aristotle's seemingly banal observation that we will get much farther praising Athens before Athenians than we will before Lacedaemonians reflects the more fundamental assumption that questions of preference are always framed by the contingencies of values and ambitions held by those whose judgment counts.

Those whose judgment counts—those who belong to a public—may include segments who lack experience in making public policy decisions and are absent the intellectual virtue of practical wisdom, but Aristotle maintained nevertheless that everyone who wished to partake in public life must understand phronêsis.

> Practical wisdom issues commands, since its end is what ought to be done or not to be done; but understanding only judges. . . . Now understanding is neither the having nor the acquiring of practical wisdom; but when learning is called understanding when it means the exercise of the faculty of knowledge, so "understanding" is applicable to the exercise of the faculty of opinion for the purpose of judging of what some one else says about matters with which practical wisdom is concerned. (1941, 1143a8–14)

By implication, Aristotle thought participation in public life required the rhetorical competence of understanding in order to render a competent judgment on issues of contingent choice, issues open to discussion and deliberation.

In sum, matters of prudential conduct are open to question. We address them properly when we reason about action or engage in practical reasoning (phronêsis). This type of reasoning addresses particular cases whose very particularity, contingent circumstances, and diverse views of the good life make them impossible to decide with scientific rules. Instead participants resolve them by exercising a quality of mind concerned with things that are noble, just, and good. This reasoning requires both individuals who are able to summarize wise thoughts of others and apply their insights with flexibility in the given case and individuals who are able to distinguish advice that is wise from that which is merely clever. The former requires phronêsis to offer sound advice; the latter requires recognition to form a sound judgment.[9]

Aristotle's analysis of practical reasoning is important in the context of this discussion because it locates within the practice of rhetoric judgment on questions open to deliberation. Judgment is not in hand from the outset as an ideological commitment that determines what should be done in the given case. Nor is judgment merely individual opinions that can be aggregated to indicate what should be done on the bases of preferential trends. *Judgment is a form of knowledge constituted by the very performance and appraisal of discourse in terms of the world our collective activity promises to frame.*

These judgments express the *common understanding* of those who are engaged, the collective understanding among those who have witnessed a public matter from their respective points of view and have taken the views of others into account while forming an opinion. This process of considering multiple perspectives coincides with the view of "representative thinking" Arendt placed at the heart of political judgment. This process of perspective taking to arrive at a collective affirmation of reality is a quintessentially rhetorical mode of thought.

Rhetorical judgment cannot escape the demand of common understanding; its validity is guaranteed only by collective agreement. Since the Enlightenment the agreements that matter as an expression of public opinion are those forged in civil society. The exchanges of commerce, fashion, the arts, the press, political parties, and the like compose the mosaic of society's continuous conversation (Cohen and Arato 1992; Hall 1995; Seligman 1992). These vernacular exchanges among strangers whose congress is independent of official fora and state or institutional control serve as society's symbolic means for affecting its own self-regulation. Civil society's mélange of vernacular rhetoric is our most sensitive locus from which publics emerge. Its agreements of common understanding are always specific, never universal; are always social, lacking validity for those who are not judges or lack access to its dominant public sphere. Importantly, common understanding reflects judgments about propositions of value and belief, such as the repugnance of Hitler's "final solution," rather than of truths or facts, such as that six million Jews were exterminated by the Nazis. In this regard rhetorical judgment becomes the vehicle for transporting us from our private and subjective existence into the common realm of shared reality and reflects our political, social, and cultural competence.

The cacophony of vernacular discourses, such as those of the Greek election, remind us that publics do not exercise their political competence only through the orderly debates of parliamentary bodies. Their deliberations take a variety of forms suited to their time and place and within the cultural understanding of their audiences while sometimes, as noted earlier, trumpeting their affiliations as literally as the raucous blare of the Athenian streets. They resolve issues through a variety of means that suggest or even urge broad-based support, sometimes even through public responses to public arguments.

A public's reasoning function requires a shared basis for under-standing vernacular "talk." The dialogic characteristics of a public sphere invest it with a conversational quality. Dialogue requires a sense of our own identity and that of the social entity we bring into being through par-ticipation in discourse, which has existence and meaning apart from our individual being. Dialogue survives by being attentive to the background consensus its participants share for the norms of conduct that apply to them as a collectivity and on which their continued interactive existence depends. Dialogue is, in this sense, *chronotopic* (Bakhtin 1981). The give-and-take of conversing creates a common discursive space shared by dialogic partners in which a complementary *I* and *we*, as discussed in chapter 3, can appear. Their movement through that space requires that partners abide by the imperative to distinguish between the *I* and *we* to retain their complementarity and prevent the *we* from disintegrating.

The complementarity of *I* and *we* does not mean that there is a con-vergence of opinion among dialogic partners but rather that they inhabit a common world of concerns that requires them to take account of one another while arriving at judgments. Extrapolating from Taylor's (1991) analysis of the atomic *I* and molecular *we* of face-to-face dialogue to the more complex multilogue from which a public emerges, the same require-ment of complementarity holds. The countless acts of publicly expressed opinions on contingent affairs require the type of social cooperation—even in opposition—that occurs when participants read the expressions of others with a degree of accuracy that permits them to ascertain the rele-vance of those expressions to themselves and the consequences for them-selves and, more importantly, the social world they share.

Common understanding of this sort would be impossible without a language of common meanings. An ensemble of individuals referred to as a "public" is, when unconstrained, liable to the contentious behaviors of factions who differ in opinions and interests, as Madison's *Publius* warned in *Federalist Paper* number 10. A public is not necessarily a group in con-sensus. The supporters of New Democracy who had demonstrated in Sindagma Square the week before the Greek election doubtless had inter-nal differences over their political and economic concerns; surely their interests diverged from those of their partisan countrymen and country-women in the rural regions, the mountains to the north, and the islands dotting the Aegean. They were manifesting every sign of deep division from their counterparts supporting PASOK, but they were not unintelligi-ble to one another as they sometimes were to American eyes and ears illit-erate in Greek politics and political conventions.

The thesis that human reality is socially constructed is by now an aca-demic commonplace. Its widespread acceptance, however, does not alter its importance for understanding the extent to which the language avail-able to a people determines the social world they share. For an ensemble of strangers to have a common understanding of reality requires more than a common language permitting intersubjective understanding. Common understanding entails a language that applies to a common reference world, even when our customs, preferences, and methods pertaining to that world are at odds. The bond of common meaning is not shared values and meanings but *the sharing of the shared world,* commonly understood even if differently lived (Taylor 1971).

One can imagine, for example, that my dialogues with my Greek hosts might have been different had we entered into discussions of our common intellectual and cultural heritage. Those discussions would have addressed our common bonds in the works and traditions of Greek antiquity and remained detached from important political decisions. Or we might have discussed the anti-American views Pampandreou advanced, wherein the economic, political, and military autonomy of Greece was compromised by the weight of American foreign policy and its military presence through NATO bases located there. Here the common ground of shared interests might have bridged apparent differences and swayed some sentiments—mine or theirs—to see Greco-American relations in a different light.

The discussions I did have revealed assumptions and impressions that often were misplaced in the context of Greek politics. The bitterest of Greek political rivals had a firmer grasp on their shared world as Greeks than any outsider could hope to attain.[10] For that reason their rivalry ran deeper and excited their political sentiments to greater passion than was possible for a witness with untrained eyes. Common meanings, after all, made their opponents all the more menacing for the transformations they seemed to propose. In this respect, the partisan expressions I had observed in Athens and elsewhere were no different from those one might witness wherever democratic politics is being practiced.

Such expressions are significant insofar as they come from a broad spectrum of society. They include more than the views of those who hold a single point of view and for that reason are different from special-interest appeals or the contentions of those who have already resolved an issue to their own satisfaction. At the same time, the realm of rhetoric is not so large as to include everyone at every moment, since the problems of complex societies outstrip the capacity of its members to attend to every problem and since some members inevitably will choose not to participate in or even attend to deliberations of public problems and hold no opinion on questions of consequence to a cross section of society. Monitoring the cacophony of vernacular exchange to determine who believes what and how strongly is essential for our social skin to detect society's climate of opinion (Noelle-Neumann 1993).

In important respects the symbolic displays of that eight-day period in Greece were rhetorical shows of strength consisting of partisan appeals to other partisans. At the same time, however, they opened the discursive spaces to which Taylor (1991) refers. The Greeks' responses to one another provided a backdrop of fervent hopes and deep divisions against which local discussions and deliberations on the election were conducted. Except when one preaches to the converted, rhetorical processes do not rest on a priori formulations of truth.[11] When they are modeled as conversational exchanges among various segments of society, the terms of the discourse more likely will produce ongoing interaction among competing interpretations of national ideals, traditions, and interests.

The Dialogical Process of Opinion Formation

There is a view of public opinion that locates its foundations in enduring values and commitments. This view distinguishes itself from alternatives that focus on fluctuations of popular opinion in which individuals seem to go with the tide, so to speak. We find its foundational position expressed in the classic works of V. O. Key (1961) and A. Lawrence Lowell (1913). But the assumption of enduring foundational commitments presupposes an environment that supports the viability of steadfastness in those beliefs as anchoring principles for political choice. A volatile milieu of unstable meanings and rapid change shatters that presupposition. When the empirical environment, such as existed during the Civil War or the Depression, challenges the efficacy of beliefs in ways that produce an epistemological crisis, it problematizes the orthodoxy contained in a stable and enduring body of opinion, in the society's understanding of the good life.

Gregory Bateson (1972) has argued that social action poses the dilemma of a world that can change radically over time while the epistemology that dominates collective choice seems to remain relatively unchanged. However, as political scientist Lawrence Dodd (1994) notes, the reality gap between ontology and epistemology becomes intolerable when the crises grow so great that a sense of group or individual powerlessness can be reduced only through epistemological change. Dodd maintains that these changes require political learning. Such learning, I would add, occurs through the processes of rhetorical dialogue by which the limits of prevailing paradigms are challenged and new alternatives are socially negotiated.

The vernacular rhetoric model seeks to account for public opinion with sensitivity to the manner in which these negotiations are conducted. It reaffirms the place of actual discourses as the locale of socially salient meaning by asserting: *the assent peculiar to public opinion is fashioned through the dialogue of vernacular talk.* It shifts emphasis from the institutional speaker or writer exclusively to include the talk of those who are members of publics that form around issues. We find these publics in civil society's reticulate public sphere and gauge their opinion through taking into account the broad range of formal and vernacular discourse by which social actors establish a common understanding of reality and chart their preferences for addressing the problems it poses for them.

Here a return to Bakhtin's (1981) insightful analysis of the dialogizing process inherent in social discourse is helpful. His discussion of the relationship between discourse in historical time and discourse in the novel reminds us that dialogue is the process whereby the meanings of words, utterances, discourses, languages, and even cultures are relativized. Challenges to the privileged positions of prevailing power structures and ideologies *dialogize* them; they make us aware of competing positions and interpretations. The spatial and temporal interactions that dialogize rival stances radiate out from the internal interactions within the subject to the farthest reaches of the external world. These radiant engagements insure that the position of the culture, the individual, the language, and the word come into contact with another position and enter into dialogue with it. As Bakhtin describes this dialogue, it interanimates language and culture; it gives new possibilities for understanding and expressing reality; it produces a polysemous state of heteroglossia.

Bakhtin holds that the conditions governing meaning in any given utterance are unrepeatable in their situatedness and make its meanings to this set of listeners at this time unlike any before or since. Discourse is heteroglossic insofar as its social reverberations go beyond semantics to penetrate the deep strata of discourse, to dialogize language itself and the worldview within a particular language. Heteroglossia constitutes the internal form of discourse. The dialogue of voices within the interior of discourse arise directly out of a social dialogue of "languages," in which an alien utterance begins to sound like a socially alien language, and in which the orientation of the word among alien utterances changes into an orientation of a word among socially alien languages within the boundaries of one and the same national language (Bakhtin, 1981, 284–85). The dialogizing of another's discourse creates contact between the material forces of alien languages within the culture; it creates the possibility for alternative suppositions and renditions of reality to affect understanding and change. The most ready example of this is our use of "she said," "they said," and "I said" in everyday speech. Our insertion of the words, opinions, and social consciousness of others in our speech is illustrative of the dialogue, even within our own discourse, between our speaker position and the positions of others. It reflects the dynamic character of alternative stances and readings of circumstances and issues, persons and events that color our understanding of experience, and even our experience itself.

The dialogical character of speech and the inevitability of heteroglossia in dialogue bear special relevance to vernacular rhetoric. Although not all theories of public opinion have promoted an examination of discourse, all are based in principle on the assumption of discursive exchanges between officials, vested interests, and those affected by an issue. As noted at the outset, the rational deliberation model presuppose that these discourses frame the final opinion and subsequent action. Importantly, the framing discourse depicted by the rational deliberation model usually follows the traditional rhetorical configurations of formal address, in which one speaks to many. Bakhtin alerts us to what this model omits: the dialogic exchanges of many to many at the informal level of society. An account of public opinion formation and ownership that begins with societal conversation introduces an important shift in focus by including the dialogues among common people, rather than those exclusively among official and empowered elites, and to vernacular expression as their medium of exchange. Vernacular "talk" is essential for a societal conversation to ensue, since conversation presupposes shared meanings among dialogic partners able to test each other's claims and find evidence from their own experiences and knowledge to evaluate the relevance of these claims to their lives.

Vernacular discourse occurs in many forms, not just in speech and writing among known interlocutors. For example, cultural forms such as films, dramas, novels, and art are significantly dialogical, as the celebrated Mapplethorp exhibit illustrated. The public controversy it provoked included the "talk" of those who joined a discussion in civil society and responded to the statements of others without using words. The nonverbal medium of the exhibit offered statements about sexuality and public persons that challenged their commonplace meanings. The fairly brisk public attendance by the denizens of Cincinnati made statements about a broad-based interest in tending to what Mapplethorp had to "say." Reactions by those who visited the exhibit also produced a dialogue in the community. This dialogue was then moved to a different public sphere when the exhibition itself was contested in a court of law. In that realm technical and vernacular modes of expression often collided, but ultimately vernacular discourse also was acknowledged as the discourse relevant to determining whether community values were violated.

Similarly consumer movements, modes of protest, public symbols, overt group expressions of sentiment, and a shelf of collective activity that permit us to navigate problematic public contexts and issues act as conversations through the shared meanings and common understandings contained in and evoked by symbolic action. Bakhtin's insight presages and complements the Burkean understanding of rhetoric as symbolic inducement in which all human symbolic forms become forms of inducement, or rhetoric.

The dialogic experience of vernacular exchange eventuates in the perception, if not the discriminable fact, of public opinion. Vernacular give-and-take is our prima facie rhetorical evidence (perhaps our only evidence) that a public exists and what its defining characteristics are. These civic conversations create the chronotopic quality of an interdependent time-space that requires participants in and analysts of rhetorical dialogues alike to read differences akin to the dialogized, heteroglossic tapestry Bakhtin finds in the novel. Movement through the discursive spaces opened by these dialogues requires skill at reading conversations that have recourse to different modes of vernacular expression if not different but nonetheless understandable tongues.

Like Bakhtin's understanding of the novel, each public sphere accommodates "a *system* of languages that mutually and ideologically interanimate each other" (Bakhtin 1981, 47). Thus, when American tourists arrived in an Athenian hotel lobby laded with PASOK's political emblems, the socialist staff immediately seized the multiple messages of their political paraphernalia, nationality, unlikely "support," and, perhaps, naïveté as a comment inserted into their restrained political dialogue with the conservative hotel manager. Here was an opportunity to violate the prohibition against political remarks before the patrons. The hotel staff could and did publicly speak the unspeakable to their boss before patrons whose display of political booty unwittingly made a statement that legitimated their response.

The innate skepticism and irony of the rhetorician's stance provide a conceptual platform from which to "see" and "hear" this conversation occurring, a conversation that cannot be detected from the positivistic platform of the pollers or the rationalistic platform of the critical theorists. It is attuned to the degree to which these multileveled, multitongued vernacular conversations intersect. To the extent that they do, there is concrete discursive evidence of a shared sentiment toward and understanding of reality, that individual expressions of particular agents have acquired the added meaning of collective expression, and that a public opinion has formed.

Tending to the rhetoric of civic conversation over an indeterminate matter is indispensable for an understanding of public opinion. These dialogues are conducted in a montage of settings and with a variety of partners who, in some way, are linked in civil society. Each extends or challenges a prevailing epistemological paradigm for explaining our shared environment. Collectively they create a multilogue from which we learn about the threats that confront us, the level of concern that our fellow citizens share, their epistemological paradigms for confronting an uncertain and perilous world, and their commitment to collective survival in the face of severe and sometimes life-threatening crises.

Participation in this multilogue informs us about the fit between our understanding of the world and the understandings of others with whom we inhabit that world. As we find our expectations defied by worldly responses to our choices for conduct, rhetorical dialogues become our source for learning about alternative models of society projected by the exemplars, tropes, narratives, and political styles (Hariman 1995) that gain currency and even dominance in vernacular and formal rhetoric alike.

These rhetorical modes of reasoning invite us to reimagine and restructure our relationships, to learn new understandings of the world that will foster survival, and to arrive at an opinion seeming to comport with the gestaltlike experience of rhetorical assessment that transpires in a multilogue on an indeterminate but, in important ways, recalcitrant world. Such an opinion becomes a *public* opinion when the dominant exemplars, tropes, narratives, and political styles of a public sphere exhibit a rhetorical pattern of understanding that structures and expresses collective judgment.

As in the case of the Greek election campaign, institutional or other leaders are often the most clearly audible in voicing images that urge the rightness and wisdom of their cause, such as Pampandreou's address to the nation at his political rally. But people also have means of publicly expressing their concerns and interests as well as responding to those of others in ways that indicate emerging patterns of sentiment, both in content and intensity. Certainly, the televised images during Pampandreou's speech are readable as expressions of public opinion. Whether a reflection of coverage conventions or editorial choices, the broadcast that night focused on the crowd, not the rhetor. For an attending nation viewing the address, the spectacle of the broadest streets in Athens jammed with an organized mass (estimated at one million) chanting and cheering its common affirmation and assent transmitted a statement seemingly as strong as the prime minister's in its impact on those viewing the broadcast with me. Although less formally argumentative, it was no less hortatory in its solicitation of agreement from others within Greece's political public sphere. And unlike poll results, it was an expression of public opinion linked to a specific set of political claims.

A public is active in ways that exceed an affirming or rejecting witness. It not only acts as a witnessing audience but also finds means to express its own views on the consideration at hand. Each manifestation of sentiment may be read as a text: consumer behavior of purchase and boycott, public letters, letters to public officials, speeches, symbolic acts, demonstrations, votes, strikes, essays, uses of public places, attendance at public meetings, graffiti, and an assortment of other forms of approval or disapproval.

Obviously this list includes means of expression that lend themselves to quantification, and numeric count can be a method for determining public opinion. Their significance as texts, however, is as symbolic forms whose meanings are uncovered by interpreting the narratives in which they are embedded. That a million Athenians had gone to the streets flowing into Sindagma Square on that June evening in 1985 made a statement of quantified support. But there was significance to their numbers that exceeded sheer volume. This mass also was providing evidence of strong feelings by its organized chants and spontaneous cheers. In addition it was providing evidence that support for Pampandreou and PASOK spanned the generations and cut across economic strata of Greek society.

Perhaps the passions being vented on Athens's streets, not to mention at its organized rallies, and the generalized public expressions of political affiliation I had encountered elsewhere in Greece exceeded that common to elections in the United States because the struggle in 1985 (as it has been so often since World War II) was between conservative and socialist political and economic agendas. Such extremes increased the stakes of political contests in ways that were apparent for every segment of society. They gave both sides impressive grounds for appeals to Greece's heritage of freedom, opposition to tyranny, and chronic struggle to provide relief from economic hardship for large segments of its citizens. The logo of PASOK superimposed on a rising sun and New Democracy's resurrection of antiquity in its party name recall former glories and appeal to their special legitimacy as trustees of continuity with the past. The presence of children at a mass rally in which they would witness the public venting of strong emotions suggests a cultural understanding of political education that links generations through the dialogue of common participation—itself dialogizing the present with ideals of citizenship from the Periclean era of the Athenian past—from preschool age on. The convention of allowing the three major parties to take their cases to the people via mass rallies in Sindagma Square reflects an understanding of participatory politics in which a show of force is a show of conviction to advance partisan claims.

In these and other ways vernacular expressions of public opinion forbear the neutrality of objectivist models of social will formation, as well as the universality that hegemonic models impose on the history, traditions, literature, and religion of a definable national group. The vernacular rhetoric model of public opinion is attached to these narratives of belonging that preserve our cultural, political, and social identities, which thereby opens it to the very features that are sui generis to the indigenous social and cultural terrain. This model rehabilitates public opinion by relocating it in the ongoing dialogue of ideas, values, and preferences that is native to social actors engaged by issues that bear on their lives.

Conclusion

Public opinion research that is faithful to the discursive processes by which social actors exchange and form their views assuredly is difficult to conduct because one must make inferences about a body of values, beliefs, and responses from evidence that is not always direct or readily available. I have maintained that publics are more complex than is suggested by public opinion polling research. Polling data provide important information about how people are responding to an event as it unfolds. However they are insufficient to disclose the shape and character of the public that actually does emerge because they are tone-deaf to the heteroglossic dialogue of vernacular narratives and arguments that give meaning to issues and express their relationship to people's lives. As an alternative, liberal democratic theory suggests that we may gauge public opinion by examining the public deliberations of active participants. However, leading voices speaking and writing from institutional seats of power are not necessarily the same as publics that weigh their advocacy; nor are their opinions necessarily identical with those judging what they say; nor are their narratives and arguments necessarily able to escape their own monologia and enter a dialogical exchange which sets ideology and lived experience in constant tension.

I have argued for a third position that focuses on discourse as it actually transpires. It regards vernacular discourse as the talk among a public's members and, therefore, as a significant source of evidence deserving intense scrutiny. The vernacular rhetoric model shifts analysis from preconceived notions of "the public" as a political ideal and from objectivist conceptions that lose the story of what active segments of society are attempting to say, to the communicative and epistemic functions manifest in the range of discursive exchanges among those who are engaged by a public problem.

I also have rejected the assumption that public opinion is the rationalistic expression of warranted assent that a reified and ideal public produces through informed and competent formal deliberation, or conversely that it is coeval with mood and attitude or even conclusions that can be learned and understood independent of discourse. My analysis insists that public opinion represents a reasoning process peculiar to practical discourse and whose character is definitively rhetorical. There can be no such thing as a public opinion independent of the discourse that tests ideas and leads to judgments. This body of discourse exceeds that of institutional speakers by locating evidence that a public has emerged, how it understands the issues, and the opinions, however ephemeral, it is forming through vernacular exchanges among social actors.

I have rejected, as well, equating public opinion with reasoned consensus or with a majority nose count. Instead I have argued that vernacular dialogues, from which we extrapolate and interpret public opinions, discursively constitute their participants' common understandings of reality. Social actors are able to construct shared social realities, even though they may not value them in like ways, because they share a language of common meaning and a common reference world. I have argued that the rehabilitation of public opinion requires according weight to opinions in proportion to the attentiveness, selectivity, and diversity of those who have engaged in a public sphere's dialogical processes. Publics may be repressed, distorted, or responsible, *but any evaluation of their actual state requires that scholars and leaders engage in analyses of the rhetorical ecology as well as the rhetorical acts, including their own, by which they evolve.* These, after all, are the conditions that constituted their individual differences. Such analysis of publics and their opinions begins with an understanding of publics as discursive formations and public opinion as a discursive expression of civil judgment on which all publics ultimately depend.

Finally, I have maintained that public opinion is an interpretation made from data, the most relevant of which is vernacular discourse. Public opinions are imbedded in the ongoing dialogue in which classes, races, religions, genders, generations, regions, and a host of other significant discriminators rub against each other, problematize one another's assumptions about meaning, create discursive spaces in which new interpretations may emerge, and lead, even if tentatively, to intersections that provide collective expressions of shared sentiments. Without attending to these dialogues we lose the narratives in which opinions are contextualized and which allow us to interpret the meaning of volunteered judgments.

Near the end of "Discourse in the Novel" Bakhtin says, "Every discourse has its own selfish and biased proprietor; there are no words with meanings shared by all, no words 'belonging to no one'" (1981, 401). The study of public opinion often proceeds on a different premise, leveling differences and emasculating the complexity and richness of our public life by treating an extrapolated interpretation as if it were descriptive of social judgments and social desires. As a result it parodies the process of individuation and the achievement of social agreement that is accomplished through discourse. In free societies we seek to learn of public opinion because in it we find how social actors are engaging in and engaged by the ongoing processes of social production. This engagement is a dynamic enterprise enacted through the uninterrupted mutual interaction of dialogue. That these dialogues are not always noble—nor do they often suspend biases for the greater good—or immune to ideological distortions is immaterial to their significance for how we monitor and attempt to influence the shape of our world. Bakhtin's words assert the place of actual discourses as the locale of meanings that social actors ascribe to their world; the words highlight the significance and promise of the vernacular rhetoric model for rehabilitating public opinion as a concept sensitive to and informative of what publics actually think.

Chapter 5

NARRATIVE, CULTURAL MEMORY, AND THE APPROPRIATION OF HISTORICITY

The struggle of man against power is the struggle of memory against forgetting.
Milan Kundera, *The Book of Laughter and Forgetting*

In his monumental study of narrative Paul Ricoeur struggles with the problem of "the vanishing reality of the past as it really was" (1990, 207) in its relationship to the present and the future. He acknowledges that we no longer think of the world, as Hegel did, by adhering to perspectives that conceptualize the past with a logic of initial terms and assumptions. Ricoeur proposes an alternative strategy whose model of understanding is based on the ideas of narration and emplotment (206). His strategy for appropriating historicity interweaves "perspectives of the expectation of the future, the reception of the past, and the experience of the present" with no impetus toward an account of totality. Drawing on the work of German historian Reinhart Koselleck, Ricoeur develops this alternative strategy in terms of a polarity between the categories *space of experience* and *horizon of expectation*.

Ricoeur argues that our space of experience emerges from our relationship to our past. The term *space* is important because it suggests both that our past always contains something foreign to us to be overcome and that how we overcome it—how we traverse its *space*—depends on the itineraries we choose for our journey. The experiences transmitted to us by past generations and by our institutions, as well as by our private experiences, are open to alternative readings joined to the future as a horizon of expectation. Here the term *expectation* is important because it includes the public and private manifestations of hopes and fears we are able to project as a consequence of the world we inhabit and the one we imagine will follow from our choices. Like the space of experience, the horizon of expectation is inscribed in the present insofar as the present is seen relative to it. That it is a *horizon*, not a *space*, indicates "the power of unfolding as much as surpassing that is attached to expectation" (Ricoeur 1990, 208). The human construction called "history" now faces this challenge:

> The task that, for our predecessors, prescribed the journey by
> pointing the way has turned into a utopia or, better, a uchro-

nia, where our horizon of expectation withdraws from us faster than we can advance toward it. And when our expectation can no longer fix itself on a determined future, outlined in terms of distinct, discernible steps, our present finds itself torn between two fleeing horizons, that of the surpassed past and that of an ultimate end that gives rise to no penultimate term. So torn within itself, our present sees itself in "crisis," and this is . . . perhaps one of the major meanings of our present. (Ricoeur 1990, 213)

Ricoeur identifies a crisis that accentuates the fragility of rhetoric in a context so overrun by alienation and difference that one has difficulty locating compelling terms that might anchor society in the silt of cultural memory. At the level of praxis, society's rhetors are custodians of history's story. By giving memorable form to distinctive episodes and persons, they evoke bonds of communal understanding and sympathy that can frame common commitments and motivate common actions. The question we face is whether the distance between the contracting relevance of the past and the fading horizon of an uncertain future precludes the possibility that we can still establish bonds of community.

Ricoeur's antidote to the fractured sense of a determined future is the interpretive power of historical narrative. His merger of past and future to the present through the story of history underscores the power of narrative form to forge and to tap cultural memory. Narrative offers a means for meeting the challenge of a past and future moving in opposite directions. His antidote also implies the centrality of rhetoric for shaping our public spheres, the publics that emerge there, and the opinions they come to express, which is to say that historical narrativity indicates the centrality of rhetoric to democracy.

The experience of democracy is not about revolutionary breaks from the past or mindless embrace of whatever now claims the banner of progress. It is rather about the ongoing *struggle* between permanence and change, tradition and transformation (Elshtain 1995, 138). This struggle involves democracies in the unending process of what Michael Leff (1995) has called "hermeneutical rhetoric," a rhetoric that constantly interprets the present and tempers future choices through its reading of communal memories.

Apropos of the hermeneutical character of struggles between permanence and change are the narratives of national identity that fueled recent Central and Eastern European revolutions conducted in the name of civil society. If 1989 was a moment of natality for nations that had experienced forty-five years of state control by alien masters, it also brought the strains of inventing publicness to peoples who lacked experience in self-regulation.

Earlier we discussed civil society as poised between the family and the state. Historically, its web of associations has been organized outside the political power of the state, though it simultaneously has sought to influence the state's policies. In its strong sense, it is the realm in which ideas and institutions incorporate their own self-interpretation as the basis for understanding national identity apart from the state. Our publicness is formed in this domain of self-structuring associations, which means that it is continually under negotiation. Consequently, the structure of civil society bears on who may appear in public, what may be said and done, and which relationships may form.

The members of civil society construct power equations among themselves and the larger systems in which they reside (Aronowitz 1988, xiii). Their self-structuring activity inevitably encounters competing interpretations that must be negotiated, so that inventing publicness invariably poses the problem of integrating conflicts. We see this most readily in the Central European struggle to establish civil society. With their traditions suspended, their national struggle under communism was to create models for integrating into a political system in which they lacked power. This effort has persisted in the post-1989 world and invariably involves an understanding of their own historicity. Appropriating historicity entails acts of selection and emphasis on which self-understanding is based and which provide the resources to invent publicness. It is a rhetorical accomplishment.

This chapter will expand on the earlier theme of civil society as the locus for publics and public spheres. It will focus on the alliance between narrative form and cultural memory, a relationship that has been observed previously (Gadamer 1975; MacIntyre 1984; Ricoeur 1981), though not quite in the context in which I wish to examine it. My discussion will concentrate on the relationship between narrative and historicity in the discursive domains in which publics are formed and express their opinions on matters that affect their interests, or the political public sphere.

After formulating an initial statement of theoretical relationships, I will turn to concrete cases of Polish and Yugoslavian discourses that reveal the place of cultural memory and narration in their most recent political upheavals. My concern is with the bridge between cultural memory and historicity suggested by their use of narrative. I will argue that this bridge at once provides the rhetoricality of a public and constitutes its place in civil society.

Rhetoric and the Active Society

The claim that discourse forms social will (Arendt 1958; Foucault 1972; Giddens 1984; Habermas 1975; Lyotard 1984; Marcuse 1964; Touraine 1981) is a modern rendition of an ancient point. The Athenians and Romans recognized political, legal, and communal realities as rhetorical achievements. This ancient insight tacitly recognizes discursive phenomena as more than *reflections* of knowledge and power. As manifestations of society's ongoing activity of asserting its identity, its discourses serve a *constitutive* function.

Social actors continually express a core of values and meanings providing an orientation to and in the world. To be of the society is to understand and respond to these expressions with interpretive sympathy, though not always with interpretive affirmation. They tell us who we are and provide models for belief and action. They are necessarily partisan because they distinguish among groups and classes in relationships that express their power differentials, alienation, and counterassertions aimed at reallocating society's resources. In this sense, as Alain Touraine (1977, 1981, 1988) teaches, societies are active, and their activity is to produce themselves.

Society's self-production is historically situated and intrinsically tied to its rhetoric. Although economic, historical, and institutional factors play important roles in the shape and direction that typify a given society, these elements are insufficient to determine a priori that society's specific contours. Rather, social actors grapple with them as among those impulses that bear on transforming society and its institutions. The catalytic agency for such transformations is society's discourse, and the resource most essential for discursively penetrating social consciousness of what is, what ought to be, and what might be is its symbols. We locate the possibilities for social action in and through our rhetoric. It is the agency by which we make and remake our political and social relations through revisable agreements, which is to say that rhetoric is among the social practices by which society constitutes itself.[1]

Rhetoric is born of conflict and uncertainty. As an agonistic practice it facilitates transforming and questioning social relations. Rhetorical praxis can shift social understandings, reorder society's sense of priority and imperative, and redirect social energies into new channels of relationship and action. In these ways discursive initiatives are reflexive, being constitutive of and constituted by society's self-understanding. This recursive characteristic of social action—this *continuity*—provides social stability. To deny members of a society their own discourse is to deny them memory.

As recollections of the past, our memories are unlike history in that their basis is retained perceptions rather than preserved and verified facts. Often their emotionally charged, selective, and arbitrary character defies a more distanced and critical stance seeking documented explanation. Our memories provide us with a living conversation with the past, infusing events and persons who preceded us with relevance to our circumstances, experiences, and choices.

Publicly shared memories function as the community's cultural repository (Ballenger 1997, 792). Stories, memorials, rituals, and the like remind us of who we are and have been. Their contents are different from reflections about the causes and consequences of events considered in terms of irreversible linear temporality and situated particularity (Katriel 1994, 1). They incorporate and refashion historical knowledge, mythologizing the past as part of a people's consciousness of identity (Katriel 1994). This consciousness is dynamic, itself a source of potent rhetorical invention and a site of contention. For example, Merrill Peterson's study *Lincoln in American Memory* (1994) points out that Lincoln as Emancipator was not the same Lincoln as Man of the People, nor Lincoln as First American, nor Lincoln as Self-made Man. Each of these images is part of the Lincoln myth; each is emphasized by different American communities as part of their own political identity. "The apotheosis of Lincoln had to do with myth as well as history," Peterson maintains. But each of these different Lincolns embodying a different ideal is an alternative resource for making public arguments; each poses an opportunity to advance different political agendas, making ownership of his mythos significant for controlling its rhetorical resources. As Peterson concludes, "Remembered history is always penetrated with myth" (26).

"Public memory," John Bodnar notes, "speaks primarily about the structure of power in society" (1992, 15). Bodnar finds that the explanation for its power is the contestive relations spawned by contradictory and polarized social forces, each seeking to ground cultural consciousness in society's material structures. Jerome Bruner suggests how this power is exercised when he advances the thesis that life and narrative are in a reciprocal bond such that "narrative imitates life, life imitates narrative" (1987, 13). The story of who we are and the events and people who shape our identity, as Stephen Browne (1995, 244) notes, are texts that are always produced by the classes within society. They are never given and are always rhetorical achievements. Further, these stories are not just about ourselves. They include the other, often as "Other," exercising power over the words, deeds, and events of which they are a part. So the question of public memory carries the questions of power into public life in at least two ways. Most obviously it raises concerns over how people find resources from their past to shape an account of their present and future. More vexingly it raises the problem of discovering the means to resist the subversive power of someone else's story to distort our own memories and appropriate our own experiences.

Although public memories may serve as a source of conflict and domination, we should not forget that, as rhetorical achievements, their life is in performance. If they can be a resource for subjugation, their indeterminacy as rhetorical inventions means they may equally open spaces for mediating difference. Every rhetorical transaction, as Aristotle taught, is a praxis created for the given case. Each rhetorical situation is marked by elements of novelty and possibility for refiguring the meaning of experience and human relations. Although society accumulates its discursive creations in rhetorical genres (Campbell and Jamieson 1978), rhetoric is not restricted to the ideological "givens," in Maurice Charland's words, "of what appears to be the delimitable rhetorical situation, where the ontological status of speaker, speech, audience, topic, and occasion offer themselves as unproblematic" (Charland 1987, 148). The critical examination of discourse permits one to decipher rhetoric's vital role of symbolically constituting experience and relations. Moreover, by examining discourse we can uncover how society invests its rhetorical creations in cultural legitimations of self-generating activities by which it produces itself: the attempts of social actors to control values and norms, to overcome subjugation from dominant groups or institutions, and to appropriate and reappropriate their own *historicity*.

The meaning of *historicity* is complex and slightly unstable, depending upon the literature in which it is used (Touraine 1977, 1988; Giddens 1984; Gadamer 1975; Ricoeur 1981). From a sociological perspective, it refers to a society's capacity to produce a model of itself based on its own actions. These include the actions of its cultural and social practices as they combine three components: knowledge, accumulation, and culture. Knowledge models society's image of itself and nature; accumulation models society's disposition of its excess resources; and culture models society's apprehension and interpretation of its capacity to act upon itself. Philosophical invocations of "historicity" are more concerned with the basis for identity of social actors than with the society itself. Here "historicity" refers to the actors' knowledge of the trajectory of history from the past into the present which, in turn, provides the condition for reflexive self-regulation manifested in history. Simply put, it is the actors' awareness of history and society as human constructions. "Historicity" encompasses the social actors' particular views of what history is. These views gain intersubjective traction through significant symbols and are, in that sense, rhetorically constituted. Principal among these rhetorical constructions is the attempt by social actors to control history. This latter sense bears close resemblance to the concern of historicity with culture, although it bears also on considerations of knowledge and accumulation. These two understandings are not unrelated, so that while my use of the term will refer primarily to its later sense, it will not be unmindful of the former.

Usually claims to historicity are contestive. In the United States, for instance, there has been a century-long struggle over the nation's root metaphor. One view has it as a *melting pot* in which various cultures contribute to an amalgam that is uniquely and uniformly American. To be American is to accept the ascendance of these new ways. In opposition there is an understanding of the nation as a *multicultural rainbow* in which its doctrines of individual freedom protect nonindigenous cultural elements from being absorbed by a uniform general culture. To be American is to celebrate diversity. Both views project an understanding of the past that legitimates alternative aspirations of class and identity to define the course of society.

The ongoing struggle of nations, classes, and groups to create their own normative universe is the sine qua non of society's dynamic character. Societies are neither stagnant nor fixed,[2] but bustling with conflict over civil rights, consumer interests, sexual mores, religious tolerance, human rights, labor conditions, peace, armaments, foreign policy, class differences, ethnicity, ecology, property, privacy, and a drumroll of similar sources of controversy that are common to postindustrial, postmodern society. Society's self-producing character questions the piety whereby rhetoric is portrayed as the pulse of community. Surely it is that. But rhetoric also enables the enunciation of alternative relations that challenge and even disrupt community. Rhetoric manifests a human capacity to deal with antagonistic relationships, precisely those relationships that typify the conditions from which publics emerge and in which societies produce themselves. Conflictive relationships equally are the wellspring from which rhetorical practices flow. A conceptual framework that understands the principal business of society to be its own self-production thus construes the social practice of rhetoric to be more than an expression of knowledge and power; it constitutes them.

Just as our conceptualizations of publics are altered by starting with rhetoric as their antecedent condition and projecting rhetoric as their creative agency, some radical consequences follow for our understanding of rhetoric's fundamental character when we situate it within a conception of society as active and self-producing. One of these is the necessity to maintain a metatheoretical union between rhetoric and society's self-production. Uncoupling this union confuses rhetoric's meaning and significance as a social practice. It reduces rhetoric to an instrumentality for some massive, lawlike set of forces determining social development, and it projects practices as the result of some anterior set of circumstances that exist beyond its bounds and shape its character. This reduction presumes that social facts exist objectively and entails an objectivist (Bernstein 1983) explanation in which actors are ignorant of the social significance of their actions.

Such confusions are avoided by coupling rhetoric with an active view of society. First, an active account rejects portraying social actors as unreflective. It construes them as *agents* capable of understanding their acts (Giddens 1984, chap. 2). Their struggles form the will and meaning of society. Societies are active precisely because at their core lies the ebb and flow of social movement produced by competing discourses laying claim to historicity. Competing rhetorics are manifestations not of historical, social, or economic determinism but of the ongoing conflict among social actors through which society produces itself. This is society's principal activity (Touraine 1981, chap. 1).

Second, an active account of society problematizes *situation* as the defining condition of rhetoric (Bitzer 1968). Situation is but one element, albeit an important one, in the larger concern with rhetoric's centrality to social action. Situations do not define rhetoric in the positivistic sense of objective contextual/environmental features calling for the actors' responses, nor is social will the product of individuals marching to the beat of necessity. Rhetorical practices and social will are the outcomes of historical agencies, which is to say groups and classes, who share a social field and are attempting to define that field's nature and meaning. The dominant power's rhetorical practices, which are typically geared toward articulating principles of unity that mask disparate visions of the desirable (or vice versa, as we shall see presently), always complicate deciphering attempts to define historicity. However, behind official visions of reality lies the fact of *relationship* as the defining condition of those who share a social field. Individual discourses may be addressed to the exigencies of the given case, but in the larger frame of social action situational responses are conditioned by the patterns among social actors who are significantly tied in bonds of historicity and class. These patterns of dependency, privilege, disequilibriums of wealth or power, or other such asymmetrical conditions define relationships that are necessarily unstable when understood as those of conflicting movements. Conflicts among historically situated actors define society by the transitory conditions that mark relationship at the moment of inspection. In significant ways these relationships are constituted by, experienced in, and sustained through society's rhetoric. In this respect, the concept of *publics* developed in chapter 1 becomes analytically useful. As emergences always in flux, they arise in the course of need satisfaction. Their interstitial character focuses our critical attention on the extensive, always emerging, and productive power of rhetoric as historicity's appearance in a social field.

Third, and significantly, these relationships define a *nomos*—a normative universe. Such a universe contains an ordering of right and wrong, paradigms for action, a world to inhabit. A nomos is held together by the force of commitments—some small and private, others massive and public—which determine our laws, customs, politics, economics, and ultimately our traditions. These commitments are captured in our mythos and borne to consciousness through narratives. Ricoeur reminds us that "the historicity of human experience can be brought to language only as narrativity. . . . For historicity comes to language only insofar as we tell stories or tell history" (1981, 294).

Gadamer (1981), among others, has argued that historicity is constituted by a culture's stories, its narratives. Our cultural identity is pregiven by the language, customs, and institutions that we share. These are imbedded with affiliations, significant events, and dispositions to respond to the world in certain ways. They tell us who we are and why we believe as we do. Commentators as diverse as Robert Bellah et al.

(1985) and Richard Weaver (1964) suggest that when a society ceases to share these bonds of common affiliation, ceases to be what Bellah and his associates refer to as a community of memory (1985, 152–55), it becomes disoriented, it begins to lose its capacity for common action, and its members find the meaning of their individual lives impoverished. To lose the capacity to respond to the stories of one's own culture is to suffer a form of amnesia whose pathology eludes medical description, since it is not at all like the loss of a psychological faculty. Such amnesia is more profound, as Gadamer observes (1975, 15), because cultural memory is an essential element of the individual's and the culture's historical being. Cultural memory places one inside a tradition in which past and present are constantly fused. A sense of history provides continuity of customs and traditions, of laws and accomplishments which fill temporal distance (Gadamer 1975, 264). It also provides models with which to respond to the present and to shape the future.

The revolutionary changes that swept through Central and Eastern Europe in 1989, and that continue to evolve throughout the former communist empire, are rich in their translation of these theoretical considerations into praxis. They afford added insight into the discursive dimensions of social action, specifically on the role of narrative, as a bridge between cultural memory and historicity, in constituting publics and public spheres with discernible differences in their possibilities for action. These paradigmatic possibilities are illustrated by the contrast in the rhetorical reconstitution of political and social relations in Poland and the former Yugoslavia, a contrast between calls for civil and uncivil society.

Memories of Hope: Poland

In *The Book of Laughter and Forgetting* Milan Kundera provides dramatic expression of the relevance a people's national consciousness bears to the political and rhetorical struggles that define society. Reflecting on the role of cultural memory in postwar Czechoslovakia, his narrator remarks, "People are always shouting they want to create a better future. It's not true. The future is an apathetic void of no interest to anyone. The past is full of life, eager to irritate us, provoke and insult us, tempt us to destroy or repaint it. The only reason people want to be masters of the future is to change the past" (Kundera 1981, 22). Certainly the political realities in Czechoslovakia following World War II, especially following the Prague Spring of 1968, weigh heavily in Kundera's words. However, they also speak to the larger issue of power equations that are at play in controlling a society's memory of its past— an imaginative product of social construction, not a factual report of information. In light of the more universal transformations of 1989 that redefined political realities for the nations of Central and Eastern

Europe and for international relations at large, Kundera provides a fortuitous anchor for examining the rhetorical forces that link narrative to the shape and texture of their changing public spheres. With this shift of power comes a search for explanations. Why these changes? Why now?

The investment in national identity is not recent in this region. Poles, Czechs, Slovaks, Armenians, Croats, Serbs, and Slovens each have longstanding cultural practices that serve as constant reminders of an identity apart from that imposed by an alien power. Among these are culturally rooted discourses that remind participants of their identity and maintain their bonds of solidarity. This play of discourses is a *recursive* social action whose continuity provides stability to national identity while simultaneously promoting instability within the larger society. Their play explains why Kundera recoils in *The Book of Laughter and Forgetting* at the communist revision of Czech history by "airbrushing" selected faces and events from the historical record. Such deletions mutilate cultural memory on which intelligible links to the shared values and memorialized accomplishments of cultural identity rest.

Certainly the political odyssey of Central and Eastern Europe following the mostly bloodless revolutions of 1989 provides an object lesson in the material process of discursive reconstruction of society from its own extant symbolic resources. Historically Poles have adhered to a national rhetoric that relied heavily on cultural memory and placed little stock in political ideology. They define national identity in terms of their traditions (Korbonski 1983). For the past two centuries Poland has lacked the guidance of a continuous state that could develop continuity from generation to generation in common political ideals. Denied continuity of a Polish state, Poles' self-interpretations have emphasized the nation and the elements expressive of it: language, literature, culture, religion, and patriotism.

There is a certain logic to Polish loyalty to tradition. Much of its modern history has been spent alienated from its state, which has been in the hands of imposed authorities. When its traditions were threatened, as when Bismarck outlawed speaking the Polish language or when the communists attempted to proscribe religious practice, Poles typically responded with fiercely patriotic acts of refusal.

One did not become Polish by an accident of birth but by living as a Pole, which meant adopting at the earliest age the ethos of a resister as a sign of one's patriotism and Polishness. Here is Ola Szczerbinska (1882–1963) recalling her initiation at the age of seven:

> My grandmother was a woman of great intelligence and strength of character. . . . Patriotism was the main motor of her life . . . and in the conspiratorial work of the January Rising [1863] she had played a prominent part. . . . The Rising's failure caused the greatest trauma of her life. Henceforward, she

always wore the same black dress, and on her finger a ring decorated with a white cross in pearls on black enamel.

—It's a ring of mourning for those who died, she said. But
when I asked to put it on my finger, she shook her head.

—You can only wear it when you're a real patriot. . . .

—And what does that mean, Grandma, "being a patriot"?

—A patriot is someone who loves Poland above everything else
in the world, and will abandon everything, even life itself, for
her Freedom. . . .

—I want to fight for Poland, Grandma, I said, only half comprehending.

After a while, my grandmother's eyes flashed.

—Yes. . . . Do you promise to fight for Poland, my child?

—I promise, Grandma, I repeated, enthralled by the ominous
feeling.

Then she caressed me, and placing the ring on my finger, held
it there tightly.

—Now there, run along. . . . But don't forget, and don't tell a
soul. (qtd. in Davies 1984, 271)

Later in life Ola Szczerbinska, like her grandmother, became a gun-run-
ner and insurrectionist. She also wedded Jozef Pilsudski, Polish general
and leader in the 1920s, who recalled a similar rite of initiation (Davies
1984, 271).

With roots so deeply imbedded in the soil of resistance, celebrating
dates of past triumphs and leaders who led them became vernacular
expressions of a Polish lifeworld in which secular and sacred acts of opposition were combined as models of patriotism. These included the martyrdom of St. Stanislaw by Boleslaw II the Bold in 1079 (though St. Stanislaw
was murdered, the act so undermined the authority of a ruler who had set
himself at odds with the rest of the nation that he was forced to seek exile),
the fight for independence in 1794 led by Tadeusz Kosciuszko, and the
war against Russia in 1920 led by Marshal Jozef Pilsudski. These were
moments of triumph and cause for national celebration. At the same time,
these moments are integrated with other, more recent dates of significant
resistance that make Polish history appear a chronology of carnage:

- September 1939—Germany and the USSR invade and occupy
  Poland.

- Spring 1940—Massacre in Katyn forest by the USSR of over 1000
  Polish army officers, all POWs and all shot in the back.

- April 1943—Rising in the Warsaw Ghetto by Jews who, refusing
  to go to their deaths unavenged, hold a brigade of SS infantry-
  men at bay for three weeks. Seven thousand fighters are killed;

121

seven thousand more are incinerated in their hide-outs; the remaining fifty-six thousand are transported to Treblinka.

- August 1944—Warsaw Rising, the largest act of resistance during the war, lasting for sixty-three days of savage combat. A quarter million of the civilian population die and the city is left in ruins while the Soviet army stationed nearby watches without aiding in the battle against the Nazi occupation force.

- June 1956—Poznan Riots in which workers from the Zipso locomotive factory take to the streets in protest against the scarcity and cost of food and the constraints on freedom imposed by the Soviet-backed regime. Poles consider this an act of national resentment against Russia.

- March 1968—A national anti-Semitic campaign is launched by the regime to deflect attention from economic difficulties and as an opportunity to quash dissident intellectuals.

- December 1970—Massacre of workers in Gdansk, Gdynia, and Szczecin seeking redress of grievances, thereby killing whatever lingering hope remains that the Party-State can be an expression of the people.

- June 1976—Repression of strikers in Ursus and Radom protesting rising food prices, ironically leading to an alliance between the intellectuals (disaffected since 1966) and the workers (disaffected since 1970) in the Workers' Defense Committee (KOR). As the immediate predecessor to Solidarity, this alliance signals the sentiment to join the struggle for free trade unions and free cultural expression.

These dates and events form a chronotope of resistance preserved in the vernacular rhetoric of generational narratives such as Ola Szczerbinska's. Recounting these episodes by grandparent to grandchild served as rhetorical triggers for the psyche of resistance common among post-war Poles.

Adherence to Poland's national traditions and native tongue were the functional equivalent of speaking a national language of resistance, for which its imposed regimes could pose no ready alternative. Given the events in Poland during the last two centuries, there was ample opportunity to become proficient at speaking a language of resistance. At the same time, Poles' resistance proved ineffectual since, unarmed, they lacked the means to overthrow masters who were armed. As social and economic conditions in communist Poland degenerated to the point where they seemed intolerable (cf. Galtung 1980; "Pope John Paul II in Poland" 1979; "Report on the State of the Republic" 1980; and Turowicz 1973), Poles faced the problem of how to initiate renewal in ways that were both nonviolent and yet more effective than previous efforts.

The interesting feature of Polish dissidence from the mid 1970s on is the way in which it confronted this problem. Predictably stories of past patriots were sources of inspiration and invocations to resistance. In addition, however, the Poles fashioned a bloodless revolution in a remarkable way. First by founding the Workers Defense Committee (KOR) in 1976, then with nonviolent strikes during the summer of 1980 and the subsequent emergence of Solidarity, and finally during the intervening period of political and economic instability in which the party eventually conceded its constitutional position as the leading edge of Polish society, the efforts of Polish dissidents were directed toward the Polish people rather than the Polish state, their foreign masters, or Western nations at large. This strategy initiated a reversal to the then-existing conditions of publicness in the public and counterpublic spheres of Polish political life. The majority of Poles, who were receptive to a dialogue on state policies that took account of national values, had been mostly ignored or excluded from the official public sphere as administratively irrelevant. KOR reversed the political valences by placing this ignored public at the center of its national dialogue on reform, while marginalizing the state. Writing in the mid 1980s, Polish dissident Adam Michnik expressed the strategic difference: "I believe that what sets today's opposition apart from the proponents of those ideas of reform in the past is the belief that a program for evolution ought to be addressed to independent public opinion, and not totalitarian power. Such a program would offer advice to the people regarding how to behave, not to the government regarding how to reform itself" (1985, xxvi).

Michnik's own letters from prison provide ample evidence of this new turn (1985). They constantly refer to the moral certification provided by tradition; it supplies Poles a tether to human dignity and condemns those adrift to moral oblivion. His letter "Why You Are Not Signing" illustrates this point. The rhetorical trajectory of this letter, written in Bialoleka prison in 1982, is interesting in several respects (Hauser 1989b), but of significance here is its contrast of worlds. On one hand, Michnik projects the militia's world through the actions and psychology of the police. His narrative construction of their brutality, their lack of integrity, and their lack of meaning in their lives apart from coercing their political prisoners provides a hermeneutic of incorrigibility. He concludes:

> To these people with their lifeless but shifting eyes, with their
> minds that are dull but skilled in torture, with their defiled souls
> that yearn for social approval, you are only raw material to work
> with. They have their own particular psychology: they believe

> that anyone can be talked into anything (in other words, every-
> one can be either bought or intimidated). To them it is only a
> matter of price to pay or pain to inflict. Although they act
> according to routine, your every stumble, your every fall gives
> meaning to their lives. Your capitulation is no mere profession-
> al achievement for them—it is their *raison d'être*. (6–7)

This contrasts with the world projected by the legacy of Polish history—
its heroes and its national life. Throughout the letter Michnik writes to a
you whose memory recalls the community of moral commitments to
which she belongs. In the midst of brutality this *you* knows that he has
been here before, has endured the partition, the German occupation, the
betrayal at Yalta. But there has always been resistance to the atomizing
attempts on national identity. With resistance comes hope. "You know
that in its [Poland's] history a loyalty declaration signed in jail has always
been a disgrace, loyalty to oneself and to national tradition a virtue" (8).

Michnik's text is an example of the resistance he advocates. Its argument, developed in terms of an ambiguous *you*, makes no pretense to conceptual sophistication since none is needed. The terms are clear: the
police have guns, *you* don't. The state cannot be overthrown through
armed revolution. And *you* are in prison, with no choice but to sign or
remain a prisoner. Yet instead of bending, Michnik finds anchors for average Poles to think and act in ways that affirm their human dignity: "Let me
make myself clear: this is not a program of romantic intransigence but
rather a strategy for social resistance" (11). Importantly, his concrete affirmations do not specify what type of community his reconstituted Poland
will have but rather more generally the attitudes and actions required for
Poles to proceed with its development. Hence the letter is organized and
articulated in terms of the quotidian experiences that give meaning to life
and hope for a future. It affirms what *you* know to be true by citing examples and relations of what *everyone* knows to be true.

Michnik's confidence that the reader and he speak the same language
precedes his skill at positioning his reader within his moral, rational, and
emotional orbit. The reader can feel his argument and make choices to
inhabit its world of amity and hope. He may make these assumptions
because the animus for his narration lies in cultural memory.

More explicit than Michnik's in its reappropriation of historicity
was the rhetorical performance of John Paul II at the time of his first
papal visit to Poland. During his 1979 visit he delivered over thirty
addresses to more than ten million Poles.[3] He delivered them at historical sites of political and religious significance. His messages organized
these sites as part of a journey from Poland's past to its future. What I
find noteworthy is John Paul II's use of Poland's Christian history to
provide an alternative *secular* awareness that fostered resistance.

By 1979 Poland's alienated condition of knowing compliance had made the hypocrisy of daily life suffocating. However, the means of escape posed a dilemma. Poles could fight for breath with the physical self-destruction of rage or fall dormant under the spiritual self-destruction of torpor. Either choice amounted to suicide. Whether the agency be blood-letting or anesthesia, these were the alternatives of a nation in extremis. At the time of John Paul's visit Poland lacked a constructive consciousness for claiming what it needed to survive and faced the real prospect that its only survivors would be the spiritually deceased whose social will had fallen casualty to national resignation. John Paul's pilgrimage to historical places was also a tutorial in inventive possibilities. Contextualized in the archive of Polish national identity, the pope's rhetorical journey articulated that community's historicity.

The Polish church's historical response to oppressive circumstances had been insistence on the right of its faithful to practice their religion, which included religious instruction in Polish and preservation of national history through significant religious events that often were acts of resisting externally imposed secular powers. The church transmitted the faith in a fashion that underwrote religious symbols with secular meaning. Poland's legendary resiliency in the face of external domination rested on a robust national identity preserved among Poles in religious sites and feast days that celebrated their identity as an ancient people—facing West toward Europe, cultured, of independent spirit, messianic, Catholic. These essentials of Poland's national identity may have been absent from the discourses of the officially sanctioned public sphere, but they continued to be inscribed in public memory through a variety of dramatic symbols—mostly vernacular but also formal expressions—that used religious signs and affiliation to make political statements.

Some of these symbols took the vernacular form of community acts and ceremonies. For example, among the more vivid portraits of the Gdansk strike in 1980 were pictures of the gate to the shipyard named for Lenin ironically festooned with religious articles—crosses, icons of the Black Madonna, and pictures of John Paul II—and used as the site for celebrating the Roman Catholic mass attended by thousands. In another example, in 1981 Poles observed the 190th anniversary of their Constitution of 1791. This first official commemoration of the constitution since World War II was held on May 3, a date that coincided with a religious holiday. The ceremony held at Holy Cross Church in Warsaw was typical. It included a concert of spiritual music. The church contained memorials for Polish writers Wladyslaw Reymont and Juliusz Slowacki. Religion was blended with literature and politics in a single celebration of national identity (Bingen 1984, 225).

Other symbols took the form of vernacular signs and monuments commemorating the unity of church and nation in acts of resistance.

For instance, during World War II a common symbol of resistance that appeared as graffiti on the walls of buildings in Warsaw combined a *P* for Poland with a *W* for Warsaw into a single sign ⚓. To casual observers this symbol appeared as *P* over *W*. However, the *W* also formed the hooks of an anchor, a traditional symbol for the church. Further, within Catholicism the anchor is the symbol for the cardinal virtue of hope. One symbol united the resisters of Warsaw with the nation and the nation with the church in a manner that refused to accept defeat. Significantly Polish graphic artists chose this symbol to remind Poles of the Warsaw Rising of 1944. For Poles "⚓ 1944" speaks of a people and its national institutions in battle for survival, memorializes their resistance to the death in every street and sewer, inflames their hatred of Russia for watching while the Nazis killed a quarter million Varsovians and reduced their city to rubble no taller than three meters at any point, and reminds them that even after their capital was leveled, the nation and its identity survive.

Equally poignant is the monument outside the Gdansk shipyard, joining church and people in a single statement commemorating Polish identity as Catholic and resisters. In 1970 workers in Gdansk who were protesting a rise in food prices were slain by the Polish army. Alarm over this experience was intensified because it was not the militia but the army, associated by Poles with nation rather than state, that executed the state's orders. Poles believed this marked the first time the state had fired on its own people. For a decade workers at the shipyard had agitated without consequence to have a monument built. At a commemorative ceremony the year before the August 1980 strikes, Lech Walesa addressed those gathered at the site. He instructed them that when they met again next year, each was to bring a rock. If the authorities would not build a monument, the people would build it themselves. As part of the Gdansk settlement, the state agreed that one would be built.

The monument consists of three gleaming steel crosses rising 140 feet. The crosses are arranged to form a triangle, with their cross pieces abutting one another. The crosses themselves form an obvious symbol of agony and death inflicted by a hostile hand. But for Catholics the cross is also a symbol for the cardinal virtue of faith, hence doubling its meaning for the memorialized as being slain and for beliefs that still live. The arrangement of the three crosses to form a triangle suggests the solidarity of the slain through the union of their crosspieces. The triangle has religious significance as well since it is a Catholic symbol for a triune God, suggesting not only their common faith but also the unity among individuals who opposed the state. On the crosspiece of each crucifix hangs an anchor. The anchor triples to represent the slain workers—shipbuilders, the church—the faithful's anchor in life, and hope. In the base of the monument, amidst the nest of steel scraps leading up to the vertical bases of the crosses, are friezes with more vernacular images showing scenes of the 1970 Gdansk strike and of the workers building the monument. As a symbol the whole monument speaks of an act that "crucified" the workers and reminds that the church suffers with them, united as one. It joins the slain workers with those who continued to resist and triumphed and with those honoring the dead. This memorial also reflects the unity and continuity of Polish experience in terms of messianic hope.[4] They suffered and died; they rose again and triumphed; they will survive as a people for eternity.[5]

The strength of these symbols, especially through invoking significant religious meanings as part of their secular message, does not indicate that all Polish Catholics were devout. The point is rather that for the vast majority of Poles during this period, their religion was an expression of national identity. Given the institutional protection of a church that acted as guarantor of national life, their religion offered vernacular expressions of identity that continually excited Poland's sense of community. Cultural memory asserted basic values that celebrated their inherent worth. More than that, as interpreted by John Paul, it invoked Poles to become *challengers* for what was rightfully theirs.

The significance of John Paul's rhetorical pilgrimage lies in this call to transcend resistance. Resisters define themselves in terms of their opponents. They stave off attempts to rob them of self-dominion. They react to threats; they do not assert a positive program. The pope's messages, by contrast, advanced an agenda of affirmative assertions. This agenda did not issue a call for insurrection but to an accounting. There is more than a hint of Enlightenment ideals of emancipation in this rhetorical embodiment challenging the rational legitimacy of state-defined reality, graced by the irony of these ideals entering public imagination through a discourse about church, family, and cultural traditions. Importantly, John Paul's own acts of direct reference and direct confrontation provided the positive model of what challengers must do.

The pope's sermons followed a similar pattern. He began with celebratory recollections of some aspect of Polish Catholicism relevant to his audience. Then he related this to some fundamental aspect of national identity. Next he considered how this aspect reflected an essential human quality. The importance of beginning with the assumptions of Polish Christian humanism were highlighted by contrasting this essential aspect with an opposing practice or ideology that seemed to deny it. Through these steps he developed an evident indictment of the state for denying some aspect of national life and human value that was the special concern of his listeners.

Often this indictment was leveled through claims linked to apparently counterfactual circumstances. Since everyone knew that the state was limiting broadcasts of his visit,[6] the pope emphasized freedom of speech when addressing those from border regions. He expressed hope that Christians in neighboring countries would hear broadcasts of his sermons. Against the party's prohibition of humanistic values from the curriculum of state-controlled education, the pope cautioned university students against measuring progress solely by economic categories since it also had a spiritual dimension. Against common knowledge that state policy restricting career advancement to party members meant Catholics would always be laborers, John Paul underscored the injustice of evident privilege for some and discrimination against others. To the faithful from regions where he was not permitted to travel he spoke of self-determination by insisting that international reconciliation rested on the right of each nation to exist, to its own culture and its own forms for developing it. Everyone knew that travel bans to worker regions grew from the state's fear that massive crowds in industrialized areas would signal the USSR that Polish workers bore greater allegiance to Catholicism than Soviet Marxism. To workers from the industrial city of Nowa Huta gathered at Mogila he celebrated the dignity of work by insisting that Christ will never approve of a system where humans are considered only as a means of production. Everyone knew this to be a direct clash with the party. The pope used Auschwitz as the setting to answer state objections to his continuing references to human rights. There he wondered how anyone could be surprised that a person who came from this region of death would express such views.

These challenges mirror the challenge the pope presented directly to the state authorities. On his arrival he was greeted formally by First Secretary Gierek at Belvedere Palace. Gierek's remarks focused on the need for détente to control nuclear weapons, the lasting benefit of Soviet friendship, and the accomplishments of the then thirty-five-year-old communist regime.

John Paul responded to this openly by speaking in terms that were understandable as criticisms and yet acceptable in the way they challenged the state to consider more fundamental issues in a broader context. Without overtly acknowledging Gierek's equation of Poland with a thirty-five-year-old state, the pope discussed the city of Warsaw as dear to every Pole and a reminder of historic service. He made special note of the Royal Castle, then under reconstruction, as speaking with special eloquence about centuries of national history. His point was unmistakable: Polish time and church time cast national identity within a different frame than the truncated one of the communists.

He responded to the first secretary's view on the beneficence of the Soviet Union by reference to the last two hundred years of subjugation. These painful and unforgettable lessons, especially those of World War II, were underscored when the pope balanced Polish gratefulness for help received with sadness that Varsovians were not spared. His obvious reference to the failure of the Soviet army to aid during the Warsaw rising offered a firm contradiction to the distortions he found in the party's rhetoric.

He also challenged Gierek's theme of peace. Although the party's rhetoric of peace appealed to a humanitarian impulse, the domination of Soviet views and of a totalitarian philosophy made the party's conception of peace alien to Polish culture. The pope called the party's hand by contending that if peace were desired it could "only be achieved on the principle of respect for the objective rights of the nation, such as: the right to existence, to freedom, to be a social and political subject, and also to the formation of its own culture and civilization." The pope's response raised the implicit question of how Poles were to take the words of their government seriously when it bowed to an external force that denied Poland its right to self-determination.

Finally, John Paul challenged the totality of the state, claiming that it was just one among various communities of which the people were members and to which the church had a temporal mission of moral guidance and humanism. He then listed the agenda of rights for which the nation must contend by asserting that the mission of the church, and by implication its members, was "everywhere and always . . . to make people better, more conscious of their dignity, and more devoted in their lives to their family, social, professional and patriotic commitments. It is her mission to make people more confident, more courageous, conscious of their rights and duties, socially responsible, creative and useful."

The Polish government may have construed John Paul's visit as purely religious. However, its political intent was apparent from his first dramatic gesture upon arrival at Warsaw's Okecie Airport: He knelt to kiss the tarmac, then rose to assert that he had come "to help to strengthen this unflagging will to live on the part of my fellow-countrymen in the land that is our common motherland and homeland." His mission was emancipatory; he had come to contest Poland's basic political definition of who they were and of what they might become.

The theme of national identity, iterated to authorities at Belvedere Palace in terms of patriotism; to the youth at Gniezno and Krakow in terms of national accomplishments; to the nation at Auschwitz in terms of victories of spirit over the horrors of "this Golgotha of the modern world"; in Warsaw's Victory Square in terms of all the seeds of blood, sweat, love, creative work, prayer, and service that have made Poland what it is, projected Poland in the chronotope of liturgical time: ancient and yet contemporary, religious and yet national, formed by a millennium of events that mark a calendar of diachronic time but are expressed in traditions of heritage that make that millennium synchronously part of the present. The dialogizing of present conditions by a continuous national culture and heritage amounted to this assertion: Poland is first a history, not a state.

What did it mean to assert that Poland was first a history? For Poles it affirmed an identity of heritage. The significance of ancestral accomplishments outweighed imposed structures. People were placed above institutions; human achievements inscribed humanistic values on the core of Polish national identity and dignified national suffering and resistance to oppression with the mantle of each individual's human and sovereign rights to freedom and self-determination. Asserting that Poland was first a history also condemned the communist state that had denied Poles their heritage by subordinating the country to its own totalitarian ideology. A person could be of any faith or even of no faith and still affirm at the level of humanistic values and beliefs that Poland was first a history, not a state.[7] Thus John Paul II led his pilgrims to rediscover and reaffirm an inheritance of national identity sealed in the blood of their forbears. It now became their right and duty as heirs to claim it, since to abandon their bequest was to beggar themselves.

The pope's authority to lead a collective discussion of national identity rested on the authenticating charisma of his believability. He used his office to open a space of appearance for a *we* of Polish identity focused on what Poland affirmed as the basis for what it rejected. His incremental recollection of cultural memories transformed a religious space into a political one. Sermons became civic conversations sustaining a projected *we* within the grand narrative of Polish national identity, recrystallizing and energizing in its members a sense of their cultural core: to be stimulated by their own cultural archive, to express it, to heed its call of duty and responsibility toward their collective identity. His celebrations of memorialized deeds were also an exhibition of the political values an authentically Polish *we* would have to perform to redeem itself. The perceptible enthusiasm with which his sermons were received signaled both submission to John Paul II's authority and discovery that their rhetorical joining was issuing a challenge.

The role of citizen as challenger, initiated at the beginning of his pilgrimage, was brought to its forceful conclusion in his final sermon at Krakow, his home city. A crowd estimated at two million had filled the great meadow of Blonica Krakowskie located at the city's center. Amid the spectacle of emotional attachment and communal celebration John Paul pointed to moral order as the lingering issue of Poland's future. Poles had to determine whether they could exhibit the discipline necessary for moral order to prevail. "In the final analysis the moral order is built up by means of human beings. This order consists of a large number of tests, each one a test of faith and of character. From every victorious test the moral order is built up. From every failed test moral disorder grows." The pope fixed the burden of responsibility on each Pole. Each had to heed the call to a new beginning. Each had to assume responsibility for personal acts that collectively would build the nation's future.

This final sermon concluded, then, with an assertion that the sphere of temporal power was the people's preserve; their temporal authority required jealous protection. Having experienced themselves as challengers for nine days, they were commissioned by him to continue on this path. Although his visit had reaffirmed that the institutional resources of the church would continue to lend its authority for acts of self-determination, the people's authority would come more fundamentally from their own discipline. At a time when Poland seemed to lack a horizon of expectation that engendered hope, John Paul II's pilgrimage revealed that the nation still was able to respond to believable appeals for moral order and courage. Equally they had shared a public experience of affirming collective goals and acceptable norms that were authentically Polish. This collective consciousness created the possibility for their challenge for freedom the following August, when labor strikes across Poland culminated in the formation of the trade union Solidarity.

The complex social conditions and aspirations that contributed to Solidarity's formation involved forces outside this study. John Paul II's rhetorical reappropriation of Polish historicity did not cause the trade union's formation, although at that time a broad spectrum of Poles maintained that Solidarity would have been an impossible development had he not visited Poland.[8] Solidarity emerged from a labor strike, and workers deserve considerable credit for its creation. Credit also belongs to intellectuals who had joined the Interfactory Strike Committee (MKS) and played a major role in the negotiations that led to the union's legalization in 1980. However, a different form of Polish public emerged during his visit than had existed prior to it. In that respect, John Paul II advanced the efforts of Poland's intellectuals who, as the leading dissidents following the formation of KOR in 1976, had been the primary force behind attempts to construct some semblance of a civil society in communist Poland.

Calls for civil society were a dominant motivation in Polish political agitation during the 1970s, and this call continued through the 1980s. Here we should revisit the earlier discussion of civil society in order to extend it in the context of Polish praxis. Z. A. Pelczynski (1988) reminds us that this idea, developed during the Enlightenment in connection with the state, underwent theoretical rupture in Hegel's work, in which it was separated from the state. Marx, though critical of the Hegelian concept of the state, accepted those portions dealing with civil society, which Pelczynski summarizes as follows:

> "Civil society" is an aspect of the modern state, which Hegel
> further subdivides into the "system of needs," concerned with
> the promotion of particular (individual and sectional) goals
> (the economic sphere of production, exchange and other
> market relations), the social sphere of classes and auton-
> omous organizations which he calls "corporations," and the
> "civil" sphere of public institutions such as the courts and var-

ious regulatory and welfare agencies. Civil society in this sense is an arena in which modern man legitimately gratifies his self-interest and develops his individuality, but also learns the value of group action, social solidarity and the dependence of his welfare on others, which educate him for citizenship and prepare him for participation in the political arena of the state (Pelczynski 1988, 364).

Gramsci (1971) reformulated the Hegelian-Marxian elements so that civil society was expanded beyond the economic sphere and beyond its adjunct status to the state. It was a sphere of autonomous activity by a range of society's organizations, and it did not perpetuate bourgeois ideology. One does not have to look far to find a Gramscian strain in the self-understanding of Poland's social actors who were advancing a rhetoric of civil society during this period.

For Poles, agitation for civil society represented a struggle to "live in truth." During this period living in truth meant establishing a place in which a moral awakening with consequences for political life would change the individual's subjective conditions. Living in truth was the alternative to passive acceptance of communist political arrangements, which meant making one's personal accommodation with a lie by agreeing to live within that lie. Living in truth was encapsulated in the policies adopted by KOR in 1976—openness, truthfulness, autonomy of action, and trust—and was part of the daily struggle to demarcate an alternative reality to the state's. Its spirit was circulated through society via samizdat writings. It was kept alive by affiliation with the church. It was even advanced by the transformation of Solidarity from a viable institutional alternative to the state to a shattered organization left materially moribund but enduring as a political myth. Timothy Ash (1988, 3) tells us that Poles and other Eastern Europeans understood civil society to refer not only to the range of associations and ties of public life independent of the state but also to the strategies of self-organization just noted to make such a public life possible. In Poland, to participate in civil society meant to be organized and civilly active, to constitute and be constituted by highly permeable arenas of a reticulate public sphere, to be part of a rhetorically formed public.

The rhetoric of this public continued then, as it does now, to draw on the reservoir of cultural memory. However, its manifestation has been significantly altered from that so effective in 1979 and is suggestive of the role of such discourse beyond the confines of the Polish situation. Normative contents, primitive traditions, and cultural affiliations give life to a resistance community that is fighting to survive against the onslaught of imposed domination by an alien power. Its effectiveness rests on its own totalizing impulse, which can be as complete as the force it opposes. But the resources of its own rhetoric can enervate the political efficacy, not to mention the moral economy, of the institutions that are its authoritative voice once conditions of opposition are replaced by more social ones of constructive interdependence. Brief observations are in order, then, regarding the rhetorical stances of Solidarity and the church following the union's formation.

The image of civil society overtook Solidarity's identity as a labor union shortly after its legalization. From its inception Solidarity's counsels were split over its identity, and its leadership, under Walesa's direction, became locked in a power struggle with other elements that wished it to move more rapidly in challenging the state. After the imposition of martial law by General Jaruzelski on 13 December 1981, the identification of Solidarity with civil society spread from the union to the entire nation. Its imprisoned leaders kept the call alive through prison writings, such as Michnik's. Although uncompromising in their trenchant criticism of the state, they were directed at Polish society with the intent of sustaining a dialogue on how a civilly functional society should be organized and about how its members should lead their lives as free men and women.

The rhetoric of prison letters, artistic works, and samizdat writings built a narrative of civil society based on the historically important themes of morality and dignity that figured so prominently in John Paul's rhetoric. These themes were developed through accounts of current events that narrated the trials of a nation willing to suffer hardships for righteous causes. Although Solidarity's leadership, especially Walesa, had been closely associated with the church and its leading figures were properly respectful of the church's institutional place in opposition to the state, its discourse did not constitute civil society through stories of church heroes and events with secular significance. Solidarity's appeals promulgated a language of citizenship, the importance of self-organization, and nonviolent revolution with secular narratives of civil society.

After the reorganization of Poland from a communist state to a representative democracy, the image of civil society Solidarity had been advancing became Poland's reality insofar as it embodied democratic principles of open deliberation and the restructuring of society based on common interests. Ironically Solidarity soon passed from the political scene of the new political order; its success in bringing about political openness created the opportunity for other interests to form and for alternative models addressed to Poland's political, social, and economic problems to vie for power.

A somewhat different pattern of rhetorical possibility has influenced the secular role of the church since 1980. Immediately after the Gdansk accords were signed, Cardinal Wyszinski urged the union to stick to labor issues and not challenge the state. His successor, Cardinal Glemp, adopted the same stance. After Jaruzelski declared martial law and stripped Solidarity of its legal status, the church once more assumed its role as the sole institutional alternative to the state. Its parish pulpits were hotbeds of dissident discourse, while parish priests were subjected to pressure from the Episcopate to desist and to physical harm from the state, including assassination.

Meanwhile the hierarchy under Glemp's leadership sought to solidify the church's legal status. Talks in 1984 were intended to change diplomatic relations between the Vatican and Warsaw. Not well received by a public then in the process of constituting Polish civil society, this seemed to be toadying to a state that was considered irrelevant to Polish political aspirations. In 1987 John Paul returned for his third visit to Poland, but to a less enthusiastic reception than before. As a symbolic gesture the church had decided to mingle its marshals with the militia for crowd control. The symbolic significance of their integration may have been in keeping with the détente the church sought with the state, but it spoke a vernacular message ill-suited to prevailing social sentiment. Poles regarded the militia, along the lines Michnik developed in "Why You Are Not Signing," as an ignorant and brutish tool of the apparatus and given to using physical force on dissidents. Their presence for purposes of "crowd control" was read as an attempt to intimidate Poles from appropriating the political content of the papal visit as it had in the past. When church marshals remained passive while militia removed Solidarity signs expressing political views, innuendo became fact, which many found deeply shocking for the divide it signaled between the hierarchy and the current state of social consciousness. Matters were worsened when John Paul's homilies failed to address their aspirations and discontents. Some felt his message was so at odds with the mood and faith of the people that it seemed intended for some other country (Mianowicz 1989).

Subsequent to the restructuring of the Polish constitution, the church has worked toward gaining increased power in matters of state. This effort is particularly revealing of the role of narrative in social will formation when conditions of society are unstable. Here Gramsci provides a helpful insight. His reformulation of the Hegelian-Marxist position specifically includes an understanding of the role the church may play in civil society in the struggle for separation of powers during specific historical periods. "In other words," Gramsci writes:

> there takes place within the society what Croce calls the "perpetual conflict between Church and State," in which the Church is taken as representing the totality of civil society (whereas in fact it is only an element of diminishing importance within it), and the State as representing every attempt to crystallise permanently a particular stage of development, a particular situation. In this sense, the Church itself may become State, and the conflict may occur between on the one hand

secular (and secularising) civil society, and on the other State/Church (when the Church has become an integral part of the State, of political society monopolized by a specific privileged group, which absorbs the Church in order the better to preserve its monopoly with the support of that zone of "civil society" which the Church represents). (1971, 245)

Gramsci's description of the church's absorption by the state accurately portrays how Poles saw its role evolving after the bloodless revolution of 1989. The church's oppositional role during the communist period positioned it to seize the new political opportunities that came with change. The church sought and received legal status; it sought to play a larger role in shaping the political posture of Solidarity in the new government, which created criticism of the church by some among Solidarity's leadership, criticism of Solidarity by some segments of society, and dissension within Solidarity over the direction its leadership was taking. The church sought to have Catholic religious instruction mandated in public schools, and succeeded. It sought to have Catholicism made the official state religion by ending church/state separation. After much public objection, the initiative was withdrawn. The church sought to have a strict antiabortion law passed, which again brought stiff opposition from Catholics as well as other segments of society.

The church has counted on its still massive numbers for support in its determination to gain a stronger voice on political matters. Despite their religious affiliation, however, Catholics have begun to form a different opinion about the church's proper role. They have used the free press to criticize it on issues of separation of church and state, abortion, and censorship of pornography and apparently have separated their religion from politics, as the 1993 national elections bore witness when *all* explicitly Catholic-affiliated party candidates were rejected ("... And Unto Poland, What Is God's" 1991, 51–52; "The Fading of the Red" 1994, 56).

The rejection of church-affiliated candidates reflects the evolutionary trajectory political discourse took once the need for resistance and structural revolution had passed. Shortly after the political upheavals in Eastern Europe at the end of 1989 Western commentators warned of the great dangers a resurgence of nationalism would bring. Ash, writing about the changes he observed as part of the immediate aftermath, noticed a different development in the language being used to describe the political and social tasks ahead: "In any case, what was most striking was not the language of nationhood. That was wholly predictable. What was striking was the other ideas and words that, so to speak, shared top billing. One of these was 'society.' In a country often stigmatized as 'nationalist,' Poland, the word most often used to describe the people as opposed to the authorities was not 'nation'; it was *spoleczenstwo*, society" (1990, 20).

In the brief time it took to remove the obstacle of an imposed government and replace it with one chosen through free popular elections, the dialectic between nation and state collapsed, and the language of civil society took its place.

The narrative of national identity is a rhetorical phenomenon, which means it has a contingent efficacy. Although the church was the steward of national identity, its role was significantly influenced by conditions of Polish subjugation. As conditions began to destabilize, alternative renditions of the Poland that drew sustenance from its cultural memory began to emerge. In retrospect, one might interpret KOR's discourse as initiating a Polish narrative in terms somewhat different from the church's but consonant with Polish cultural memory and the ongoing struggle of its people to reappropriate Polish historicity. KOR's policies for living a public life were the basis for a civil society in which individuals were awakened to their subjectivity and the moral consequences of their choices. As Poles sought an alternative vision of themselves to that of "deviants" and "incompetents" fostered by the state, KOR emphasized the primacy of personal dignity and the individual as the basis on which to establish a viable moral economy. KOR developed an alternative story of Polish aspirations for politics and society to that of the state's.

On the one hand, under prevailing conditions of a communist state, KOR's rendition had less power than the church's for reasons largely related to the church's historical role as protector of Polish national identity against a state often controlled from outside. On the other hand, after the state's collapse in 1989, the caesura between state and nation evaporated. Quite different political realities emerged that account for "society" sharing top billing with "nation" in the discourse on Polish identity Ash observed in early 1990.

In terms of the narratives of cultural memory, the significance of this shift lies in moving discussion away from the concept—*nation*—that underscores the centrality of the Roman Catholic Church to Polish civil society as a realm apart from the state. Not only is the nation/state split no longer the defining condition of Poland's dialogue on identity, but the introduction of *society* as a pivotal term has moved consciousness away from the isolated relations that were validated as truly Polish by the church. Instead the dialogue has defined Poland in the larger sphere of civil society, with comparative models from across Europe and with its own sphere intersecting the spheres of the European community, free market trade and the global economy, NATO, and its own laws and codes of social conduct chosen in open deliberation rather than dictated by religious dogma but supported nonetheless as an act of opposition to an imposed state.

Instability does not dislodge the narrative function of appropriating historicity; however, it does link its rhetorical efficacy to the relative condition of life practices. In the church's case, opposition to the communist state gave it proprietary rights to articulate popular aspirations in terms of the nation's historical archive. The church extended its institutional position on the leading edge of opposition by insisting that the faithful refrain from criticism of church practices and political arrangements. Faithful who did raise criticisms were excoriated as sympathetic to the communist regime. Moreover, restricting involvement to the church's hierarchy did not encourage participation by the laity in the official public sphere. The resulting bimodal mentality imposed by the church on all public issues—one either supported the church or the regime—denied its members an opportunity to enter deliberations on matters that were consequential for their lives.

Policies of rigid control may be effective for dealing with specific situations and adversaries. However, when conditions change, the terms of the relationship may no longer apply, making the need for silence obsolete and offering no ongoing context of alternative considerations that can only develop through an openly deliberative praxis. Moreover, rigid control denied the church the opportunity to develop effective structures for deliberation of controversial matters. Consequently, when the church became aggressive in changing its terms of relationship to the secular realm through pressure to require religious instruction in schools, eliminate the separation of church and state, and legally prohibit abortion, criticism gravitated to the multiple arenas of a political public sphere. The strength of opposition has made it difficult for the church to continue its agenda for influencing the secular course of Poland and has provided a clear indication that political dialogue has shifted from terms of national identity to those of an evolving civil society.

The search for Polish identity continues to extend from John Paul's visit and Solidarity's meteoric journey from trade union to political institution to myth. The conditions of that search, however, have been marked by the instabilities of a legalized alternative to the Polish Workers Party (PZPR), a state of martial law, a failure of the state to motivate social will to escape economic collapse, the relegalization of Solidarity, a power-sharing agreement between the party and openly elected representatives, the disbanding of the Communist Party, the shift of the controlling political image from "nation" to "society," the attempt by the church to secure secular authority, the rejection by the voters of church-affiliated candidates thereby indicating it no longer is the controlling voice in the dialogue on society's course, and the reemergence of former communists as the elected party in power. Instabilities of life practices, such as these, are accompanied by destabilization of information. Under this quintessential postmodern condition narratives with social, political, and economic traction become a function of community criteria for acceptable renditions of reality. For any discourse to have social consequences it must draw on the cognitive, emotional, and normative dimensions that make a culture a system of meaning. Yet there are no guarantees. People respond to culturally resonant rhetoric because it provides salience and bears fidelity to their lives. But such rhetoric is always riddled with myth, making relationships of affiliation and acts of dissociation it invokes and sustains rest on a construction of life's events whose truth may be no more than apparent.

Memories of Despair: Yugoslavia

Poland's cultural memories were not entirely beneficent. Its inventional possibilities included strains of antisemitism and protofascism as much as those of individual worth and responsibility. That the latter were selected is, perhaps, a sign of practical wisdom among Poland's dissident leaders. Regardless, it certainly was a choice of consequence for the reinvigorated civil society Poland actually did experience. As much was not universally the case among the other formerly communist nations that began refashioning their political identities in 1989. No one should have been surprised, therefore, when, hard upon shedding the yoke of totalitarian rule, the warm afterglow of Central and Eastern Europe's rekindled freedom soon cast ominous shadows. The endemic ethnic differences of these regions became rhetorical anchors for nationalistic appeals promoting incompatible political aspirations locked in a death struggle for dominance. No country more completely manifested these conflicts than the former Yugoslavia. This country, whose republics collectively had been free longer under Communist Party rule than at any time in their respective modern histories as autonomous national entities, lost a center that binds.

The people of the former Yugoslavia came from six multicultural republics that spoke four different languages. They wrote in two alphabets (Cyrillic and Roman) and, in most republics, practiced three religions (Catholicism, Islam, and Orthodox Christianity) and a fourth (Judaism) in Bosnia Herzegovina. More a federation of multicultural federations than one nation-state, its citizens possessed markedly different cultural impulses and affiliations: one set with Europe and the West, the other with the Balkans and the East. During the period leading to Yugoslavia's dissolution, Croatian, Serbian, and Slovenian rhetorics respectively made reference to national myths that called for quite different political realities (Kovacic and Travica 1992). When the republics declared themselves to be independent nations, a nationalistic anti-Muslim rhetoric quickly followed suit.

In the late 1980s and early 1990s Croatian and Slovenian separatists propagated stories of a previous age in which their land and their people's accomplishments were wedded to an autonomous nation that spoke its own language. These narratives supported a relationship of confederation, at best, with the other Yugoslavian republics. For Serbs, medieval stories of Serbia's imperial status supported their insistence on maintaining the republics in a single, centrally governed state in which Serbia would play the leading role. Matters were similar for Croats who wished no part of a Serbian empire but sought national autonomy. For instance, Michael Scammell reported visiting the Democratic Union's election headquarters in Croatia, where he: "found the campaign workers put heavy emphasis on Croatian history and Croatian national traditions. The walls were decorated with pictures of medieval Croatian rulers and coats of arms of Croatian cities, where the campaign literature had much to say on Croatian folklore and customs" (1990b, 44). These stories of a glorious past carried memories of an alternative reality to that invoked by Serbian ambition.

In "The Storyteller" Walter Benjamin (1969) wrestles with the problem of explaining how stories gain so deep a hold on the human imagination that they become a vehicle for exchanging experience. Stories are different from information. Information lives for the moment in which it is new; it must be explanatory to the moment when it is presented. A story, on the other hand, does not expend itself at the moment of utterance. Its release is over time, its power sustained by its capacity to thrive in the milieu of the listener's memory. A story does not require technical knowledge or ideological commitment from the listener. Instead, through tone and shade, form and action it colors imagination. A story portrays with images that, on hearing or reading, evoke memories of what we have seen and done in similar circumstances and of our soul's responses to real moments in our lives. An artisan mode of communication, its moral unfolds beyond the moment of its invention. Each iteration announces itself to new listeners in differing circumstances and, through its common theme, binds them in a community of memory. "Seen in this way," says Benjamin, "the storyteller joins the ranks of the teachers and sages. He has counsel—not for a few situations, as the proverb does, but for many, like the sage" (108).

In subcultures that are repressed by the state or by the majority culture, resistance to assimilation often is engendered by a process sociologists call *primary socialization*. Beginning with preschool interactions in the family and with closest friends, children receive instruction in the language, customs, religious practices, and national consciousness that provides their sense of social integration. Stories of family struggles against oppression, accounts of civil society before the loss of autonomy, and tales of past heroes who embodied ethnic ideals, exposure to symbols, and participation in rituals that link the individual to a past when they were publicly practiced provide intergenerational interaction and integration into a shared identity. Hank Johnston (1994) observes that the private character of these interactions makes them impossible for the state or the apparatus to control and places them beyond its penetration. Narrative sharing gives each individual continuity with the past and a common identity with individuals with whom they otherwise are unconnected.

For the ethnic groups of Yugoslavia, the vernacular rhetoric of iconic displays and tales that referenced traditions of glory and struggles of oppression offered political counsel to their respective peoples. Speeches and writings laced with these stories gave expression to long-harbored discontents and provided visions of a new order. Outside eyes read these same discourses, which drew upon myths of origin, tales of grievance, or stories of confrontation and conquest, as promoting a sense of national exclusivity along ethnic lines. Certainly they did that, but the plot does not end there. The perception that the Balkans' current horror was *caused* by ethnic antipathies is an oversimplification of more complex historical relationships that involved an alternative identity to the one projected by official versions of nationalist leaders.

For fifty years Yugoslavia stood as the most apparently liberal of Europe's communist states. In contrast to Western European nations in which there is relative cultural purity, and sometimes, as in Germany, where citizenship is based on bloodlines rather than place of birth, Yugoslavia was a model of multiculturalism. Croats, Muslims, and Serbs intermingled throughout the country. They worked together, lived as neighbors, and intermarried. They could not be distinguished by physical appearance, occupation, or other observable features except religious practices. Yet, according to Noel Malcolm (1993), Christianity and Islam had intermingled for over five centuries, so that at the level of folk beliefs they were not remarkably different. Most experts agree that Yugoslavia was not a confessional society[9] in which religious differences were divisive. Although there have been attempts to characterize Bosnia's Muslims as fundamentalists, perhaps aspiring to a fusion of Islam with civil society and the state in the fashion of Iran, their actual practices followed the general pattern of Bosniaks who, by 1990, included only 17 percent who declared themselves believers. For many being a Muslim in Bosnia was like being a Jew in the United States: it marked a person's self-definition but did not necessarily indicate the fervor of one's worship (Laber 1993).

Religion gave a less accurate account of allegiances among Yugoslavians than group difference inspired by regional power struggles. For example, struggles between the Austro-Hungarian and Ottoman Empires divided neighboring republics from one another. Although these empires no longer exist, the expansionist designs of its neighbors, particularly Serbia and, to a lesser extent, Croatia, have kept tensions alive in Bosnia. Caught in these struggles since 1870, the peoples of this region have been forced into divisive choices of fealty.

Communism held these republics together as a national whole, but it did so through a curious jumble of cultural contradictions. In the interest of national unity, it suppressed national and ethnic interests by denying them a place in civil society and controlling them in matters of governance. To cite one case, neither Serbs nor Croats could unify their republics as ethnic entities since substantial numbers of their populations had a long history of living elsewhere in the nation. Still Tito governed Yugoslavia with a policy of multiethnic federalism, based on the assumption that national welfare required keeping traditional rivalries in check. Given the ethnic diversity of each republic, he believed he had to achieve ethnic balance in administering the country. To this end he reduced Serb influence in the federal system in Belgrade but increased its influence elsewhere by inserting Serbs into positions of power in places such as Croatia.

Sometimes the state adopted policies in one area that created ethnic strife in others. For instance, Hungarians and Albanians also lived in Yugoslavia, with substantial numbers in Kosovo, Vojvodina, Southern Serbia, and Macedonia. Under Tito's multicultural policies they were eligible for civil service positions. The power of the majority to control the language of all official communication led to the exclusive use of Serbo-Croatian on television, in the schools, and in many parts of the universities regardless of whether that was the language spoken by the majority in the town or region. Inscribing official language as a polysemic performance of vernacular rhetoric backfired, however, as Hungarians and Albanians acquired relevant bilingual proficiency more readily than Serbs or Macedonians. When civil service positions became vacant in regions with heavy concentrations of Albanians or Hungarians, bilingual skill was an important employment consideration. This created a serious patronage problem, since Hungarians and Albanians were now advantaged over Yugoslavians in gaining these positions. Although language proficiency helped to turn the wheels of local administration more smoothly, over time the perceived unfairness of this advantage gave rise to collective resentment (Kovacic 1994).

Yugoslavia had developed a system of self-management which included everyone as part of a public sphere and public whose opinion, in theory, mattered in local decision-making. However, as these examples illustrate, the state did not promote strong structures that would have permitted self-management to supersede ancient ethnic divisions. Attempts like these to stifle ethnic differences actually accomplished the opposite, since the state's policies were a constant reminder that ancient rivalries were never far from the surface but lacked a way to be expressed or a place in civil society. They evoked an "injustice frame" (Johnson 1994) in which everyday interaction with the ethnic Other became an opportunity for perceived slights. In this state of quotidian destabilization, in which comments by and encounters involving the ethnic Other are perceived as grievances, the aggrieved party dissociates at the mundane level of shared experiences from neighbors perceived as privileged at his expense while bonding in ethnic (or nationalist) solidarity with strangers otherwise unconnected except for their participation in a common story. Little "injustices" of everyday life pertain immediately to a person's life, making perceived insults from the Other invasions of personal identity. Quotidian destabilization reinforces stories of identity and difference in a way that, harbored over time, intensifies emotions of opposition.

Although simultaneously stifling expression of national and ethnic interests and reminding everyone of their presence, Tito did not develop democratic traditions by which the political process could evolve alternatives to nationalistic understandings of economic and social problems. Yugoslavia's multicultural public, which should have been an empirical model of socialist possibilities, was eclipsed, and with that the prospects for resolving differences through deliberative rhetoric also faded. Instead ancient quarrels and strivings which lurked in the background were a rich vein of stereotypes waiting to be mined. Milovan Djilas, Tito's long-standing archrival, commenting to British journalist Michael Ignatieff (1993a) on this policy of repressing the development of democratic procedures, found irony in the fact that Stalin's opponent behaved as a Stalinist in the end.

Misha Glenny implies the correctness of Djilas's analysis when he develops the thesis that ethnic differences were not a major source of division in Yugoslavian society until the party began to lose its grip and its leaders determined to retain their power by inciting nationalistic emotions on lines of ethnic purity (Glenny 1992, chap. 1). For example, there are many ways to be a Serb, such as identifying on the basis of religion or through common affiliation as a Slavophile. Atomizing, instead, in terms of ethnicity served a politically useful function for those in power because it produced solidarity in terms of a background consensus on *difference*. A rhetoric of *difference* encouraged perceiving those who opposed its division as traitors to their own people.

In multicultural republics national identity must be understood in relative terms to achieve inclusive solidarity. Without flexibility, membership in the nation becomes a source of conflict because *difference* gets defined as disagreement and requires that the majority, by granting membership, include the Other in a political accommodation. Posing the terms of relationship as *political accommodation* rather then as *interdependence* and *tolerance* made exclusion of the Other a far easier path to promote. Regrettably, official versions of what it meant to be a Croat, Serb, or Bosnian, which parsed along these atomizing lines, became the rhetorical invocations for Yugoslavia's peoples to appropriate their own past. Without an alternative framework for analysis of the new national situation Croats and Serbs found themselves speaking a tongue that reduced their identity to their ethnicity. Ignatieff (1993a, 3) supports this view with the contention that Yugoslav conflicts were not produced by *historical* differences. Rather, they were the manufactured fables of ideologues that portrayed the other side as committing monstrous acts of genocide and their own as untainted victims. Without a tradition of open political deliberation in which differences were settled on their merits, nationalism was the only language available for political appeal once communism dropped into its political free fall. Slavenka Drakulic (1993) observes that this language expressed political relations in terms of national pride and grievance by voicing exclusionary longings and fears.

Closer inspection of the issues confronting Yugoslavia's republics in the late 1980s suggest that the communist regime began to unravel over regional differences that transcended ethnicity. For example, there were economic issues concerning the republics' disproportionate contributions to the national treasury as compared to their respective political power. The exclusionary fears and longings evoked by a rhetoric of national pride and grievance had little to do with addressing their causes or advancing solutions. Thus, when Slovenia began speaking overtly of secession, its grievances were not just that Slovens felt an ethnic aversion to Serbs. With 8 percent of the population Slovenia was producing 20 percent of Yugoslavia's GNP, 30 percent of its exports, and 27 percent of its budget. Yet it lacked a commensurate measure of political power to feel that it was being treated as an equal political shareholder (Danforth 1990; Denitch 1989). Although burgeoning nationalistic rhetoric exacerbated ethnic strife, material relations such as these stirred the Yugoslavian republics to search for instruments that might reconstitute social practices in terms more favorable to their respective interests. Without a democratic political culture to thematize material differences in compelling terms, Yugoslavians had emaciated potential for understanding issues. Recondite premises of economic interest and its relation to power carried far less rhetorical intensity than did regional (and latent ethnic) interests. Without alternatives to the language of nationalism for expressing economic, political, or social grievances, Yugoslavians were vulnerable to reductionistic propaganda that played upon ethnic differences. Echoing Kundera, Ignatieff concludes that "it is not how the past dictates the present, but how the present manipulates the past which seems decisive in the Balkans" (1993a, 3). A similar conclusion is drawn by the International Commission on the Balkans, whose final report rejects the popular explanations for Yugoslavia's unrest with the observation:

> The principal responsibility for the recent war in former Yugoslavia rests with those post-communist politicians throughout Yugoslavia who have invoked the "ancient hatreds" to pursue their respective nationalist agendas and deliberately used their propaganda machines to justify the unjustifiable: the use of violence for territorial conquest, the expulsion of the "other" peoples, and the perpetuation of authoritarian systems of power. In that process, they manipulated fears through misinformation and incitement to hatred. (*Unfinished Peace* 1996, 22)

During this period of the early 1990s, the most notorious leader to rely on a nationalistic rhetoric has been Serbia's head of state,

Slobodan Milosevic. The breakup of communist control of Yugoslavia in the mid 1980s and the increasingly overt expression of secessionist aspirations by its republics created the conditions in which Milosevic wrote his 1986 Serbian Academy of Arts and Science Memorandum advocating a greater Serbia reconstructed from the rubble of Tito's quickly crumbling state.[10] If the other republics were not prepared to accept Serbia as its political epicenter, Milosevic was prepared to incite Serbian segments in those republics to demand Serbia's protection of them from the other indigenous peoples who were their neighbors (Ignatieff 1993a).

Incredibly, Croatian leader Franjo Tudjman seemed determined to accommodate the appeals of Milosevic's nationalistic narrative by overtly discriminating against its Serbs, estimated to comprise between 12 and 20 percent of Croatia's population. Croatia, in its zeal to emulate the West, strove to model itself along lines of cultural unity that mark most Western European countries. Hence, Serbs were stripped of their status as a constituent nation within Croatia. Literary Croatian, written with the Roman alphabet, was declared the official language, thus barring the Serbs' native Cyrillic script from official documents. Serbs were denied cultural autonomy, including control over schools in which they were a majority. In these same districts Serb police were replaced by Croats and Serb officials were dismissed.

Most incredible of all, the Tudjman government replaced the red star, which had symbolized Yugoslavia, with the insignia of Croatian statehood, the red and white checkered shield, or *Sahovnica*, which had been the historical coat of arms of the Croat kingdom. A version of the Sahovnica also had been used widely by Ustashe, a murderous Croat fascist organization installed as rulers of Croatia in 1941 by the Nazis. Serbs memorialize the deadliness of Ustashe with the story of the prisoner camp at Jasenovac. Trainloads of Jews, Serbs, Gypsies, and Croatian communists were interned there behind the barracks' barbed-wire fence. "They were put to work in the brick factory, and when they were used up they were burned in the brick ovens or shot in the back of the head and then dumped in the Sava River" (Ignatieff 1993b, 32). The number killed is uncertain, and Serbs and Croats offer wildly different estimates. Serbs say 700,000, while Croats claim it was no more than 40,000. Independent researchers estimate that around 250,000 died there (Ignatieff 1993b, 32).

Here, as in much else that is contested between these warring people, Tito did not commission the writing of an objective history to provide an authoritative account (Gutman 1993, xxi). All that remains is the account preserved in tribal memory, giving the Sahovnica ominous associations in every Croatian Serb village. Consequently, when it replaced the red star, which was regarded by Serbs as a symbol of their equality with Croats, Croatia's indigenous Serbs felt a mounting urgency to act. The red and white checkered shield was interpreted as a symbol of Croat hegemony, domination, and virulent commitment to ethnic genocide. Although the Sahovnica may have been no more than an innocent traditional symbol of Croatian independence, its vernacular meaning for Serbs invoked a narrative that required no second thought for them to feel threatened or for Milosevic's nationalistic exhortations to acquire new credence.

Such acts unwittingly abetted Milosevic's own expansionist designs by helping him whip Serbs in Kosovo, Croatia, and Bosnia to hysteria. His claims (supported by old World War II photos) that their minority status placed them in imminent danger of being slaughtered seemed incontestable to Serb eyes witnessing the actions and symbols of Croatia's newly asserted nationalism (Laber 1993, 6). Croatia's policies of advancing politics and culture based on ethnic purity fueled cries for Serbia to protect its people from a pogrom and provided Milosevic with his pretext to send in the then Yugoslavian army, which Serbia controlled, to protect the Serb minority in Croatia.

When hostilities erupted in Bosnia, the forces of ethnic rivalry coalesced to produce unimaginable atrocities. At the outset of conflict Bosnia was a country of slightly more than four million: about 52 percent Muslim, 31 percent Serb, and 17 percent Croat. Bosnia's Muslims were mostly urban and middle class. In Sarajevo and some other cities they formed a professional cadre more affluent and sophisticated than the Serbs who lived in the rural regions. Rivalries between urban and rural were real in Bosnia, as they are in many other places, but that had more to do with class than ethnicity.

Urban Sarajevans oriented to Western Europe. They were like other Yugoslavians who enjoyed their distinction among communist countries of having an open border. They had passports, could travel, found ways to exchange excess dinars on the black market for hard Western currency, visited Western Europe, and bought Western merchandise. The words of Croatian journalist and writer Slavenka Drakulic explaining the calamities of Yugoslavia as a whole apply with equal force to the cosmopolitan Bosnians. When asked by an American friend to explain how this tragedy could befall the most liberal and prosperous communist country she responded, "We traded our freedom for Italian shoes" (Drakulic 1993, 16). Her explanation reads as a classic example of civic privatism: "This freedom—a feeling that you are free to go if you want to—was very important to us. It seems to me now to have been a tacit agreement with the regime: we realize that this government is here forever, we don't like you at all, but we'll compromise if you leave us alone, if you don't press too hard." Then, catching the irony of her analysis, she adds, "Lucky Hungarians, for they suffered in 1956; lucky Czechs and Slovaks who suffered in 1968."

Rural Serbs, on the other hand, are both farmers and warriors. Bosnia's Dinaric Alps are steep and rugged. They form a natural fortification that poses a significant obstacle to any invader. This point was not lost on Tito, especially in light of his antagonistic relations with Stalin and the Soviet Union and his uneasy relations with the West. Although Yugoslavia's eastern and western flanks were vulnerable to military attack, eventually hostilities would reach the mountains where armed defenders could withstand an invader indefinitely.

Every Yugoslavian male was armed and trained for military service. However, for those lacking bright economic prospects, the military offered an opportunity for material gain, since all ranks below general were based on merit. Consequently, the incentives of upward mobility attracted a disproportionate number of Serbs to became professional soldiers (Kovacic 1994), many of whom Tito had armed and trained for this defensive military role. Whatever estrangement may have existed between rural and urban life was further aggravated by the distance between the cosmopolitan understanding of people and events cultivated in Bosnia's cities and the provincial nationalism that the state cultivated in these farmer-warriors removed from the complexities of interdependence and cultural intermingling of metropolitan centers. Of course, this difference was especially deadly given that those most susceptible to nationalistic rhetoric were also those who were armed.

Although its Muslims did not have a compelling narrative of nationalistic aspiration (the Ottoman Empire is no more), there were real class differences that separated them from the Bosnian Serbs: urban/rural, professional/peasant, cosmopolitan/local, have/have not. Exposed to Milosevic's propaganda of ethnic strife in which minor differences were magnified in a distorted fable, Serb peasants vented these class antagonisms through ethnic hostility.

The genocidal passion with which Serbs prosecuted their policy of ethnic cleansing has been a source of perplexity and moral indecision in the West, leading us to ask what "ethnic cleansing" might mean in a multicultural society whose people lived in relative harmony since World War II. Michael Sells (1996) makes a compelling case for religious stereotypes as the most basic divide between Yugoslavia's ethnic groups. Although religion is not a dominant lived difference among them, it lurks beneath the surface as part of cultural memory's mythos. Primary among religious antagonisms is the construction of Muslims as Christ slayers.

How could followers of a religion founded six centuries after Christ be blamed for his death? The answer lies in the messianic construction in Serb memory of Prince Lazar, a fourteenth-century leader who was killed in battle with the Ottoman Turks. In Serb tradition his death marks the end of Serb independence and the onset of Ottoman rule (Sells 1996, 31). During the nineteenth century Lazar was transformed into a Christ figure. If his martyrdom symbolized the death of the Serbian nation, it could not be resurrected until his murderers were slain. On this premise hung the fate of Bosnian Muslims, who, seen as direct descendants of Ottoman Turks, were constructed as Christ slayers who must be purged from the face of the earth.

The antipathy toward Muslims was performed in memorable ways. In 1814 Vuk Karadzic wrote this curse on those who refused to fight at Kosovo, where Lazar fell, and subsequently became Muslims under Turk rule: "Whoever will not fight at Kosovo / may nothing grow that his hand sows, / neither the wheat in the field / nor the vine of grapes on his mountains" (Sells 1993, 38–39). Another construction was in cultural practices, such as resolving a blood feud. Serbian and Montenegrin tribes held that reconciliation could be achieved in a blood feud through the godfather ceremony (*kum*). In *The Mountain Wreath* (Petrovic 1986) the extermination of Muslims is placed outside this practice. When a blood feud arises between the novel's Muslims and Danilo's men, the Muslims suggest a kum to resolve it. This proposal is rejected because the ceremony requires baptism. There is no reprieve from "extermination of the Turkified" (Sells 1993, 42). Or again, in *The Bridge on the Drina* (Andric 1959) Muslim inhumanity is portrayed by the impaling of a Christian peasant suspected of attempting to sabotage the Turks' bridge project. The scene offers a graphic account of a stake driven up the length of the victim's body, at an angle calculated not to harm any vital organ, and exiting at the shoulder. He is then raised on a platform at the top of the bridge and left there to suffer his death in public view of the citizens as a warning against disobeying Turkish orders.

These performances of otherness made Muslims' Other and references to "ethnic cleansing" euphemisms for their liquidation and dehumanization in the process. Reports of the Bosnian conflict's astonishing savagery are framed ultimately by the relations between the combatants and their victims. In reality, the "enemy" was friend, neighbor, and even relative, which should have made Bosnia's strife improbable under the conditions of its populace's actual relations. As leaders persuaded their people to inscribe their friends and neighbors instead as the ethic of her, bonds of affiliation acquired an incomparably tragic twist. Most revolting were assaults on captive women who were repeatedly gang-raped over a period of time. Their assaults were made more horrific by the identity of their violators. Jeri Laber (1993, 3) reports the testimony of Fatima, a forty-year-old Muslim nurse, recounting how she was first raped by a Serbian doctor who called her name from a list. "Now you know how strong we are . . . and you will remember it forever. Where is your Izetbegovic [Bosnian Muslim leader] now?" She continued: "He was a *doctor*. . . . I would have expected him to be different from the others. . . . I knew him for ten years. We were in the same hospital circle. I saw him every day in the restaurant for hospital personnel. We talked, we were acquaintances, I never sensed any hostility. He was a golden guy, refined, polite." Her experience was not isolated. Laber, who interviewed rape victims from the Bosnian war for the U.S. Helsinki Watch Committee, was charged to gather credible testimony. She found several different patterns to the rapes there. However, "More often than not the rapes take place in public or are committed in front of witnesses, and they include a variety of sadistic acts intended to degrade and humiliate the victim still further. Women are raped without regard for their age or appearance and are threatened with the traumatic prospect of bearing 'Serbian babies.' All too frequently the aggressors are known to the victim: 'They were our neighbors' is a common refrain" (4).

The shared personal past of assailants and victims was a living refutation to the depraved narrative of ethnic propaganda. Rape as a war crime is unlike civilian rape. The violated woman cannot call to neighbors for help, seek police protection, or prosecute her assailant in court. She cannot seek medical attention or psychological counseling. None of the resources civilized society marshals to the aid of civilian rape victims is available to her. She is thrown to her own inner devices to cope with the dehumanizing brutality inflicted on her. Rape as a war crime is different from civilian rape in another way. We understand civilian rape as an assertion of power by the assailant in an attempt to subjugate his victim. Rape can exist as a war crime only in the context of a discourse. It requires a frame to legitimate the systematic degradation of captured women.[11] In the case of Bosnia, that frame was provided by virulent anti-Muslim discourse that portrayed them as Christ-slayers from within who had to be purged from the land. And what better denial of their victims' identity within this frame than to cloak them in the anonymity of mass assault? By maiming and disfiguring faces and bodies; by taking the other side's women to holding places where they were repeatedly, often publicly, gang-raped; and by slaughtering noncombatants in an ambush and then dumping their dead bodies in a mass grave the aggressors physically stripped their prey of their subjectivity. When Muslims were objectified in this way, it was easier to act with vengeance against them as the symbols of oppression in an ancient and bitter blood struggle whose narrative portrayed these aggressors as themselves the blameless victims.

On the other side, those who were engaged in killing and raping depicted themselves as prisoners of necessity. Robert Block reported an example of this thinking in his interview with a member of a Croat paramilitary unit then operating out of Mostar (18 November 1993). This unit was notorious for being killers. Branimir, the subject of the interview, was twenty-four, soft-spoken, good-looking, even angelic according to Block. Branimir reasoned how he had no choice but to kill civilians, since his paramilitary unit lacked back-up to take prisoners and he was fearful that if they were to be set free they would shoot him and his comrades in the back. So they had to be executed. This was not what he wanted, but events caught up with him and made him choose: take your stand or slink away like a traitorous dog. "I no longer have any of the friends I grew up with. They are all on the other sides. Serbs among Serbs. Muslims among Muslims. If I meet them again I wouldn't know what to say to them. There's no turning back now. The only thing left is to fight for Mostar" (9). After a pause he added the reflection, "In everything I ever did I only wanted to be perfect." Being "perfect" for Branimir meant putting into practice the art of killing taught him by a British mercenary: Locate a target populated mostly by women, children, and elderly; attack at night; create panic so that they flee by the only open route; set an ambush; slaughter them all. "I really don't hate Muslims," he told Block, "but because of the situation I want to kill them all" (10).

Each side told these tales to official panels and journalists. Each telling contributed to a narrative of alienation from ethnic "enemies" and of justification for retribution against their military and civilian populations. These tales also provided counternarratives of "civil war," of resurfaced "ancient hatreds" and "blood feuds" beyond comprehension to outsiders, of military risks posed to any intervening force by the Dinaric Alps, and of no strategic interest to the geopolitical order of the West. Although they provided a rhetoric of identity and justification, these narratives did not advance a political point that might compel international intervention or promote internal détente. In Ignatieff's words, "Hence, there was no narrative of neo-imperial interest to add pragmatic weight to moral concern" (1994, 3).

Nor did fear of an uncertain political horizon encourage a shared rendition of a common past. Although the history of Yugoslavia and the indigenous peoples of its republics offered alternative versions of past experiences from which to interpret their present and project their future, within the injustice frame of ethnic grievances every vernacular exchange of difference posed one more threat. These narratives did not dramatize the historicity of Yugoslavia or its traditions of multicultural community. They related alternative versions of historicity that produced models of self-selection based on aspirations for an ethnically pure national identity. Themes of difference and victimization invoked a historicity of blame and vulnerability sufficient to motivate both self-protection and an active policy of terror to achieve ethnic cleansing.

Accepting nationalistic narratives involved the Yugoslavian peoples in a very different story from that expressed during their lifetimes and called them to an ancestral identity predicated on eliminating the bonds of family and friends that had prevailed for decades and, in some cases, even centuries. They embraced a world exemplifying the Ricoeurean problem of the field of experience and horizon of expectation moving so rapidly in opposite directions that the present itself loses its meaning. Bosnian journalist Zlatko Dizdarevic captured the enormity of its anomie in her recollection of her last visit with her father:

> We spoke at length about life, about the past, about his grand-
> children. We didn't say a word about the future since we both
> figured it was better not to say anything about it. Accompanying
> me, as always, to the door of his house, my father said: "You
> know, Zlatko, I really don't have anything left to live for.
> Everything I've got in my head no longer applies. It was all a lie.
> I'll never see my grandchildren again. I'll never see Mostar, not
> the Old Bridge that I grew up under. I don't even have my vio-
> lin anymore since it was blown to bits a few days ago by a shell
> that hit next door. I think I'm going to die." (1994, 68)

The next day he did die, his spirit apparently having fallen victim to the haunting matter-of-factness of Branimir's summary that serves as the region's epitaph: "I really don't hate Muslims . . . but because of the situation I want to kill them all."

The ethnic narratives that fueled competing rhetorics of nationalistic aspiration were antithetical to a discourse of common understandings that might have fostered accommodation. How were these antagonists to engage an opposing viewpoint whose authors were dehumanized by powerful stories of identity? These antecedents incited forceful counter-rhetorics of ethnic insurgence. The mythos of conflicting cultural memories that portrayed neighbors as the menacing "Other within" produced a vicious cycle of nationalistic paranoia. Conflicting stories of victimization provided mutually exclusive justifications for policies and acts of mutual extermination and perverted the rhetorical possibilities of quotidian experiences that supported multicultural tolerance. Their common meaning of Yugoslav *difference,* now turned inward, made each an "expert" interpreter of the Other's subtlest signs. Each was able to detect "evidence" that "proved" he was in jeopardy and, therefore, must strike swiftly with deadly force or be killed. The only common understanding in this world seemed to be that Bosnia's Muslims, Serbs, and Croats should kill one another until the last drop of blood was spilled. This is not the lived experience of a common reference world; it betrays retreat to isolated archipelagos of mutual exclusion incapable of functioning as arenas of negotiation.

Contrasting Stories, Contrasting Possibilities

Viewed as a resource that contributes to self-production, the apparent ethnicity of Yugoslavian rhetoric is in stark contrast with the quite different story that was told through the frequent spontaneous outbursts of the national anthem and "International" by the Chinese students who occupied Tiananmen Square during April/May 1989. Nevertheless, both discourses appropriated a cultural model from which they could construct social transformations. Strong claims to patriotism and loyalty to national aspirations invoked by culturally shared stories and significant symbols are an acknowledgment of themselves as producers rather than consumers of their social situation, even when that production is itself tragically destructive of those who are not supported by its story line.

Such narratives demonstrate how partisan assertions of identity must be. Our cultural memories are necessarily prejudiced because they contain a pattern of associations and events that provide us with our place on the trajectory of history (Gadamer 1975, 323). They inform our historical consciousness by inserting us in a tradition that interprets events from a certain point of view. They contextualize current events and circumstances in a tradition of beliefs, values, and actions that retains the patina of life but that also may promote violence against its thematized villains.

To share in cultural memory is to feel the force of its valences, to know how to respond to them and apply them to one's own circumstances. In turn, stories and symbols draw on memory's communal force only if they fall within its orbit of good, beauty, virtue, and desire (Wells 1996). Put differently, shared stories and symbols derive their force from their connections to cultural memory. For example, the Communist Party may have been beset by its inability to resuscitate the Polish economy. However, of equal significance, it lacked access to the most fundamental beliefs that define Polish national identity and that rally allegiance and support, namely its historical resistance to externally imposed masters. The very existence of the *nomenklatura* identified the communists with an enemy (Russia) that countless generations of Poles had battled. The party fitted into Polish cultural memory of past oppressors.[12] This negative bond predictably encouraged Poles to do exactly the opposite of whatever the party advocated, since individuals or groups in a negative bond define their identity by division rather than by identification (Sennett 1980, chap. 1).

The partisan character of cultural memory, with its concomitant social discourses, adds further strength to the claim that social identity exceeds its spatial and temporal conditions. Cultural memory invokes relationship over exigency, thereby grounding social identity itself in relational terms. That is why, for example, the trio of forces creating the tragedy of Armenia is so resistant to a political bridle (Danielian 1992). The union of Karabakh with Azerbaijan since the 1920s leads the Azerbaijanis to consider Karabakh as now part of their republic. Armenians, who comprise the majority of Karabakh, see themselves in a different time frame and compass of cultural relationship, bearing affiliation with Armenia. Moreover, prior to Armenia's separation from the former USSR, Moscow found itself in a constitutional dilemma with serious political implications if it directly intervened and hence adopted a policy of de facto support for the Azerbaijanis and repression of the Armenians. Such instances remind us that groups and classes experience themselves in relation to other groups and classes, which makes status relative and necessarily produces disequilibriums of power, alienation, and counterassertions by the marginated aimed at reallocating society's resources. The conflicting stories whereby the Armenians and Azerbaijanis narrate the identity of Karabakh reflect these patterns of appropriating and investing the resources of history and cultures in their struggle to control their own self-production.

Finally, and significantly, the political upheavals in Poland, the former Yugoslavia, and the other Central and Eastern European nations generally suggest that the self-producing activity of a society's rhetoric depends less on forging consensus than on sharing a *common reference world*. Conflict confronts us with the paradox of inventing a public space in which to disagree. Antagonists must cooperate in order to air their disagreements. This need stands behind the call for civil society. Without civil society's ensemble of free associations, it is impossible to open a space for disagreement. Without a space of disagreement, the *we* that is the discursively created basis of social and political relationship could not emerge. A mosaic of competing interests cannot coexist as a society without a space for disagreement. When we create such a space, paradoxically, we open the possibility for the cooperative acts of mutually sustained dialogue on which a *we* depends. This dialogue depends on language that is understood, even by those whose views and yearnings do not coincide, and that projects a world shared in some meaningful way. None of these conditions requires consensus. Conversational associations in a public arena actually may be marked by intense disagreements. These disagreements arise and lend themselves to rhetorical development only because there is a shared understanding of what is significant even though the ways in which it is framed and its implications are projected may be hotly contested.

In the Warsaw Pact nations the party never overcame the profound gulf between its officially invoked reference world and that of the indigenous culture. The dissident factions of these societies were in apparent disagreement with the policies of the Communist Party. At every turn the party's insensitivity to the call for civil society, in which matters of national and social identity could be formed and celebrated, reinforced the conclusion that life was unbearable because it was false. The early secessions of Lithuanians and Ukrainians from the USSR, the objections of Croats and Slovens to continuing the status quo of Yugoslavia (Scammell 1990a, 1990b), and even the dissent of Chinese intellectuals, such as Fang Lizhi (1989; Link 1989), to the impositions of a central government were so pointed in their denial of the official stories as to suggest that such stories were invitations to live a lie. One finds similar characterizations by Poles of their national life just prior to the formation of Solidarity (Galtung 1980; Norr 1982). In each of these cases, in which the state impeded the invention of a public space, the possibilities of a common reference world receded.

Having noted the similar depictions of national life without a vibrant public sphere, one must also add that these nations are vastly different in their levels of diversity, which led to different narrative possibilities for forging their futures. Poland and the former Yugoslavia, for example, provide a contrast of ethnic homogeneity vs. heterogeneity, of unitary national history vs. plural regional histories, of unilingualism vs. multilingualism. Yugoslavians had been steeped in a rhetoric of nationalism that emphasized cultural differences and that required political accommodation rather than advancing shared multicultural identity as an achievement to be celebrated. As narratives of diversity retreated to themes of differences that had to be contained, the possibilities of a reticulate public sphere evaporated. The diversity of Yugoslavian reference worlds made it difficult to speak a language of common meaning once its republics set on a course of national identity based on traditional ethnic grounds. They required a common field of past experiences that would provide contesting ethnic groups with warrants for a future political accommodation. Instead it was as if their shared history as Yugoslavians were a caesura in public memory. The absence of an intervening tradition of democratic deliberation diminished whatever pragmatic weight might have come from the common reference world of class and regional grounds for identification. Indeed, the absence of a common reference world led to a rhetoric that emphasized differences, that presented obstacles to forging coalitions, and that encouraged lapsing into a paranoid political style.[13]

In obvious ways the language available to a people will circumscribe their possible social worlds. For an aggregate of strangers to have a shared understanding of reality requires more than a common code permitting intersubjective understanding. Since the world is seen from many perspectives, we are most certain of its realities when what appears before us is confirmed by the shared sense that its presence is noticed irrespective of our differences (Arendt 1958; Bowers et al. 1993). The writings of Hannah Arendt (1958; 1977) and Charles Taylor (1971; 1985) suggest that a *common* sense of reality entails a language that references a common world, even when our customs, preferences, and methods pertaining to that world are at odds. The diversity of complex societies and the range of social conversations in which the modern social actor participates carry the intimation that the demand for a common language is at once unreasonable and insufficient. No single language can encompass the diversity of interacting perspectives that bear on society's problems. Yet to understand and effectively participate in society's conversation requires literacy in the multiple vernacular and formal languages in which issues are explored and deliberated as well as sensitivity to the bonds of common meaning that dissect the heteroglossia of vernacular dialogues. This *common* sense entails a language that references a common world, even when our customs, preferences, and methods pertaining to that world are at odds.

The bond of common meaning is not shared values and beliefs but the sharing of a *shared* world, commonly understood even if diversely lived.

Adam Michnik (1981) provides ample testimony to the conscious awareness Polish dissidents had of the significance of a resonant vernacular language for the events that brought Solidarity to birth. In a speech delivered in November 1980 he explained why the communists were unable to resolve the problems of the country. He rejected the premise that submission to the terror of Stalinist Russia induced Poland's lassitude. Rather, he offers:

> The communists who arrived at the end of the war succeeded in imposing false solutions because they succeeded in imposing their language. I would even say that the debate over language is the debate concerning the entire intellectual life of these past 36 years. This debate over language leads us to reflect on the technique that governs communications between men. During the course of those years, most of our society lost its language. The reality was terrible and we could not find appropriate terms to describe it. (Michnik 1981, 67)

Michnik's view, expressed in the days when Poland's Solidarity movement was still heady with that summer's success at Gdansk, recurred as a leitmotiv throughout the succeeding decade. One cannot help but notice, for instance, that the dissident groups of Central and Eastern Europe strove to establish a realm where a nationally relevant discourse might occur. How else is one to decipher the agitation for access to television or the underground video productions and references to culturally significant events than as manifestations of the aspiration to use an alternative—in many cases vernacular—language capable of conveying relevant information and offering individual interpretations of ongoing events? Along lines we explored earlier, Central and Eastern European dissidents commonly understood the necessity of an open public sphere for informed political participation and to forge an authentic social will. Having won that battle, most of Central and Eastern Europe now is beset by the problem of multinational states being divided into ethnically pure ones. Serious social and political turmoil has accompanied attempts to limit vernacular and formal discourse that is inclusive and mindful of history.

This divisiveness is illustrated by some of the acts of those who have entered the political public sphere only after the communist regimes were deposed. In Czechoslovakia this element, in control of its legislature, passed the Lustration Act in October 1991. Lustration adopted a blanket assumption of guilt toward any member of society who had any association with the communist state. The act's arm reached to anyone who had engaged in any state-related activity, no matter how remote or insignificant, and bared that person from holding any civil position for five years. Those who were most aggressive in seeking vengeance had not been Czech and Slovak dissidents who suffered for their political commitments but those who remained on the sidelines during the communist rule. Laber characterizes them as coming "from the 'gray zone'—neither Communists nor dissidents, they sat back, did nothing to incur disapproval, and were not prosecuted" (1992, 7). One theory holds that their spirit of reprisal sprang from a guilty conscience. Whether or not that is so, Havel caught the felt contradiction in these legislators' ambivalence toward Czechoslovakian struggles over historicity when he characterized the law as symptomatic of a more profound problem. "We have not yet found a dignified and civilized way to reckon with our past," he told Laber (8).

In a similar vein Michnik (1993) upbraided those who sat on the sidelines during the communist reign but who afterward led the charge to discredit those who took a stand. In Poland these critics claimed that dissidents actually had prolonged communist rule. Michnik found this charge absurd on its face and insulting given its source. While the forces of Polish and Czech liberalization lost their battles of the Prague Spring and the Polish October, these dissident movements produced KOR in Poland and the Czech Charter 77, both of which expressed a new political consciousness. Moreover, both the Prague Spring and the Polish October reflected a crisis within the Communist Party, in which large numbers refused to obey the orders of the nomenklatura on the basis of moral principle. For those who were on the sidelines to say that these were mere interparty squabbles rather than turning points in recent history, he argued, "is to deny an important moment in national history, and to falsify collective memory" (Michnik 1993, 20). Moreover, since these accusers had chosen the alternative of accommodation over opposition, while others were taking risks and going to jail, they were living and working in safety within the official legal structures. One cannot reproach those who behaved this way. But Michnik professed his astonishment to hear those who, through their silent cooperation, had joined hands with the party—the "prudent, with clean hands" who had kept themselves at a distance from political conflict—accuse activists of having maintained links with communists.

Observing such struggles over matters of definition and technicality concerning who is to blame for the past, Havel expressed fear that their futility would provide the grounds for national demise. In his address to the General Assembly of the Council of Europe he warned that the velvet revolution would fail if "we believe . . . we need no more than discuss endlessly, or, more precisely, argue endlessly over technical matters without ever attempting to change anything in ourselves or in the habitual motives and stereotypes of our behavior" (Havel 1993, 3).

Here we come full circle, for a common reference world, as I have described it, would be impossible without cultural memory. As noted earlier, people form their knowledge of the progressive possibilities of their histories from experiences that have endured as significant moments and that resonate with the current times. The preserved and shared past becomes a vernacular inscription of deeds and values. It permits intelligible discussion of fundamental commitments and recognition of virtuosity. Without cultural memory social actors are denied the very terms on which they might understand their own reflexivity in creating their identity. They are denied, as well, the precondition for confronting the past. They are reduced from participants forging their future to spectators doomed to live a future in conformity with the past (Arendt 1965; Ash 1995).

This idea is expressed differently, but apropos of events in 1989, at a later point in *The Book of Laughter and Forgetting*. Kundera engages his friend Milan Hubl about the systematic dismissal of the historians from the Czech universities after the Russians have imposed Gustav Husak as their puppet president. Hubl was one of the 145 dismissed.

> "The first step in liquidating a people," said Hubl, "is to erase its memory. Destroy its books, its culture, its history. Then have somebody write new books, manufacture a new culture, invent a new history. Before long the nation will begin to forget what it is and what it was. The world around it will forget even faster."
> "What about language?"
> "Why would anyone bother to take it from us? It will soon be a matter of folklore and die a natural death." (Kundera 1981, 159)

To Kundera's mind, Hubl has posed the critical question. "Was that hyperbole dictated by utter despair? Or is it true that a nation cannot cross a desert of organized forgetting?" Events of the recent past suggest that the former was the more accurate interpretation. At least for these nations, the "desert of organized forgetting" was a compromised landscape, dotted with the oases of cultural models brought to consciousness by narratives of national tradition. They provide vernacular expressions of the stakes at issue in the clash with the authorities: social relations, and therefore power relations, that allow for the possibility of authentic social practices.

Conclusion: The Narrative Bridge from Tradition to Historicity

Insofar as the stories I have been sketching project a future through appeals to a people's destiny, they flirt with being grand narratives (Lyotard 1984). For these societies, and perhaps generally for societies during periods of focused resistance, there is great susceptibility to the persuasiveness of stories that direct coordinated actions with a script of identity. The images of the subjugated or marginalized of society may not be those which its vested and empowered segments choose to illumine with publicity, but the very fact that "official" images can be resisted indicates that society cannot be reduced to a self-reproducing organism. Although such stories may lack applicability beyond a specific national border or beyond an extreme set of circumstances, they nonetheless illustrate Gadamer's (1981, 41) point that a society has the capacity to posit the order of its own representations, to create its own historical environment.

This positing, it seems to me, is linked fundamentally to cultural memory. The rhetoric that accompanied the turmoil and change in the former communist states shared the use of stories from the past to advance alternative modes of governance, distribution of power and wealth, and assertions of self-awareness and identity. Cultural narratives were used for more than inspiration; they were a vernacular source of models for the type of society to which they wished to belong. These alternatives refrained from the neutrality of a scientific model or the universality of a hegemonic ideological model toward the history, traditions, literature, and religion of a definable national group. These models for belonging were located in the very features that were sui generis to that society. They were also qualitatively different from the controlling quiescence often induced by administrative narratives of nostalgia. These models were appropriated not as patterns to be reproduced but as a stock of resources with which to reframe political realities.

The use of cultural models as a means of production leads to a related conclusion: narratives that grow from cultural memory can be used to build a politics and society rather than as forms of popular consumption. That is to say that the narratives of these political actors were used differently than as cultural artifacts whose sole utility was entertainment or spectacle. The world of prudential conduct requires the capacity to act. Modes of communication that induce passivity are destructive of politics. Hannah Arendt (1968) has warned that the stories of historians and poets are debilitating modes because they render the audience spectators of the passing scene without the capacity to render judgment. Doubtless when politics is conducted through deliberate attempts to pacify with stories of leaders experiencing emotion or the drama of their actions to combat "wickedness" or justifications of policies disconnected from existing conditions that nonetheless are psychologically compelling nostalgic gratifications, this indictment is telling (Edelman 1988). But the important lesson of the tradition-based narratives I have been discussing is their presentation of an alternative world which a public could populate only through actions that reflected conscious choice.

Publics certify the validity of actions through judgment of their moral and aesthetic efficacy. These are contingent judgments pertaining to matters of public opinion; they do not necessarily lend themselves to verdicts of truth or falseness. Narrative form doubtless is rooted in the praxis of the historian and storyteller, as Ricoeur (1981) has indicated. However, it assumes rhetorical significance as it escapes the retrospection and spectatorship these forms encourage. There is a significant difference between the narratives of Central and Eastern European dissidents and the traditional tales of their bards (see Lord 1971). The present has its own reality which must be claimed through an interpretation. The point of the historical references we have been considering is not to situate their publics in the context of the historical past but to interpret the present in terms of an inherited culture and tradition. The Central and Eastern Europeans' *sense* of history contains more than a knowledge of or even a feeling for the past; it is an act of intervention by which they continue to shape their own destiny through their ongoing reacquisition of their respective traditions.

Of course, to intervene with narratives against a dominant rhetoric of totality requires the creation of conflict, from which social construction may develop, and a discursive space in which to raise it. A society's symbolic capacities and resources can be appropriated by its members to create knowledge of who it is and of who it wishes to become. We are instructed by the manner in which dissident and also exclusionary narratives invoke historicity. Their references to historically significant events move beyond the Gadamerean observation that every tradition contains its own prejudice. Although true, the Polish narratives contain more than simply substitution of one set of prejudices for another. By design they do not ask for commitment to a particular program but for disengagement from an existing one. The extreme case of the former Yugoslavian republics, by contrast, indicates that a narrative of national identity absent a positive program of inclusion cannot sustain itself over prolonged experience. One invites a public sphere of high participation and with openness to resolutions that can cut across narrow ideological commitments; the other invokes a sphere more constrained in whom it will admit and what its participants may say.

Nonetheless the Balkan lapse into internecine conflict and the Polish accomplishment of a bloodless revolution are similar in their invocation of narratives that appropriate a specific historicity through which they project images of a future somehow better for its embodiment of national ideals, even if its pragmatic policies remain unformulated. Their historical orientations and the relations they made possible were as if manifestations in politics of a Ricoeurean hermeneutical *distanciation* (1981) from the managerial power of the state or nation with which they were at odds.

Ricoeur discusses distanciation as a hermeneutical experience whereby the interpreter places distance between herself and her historical situation such that the conditions of subjectivity are no longer given in the discursive situation but are created by the discourse itself (1981, 143). Distanciation becomes the counterpart of *appropriation,* allowing the actors—those engaged in an active public—to understand at a distance the world that is "fore-given," or in front of the social texts to be appropriated. It is not an alignment of the present with the past so much as a construction of the future from an interpretation of the present.

This interpretive possibility is not unconditional. The Yugoslavian republics, for instance, experienced competing claims to historicity. Moreover, Yugoslavians lacked a vibrant civil society from which to draw a cultural narrative that celebrated their achievement of a multicultural society. The absence of a viable civil society coupled with federal policies to keep conflicting narratives in check strongly intimated that historical differences and grievances were important discriminators of identity. These conditions neither encouraged the emergence of an alternative sense of historicity nor defused the explosive force of ethnic narratives. They placed boundaries on the range of the "fore-given" world to be appropriated.

These boundaries bear on the availability of rhetorical resources to address rapidly changing social conditions. The degree to which the state and institutions succeed or fail at providing opportunities for broader participation in its official public sphere is attached to the possibility for critical dialogue to develop. In this respect, the postcommunist Polish church is not unlike the former Yugoslavia in its limitations. On the other hand, we must also note that unlike in Yugoslavia, Poland's embrace of civil society made it possible for new culturally relevant narratives to emerge and for rhetoric to play a central role in its ongoing self-production.

At the level of historicity, society is constructed as a normative world. For members of the public initiating change, reconstituting the existing order through distanciation from its apparatus suggests that the subject decouples from the apparatus. Put differently, these political transformations reveal the profound implications of narrativity for the emergence of the subject because they rest on acts of appropriation in which meaning is constituted by an investment of cultural resources that detach the managerial power of the state from the individual. At the level of the subject, we are led to conclude that narratives bringing historicity to consciousness construct rather than consume society.

The challenge to Poland and Bosnia, as to every complex society, is to build upon the resonance of its founding moments in public imagination. Sustaining a society capable of maturing and growing through themes that tolerate differences is an arduous task that requires a shared search for common direction and common action as the outcome of deliberation and choice. It is a task that requires attention to constituting publics enabled to form and express informed opinion, which is to say publics capable of recognizing and understanding phronêsis. As we have seen here and will see again in chapter 7, sustaining such a public is a fragile enterprise, easily undermined when political ambition supersedes an interest to deliberate the issues on their merits.

Finally, the narrative bridge between tradition and historicity provides insight into the role of narrative in legitimating political action. The discourses of Poles and former Yugoslavs decidedly are concerned with issues of economic and political power and of territorial integrity. Yet their opposition to or even disregard of the state proposes that responsible and meaningful political action is impossible without a tether to a people's national aspirations. Legitimate civil and political affiliations reflect the actors' sense of order in the world. It is significant that Polish narratives, for example, which borrowed heavily from religious tradition, did not use religion as the basis for constructing a God-centered society. These references were used almost always to emphasize a point about the individual. They were a basis for an alternative politics and, in the wake of the failures of the party's state-centered policies, made the party irrelevant to constructive thought about the future.

Examining a public engaged in structuring the present through acquisition and reacquisition of its tradition reveals how central historicity is to the interpretive enterprise of constituting our commitments. Our laws, customs, politics, and ultimately our traditions have force because we share a body of commitments to norms of dedication, acquiescence, acceptable contradictions, and even resistance. To be of the culture is to resonate to the call of its normative universe, to participate in its imaginative projection of an orderly world, to accede to its mythos as paradigmatic for behavior. The cultural bedrock, its sedimentary forms, are contained in its narratives. These bring to language the cultural consciousness that is essential to historicity and its creative possibilities for framing an alternative reality, a world that is other than given. They are essential to common action because they provide a means for shaping a common interpretation and evaluation of events. They give vernacular expressions argumentative value beyond their seeming mundanity through their dialogical presence in the practices of class and identity. They permit us to frame the civil judgment that emerges from the intersection of narrativity and historicity, to populate a world in which our words and deeds may be certified as sane.

Chapter 6

RESHAPING PUBLICS AND PUBLIC SPHERES: THE MEESE COMMISSION'S REPORT ON PORNOGRAPHY

> The plan was to have described to them, in the greatest detail and in due order, every one of debauchery's extravagances, all its divagations, all its contingencies, all of what is termed in libertine language its passions. There is simply no conceiving the degree to which man varies them when his imagination grows inflamed. . . . It would thus be a question of finding some individuals capable of providing an account of all these excesses, then of analyzing them, of extending them, of itemizing them, of graduating them, and of running a story through it all, to provide coherence and amusement.
>
> Marquis de Sade, *The 120 Days of Sodom*

We experience our bodies in incongruous ways. The privacy of our sensations, the personal awareness derived from physical acts, and the joys and pleasures aroused through intimate contact with other bodies teach us profound lessons about our personal identity and self-sufficiency. We experience our own body in ways that are unavailable to the inspection of others. Our pain or ecstasy is our own and known only secondhand to those with whom we share its secrets. But our bodies are also in the world. Like Adam and Eve after the fall, we encounter strange and unlike things; our innocence is lost, and we experience shame in our nakedness. Beyond the gates of our privacy we become aware of our flaws and experience rebuke for our personal insufficiency.

Richard Sennett's *Flesh and Stone* (1994) argues that we structure our public spaces, principally our cities, in ways that mirror how we experience our bodies. The incongruity between personal lessons of self-sufficiency and public ones of insufficiency is transferred to the tension between domination and civilization in urban spaces. We attempt to shape a civic realm that can protect us from our own weaknesses and those of others but also can accommodate our desire to turn toward those others and be open to experiencing them as the Other. The urban experience that Sennett describes is one of publicness. In the city we publicly encounter a discourse about privacy: the experience of the body, including the most intimate aspects of its private contact with other bodies.[1]

This urban discourse is part of a larger historical and cultural dialogue on the body. The voices engaged in this conversation speak in many arenas: the pulpit and confessional, medical practice, psychotherapy, the legislative assembly and the courts, urban and architectural design, fashion design, the arts, and, of course, the streets. These discursive arenas transform the personal and private experiences of the body into an object of public expression. As they acquire official status, whether by virtue of trust (as in the efficacy of medicine), faith (as in the redemptive power of religion), or ballot, they speak a discourse of power in which the individual's self-sufficiency is made the object of protection and regulation.

The incongruity between private experience of personal awareness and public experience of the body as an object of discourse, between private awareness of self-sufficiency and public rebuke for personal insufficiency, between private freedom of personal expression and public regulation of bodily expression renders these public discourses on the privacy of the body sites of contention. The deep discord they provoke within and across dialogized domains is most evident in discourses on sexuality. In the arts and in the streets, human sexuality is often explored as an avenue to self-awareness and self-expression. Historically their dialogized formation of the body has conflicted with more institutionally based discourses, such as those of religion and the state. Michel Foucault (1980) has argued that these attempts by religion and the state to regulate what may be written, spoken, or displayed about human sexuality are themselves discourses of power. Such discourses regard the body's sexuality as an object of knowledge controllable by an authoritative discursive practice. They censor unauthorized discourse on the body as pornography and ban it from the public sphere. Yet they don't speak uncontested.

Pornography comes from the Greek *porne,* meaning prostitute, and *graphein,* meaning to write, or literally writings of prostitutes. It is a form of communication that has existed since antiquity as an expression of humankind's sexuality. As a form of popular culture, it is a vernacular genre. Because censorship by church and state frequently have denied eroticism's legitimacy as a discursive exploration of the body, pornography has had to spend much of its existence as a clandestine discourse. Its shadowy reality has carried consequences for its readership. For some, its tenebrous existence has been symptomatic of pornography's exclusion from the literary public sphere and readers' access to the genre. Similarly, there are conflicting views on its admissibility in larger cultural projects of open discourse on representations of the body or political regulation of the body in the privacy of the domestic sphere (Downs 1989; Tisdale 1994).

Historically the forms of subjectivity whose roots lie in human sexuality have found haven from repression and domination by constituting themselves as a literary counterpublic sphere (Eagleton 1984). Literary counterpublic spheres are discursive domains in which censored works of art encourage self-reflection on taboo subjects. Pornography speaks a vernacular language of power related to libidinous urges and, as such, constitutes a site outside the disembodied rationality of the bourgeois public sphere that includes both pornographic works and discussion of the meaning and relevance of pornography to social experience. Its bonds of association are private experiences discussed by private citizens in private places in a social discourse about their subjective autonomy.

Yet their enclave is never completely isolated. As Marquis de Sade knew, "there is simply no conceiving the degree to which man varies [the possibilities of erotic pleasure] when his imagination grows inflamed." Quite apart from religious or cultural values, the bond between sexual intimacy and subjective autonomy makes pornography a continuing matter of public concern. Even when banned from civil society's literary public sphere and forced to constitute itself as a discursive formation within a literary counterpublic sphere, it has enjoyed continual thematic life in the institutional public spheres of politics and legislation. These open discussions have concerned social attitudes toward the explicit portrayal of sexual subject matter and the judgments of society on the manner in which sexual subject matter is portrayed. For example, often pornography has depicted women and children as sexual partners lacking power and therefore vulnerable to degradation and humiliation. Its proponents have argued that pornography is an artistic extension of human sexuality and, like all art, can lead us to deeper understanding of ourselves and the human condition. Censoring erotic productions is an infringement on rights of free expression. On the other hand, opponents have maintained that since it is a mode of expression that degrades women and children as inferior or powerless, it is a source of political imbalance with dangerous social implications and must be controlled. This is to say that pornography is a source of complex social issues (Downs 1989) and, therefore, interesting in itself as an object of discourse in society's continuing project of self-production. The form and function of society's public spheres in disposing of these issues promise insight into their self-understanding.

In a significant sense the shape of the reticulate public sphere in which an issue such as pornography is discussed serves as a barometer of a society's freedoms. Its structural requirements of accessibility, availability of information, means of dissemination, and audiences qualified to form as publics (Habermas 1989) presuppose, as we noted earlier, that certain rhetorical antecedents are met: that ideas may move across spheres, that dissident views may be expressed openly, that the language of deliberation has vernacular resonance, that participants are aware of their freedom of choice, and that tolerance for difference is valued. Satisfying these conditions is necessary for social actors to achieve autonomy; their absence tends to promote domination. Consequently, the unique character of a given public sphere sets parameters for the rhetoric a society can accommodate. Altering its character introduces corresponding effects on society's self-understanding. Possessing or losing one's franchise to participate in a public sphere alters power, shifts freedoms, and redefines the normative structures on which social relations hinge (Giddens 1984). As Alain Touraine (1981) has argued, one cannot escape domination without first appropriating historicity—one's capacity to define one's own meaning and the legitimacy of one's place and aspirations as a social actor. A shift in the character of the public sphere was precisely the action proposed in the *Final Report of the Attorney General's Commission on Pornography* (United States Department of Justice 1986).

The *Final Report* of the so-called Meese Commission, issued in 1986, became an instant source of controversy due to the way it chose to address these complexities. It called for radical initiatives with profound implications for what could appear in the literary public sphere and, ultimately, for the shape and character of that sphere itself. Its understandings of the body, vernacular discourse on the body, and the literary public sphere and its recommendations were themselves results of the type of public sphere the commission had made of itself. In this chapter I will examine the report as a source of controversy in relation to these public spheres. My focus will be on the contrasting formal and vernacular rhetorics of its internal and external representations of pornography. I am interested in how the report served as a legitimating instrument for extralegal regulation of the literary public sphere, how it became a contested site for the right to speak and be heard, the consequences of its rhetorical animadversions for symbolic constructions of the body, and the implications of these considerations for our understanding of the reticulate public sphere itself.

A Call to Reshape the Literary Public Sphere

In 1970 the President's Commission on Obscenity and Pornography reported that it could find no public harm caused by pornography and obscenity. That commission's report did not receive a warm reception from the Nixon administration or Congress. But its finding seemed in keeping with a Supreme Court decision that thirteen years earlier had afforded First Amendment protection to all materials except those that could be considered as "utterly without redeeming social importance" (*Roth* v. *U.S.*). Nor was it removed from the mood and tenor of a nation emerging from the Sturm und Drang of national protests over the war in Vietnam, civil rights, and university policies, not to mention the so-called sexual revolution.

The years following the commission's report saw a proliferation of sexually explicit books and magazines, music, film, and photographs available for public consumption. Moreover, the market for these materials seemed strong and growing throughout the 1970s. For example, the monthly circulation for the thirteen most widely distributed male entertainment magazines crested at approximately 16.5 million in 1980 (United States Department of Justice 1986, 1410). In the 1980s this volume subsided, most likely with a shift of consumption patterns to sexually explicit fare accessible on cable TV and in videocassettes. The expanded availability of pornography also increased its variety, ranging from nudity to the disturbing extremes of sadomasochism and pedophilia.

The Supreme Court's refinement of *Roth* in *Miller* v. *California* (1973) left each community with the responsibility of determining its standards of obscenity. Although some might say that during the period following the 1970 report America's taste for erotic and pornographic materials went from the risqué to the raunchy, the fact remains that few obscenity cases were successfully tried. The reluctance of most communities to introduce more conservative norms of censorship within the literary public sphere served as a tacit endorsement of the 1970 commission's views. The report did not endorse pornography but did endorse its right to appear, suggesting that without proof of social harm caused by pornography, wisdom lay in tolerance.

Sixteen years later, with *Playboy* and *Penthouse* having become common items on convenience-store shelves and with *Deep Throat, The Devil in Miss Jones,* and *Debbie Does Dallas* having entered the arena of middle-class experience, the Reagan administration determined to have the harmful effects of pornography on society reexamined. On 22 February 1985 Att. Gen. William French Smith established the Attorney General's Commission on Pornography. The rationale behind the commission's formation remains a point of controversy, though the ostensible reason was the enormous technological change that had transpired during the intervening years since 1970. Basically there was more porn more readily accessible to more people, which led moral conservatives, religious fundamentalists, and selected feminists to sound an alarm.

One year later, on 9 July 1986, at a Justice Department news conference held under the gaze of the "Spirit of Justice," French's successor, Att. Gen. Edwin Meese III, accepted the commission's report. The irony of the scene—America's chief law enforcement official accepting a commissioned study on the ill effects of public depictions involving sex while the Reubensesque statue symbolizing his office looked over his shoulder, arms uplifted and right breast exposed—escaped few, least of all that element of the press aching for a fight over a perceived attack on an area of First Amendment rights (Kurtz 1986; McDaniel 1986; Stengel 1986; Wines and Sharbutt 1986). The report triggered an immediate controversy that sustained itself in the popular press for the balance of the summer.

The expressed hope of the commission report was to encourage public discussion of pornography's effects on its consumers and on the community. Commissioners Becker, Levine, and Schauer, in fact, explicitly emphasized this hope in their personal statements (United States Department of Justice 1986, 179, 195). Surely this was an important objective in light of the growing concern of many over the effects that explicitly sexual depictions have on public and private perceptions and behaviors. Dismay over the characterization of women as sex objects had long been voiced by feminist critics of male-oriented magazines. While one may quibble over whether the contents of *Playboy* display liberated sophistication or adolescent fixation, serious concern had been raised about literature that depicts women as objects to be attacked, humiliated, mutilated, and raped, as enjoying physical abuse, or as consumed with desire for bestiality. Moral objections had also been raised against the depiction of pedophilia and the uses to which such portrayals were sometimes put as lures for children to cooperate as subjects of pornography or as sexual partners.

For many groups these matters appeared to support the formation of the commission and to invest it with the hopes of those who either saw themselves as victims of exploitation and violence or questioned the redeeming social value of such portrayals. Yet these hopes were denied because, from the moment of its inception, these normative concerns never became the focus of the debate. Rather the focus was the commission itself (Fielding 1995; Palczewski 1995; Stewart 1991). Why was this so, especially when the commission offered a report seemingly understanding of and sympathetic to these very concerns? I believe the answer lies in the manner in which the commission itself and its *Final Report* were perceived as a threat to the multiple public spheres in which pornography and its attendant issues and problems are discussed.

The commission's charter charged it "to determine the nature, extent, and impact on society of pornography in the United States, and to make specific recommendations to the Attorney General concerning more effective ways in which the spread of pornography could be contained, consistent with constitutional guarantees" (United States Department of Justice 1986, 215). The charter went on to outline a mandate of broad scope, including such items as studying "the dimensions of the problem of pornography," reviewing "the available empirical evidence on the relationship between exposure to pornographic materials and antisocial behavior," and exploring "possible roles and initiatives that the Department of Justice and agencies of local, state and federal government could pursue in controlling, consistent with constitutional guarantees, the production and distribution of pornography" (United States Department of Justice 1986, 1957).

Thus charged with finding a remedy for an assumed evil, the commission had its subject and its publics identified. Unfortunately, it found great difficulty in constructing an operational definition of the subject matter that constituted this evil (United States Department of Justice 1986, 227–32), a problem that eventually bedeviled its findings. After reviewing the difficulties encountered in providing a generally acceptable definition of hard-core pornography, the commission reported that it sided with Justice Stewart, who, although also unable to define hard-core pornography, admitted, "I know it when I see it" (United States Department of Justice 1986, 229).

The commission's publics were easier to identify. The examination of pornography as a problem of social significance had potential publics of wide scope: women, parents, and practicing members of organized religions come immediately to mind. At the same time, that segment of society already actively opposed to pornography and committed to curbing its spread was much narrower. Here is a list of those who, in keeping with what the *Washington Post* reported as the Moral Majority's[2] call for 1985 to be the year to clean up "filth" (Duggan 1985, C1), organized against pornography at the time the report appeared: The National Federation for Decency, Women Against Pornography, Citizens for Decency Through Law, Inc., Parents Music Resource Center, Concerned Women for America, Eagle Forum, Liberty Federation, Morality in Media, Citizens for Legislation Against Decadence, and Feminists Against Pornography. The leadership and agenda for many on this list embraced assumptions with a narrow band for accommodating diversity: moral conservatives, religious fundamentalists, and law enforcement officials were commonly in this constituency. Added to this list were selected feminists who defined the issue in simple causal terms. These were not the assumptions of liberals, the publishing industry, or a substantial number of feminists who defined the issue in complex terms of power and health. Such groups included: The National Coalition Against Censorship, The Media Coalition (drawn from publishers' associations), and the Feminist Anti-Censorship Task Force. Nor, apparently, were the commission's initial assumptions shared by a substantial portion of Americans, many of whom consumed pornography for enhancement of their sex lives. For example, a few weeks before the *Final Report* was issued, the citizens of Maine rejected a referendum much in the spirit of the report in its proposed curbs on pornography. The margin of defeat was two to one.

This division of perspectives, present from the commission's formation, had serious consequences for public response. Endorsing the report was framed as endorsing a morally conservative and Christian fundamentalist interpretation of an issue of personal and ethical concern. It also imposed serious restrictions on what might appear in the literary public sphere. Opponents portrayed the report as a threat to open and honest dialogue and debate on the issue. At the same time, the moral stigma associated with pornography carried equally weighty consequences for the public dialogue. To oppose the report required dodging the appearance of favoring sexual abuse of women and children and subordination of community moral norms to unqualified First Amendment protections for vile and degrading portrayals of sexual relations. The public debate may have centered on the commission and the validity and balance of its report; however, the transcendent issue spawned by the report was whether or not the literary public sphere was properly limited from outside in portrayals of human sexuality and critical dialogue on their meaning for constituting subjectivity.

The *Final Report:* Version I

Were one to read the commission report without prior knowledge of the venomous attacks to which it was subjected, one might conclude that it was at least struggling to present balanced and responsible analyses and recommendations, especially if one focused on the first quarter of the two-volume document or its initial 458 pages (Vance 1986, 78). These contain the specific statements of the commissioners, occupying nearly 200 pages. All express their views on selected issues addressed in the report, their reasons for the positions they took, their general endorsement of the report itself, and their disclaimers about time, money, and the recognition that not every recommendation was unanimously endorsed. This section also contains a dissenting opinion authored by two members, Judith Becker, associate professor of clinical psychology in psychiatry at Columbia University, and Ellen Levine, editor in chief of *Women's Day* magazine and a vice president of CBS Magazines. This is followed by a 218-page statement written by Frederick Schauer, a commission member and professor of law at Michigan, and endorsed by the other members. The Schauer statement offers the commission's analysis and argument. This is followed by a section specifying ninety-two recommendations to curb the spread of pornography. The remainder of the 1,960-page document consists of selected testimony and evidence, excerpts from pornography, summaries of pornographic books and movies, a rather extensive bibliography of pornographic literature and videos, and photos of the commission in action. These materials composed by the commission staff, more strident in tone and less thoughtful in analysis, led Becker, among others, to encourage readers to stop upon completing the Schauer report.

The Schauer statement is a smoothly written document that is scholarly in tone. It recognizes the complexity of its subject matter and is peppered with qualifying statements suggesting the need for caution in drawing conclusions. In this sense, it does not read as the conservative broadside the liberal community had anticipated and feared but rather appears to argue a reasonable position. It recognizes that the term *pornography* is problematic because it conveys a conclusion (227–32). It elects to favor the word *obscenity* instead because it has a legal meaning and therefore will enhance objectivity and fair treatment. The statement recognizes that recommendations to limit pornography are warranted only if harm is shown but is candid in admitting its inability to provide scientific demonstration of the causal link between pornography and harm (299, 306–12). At the same time, it acknowledges the complexity of establishing social causation and the danger of simplistic reduction to one variable as definitively causing a social consequence. While admitting the limitations, therefore, of a strictly positivistic approach to drawing inferences about pornography and public harm, the Schauer report offers a substitute argument for multiple causation, with a criterion of "common sense" (360, 381), to determine whether pornography was a likely contributing cause of the harm. For example, it is not in the best interests of a child to be sodomized or raped for purposes of making a pornographic video, nor is it in the child's interest to have his or her introduction to human sexual relations through exposure to such materials. Although it is impossible to show that adult antisocial behavior was caused by childhood experiences such as these, "common sense" suggests that these would not likely act as deterrents.

To illustrate the commission's argumentation invoking its "common-sense" criterion, consider this example of one of the milder depictions of the problems associated with pornography, the typical peep show:

> The peep show is often separated by a doorway or screen from the rest of the establishment, and consists of a number of booths in which a film, or, more likely now, a video tape, can be viewed. The patron inserts tokens into a slot for a certain amount of viewing time, and the patron is usually alone or with another person within the particular booth. The peep show serves the purpose of allowing patrons to masturbate or to engage in sexual activity with others with some degree of privacy, at least compared to an adult theatre, while watching the pornographic material. In a later portion of our report describing these establishments we note in detail the generally unsanitary conditions in such establishments. The booths seem rarely to be cleaned, and the evidence of frequent sexual activity is apparent. Peep shows are a particularly common location for male homosexual activity within and between the booths, and the material available for viewing in some of the booths is frequently oriented towards the male homosexual. (290)

Even if this does not establish a causal link to social harm, the repulsiveness of the scene encourages a "commonsense" conclusion that such establishments are a blight on the community. "Common sense" suggests that eliminating certain kinds of pornography and restricting others would eradicate this social cancer.[3]

The committee continues to recognize that not all pornographic materials are of this nature and to recognize that all legitimate First Amendment protections must be honored (250). Hence it divides pornography into three classes: sexually violent, nonviolent but degrading, and nonviolent and nondegrading materials (323–49). The first two require government and citizen action, while the third is beyond the realm of official redress since it clearly has First Amendment protections. Finally, the Schauer report leaves the reader with a series of recommendations that place emphasis on citizen action (433–58). It recognizes that the courts will not prohibit the distribution and sale of lurid materials and accordingly instructs the public on the stance to take on this issue. The public is encouraged to exercise its options of dissent through pickets and economic boycotts as effective local means to discourage the accessibility of pornography in the community (300, 361, 419–29).

These may be conservative claims, but they are not unreasonable or necessarily oppressive. Why were they perceived by opponents to represent a threat to the literary public sphere? To answer this question we must examine the commission and its report in terms other than its apparent presentation on pornography. We must examine how the *Final Report* was portrayed in the public press.

The *Final Report:* Version II

The Meese Commission Report may have experienced brisk sales, but the report that the general public responded to was the one that appeared on the pages of America's newspapers and magazines. Although sparsely covered by television, the report became a source of national debate at the newsstand. Its notoriety was principally attributable to American Civil Liberties Union (ACLU) attorney Barry Lynn, who, as a self-appointed commission watchdog, followed the panel to each location, securing court orders for the release of information and providing the working press with a steady stream of information and quotable interviews. From its inception through the *Final Report*'s reception and debate in the popular press, Lynn successfully galvanized a press portrayal of the Attorney General's Commission as an object of suspicion to the liberal community, as anathema to the publishing industry, and as a palpable threat to the civil liberties of the average American.

The generally negative reporting and commentary on the commission's activities and findings insinuated that the validity of the report was questionable along several lines. In part, the commission itself was an obvious target for Lynn and press attacks against its legitimacy as a body capable of dispatching its charge, especially since its charter foreordained it to collide with its 1970 predecessor. But the contrast between it and the President's Commission on Obscenity also strongly suggested that the current panel was a stacked deck appointed as a payoff to religious fundamentalists and the radical right who had staunchly supported President Reagan. This suggestion was enhanced when the press embellished on these differences in a manner intimating that the Meese Commission's findings should be regarded with caution (Hertzberg 1986, 21; Lipton 1986; Scheer 1986b, 160; Vance 1986, 78–79).

The 1970 commission was given a budget of $2 million and two years to complete its task. It was chaired by the dean of the University of Minnesota Law School, a renowned constitutional law scholar; its executive director was a social scientist; its staff consisted primarily of trained social scientists; its membership included representatives from law, medicine, the publishing and film industries, education, the social and behavioral sciences, and the clergy. Of its eighteen members, only the three clergy and one other had publicly expressed a prior view about pornography. The commission saw its work as establishing scientifically valid findings on which to make recommendations. Hence, it held only two public meetings but commissioned eighty studies to gain information relevant to its charge. Critics of the Meese Commission suggested that such factors lent credibility to the 1970 panel's conclusion that one could not demonstrate a causal relation between pornography and social harms.

By contrast, the Meese Commission was portrayed as a partisan effort intended to gloss over analysis while advancing a politically expedient recommendation. It had a budget of $500,000, or sixteen times less than its predecessor in real dollars, and one year for its work. The chair and executive director of the 1986 panel were local prosecuting attorneys who had achieved successful records prosecuting pornography. Its professional staff included three attorneys, and three of its full-time investigators were police officers. Eight of its eleven members had publicly expressed opposition to pornography prior to joining the panel. The 1986 panel saw its work as curbing pornography. Since this charge assumed that pornography had harmful effects, the panel commissioned no studies to determine the effects of pornography. Instead, the report relied on extrapolations from the existing literature to form "scientific" support for its recommendations while documenting the effects of pornography on social behavior through excerpted testimony found in other venues and contexts (actually included in the *Final Report*) and personal testimony recorded (although modestly included in the *Final Report*) in meetings of several days each held in six different cities. Even panel members were critical of relying exclusively on open sessions to receive testimony, since this denied them an opportunity to explore sensitive accounts in private where witnesses might be spared press coverage of their private consumption of sexually explicit materials (United States Department of Justice 1986, 196–98).[4]

As a federal commission, the panel spoke with an official voice. It was a body charged to study a problem of national concern and to make recommendations. The trappings of authority graced its findings, whatever they might be, giving them the weight of legitimation. Critics saw the combination of official charge to a panel with this one's predisposition as legitimating conservative and religious fundamentalist views that, in another form, would have been subject to challenge (Vance 1986, 78). Hence, the qualifications of the Meese Commission, as an official body, were questionable from the outset, and critics responded to it skeptically by making the commission itself the issue (Clark 1986; Kurtz 1986; Shenon 1986b; Smith 1986; Wald 1986).

Further, the commission's methodology aroused concern. If the press harbored reservations about the panel's composition, it was derisive in its portrayal of how the commissioners collected data and drew inferences. Commissioners Becker and Levine's dissenting statement had already commented on the one-sided testimony received in the public hearings and on the difficulty of drawing valid inferences when such partiality could distort the panel members' judgment "about the proportion of such violent material in relation to the total pornographic material in distribution" (United States Department of Justice 1986, 199). Their view was extended in the coverage available at the newsstand. Press coverage highlighted examples such as the above-mentioned visit to a Houston peep show (*People* 1986, 28–29), the scarcity of witnesses from the book industry (Bob 1986, 39), the selectivity with which witnesses were chosen (Hefner 1986, 58), and the extreme nature of the testimony received (Stengel 1986, 14–15). These reports and commentaries strongly implied, and sometimes asserted, that the commission received, reported, and based recommendations on seriously skewed data.

The briefest consideration of consumption data indicates that depictions of the panel as prudish, at best, spoke to a broad-based predisposition concerning sexually explicit materials. Since 1970 the pornographic movie and publication industries had thrived. More important, in 1970 the home video business had not existed. Its explosion since 1980 had made the consumption of X-rated movies common. As many as 40 percent of VCR owners reportedly bought or rented X-rated cassettes during 1985, and adult tapes were estimated to account for 20 percent of the total video market (Duggan 1985, C4). The growth in public distribution of X-rated videos coupled with continued substantial sales of male-oriented magazines were meaningful data supporting a counterclaim that significant numbers of adult Americans consumed pornography without apparent ill effects. Such liberality in private consumption of sexually explicit materials may explain why few public prosecutors had been willing to bring suit against producers or distributors of erotica. In addition to First Amendment guarantees, community standards exhibiting tolerance made a successful action extremely unlikely.

Such data also suggested a widely shared but not commonly disclosed predisposition toward debunking the *Final Report* while simultaneously jeopardizing the likelihood of balanced commission findings. Typically adults watch and read pornography for sexual stimulation. This private motivation is not commonly made a theme of public discussion. Consequently, although large numbers of Americans may have consumed and approved of certain types of pornographic literature, magazines, films, and videos, few were willing to appear before the commission to testify that they consumed erotica for personal sexual fulfillment without suffering harmful side effects. The lack of such witnesses deprived the commission of testimony that could have confirmed or denied whether the extreme forms on which they had focused were representative of the mainstream or were giving sex a bad name. In light of the apparent widespread consumption of sexually explicit materials without corresponding social harms in the vast majority of cases, the press portrayal of the Meese Commission's findings made them appear a one-sided fait accompli.

Beyond its implicit assumption of harm, the methodology was indicted for its witness testimony. The press focused on the types of witnesses that appeared and the special views of pornography they held. Most witnesses who testified against pornography had opinions colored by negative and extreme circumstances of sexual experiences accompanied by violence. For example, in the Chicago hearings a woman who reported having been sexually abused from the age of three by her father connected his sadistic behavior to pornography in this way: "[He would] hang me upside down in a closet and push objects like screwdrivers or table knives inside me. Sometimes he would heat them first. All the while he would have me perform oral sex on him. He would look at his porno pictures almost every day, using them to get ideas of what to do to me or my siblings" (788). Such witnesses, accounting for 77 percent of those who testified, called for greater control or elimination of sexually explicit materials. The force of such numbers was undermined, however, by allegations that only those with a supportive view were invited to appear. Rather than engaging these voices in a serious and sensitive dialogue on the issues their violent sexual encounters raised, they were dismissed on the technicality of perceived police bias. As one critic wrote, "The vice cops on the staff energetically recruited the alleged victims to testify, assisted by antipornography groups and prosecutors. The same zeal was not applied to the search for people who had positive experiences" (Vance 1986, 77).

Law enforcement officers comprised a significant number of witnesses (68 of 208). They opposed pornography because they associated it with crimes they had investigated: vice, rape, and child abuse, to name a few. Victims of incest, child abuse, pedophilia, mutilation, and rape as well as former porn queens and hookers opposed pornography because they associated it with the degradation to which they were subjected in contexts of sexual contact or the production of lurid materials. The popular press depicted their accounts in a manner that made them seem extreme and questioned their conclusions. For example, *Time* inscribed the testimony of Larry Madigan, thirty-eight years old, with quotation marks of incredulity: "[Madigan] told the commission he had been 'a typically normal, healthy boy,' whose subsequent life of solitary masturbation, bestiality and drug addiction could all be traced to finding a deck of pornographic playing cards when he was twelve" (1986, 15). *Time* cited Madigan to illustrate its claim that "there were times when the commission seemed to be on a kind of surrealist mystery tour of sexual perversity, peeping at the most recondite forms of sexual behavior known—though mostly unknown—to society" (14).

If this were a mystery tour, the commissioners were not unaware of the terrain they were covering. One commissioner described the experience of gathering data and taking testimony on the degradation reported as akin to sailing through a sewer in a glass-bottom boat. Doubtless such a depiction was in part due to the commission's scatological fascination. Even the most casual perusal of the descriptions of pornographic materials examined by the commission reveals a striking preoccupation with degrading acts involving fecal matter. Sexual depictions involving animals were another frequent inclusion. Press accounts used such details to suggest that the commission's concerns were with materials far beyond the mainstream (e.g., Grove 1986, D1, 8–9). At the same time, with a limited range of witnesses, the panel was vulnerable to the objection that its conclusions sprang from a biased sample that encouraged identifying depictions of rape, incest, bestiality, and sexual violence as typical pornographic fare. Undoubtedly the police officers to testify were competent investigators of criminal offenses involving sex and pornography. Equally, there was no reason to doubt the devastation of sexually abusive behavior on the witnesses who testified. But press portrayals urged that credibility required more than deference to authority or compassion; it required detachment and objectivity to entertain the possibility of alternative accounts. Again, the accounts themselves were not engaged. Their issues were displaced by deep suspicions over the commissioners' predispositions.

Although Meese made much ado over the commissioners' qualifications to deal with the subject, press focus on the commissioners' qualifications suggested that their religious biases and experiences as proactive agents opposed to pornography or as dealing with victims of sex-related offenses were signs that they would have difficulty being objective judges of testimony. Their vulnerability to this characterization surfaced at the commission's first meeting in Washington. One of the witnesses, Bill, recounted his molestation of two fourteen-year-old girls who were visiting his home. Bill was prepared to tell the commissioners what he had done and the role pornography played in his actions. His account was so pat, in fact, as to raise doubts in Commissioner Levine's mind. She cross-questioned him as follows:

> LEVINE: Can you tell me whether drinking was also a problem of
> yours and whether or not it continues to be?

BILL: Drinking was a problem in my life. I was drinking approx
imately two to three six-packs of beer daily.

LEVINE: Was drinking in any way one of the triggers that allowed
you to do things that otherwise you wouldn't have done?

BILL: Yes, it certainly was.

In an analysis of the commission's work published by *Playboy*, *L.A. Times* writer Robert Scheer observed that when Levine suggested to commission chair Hudson in private that the witness appeared to be coached, her concern was evaded. Scheer concluded, "The commission's questioning of Bill was typical of what would happen for the rest of the year—pandering to the antiporn witnesses to buttress the case and attempting to discredit those with a different position" (Scheer 1986b, 160).

At issue, then, were the witnesses' qualifications to determine the role of pornography in the behaviors they reported. And as a corollary, at issue was the level of understanding the commissioners were able to form of the problem from such a sample. These concerns, commonly appearing in major newspaper and magazine opinion pieces, portrayed a version of the *Final Report* that went beyond the commissioners' own statements and Frederick Schauer's report. They drew on materials appearing elsewhere in the document and on which the commission's findings seemed to rest. To place the matter in context, we must turn to that data to determine how they were presented in the report and in the press.

The graphic excerpts of testimony cited to support claims about pornography's adverse effects (767–835) engage the reader with brief depictions that can only be described in terms of distress, shock, and rage. These excerpts are provided to support the report's characterizations of the ghastly consequences witnesses had attributed to pornography:

A. Physical harms of rape, forced sexual performance, battery, torture, murder, imprisonment, sexually transmitted diseases, masochistic self harm, and prostitution.

B. Psychological harms of suicidal thoughts and behaviors, fear and anxiety caused by seeing pornography, feelings of shame and guilt, fear of exposure through publication or display of pornographic materials, amnesia and denial and repression of abuses, nightmares, compulsive reenactment of sexual abuse and inability to feel sexual pleasure outside of a context of dominance and submission, inability to experience sexual pleasure and feelings of sexual inadequacy, feelings of inferiority and degradation, feelings of frustration with the legal system, of alcohol and other drugs abuses.

C. Social harms of loss of job or promotion, sexual harassment, financial losses, defamation and loss of status in the community, promotion of racial hatred, loss of trust within a family, prostitution, and sexual harassment in the workplace.

The pathos of the testimony narrating this scene is wrenching. And the reader cannot avoid noticing this section's common reference to magazines such as *Playboy* and *Penthouse* as sources of sexual stimulation for their attackers. This joining carries the obvious implication that male-oriented entertainment magazines caused these horror shows. Although the Schauer report explicitly qualifies its stance so as not to call for action against this genre, the "testimony" section suggests that this genre is indeed among the culprits. For example, a woman alleged that her father used *Playboy* as an enticement to his molestation of her as a small child. The text reads as follows: "This father took a *Playboy* magazine and wrote her name across the centerfold. Then he placed it under the covers so she would find it when she went to bed. He joined her in bed that night and taught her about sex" (United States Department of Justice 1986, 775).

As in this excerpt, much of the evidence in this section is staff reportage, not direct quotation, of witness testimony. Further, this report, as with those throughout this section, contains no indication of witness interrogation. Similar traits characterize the following account by a mother whose son committed autoerotic suicide:

> My son, Troy Daniel Dunaway, was murdered on August 6, 1981, by the greed and avarice of *Hustler* Magazine [*sic*]. My son read the article "Orgasm of Death," set up the sexual experiment depicted therein, followed the explicit instructions of the article, and ended up dead. He would still be alive today were he not enticed and incited into this action by *Hustler* Magazine's [*sic*] "How To Do" August 1981 article; an article which was found at his feet and which directly caused his death. (797)

A reader must take or leave these accounts at face value, including, by their featured roles, the clear implication of *Playboy* and *Hustler* in the crimes reported.

Such presentations created complications for the report's recommendations. The severity of their violence demanded attention and remedy. At the same time, because they raised issues of human degradation and civil liberties that cut so deeply to the core of what it means to live in a civilized society, these traumatic episodes required more careful analysis than the witnesses themselves could provide. Here is a typical instance of victim testimony that illustrates the analysis witnesses often provided:

> When I first met my husband, it was in early 1975, and he was all the time talking about Ms. Marchiano's film *Deep Throat*. After we married, he on several occasions referred to her per-

formance and suggested I try to imitate her actions. . . . Last January . . . my husband raped me. . . . He made me strip and lie on our bed. He cut our clothesline up . . . and tied my hands and feet to the corners of the bedframe. (All this was done while our nine month old son watched.) While he held a butcher knife on me threatening to kill me he fed me three strong tranquilizers. I started crying and because the baby got scared and also began crying, he beat my face and my body. I later had welts and bruises. He attempted to smother me with a pillow. . . . Then, he had sex with me vaginally, and then forced me to give oral sex to him. (774–75)

Without further comment of its own, the report invites the reader to regard this and the other accounts as leading to a self-evident conclusion. In fact, the report explicitly eschewed any commentary on findings. In its own words, "We have tried in this chapter to allow victims to speak in their own words, without interpretation or commentary" (769). Thus a reader is left with witnesses' analyses, often based on the emotional distress that accompanies the degrading violence of sexual assault to which they were subjected. The reader is not asked to make a rational inference of causation but to deal with the victim's hurt. Without further discussion the rhetorical dynamics of inflammatory testimony of this sort enrage and cry for action. They preempt the ethical foundations of the issue, making it difficult to question the implied causes or to advance remedies without appearing to lack moral sensitivity.

Of course no one, except possibly the staff who authored this vital section, could reasonably expect this testimony to dictate action without further discussion. The question was how such discussion should proceed. Here we should recall our earlier consideration of the difference between Enlightenment standards of rationality and rhetorical modes of reasoning. By Enlightenment standards, facts cannot be fully meaningful without locating their causes, whereas the premodern discussion of issue formation located the *causa,* or cause, of the issue in the facts themselves.

For adherents to the scientized epistemology of modernism, the objectivist/relativist binary dictated that this evidence was deeply flawed. For example, it suggested that the general indictment of magazines such as *Hustler* as causes of sexual violence was an oversimplification at best. Were it true, the several million monthly readers of these publications would have constituted a massive public menace, not to mention the corrosive effects on the commissioners who were steeped in far worse for a full year.

One might then have wondered at the types of conclusions permissible from the savage assault allegedly sparked by *Deep Throat.* Was it evident that this would not have occurred had the perpetrator not seen *Deep Throat,* or that pornography or certain types of pornography or too much pornography caused crime, or that sexual relations or certain types of sexual relations were dangerous? Was it evident that the husband required psychological treatment? And what of the lurking hints that there may have been drug or alcohol abuse, or that the husband may have had a problem accepting his role as father, or that the marriage was generally troubled? Nor did the reader know of the events prior to the episode that may have acted as a trigger. In the context of a report charged to suggest legal remedies for the spread of pornography, these questions went begging. Without the antidote of wider, perhaps more analytical testimony, however, the commission may have denied itself a repertoire of alternative accounts for critical assessment of its evidence. Moreover, it made the procedure and perceived bias of the commission itself the source of controversy.

The provocative nature of this testimony, coupled with the absence of analytical assessments of witness accounts, only further fueled the dialogizing depiction of the commission as engaging in an ideological witch hunt. Doubtless there was little rhetorical advantage to be gained by challenging the victims' analyses of such overwhelmingly vicious attacks, but equally, once the focus shifted from discussing the public and personal harms of pornography to the threat posed by a "witch-hunting" committee, the attending public had little chance of connecting with the pathos of these accounts because they were seldom publicized.

I have examined the accounts in the *New York Times*, the *Washington Post*, the *Los Angeles Times*, major newsweeklies, and other magazines that engaged in reporting and commenting on the commission's work. The more than 250 newstories and commentaries I examined contained not a single verbatim report of a woman's testimony. The few mentions of witnesses that did appear characterized them in ways that reflected more on the commission as a source of controversy than on those who testified to tell their stories. For example, Carole Vance asserted: "The commission's 300-plus hours of public hearings and business meetings featured zany, if unintended, comedy: vice cops, born again Christians and prosecutors thundering indictments of pornography and its progeny" (1986, 65). Testimony that was reported typically was by contrite men whose accounts of abuse involved admissions of alcohol and drug abuse at the time of their acts, or stories so extreme in their perversity that the reader was invited to suspect the person had a psychological disorder. In these cases the stories were treated as anecdotes that could not establish a causal relationship between the consumption of pornography and sexual violence. Tragic as any individual case may have been, it came to the reader through the filtering process of press and commentator or special-interest voices intent on debunking the commission as embarked on a witch hunt.

The women lost control of their story; we are not engaged *by* the plight of their bodies but through redacted versions that are *about* their plight. Unlike the hunger striker, for example, who uses the body to make a point, the sexually abused body does not present itself directly to us. It comes to us through a discourse several steps removed from the physical body in pain. Rather than a discourse *of* the body, it is *about* the body. It is a discourse about words and images whose consequences are subject to myriad interpretations. The bodies depicted in sexually explicit materials, ranging from erotica to the extreme of obscene depictions of abuse and degradation of the subjugated partner, became the source of a complex discourse difficult to confine to an overriding issue. Was the question of pornography really about freedom to engage in erotic expression, or violence, or public health? In the discussion of a public problem they do not own (Gusfield 1981), the victims were unable to control their own narratives. Their bodies' synecdochic representations of the issues were lost as their stories were appropriated by others as anecdotal and became no more than more data to consider.

Even the *Final Report* itself co-opts the bodies it purports to protect. Its chapter offering testimony on sexual violence provides excerpts from testimony and letters ostensibly directed to the commission. Of the testimony reported, however, only a fraction was presented to the commission itself. The majority was excerpted from the Minneapolis City Council hearings on 12 and 13 December 1983 regarding a proposed city ordinance to restrict pornography and inserted in the commission's own contexts to support its points. These points were then later challenged in the cultural imagination by works, such as Sallie Tisdale's defense of erotica *Talk Dirty to Me* (1994), in which comparable narratives were inserted into benign contexts. The instability of meaning attached to these bodies opens them to multiple readings that deny them the force of, say, the hunger striker's starving body wasting to extinction before our very eyes and its identification with the cause for which it is starving itself to death.

Without any internal interrogation of these bodies, their pain lost its rhetorical force. Lacking an operational definition of what constituted pornography, the commission could not specify precisely what caused the misery parading before it. Without the methodological requirements of cross-examination or the presentation of expert interpretation and analysis of testimony, the commission's thinking could be portrayed as reductionistic. The commissioners' report discussed the testimony only in terms of the presumed problem of pornography and the presumed solution of legal changes. On the other hand, the debunking version suggested that pornography was not the real problem, from which it followed that the report's recommendations were no cure (Goleman 1986, A35; Hefner 1987, 28–29; Scheer 1986b, 167; Shenon 1986a). The report was challenged for the unrepresentative sample of pornography examined and for being prudish in its shock at what millions of middle-class Americans take as commonplace (Nelson 1986). Press accounts and critical commentaries suggested that it was plausible to ask whether the victimage examined was more basically a problem of health and welfare requiring a completely different analysis and remedy than a problem of sexual portrayal requiring legal remedy.

In light of the profound implications for a democratic society that accompany any restrictions on its access to the public sphere, the aforementioned concerns made the Meese Commission and its report seem threatening to a significant range of citizens—journalists, publishers, physicians, lawyers, and educators, among others (e.g., Wines and Sharbutt 1986). Consequently, the findings themselves were challenged on the grounds that the commission had failed to establish a causal relation between pornography and sexual violence and that it was using an emotionally loaded topic to abridge civil liberties. By these turns in the public controversy surrounding the report, the women's voices effectively were silenced, as the commission's major burden of proof became demonstrating causality between pornography and physical, psychological, and social harm.

Attacks demanding causality were widespread in press coverage of the report. No fewer than thirteen articles and editorials appeared between 11 May and 20 July in the *Los Angeles Times,* the *New York Times,* and the *Washington Post* objecting to the failure of the commission to demonstrate causality. Specifically, the commission was pilloried for its failure to base its recommendations on a scientifically established causal relation between pornography and harm.

Certainly this objection was not a distortion of the commission's position, since the commission had not advanced a scientifically based argument for causation. Instead it had argued that social behavior had multiple causes which could not be accounted for in social scientific research. The "commonsense" criterion was advanced in place of direct causation, buttressed with extrapolations from social science research on pornography. The commission concluded, for example, that extended exposure to increased aggressive behavior directed at women will increase one's level of sexual violence and that substantial exposure to violent, sexually explicit material will cause an increase in the rape myth (United States Department of Justice 1986, 325, 327).

Press accounts used the admitted absence of the strongest possible causal claim as evidence of the commission's problematic reasoning. The press paid scant attention to the commission's rationale of complexity but embellished on the absent evidence of direct causation as proof of the commission's inquisitional leanings. The commission's predisposition to curb pornography was portrayed as leading it to raise a smoke screen on the causal issue because no causal relationships existed. The commissioners' actual argument for a "commonsense" criterion was not engaged. News coverage pointed, instead, to social scientists who had appeared before the commission but did not believe their studies supported the causal claim the panel was alleged to have advanced. The incriminating evidence was not the Schauer report but the aftermatter, especially its reportage of sexual violence. Speaking in the *New York Times,* University of New Hampshire sociologist Murray Strauss observed, "The panel seems to have deliberately released its findings before we [the social scientists who testified or were cited by the commission] could meet [at the Surgeon General's request], because they were afraid that the social scientists' conclusions would contradict theirs. . . . I dispute their conclusions because they are not in accordance with my understanding of the scientific data" (Goleman 1986, A35). The article continues to cite Professor Strauss's report that although social scientists have found eleven factors correlated with rape, none was related causally. Moreover, the rebuttal emphasized the scientific community's contention that sexual assault was not a problem of pornography but of violence.

As already noted, the research cited to support the point did not specifically investigate the relationship between violent pornography and sexual behaviors. It was more concerned with violence than with sexuality. The assumed relationship between pornography and antisocial behavior became self-confirming when the panel interpreted aggressive behavior toward women as a portent of a *sexual* offense rather than one of violence, as the researchers maintained (e.g., Donnerstein 1986). The irony of this shift in focus was underscored by Michael Kinsley, who remarked in the *Washington Post* (1986, A25) that one could not conclude that viewing sexual violence induced violent behavior with any significance beyond that encouraged by, say, slasher films or a steady diet of Sylvester Stallone.

Anyone who accepted the press's reading of the report could hardly avoid the strong impression that the commission's contention of a link between pornography with violence was reinforced by the skewed body of testimony it received. Many of the witnesses who averred that pornography caused irreparable tragedy were not in a position to form an objective or competent opinion: law enforcement officers, who formed judgments based on their encounters with a highly selective sample of society and always in the context of crime; religious fundamentalists (Hiaasen 1986, 53); and victims, whose own tragic circumstances tended to confuse consumption of pornography with the fact that they were victimized by another's sexual behavior.

Finally, the dissenting members of the commission, Barker and Levine, were commonly cited in front-page coverage of the report upon its release. They also were invoked by the report's antagonists as specifically arguing that the conclusion of causality could not be teased from the data at the commission's disposal. Their demurrer suggested that, in the presence of substantial methodological flaws, one reached the claimed causal link only by smuggling in an ideological bias (Fields 1986, 14).

Collectively these difficulties with the commission's methods and assumptions transformed the seemingly evenhanded and well-reasoned

Schauer report into a threat to the literary public sphere and to selected publics of some significance. The Schauer section discussed pornography in terms that are more general than the examples I have been considering. But the extreme nature of examples that appeared in latter portions of the report suggested that they were the norm. Consequently, despite the commissioners' disclaimers, when the Schauer section was read in light of what appeared after it, the report left the impression that pornography is pornography is pornography. To protect the community, it had to be banned entirely from the literary public sphere.

By contrast, the press version strongly intimated that freedom of speech was the central issue, albeit one given relatively little consideration, consistent with the commission's determination to focus its attention on materials that would satisfy a legal test of obscenity. Freedom of speech was discussed by Schauer as a "constraint" on what the committee might recommend, and it also received consideration near the end of the report when social scientific and legal evidence bearing on the harms and regulation of pornography was considered. Indeed, out of a total report of nearly two thousand pages, slightly fewer than eighty were devoted to this topic, a disturbing balance in light of the panel's charge to honor First Amendment protections. By contrast, press accounts were ashimmer with reminders of First Amendment rights (e.g., Kurtz 1986, A8; "An Issue of Consent" 1986; Shenon 1986b; Smith 1986; Wald 1986).

Reconstructing the Public Sphere

Had Version I—the first 458 pages containing the commissioners' individual statements, the Schauer report, and the commission recommendations—remained uncontested regarding the commission's composition and methodology, a national debate on pornography conceivably might have ensued. But Version II, or the version that was constructed through press accounts, so challenged the credibility of the *Final Report* as to make the commission itself the focus of controversy (e.g., Scheer 1986a). On the one hand, it portrayed itself as a champion of the public sphere, of the public's right to know, to discuss, and to decide. Conversely, by virtue of seeking legal restraints on what may appear in public, it acted as an antagonist toward the literary public sphere. The commissioners could protest in the public press as loudly as they chose about the balance and responsibility of the report, but its purported argument shouted a completely different message. Inflammatory testimony coupled with specific recommendations for public action gave the document incendiary potential, especially for local mentalities distrustful of a complex world and fearful that it meant them harm.

For the vast majority of Americans whose knowledge of the commission's findings were informed by the press, the document was portrayed to argue for an interpretation of all explicit treatments of sexual relations as deleterious to the public welfare. The vernacular rhetoric of pornography was dangerous. It threatened the literary public sphere much as ancient Athenian critics of political rhetoric feared it threatened the civic arena. The skillful orator could raise the body's heat with words chosen to inflame strong emotions. Bodies convulsed with passion did not lend themselves to collective control.[5] Nor were bodies aroused by this vernacular genre prone to self-control. The community had to be protected from the wild behavior loosed by its graphic sensuality.

Interpreted in this way, the report seemed to address particular audiences who were either vulnerable to or receptive of appeals that confirmed predispositions opposed to sexually explicit depictions. To readers of the press version, one audience lacked experience with pornography. They were most vulnerable to inferring that mayhem loomed were this rhetoric of the body not banned. For that audience, pornography appeared as the clear cause of child abuse, incest, rape, physically violent sex, pederasty, and homosexuality and as contributing to the welfare of the underworld and to urban blight. The press version portrayed a second audience composed of moral conservatives and religious fundamentalists, for whose views the report provided legitimation now authorized by the government's voice. A third audience was projected as those who shared feminist concerns about the relation between pornographic portrayals and the specific issue of sexual crimes as well as the larger issue of stereotyped and degrading depictions of females as sex objects.

For those who may have been consumers of erotic literature and films, the press accounts of the report depicted an environment hostile in its judgment of their private lives. Reports of the commission's leanings reinforced the taboo pornography carried in American public culture. Rather than encouraging dialogue, the press version introduced the threat of moral predispositions that could only discourage them from speaking out.

Hard-core pornographic films and writings already live a shadowy existence. In the United States urban zoning ordinances protect cities by segregating movie houses and adult bookstores specializing in hard-core pornography from mainline commercial districts. The literary public sphere ignores its productions. Films and books that are difficult to convict in court as obscene are commonly judged to be so by editors, critics, and public intellectuals. The fact that they are ignored as literary trash sets them apart from other erotic discourses that have been hotly contested in the literary public sphere as well as in the courts, such as those of James Joyce and Henry Miller (Eberly 1994). Only works regarded as having literary merit become a source of opinion and debate, as was the case with Brent Ellis's *American Psycho*, a novel dealing graphically and repeatedly with themes of violence in connection with sexual acts, whose appearance provoked a controversy that attracted such luminaries as Norman Mailer as its literary arbiters. The distinction between pornography with literary merit and obscene trash runs so deep that when noted feminist author Andrea Dworkin's *Mercy*, a novel that uses explicit depictions of traumatizing sexual abuse since childhood to explain the consciousness of a woman who becomes a guerrilla warrior dedicated to killing men, was ignored by the literary public sphere, it became a source of inquiry into the relationship of its discourse on the body and the nature of the sphere itself (Eberly 1993). When the topic shifts from literary merit to a serious defense of pornography, as occurred when writer Sallie Tisdale published an essay in *Harper's* (Feb. 1992) in which she argued her case in graphic terms that described her own viewing experiences, it provokes strong reactions, including condemnations of the social and moral consequences of graphic sexual depictions on individuals and the community and also condemnations of favorably disposed critical commentators themselves for their apparent endorsement of abusive sexual practices ("Letters" 1992).

More than anything, within this general climate of public discourse the press version encouraged a spiral of silence, a condition of public expression in which the individual's sense of what everyone believes provides an indication of what one must or must not say in public to be acceptable, a judgment made irrespective of personal beliefs or commitments (Noelle-Neumann 1993). Freighted with these associations, there was too much ground to defend. The press version highlighted and intensified the dangers of speaking out; prudence dictated safety in silence.

For those who chose to address the issues being contested in the national debate, press focus on the commission itself proved counterproductive for enlightened discussion of the serious problems associated with hard-core pornography. By underspecifying the cause of the harms it reported, the *Final Report* served more as an invitation to polemics than to discussion. Version II reflects the consequences of a public document perceived to leave no ground for disagreement without appearing supportive of the morally reprehensible practices depicted in the cited testimony or callousness toward the cruelty to which many of the witnesses were subjected.

With pornography itself thus suppressed as a viable issue of debate, dissenting voices gravitated toward the quality of the report's reasoning. The problematic character of the causality claim made the specific recommendations of the commission necessarily appear as a form of censorship (Baker 1986; Hefner 1987, 27–28; Hertzberg 1986, 24; Vance 1986, 81). Especially troubling was its invitation to form citizen watch groups for surveillance of merchants trafficking in pornography. It made the explicit recommendation that they picket and boycott to exert economic and moral pressure. For many this appeared an open invitation to vigilante action as a form a censorship. The potential to intimidate patrons from doing business with a merchant extended clearly beyond "adult only" establishments to enterprises that carried such items as *Penthouse* or X-rated films in their inventory but were not devoted primarily to the sale of pornography.

This fear was not unfounded. The call apparently was heeded, if increased mobilization by antipornography groups shortly after the report appeared was an indicator (Kurtz 1986; Quinn 1986; Rangel 1986; "Clerics Sign Antismut Statement" 1986; Sharbutt 1986). And the fear was only intensified by the infamous Sears letter. Alan E. Sears, who served as executive director of the commission, sent a letter to convenience stores following the testimony of the Reverend Donald Wildmon, a notoriously outspoken opponent of all sexually explicit matter. Included in his crusade were magazines of the *Playboy* variety and their common outlets, America's convenience stores. Mr. Sears's letter outlined Reverend Wildmon's charges and offered the accused an opportunity to reply. In an act of questionable judgment, he warned that failure to respond within ten days would be taken as an indication that they did not contest the claim. A substantial furor ensued, which led to a court order that the letter be withdrawn. Nevertheless, the 7-Eleven chain took *Playboy, Penthouse,* and their likes off its shelves. The public reason for its action was 7-Eleven's own polling data that showed its customers wished these magazines withdrawn from display. Whether the chain was responding to its poll findings or to its perception of a new moral militancy with which the commission was in tune, the fact remains that a form of coercion tantamount to censorship was being exercised. The parent Southland corporation no longer considered it safe to display these magazines. In effect the vernacular appeal of Southland's actions made it complicitous in a spiral of silence by intensifying the perception that it was dangerous to be identified publicly as a consumer of sexually explicit magazines.

The aura of moral militancy encouraged by the commission's urging of citizen action and the Sears letter spoke in harmony with the Reverend Jerry Falwell's much-publicized crusade against *Playboy.* Two weeks after the *Final Report*'s release, *Newsweek* (McDaniel 1986) suggested that this mood was spreading when the Wal-Mart chain ordering its 890 outlets to remove thirty-two rock magazines from store racks. The *Washington Post* (Mann 1986, B3) suggested that the Reverend Jimmy Swaggart's criticisms of rock magazines as a form of pornography had done its part in encouraging the wisdom of such a decision. In light of the massive television audiences commanded by fundamentalist evangelists, the threat of citizen action leading to mass censorship seemed more likely now that the commission had given its legitimating endorsement.

For the concerned citizen reading of such events in the daily paper, the authoritative speech of the report was enacting a Bakhtinian reversal by publicly dialogizing a vernacular rhetoric of the body in a way that distorted the civic public sphere. Its message was clear: it was not safe to say that one read erotica; it was not safe to deny that pornography commonly turned its consumers into antisocial maniacs. The very terms in which the issue was presented made such admissions of practice and belief equivalent to relinquishing one's claim to being a moral person.

Thus, the argument of the report, especially the portion written by Frederick Schauer, was perceived as encouraging legislative and citizen initiative for a conservative and fundamentalist interpretation of sexually explicit matter. Moreover, the sobriety and moderation with which the Schauer portion was written made the *Final Report* appear to legitimate this interpretation with its own voice. Schauer wrote with an audience in mind, having been prompted by the blatant overstatement of the commission's work which he professed would not be acceptable for any responsible person to sign. His massaging of the data put them into more temperate language that saved the report and the commission from being publicly laughable. It was now a document to be taken seriously, with potential to encourage action with weighty implications for freedom of expression in the United States on sexually related matters. The more extreme views presented in the report's later sections, moderated by Schauer's temperate and decorous tones, made the commission report a threat to the shape of the literary public sphere. Ironically, it discouraged enlightened social dialogue on the body as a locus of tension between the self-sufficiency of an autonomous subject and the personal insufficiency of a subject objectified through an imbalance of power that required civic protection and regulation.

Conclusion

The Meese Commission did not have a profound effect on the spread of pornography. The antipornography initiatives that did surface during the Reagan administration issued primarily out of the attorney general's office. One reason for legislative distaste over pursuing the commission's recommendations is found in the Maine referendum noted earlier. Given the chance to endorse measures in the spirit of the *Final Report*, two out of three Maine voters said "no." The message was clear to politicians looking for votes.

But there is another reason for the report's apparent lack of impact. The stated intent of the commission was to provoke an informed dialogue on pornography. But it was impossible to have a dialogue when the methodology of the report seemed to satisfy voyeur interests with de Sade–like skill at presenting sensational testimony accompanied by summaries and bibliographies of the most degrading pornography available. How was it possible to have a dialogue when the report made it impossible to advocate the opposing side without indicting oneself as morally corrupt? Equally, how was it possible to have a dialogue when the women's voices were portrayed in a way that made their stories dismissable as merely anecdotal. The stories of women who had been subjected to horrendous forms of degradation and humiliation were urgent pleas by bodies in pain for a civil society's compassionate intervention. However, their transportability to multiple contexts made each woman's story just a story. Ultimately, their inability to control their own narratives or their treatment as personal stories and, therefore, their evidentiary status prevented the vernacular rhetoric of their bodies from becoming paradigmatic in a way that compels social action. For citizens whose issues were other than legal, the skewed public sphere of this debate was lacking as an informed context for discussion, although it was well suited for polemics and ridicule. The *Final Report* did not promote discussion on pornography because it did not provide insight into pornography.

In terms of larger theoretical concerns, the report's failure to produce a meaningful dialogue from which a stable public opinion could emerge provides confirming evidence for the rhetorical conditions that temper the shape and function of the reticulate public sphere itself. The mosaic of discursive actively within the reticulate public arenas considering a public problem will test the permeability of each public sphere's respective borders. Publics form through bonds of association that must, of necessity, forge links to those engaged in other arenas. When this does not occur, those who are advocates for a particular point of view are reduced to the status of a special interest. Whatever authority insular groups may possess or attempt to possess becomes a display of power rather than a shared basis for public action. The exclusion of alternative voices from the commission's witness list undermined its own authority as an inclusive public sphere. Since its authority ultimately rested on its power to persuade Americans to engage in concerted citizen actions of protest and boycott, its failure to be inclusive gave the commission the appearance of catering to special interests. By attempting to fortify its own boundaries against dissident voices, its conclusions and recommendations lacked the associative bonds that could command general endorsement beyond those who shared its a priori disposition toward the issue. Instead of a dialogue on pornography, it promoted a metadialogue on the commission itself.

In addition to providing evidence of negative consequences that can result from a failure to maximize the permeability of boundaries and admit diverse voices to its conversation, the controversy over the commission itself produced a dialogue on the body that was disjointed and continually struggled to find a contextualized language. This failure reflects, in part, the public envisioned by the commissioners and the public sphere that would accommodate them. The commission posed the problem of pornography in legal terms. It then produced an aura of intimidation by the exclusion of witnesses who would challenge its assumption that pornography caused acts of physical abuse or who would speak about pornography in terms that better captured differences between obscenity and eroticism, and by direct acts of the commission itself, such as the Sears letter.

The innuendos of immorality through resistance to the report's rendition of pornography had profound implications for reconstructing the institutional public sphere, in which laws are made and enforced, along conservative and religious lines. The report promised to distort the civic and literary public spheres along similar lines with legal and social restraints that prohibited either one from accommodating an open dialogue among those looking beyond the legal restrictions on pornography. In its open instruction on citizen action tactics, the report became an invitation to vigilante disruption of discursive spaces. While citizen dissent has been a strength of the American political process, heretofore it had not been officially authorized to contravene private rights.

In its silence on the public welfare and health issues and its insistence on treating social and cultural questions of gendered power as legal problems, the panel subordinated an alternative analysis of pornography to a conservative legislative agenda. In its presentation of data in a sensationalistic fashion and in its method for selecting witnesses and deriving conclusions it projected a public more attuned to respond to titillation and power than analysis. These left a great vacuum of silence for a significant body of opinion otherwise expressed and reinforced in the ongoing dialogue that was reflected by American consumption data. By reading or viewing pornography these Americans had entered a discourse on the body that spoke a vernacular language of desire and self-awareness but also power and depersonalization. They set alternative terms to those of religious and moral decay and of seemingly extravagant causal assertions without the benefit of supporting evidence. Equally, the report encouraged a burlesqued language of political agreement in which leaders of the religious right were speaking against pornography as if they subscribed to radical feminist thought.

The report created a lacuna between the rhetorically salient meanings the commission invoked and those held by the silenced. The ensuing metadebate about the commission's methods and agenda suggests that without a common language to frame the problem, the public sphere parodies itself by appearing to address substantive issues that are removed from actual sources of public discontent. Ironically, the commission's rhetoric replicated the terms of relationship whose extreme it was attempting to eradicate. It was difficult for those who were being asked to join in community action to imagine common cause with strangers whose discourse was so easily caricatured as foreclosing open dialogue.

Critics of the report may have won the public debate about its value on a censorship issue; however, that did not remove the intimidating effect of the report on open discussion of sexually explicit materials. The commission's failure was not in its inability to reconstruct the multiple public spheres in which dialogue on the body occurs, but in its failure to explore its possibilities for open discussion in these spheres of a complex mode of communication with enormous implications for intimate and public life. Ultimately the commission reflected a failure to understand the rhetorical character of reticulate public spheres and the possibilities of genuine dialogue they offer.

Chapter 7

TECHNOLOGIZING PUBLIC OPINION: OPINION POLLS, THE IRANIAN HOSTAGES, AND THE PRESIDENTIAL ELECTION

> If a president's policy is right, debate will strengthen the national consensus. If it is wrong, debate may save the country from catastrophe.
> Sen. Edward M. Kennedy, Georgetown University Address, 1980

> There's only one poll that counts, as my wife said on the "Today" show this morning, and that's the final vote.
> Jimmy Carter, Remarks to Gannett Newspaper and Broadcast Executives, 13 December 1979

This chapter explores public opinion: how politicians frame it, respond to it, misconstrue its character, and ultimately get trapped by it. It questions whether the data reported by polls—those taps on the mercurial fluctuations of popular mood—are really *public* opinions. In the following pages I try, through innuendo as well as explicit argument, to aggravate the reader into thinking about the nature and function of public opinion in a nation such as the United States, especially with respect to the "publicness" of it—where public opinion is formed, how it is influenced, and what it represents.

In chapter 4 I developed a rhetorical perspective on public opinion that places rhetoric, not survey research, at its center. This perspective assumes that *publics* are rhetorically constituted, and therefore their opinions are not deeply captured as an aggregate from measures of private opinions or as the outcomes of idealized rational deliberation. The vernacular rhetoric model assumes that publics emerge insofar as interested citizens, often out of concern for the common good, engage in dialogue on the issues that touch their lives; and further, that individual publics are not conceptual but real—although not ideally real. To render these assumptions intelligible, I revisit earlier themes on the rhetoricality of public spheres and public opinion to frame the problem of a technologized and manufactured public opinion. This framework will then be brought to bear on a specific case that illustrates a number of problems with our understanding and use of public opinion in American politics: the Carter administration's rhetoric concerning the Iranian hostage affair.

The Problem of Public Opinion

Governance and social action in complex societies rely on discursively formed coalitions of interests to establish social will. As researchers who investigate social practices remind us, the realities of praxis often temper the transcendent values of community. Opinion poller Samuel Popkin points out, for example, that citizens typically are most aware of the facts of daily life. The cost of groceries, the line at the gas station, and the general state of employment among friends and neighbors are data immediately available. Developments detected through the media often appear to be distant and unconnected to our lives. We require assistance, whether from an opinion leader, a media analyst, or a presidential speech, to link social conditions with actions by the government (Popkin 1991, 27–28). Further, pluralistic societies seldom subscribe to universal goals except in times of crisis, such as war or economic collapse. Even at such moments governance and social action rely on coalitions of interests, each responding for reasons that mark them as distinct, albeit interdependent.

These coalitions have had various titles, such as "the people" or "the citizens," each reflecting its historical version of the ancient cry "*Vox populi, vox Dei*" (Boas 1969). Modernized as *the public,* this title expresses the democratic ideal that power resides with the governed. The people are a source of endorsement and certification for ideas and actions in various arenas of public life who express their warranting force as *public opinion.*

The concept of public opinion is used in a variety of contexts and for quite different purposes, as is illustrated by our everyday encounters with its use to indicate economic tendencies in the marketplace, organizational preferences at work, or popular fashion. As I use it here, *public opinion* assumes my earlier discussion of the vernacular rhetoric model. A dialogizing process (usually but not always deliberative) of formal and vernacular rhetorical exchange is essential to its formation and to whatever sociopolitical coordination may follow from it. Public opinion always carries *political meaning* in the general sense of *an expression of interest which bears on relationships among strangers relevant to it, on how they will act and interact.*

Historically, "public opinion" has referred to community-based views. But since 1940 this concept has been technologized to refer to data acquired in opinion polls.[1] The ideals set forth in liberal democratic theory are in sharp contrast to the objectivist version of public opinion advanced by the applied method of opinion polling. From responses to specific questions by a random sample of a defined population, survey researchers are able to portray the belief patterns of that population at any given moment—or even over time. Their methodology forgoes the ideological privileging of a specific political process and instead attempts to ascertain trends in popular beliefs through empirical data. These trends become the operational meaning of public opinion, and opinion pollers purport that polls measuring these trends provide a more realistic account of public opinion content. This is not an idle claim.

Contemporary pollers are skilled predictors. Their survey techniques transcend the limitations of preference-type questions to forecast the behaviors of sampled populations. By using semantic differential-type questions and regression analysis, pollers are able to diagnose opinion through second cuts at prevailing inclinations, susceptibilities, and beliefs. These methods locate salient factors which are further examined in focus groups. The responses of these groups to a range of specific, often open-ended questions, concerns, and choices are scrutinized to gain deeper knowledge of discriminations and perceptions that alter popular sentiment and influence behavior. Regardless of one's research tradition, at the very least the information produced by survey research is valuable for the evident accuracy with which it monitors the pulse of opinion groups and the insightful leads it provides for discerning the characteristics of aggregate choice.

However, survey research also has been subjected to a variety of criticisms, the most telling of which suggest that it produces results that can be grossly insensitive to the phenomena under investigation, if not outright misleading. Survey research administers predetermined questions in a controlled fashion to a random sample of a specified population in order to locate correlated factors. It determines relationship through patterns of statistical inference that meet the technical definitions of significance. Its methodology assumes that everyone has an opinion. Consequently, it substitutes a *general populace* for an actively engaged *public* in framing political issues and shaping responses. It assumes that everyone can be meaningfully interrogated on a public topic because people are omni-opinionated, so that *randomness* replaces *discrimination* in determining whether an opinion bears on an issue. Survey research assumes that all opinions carry equal weight, which justifies reliance on *quantification* rather than *intensity* and *duration* in deciding the weight to ascribe to a reported view. And it assumes that there is consensus about which problems make certain questions worth asking, thereby privileging *standardized responses* over *rhetorical messages* to locate salient opinions. In other words, survey research transmutes public opinion from a discursive phenomenon to be interpreted and studied critically into a behavioral phenomenon to be quantified and studied scientifically. Without gainsaying their methodological rigor or denying their value, even the most rigorous polls require cautious use when they are the bases for interpreting public sentiment.

These differences are important because they entail an ontology of discourse at cross purposes with the ontology of political relations they purport to measure. Pierre Bourdieu's (1979, 124–30) celebrated critique of opinion polling raises the objection that its prevailing assumptions lead to distortions. Specifically, Bourdieu points to a fundamental problem of interpretation imbedded in survey research of political behavior.

Survey research is aware that the questions asked influence the responses given. Changes in wording or order elicit different responses. Further, political scientist Christopher Achen points out that researchers must rely on a mathematical theory of survey response to choose between "competing simulations of measurement error" (1983, 80). In other words, their discriminations are not based on a theory of political behavior but on one of statistical inference. Years of attention to the fact that differences of wording or question order alter responses have failed to yield a good theory to explain the impact of these permutations. This theoretical weakness leads Achen to conclude: "Bluntly put, political scientists do not know what survey responses are measuring" (80). Without a theory, political scientist John Dryzek wonders, "how can a meaningful instrument exist" (1990, 158).

I wish to emphasize that the problem here is not whether inferences about public opinion can be drawn on the basis of numerical count. The idea of public opinion inherently involves a sensed assessment of the common mind. Historically this sensed assessment has been conceived as a question of an idea's relative strength among community members, which in some way requires gauging the comparative size and strength of commitment among those who held this or that view (Boas 1969; Herbst 1993; Noelle-Neumann 1993; and Speier 1950). Rather, the basic problem lies in a confusion between a sociology of science, as reflected in Leo Bogart's previously noted view (cited in Yankelovich 1991, 39) that public opinion means what opinion polls report, and a philosophy of science, in which the status of a claim is determined by its ontological fidelity to the phenomenon it purports to describe.

This relationship of claim to ontological fidelity has been a problem for opinion polling as an applied methodology almost from its outset. The contest between the social determinism of Lazarsfeld's Columbia group and the social psychologism of Miller's Michigan group resulted in a general consensus in Miller's favor. However, this debate failed to provide a theory for differentiating political from social or economic behavior. The absence of such a distinction is important, since political behavior in a democratic society makes important assumptions about the role of discourse in establishing relations.

Politics, by definition, involves discussion among those in a democratic polity. Presumably, their political decisions are open to conversations with neighbors, coworkers, and friends as well as public deliberations of a more formal sort. These informal conversations and more institutionalized discussions, speeches, essays, and debates involve the individual in an array of interactions focused on locating and clarifying interests, weighing alternatives, and advancing reasons addressed to how we will act and interact. They place participants in relationships that involve the future shape of their shared world. Dryzek (1990) has advanced the telling observation that survey research is problematic for studying this phenomenon because it fails to account for the discursive process by which publics and public opinion emerge. Instead, it measures beliefs, attitudes, and opinions an individual is capable of holding about politics outside of and independent of political discussion or action.

In addition to ignoring political discussion or action in the measure of political behavior, political pollers are in disagreement about the potentially distorting influence that discourse might have on poll results. Whether looking at panels sampled in waves (i.e., at different moments in time) or in focus groups, involving participants in discussion can encourage otherwise disengaged individuals to act as if they are interested (Clausen 1968). Dryzek makes the point that the survey instrument assumes that "an individual's beliefs, opinions, and attitudes about politics are invariant across the degree of action or inaction involved in a situation (though of course survey researchers are interested in how attitudes change with time and political history, e.g., between two waves of a panel survey)" (1990, 160).

These psychological assumptions about individual behavior, based on individual attributes of attitude, belief, and opinion, do not take into account (or account for) the discursive character of political behavior. Consequently, of the many possible political worlds that can be and are brought about through the discursive nature of political relations, survey research projects only one: a political world in which the individual must choose sides among contesting forces. Dryzek concludes that in this world the only rational choice is to choose the side that best advances one's interests, thereby making rationality consist exclusively of instrumental action.

Instrumental Rationality and the Technological Production of Public Opinion

Polling accounts of political behavior are ironic. Though they ignore the actual discursive enactments by which political relations are established, polls are an intensely political mode of discourse. There is a natural political relation between the designer of the survey instrument and the respondent. Survey methodology assumes that truthful responses depend on the respondent not knowing what the investigator seeks to learn. To keep the respondent in the dark about the designer's purposes, she must dominate the relationship. Hence the survey instrument is developed as a form of discourse that is intended to hide its maker's intent in order to preserve her power (Dryzek 1990, 162). This power becomes dangerous when the telos of scientific description is replaced by pragmatic ones, raising significant issues beyond methodological and conceptual ones regarding the impact of polls on opinion formation.

As disconcerting as we may find the level and accuracy of disclosure possible through opinion polling, the subsequent uses of this information are more alarming. Polling information may be benign, but in the hands of those whose economic and political resources facilitate control of information and access to the media, polls become an instrument for *technologizing* the production of public opinion. The salient factors they locate through the various research methods mentioned above form an information base of popular perceptions and susceptibilities on which to build persuasive appeals.

The resulting media campaigns and public messages designed to evoke the worst fears (*negatives*) in connection with the object of opposition and to allay fears and reinforce hopes (*positives*) concerning one's own cause have generated a firestorm of criticism and controversy, such as that aroused during the 1988 presidential race by the Bush campaign's Willie Horton ads that targeted Michael Dukakis's prison furlough policy. The negative campaigns that now seem endemic to American politics reinforce questionable stereotypes and frame misleading associations, not to mention exercise questionable ethics.[2] Whether one typifies such practices as the beneficence of pragmatic deception for noble ends or the maliciousness of demagoguery, their conceptualization of publics remains the same. Their appropriation of the opinion-poll model transmogrifies publics into incremental assemblages constructed technologically via verbal and visual stimuli that target salient susceptibilities.

The danger of such information-gathering technologies stems from their restricted use by elites with resources of wealth, position, or technical knowledge. When the power to gather and use poll data is limited to the few who are among the technically, politically, and economically vested, those who own them tend to use polls as instruments of control, as the practices of PACs in recent years illustrates. Rather than entrust consensus to the power of reasoned argument, their owners gravitate toward using scientifically derived data in a means/ends calculus to achieve desired outcomes.

This pattern of analysis is a pragmatic extension of the primacy of scientific thought in Western society. The modern conception of communication that aligns logic with scientific investigation, that locates the logic of discovery exclusively in science, and that tends toward proof based on external and objective data is an extension of the division of dialectic from rhetoric begun in the late Renaissance and deepened with the work of René Descartes and then of Francis Bacon. It represents a significant departure from the Greco-Roman ideals in which logic and rhetoric were united, in which there was an emphasis on rhetoric's inventional system as a logic of discovery that devised subject matter, and in which mental interpretations took priority over facts as the starting points for arguments (Howell 1966).

The rise of science and the extension of its epistemology into the domain of human affairs altered the manner in which Western democracies managed their political relations. The rationalist conviction that there was a reality outside the human knower, that it could be known and its behavior predicted and controlled, displaced reliance on communication to establish social and political affiliations. Knowledge and power in the polity no longer resided with those who were rhetorically adept at crafting persuasive arguments. The reins of governance passed to a new elite who were versed in the scientific measurement of social variables on which policies would be based. A corresponding objectivism now set standards for policy decisions, including its application to matters of value and morals. The shift from a discourse-based model for political decision making to an objectivist one carried a corresponding but seldom noticed addendum for explaining political reasoning among the governed. Although discourse remained nominally present, it was displaced by the means-ends epistemology of technology.[3]

More specifically, the extension of the Enlightenment program into affairs of state has fostered the negative consequences associated with *instrumental rationality*. Scientific inquiry models phenomena as naturally occurring entities, events, and processes. They are subject to observation, and their variables are precisely measured in an attempt to discover underlying causes. Knowledge of these causes permits answers to questions about their uniquely identifying traits, groups them on the basis of shared characteristics, and accounts for their behavior under specified conditions.

The application of technology transforms the benign practices of science, with its detached concern for exact knowledge of the intransitive objects of inquiry, into a pragmatic activity. Whereas the scientist observes natural phenomena in order to describe with precision their innate properties and characteristics under specifiable conditions, the technologist invades nature for purposes of transforming it to achieve some predetermined end, such as overcoming gravity, altering a genetic map, or changing Earth's topography. Technology is the quintessential embodiment of instrumental rationality, since its raison d'être is to find a means to a desired end. Applied to social actions, this epistemology models them in ways that necessarily emphasize observable aggregate characteristics. The identifying marks of aggregate behavior lend themselves to instrumental reasoning, in which social action is guided toward desired outcomes.

Applied to social practices, instrumental rationality assumes, as Dryzek remarks, that humans have "the capacity to devise, select, and effect good means to clarified ends." Of course, a model in which science, technology, and economics flourish as the principal avenues for means-ends accommodations only makes sense in an orderly world (1990, 3–4). In the real world, much less tidy in its compass of human relations, the consequence of instrumentalism is the "iron cage" around human existence that Weber forecasted as the result of a bureaucratized civic life (1968, 956–1005).

This less than sanguine interpretation of instrumentalism's extensiveness is empirically derived. Democratic societies have always had to balance power between common citizens and those advantaged by birth and wealth. Instrumental rationality adds the complication of exclusionary discourse rules. They limit evidence to that which can be quantified and restrict access to the policy-making sphere to elites with technical expertise, in addition to the well born and the wealthy (Lyotard 1984). Meanwhile, the publics affected by policy decisions are rendered mute in discussions that directly bear on their interests. Added to the aristocracies of birth and wealth, epistemic elites comprise a new element of a power elite that controls the apparatus for framing public policy. As Habermas has argued, the tendencies of instrumental rationality are antidemocratic. The forces of profit and power apply the technical influence at their disposal to invade and subsequently colonize the lifeworld (Habermas 1971a, 1975, 1987, 1989). Rather than swelling democratic participation, instrumentalism has restrained it; rather than expanding the accessibility of economic and social opportunities, it has narrowed them.

These concerns bear special relevance to the character of public discourse today, since instrumentalism carries serious implications and can have profound consequences in the domain of practical conduct. The opinion-poll model itself tends to treat discursive phenomena as if they were behavioral ones. Appropriated by instrumental rationality, social action becomes technologized into controllable behavior through structures that organize human activity, information, and rewards along the axis of mean-ends equations. This produces a vicious cycle that distorts political rhetoric.

On the one hand, survey research can reveal what is popular at any given moment. It can reveal, as well, selected factors that enhance or diminish an item's popularity. Used as the basis for public communication, it encourages discourse that sequences appeals targeted to specific audiences on the basis of their susceptibilities. Strung together, these pockets of assent become an incrementally assembled public. This is a world where messages are tethered not to issues and principled positions but to what will provoke a desired response. This public and its reactions, identified as "public opinion," are instrumental constructs built through the technological application of polling data to message design. As soon as conditions change, however, the popularity of persons, programs, issues, and so forth may alter so drastically as to vanish from view. In the hands of the powerful (and assistants to the powerful) a technologized view of public opinion encourages emphasis on the popular, stresses the efficacy of themes that accentuate popularity, and promotes keeping "helpful" concerns before the citizenry as long as possible. It does not project a public as actively tending to and even participating in the discussion of an issue but as an incremental assemblage of responses to be arranged and rearranged in various combinations as may suit the ends of those in power.

On the other hand, the news media's heavy reliance on opinion polls as evidence of public opinion engrains objectivism as a rhetorical phenomenon and as the basis for social action. This reliance substitutes quantification for discourse to inform community understanding of the body of opinion within the community (Dryzek 1990; Habermas 1989). Consequently, individuals responding in isolation provide an evidentiary base of patterned response that lends itself to interpretation, though the database lacks significant information that bears directly on its meaning. Each person's response counts with equal weight, and each numerical weighting of approval or disapproval becomes part of an aggregate score that is narrated as "public opinion." Absent indications of the respondents' individual or collective knowledge of the issues, or the respective contexts in which they are interpreting what they hear, or their own accounts for why they find a politician's ideas appealing or objectionable, the raw data create an impression of the sample population's approval/disapproval tendencies. The logic of the news media's methodology for gathering and interpreting the data of public opinion completes the circle. These tendencies are then "validated," and their meaning as public opinion is interpreted when "expert witnesses" appear on radio or TV networks or in print media to analyze the data's significance for detecting *the* public's thinking. They substitute expert discourse for the vernacular exchanges of the interested populace and give the data set rhetorical weight as *the* public's judgment.

This transformed sense of *"the* public*"* into a data set highlights the danger of technologizing public opinion. Even in the hands of well-intentioned leaders, the frequent measurement of opinions on policies, programs, job performance, and the like may distort their perceptions. Peter Hart, a poller for Democrats, describes how a government held captive by the latest poll conducts the people's business:

> The world of public opinion has come into great collision with the art of governance. In the old Washington there were two or three polls, principally Gallup and Harris, and each one took a couple of weeks to do, going door-to-door. . . . Now, with new kinds of telephones and computers for tabulation, in a half-hour you can come back and say, "This is what the public thinks." And the polling is "spin numbers," that is, "advocacy analysis," done by parties, by associations, by corporations, by networks or newspapers who can use or release only the questions or answers that suit their narrow purposes, which often comes down to changing a number or a word in complex legislation. One word, one number, one comma means someone or some interest gets a few million dollars or someone else does not. (qtd. in Reeves 1995, C3)

In short, our public officials gauge our concerns, preferences, and commitments on the basis of rapidly conducted telephone surveys. Then they inform us of what our fellow citizens believe with selectively released information that supports a particular point of view or policy.

Rather than providing officials with insightful information on what people believe and why they believe it that might help to shape a serious public conversation, polls of the sort Hart describes substitute widespread but evanescent factors like mood for *public* opinion (Nisbet 1975). The public official committed to a legislative agenda can find violent fluctuations of popular attitude diminish her willingness to engage in serious public discussion, especially when the technology of polling can make instant reaction appear as settled judgment. The uncertainty of mood coupled with the way polls can be used to provide backing for a position as either in or out of tune with the will of the people encourage a rhetoric of pragmatic deception for noble ends: "I can't get my bill passed without voter support, I can't get voter support unless I say what they want to hear; thus I'll speak their mind rather than my own." Meanwhile, the logic of the news media's methodology for gathering and interpreting the data of public opinion keeps the circle closed. The media substitute expert discourse for the vernacular exchanges of the interested populace and give the data set of survey results rhetorical weight as *the* public's opinion on the questions of the day.

The point I wish to stress is that the tendency of polls to transform a discursive phenomenon—the formation of opinion through processes of publicity and deliberation—into a technological one impedes the community from reaching a common mind, much less an understanding of its contents by those who lead. Their tendency is to construe problems of connecting with the public mind as a technological failure that can be repaired through improved techniques for gathering data.[4] However, improved methods for gathering survey data ignore the more fundamental conceptual oversight of ignoring the heteroglossic character of a reticulate public sphere and the necessity for dialogue to generate public opinion. Modeling public opinion as an inference from fixed data points that can be measured while ignoring the essential dialogizing element of contestive discourse inevitably results in a quandary. It offers a technically proficient measure of mood and attitude which is unable to disclose the political reasoning that underwrites it. These criticisms provide a backdrop for viewing the way Jimmy Carter and those in his administration thought about and spoke to the American public during the 444-day captivity of their fellow citizens in Tehran.

Transforming Victims into Heroes

On 4 November 1979 Iranian militants stormed the American embassy in Tehran as a protest against admittance of the deposed shah to the United States for medical treatment. More than sixty Americans fell victim to this angry mob. Officials and staff prisoners were held as hostages while the militants issued various demands to the government of the United States; fifty-two of these hostages were incarcerated for more than a year.

Public exchanges between the two governments instantly precipitated and then sustained an international crisis that remained in the glare of public light for the episode's duration. When the hostages were finally released, these apparently innocent victims—individuals who prior to captivity were engaged in the "normal" activities of embassy personnel—returned home to heroes' welcomes. But the president who negotiated their release had already been turned out of office, in part for his handling of the situation. Why did Americans lionize their captive countrymen and women while rejecting the president whose diplomatic efforts ultimately prevailed?

The answer to that question lies, in part, in the way the Carter administration talked to the American people. Its statements embodied the tension between public opinion as a discursive phenomenon and an antecedent technologized understanding of public opinion that shaped the administration's rhetoric. I will argue that Jimmy Carter's rhetorical choices encouraged a heroic view of the Tehran captives. By exploring how those choices were guided I hope to reveal, in part, why the electorate lost confidence in his leadership.

To begin this discussion we should note that the homecoming of the captive Americans was not entirely typical. For example, returning sailors held captive aboard the *Pueblo* and *Mayaguez* were not similarly feted. More darkly, why were these apparently innocent victims, who had engaged in no extraordinary acts on behalf of their nation, treated heroically, while returning veterans and prisoners of war from Vietnam—men and women commissioned to risk their lives and subjected to much greater physical danger—were treated as outcasts? Among the hypotheses advanced to explain the returned hostages' reception, we cannot discount the likelihood that the rhetoric of the Carter administration energized a public sphere for the American discussion of the hostage-taking—insinuated itself into it, molded it, constrained it, and thereby influenced the formation of public opinion concerning the hostages and the American values they represented.[5] That is the first hypothesis I shall explore.

Three dimensions of the Carter administration's rhetoric are noteworthy. First, the administration seemed to go out of its way to impress upon the American public that securing the hostages' release was a matter of preeminent magnitude. The event naturally attracted attention and concern; an embassy seizure is, after all, an international news item. However, seizure of the Dominican embassy in Colombia on 27 February 1980 received far less public attention despite the fact that Americans, including Ambassador Diego C. Asencio, were taken hostage. Indeed, a search of the *Department of State Bulletin* and the *Weekly Compilation of Presidential Documents* failed to locate even a short press statement announcing Ambassador Asencio's release after sixty-one days in captivity. The qualitative difference in the Iranian hostage matter was the Carter administration's willingness to participate with the Iranian parties in an exchange of public acts.[6] In the immediate aftermath of the embassy takeover these acts heightened the drama of the event, riveted continual attention on it, and suggested that the hostages' incarceration was a matter of sustained national emergency.

Dramatic events occurred in rapid succession. The interim government of Iranian prime minister Mehdi Bazargan fell. Ayatollah Khomeini refused to meet with presidential envoys Ramsey Clark and William Miller. Crowds took to the streets of Tehran, creating the recurring spectacle of multitudes chanting anti-American slogans and hectoring foreign reporters. Iranian militants were televised using the American flag to haul garbage. Sketchy information created ambiguity about the numbers actually held hostage, and anxiety over this was compounded by the militants' threatened actions against the hostages. Six hostages escaped with the aid of Canada, signaling an interim victory over a clearly defined villain.

American responses of United Nations Security Council resolutions and a plea before the World Court were equally dramatic. Personal acts of Carter added to the drama's intensity: he stopped delivery of $300 million in spare military parts bought from the United States by the shah, issued a deportation order for Iranian students with visa irregularities, suspended importation of Iranian oil, dispatched the carrier *Midway* to the Arabian Sea, and froze $8 billion in Iranian assets. Such reciprocated hostilities focused public attention on the affair and confirmed that these hostages were extremely important.

The administration's communications to the American people reinforced a perception of the hostages' significance by proclaiming that the crisis stood at the center of American foreign policy. Though the administration initially called for quiet, patient diplomacy, for restraint and firm negotiation, its practice was not calming. The United States cajoled other nations to line up either "with us or against us." The White House issued a flood of words informing Americans about its responses and initiatives, indicting and denouncing Iran, and otherwise publicizing the hostages' plight.

Nothing communicated urgency more than the president's own behavior. In the early going Jimmy Carter secluded himself at the White House by cancelling meetings abroad and at home. Soon the president announced he was canceling his political activities to stay close to the scene (United States Department of State January 1980c). As the primary election season arrived, Carter's preoccupation with remaining in Washington mushroomed into his celebrated "Rose Garden strategy."[7] The style of his conduct sent Americans an unmistakable message: the Iranian situation was so volatile, required so much executive attention, and was so important to the nation that the president could not leave his post. In the phrase often repeated by the administration, it was his "abiding concern." White House words and actions sustained the Americans' perception that the Iranian affair was an important problem by keeping it in the glare of public light.[8]

Carter's rhetoric asserted the precise importance of the hostages by repeatedly linking them to national character and honor. He told the nation that these "American citizens continue to be held as hostages in an attempt to force unacceptable demands on our country"; that our concern was for the "lives of these brave hostages—our nation's loyal citizens and faithful representatives"; and that our national response was not just anger, outrage, and concern but "pride in their great courage." He stressed the significance of their detainment for the nation: "No single situation so aggravates the American people, so tests our maturity, so tries our patience, so challenges our unity, as does the continued captivity of American hostages in the Tehran Embassy." And as if presenting them as the heroic symbol of national character were not enough, the president magnified their meaning in a textbook example of condensation when he proclaimed, "The lives of over *50 innocent people* are at stake; the foundation of *civilized diplomacy* is at stake; the integrity of *international law* is at stake; the *credibility of the United Nations* is at stake. And at stake, ultimately, is the maintenance of *peace in the region*" (emphasis added) (United States Department of State December 1979a, 50; December 1979b, 18; May 1980I, 3–4; February 1980e, 53).[9]

Thus the course of events and the behavior and rhetoric of their leaders told the American people that this was a singularly important episode; that its significance was no less than the honor and character of the nation itself; that the foundations of civilization and of peace were symbolized by their brave and faithful representatives; and that this matter of grave import presented Americans their opportunity to rededicate themselves to the ennobling principles of freedom and decency through national unity, resolve, sacrifice, and support of its dauntless leadership.

Had the Carter administration adopted a policy of quiet diplomacy and done all within its means to minimize public preoccupation with the hostages, its behaviors and rhetoric might have projected other matters into the limelight of national discussion, leaving the hostage-taking for necessary but perfunctory news releases. But the opposite decision was firmly made—a decision, in the words of Cyrus Vance, that "as long as their cruel torment continues, this matter will remain in the forefront of our national agenda" (United States Department of State May 1980d). Once the administration placed this incident within the arena of public discussion and made it a uniquely salient matter for public opinion, it then had to keep opinion solidly unified behind the president and focus attention on issues that would serve administration attempts to secure the hostages' freedom. To these ends the Carter administration attempted to manage topics admitted into the public sphere of national discussion now consumed by the incident, with the result that the information made accessible to the American public encouraged its perception of the hostages as heroes. This is the second feature of Carter's rhetoric contributing to the hostages-as-heroes perception.

Mostly the president wished the American public to entertain certain obvious topics that, predictably, worked in the administration's favor. There were official acts: the United Nations resolution, the World Court proceedings, the freezing of assets, the deportation of Iranian students, the embargo on Iranian oil, the waving of diplomatic relations, and other actions of an official nature. There also were strategies to place pressure on Iran: the administration publicized the principles that would guide its responses to the situation, made attempts to solidify foreign support through shared actions, and made ominous references to unspecified military options. And it reported attempts to negotiate a settlement in press releases laced generously with descriptions of weird politics involving the street, the embassy, and a strange mélange of militant-president-mosque-parliament-potentate-minister. Politics of this sort soon appeared to be "typically" Iranian.

But there also were topics of a less obvious nature. For example, the administration reiterated the commonplace of American unity. Citizens were repeatedly reminded that they were in "unanimity," "galvanized" in "public unity," "dedicated to the principles and honor of our nation," standing "as one people."[10] In the words of United Nations ambassador Donald McHenry:

> There is in the United States a unity of purpose, a disciplined sensitivity to the needs of peace, a determination to search out all peaceful means to bring this dispute to a just conclusion, and also a determination to do what must be done to protect our fellow citizens and the rule of law. That unity of purpose is shared by all Americans. But make no mistake. Beneath that discipline is a seething anger which Americans properly feel as they witness on daily television new threats and outrages against their fellow citizens. The hostages must be freed (United States Department of State January 1980b, 52).

Like the general public in the movie *Network*, the citizenry was portrayed as ready to pull up windows and shout, "I'm mad as hell and I'm not going to take it anymore!" According to the administration, these hostages had given the country a renewed sense of patriotism. With hindsight we can see how rhetoric inflected with the people's renewed sense of national pride encouraged lionizing the symbols who evoked that patriotism.

A more peculiar topic was that of America's energy needs. National energy problems were repeatedly associated with the hostage taking. To the Thirteenth Constitutional Convention of the AFL-CIO, Carter stated, "The developments in Iran have made it starkly clear to all of us that our excessive dependence on foreign oil is a direct, physical threat to our freedom and security as Americans." But, he continued: "Our love of freedom will not be auctioned off for foreign oil. Hundreds of thousands of our forebears gave their very lives for our freedom. Our freedom is not for sale—now or ever in the future" (United States Department of State December 1979b, 19). Two weeks later the president linked energy to the hostage issue when he proclaimed, "We stand as a nation unified, a people determined to protect the life and the honor of every American. And we are determined to make America an energy secure nation once again. It is unthinkable that we will allow ourselves to be dominated by any form of overdependence at home or any brand of terrorism abroad. We are determined that the freest nation on earth shall protect and enhance its freedom." Carter's State of the Union Address continued this theme, claiming that the events in Iran and Afghanistan dramatized the fact that a clear and present danger to national security was created by our excessive dependence on foreign oil (United States Department of State January 1980c, 1; February 1980b, C).

These references carried twofold implications for America's energy needs: our energy dependence kept us vulnerable to future humiliation by unstable OPEC regimes, and it jeopardized national freedom. Carter thereby linked national security to the hostages' status. Not only was Carter using the hostage crisis to support his energy program, but he was also making support of energy conservation and related legislation appear a patriotic duty that would somehow assist in securing the release of the hostages and defend the nation's honor and security.[11]

Topics Carter did *not* wish to open for discussion are equally interesting. From the outset he determined that grievances voiced by Iranians against the shah were inappropriate matters for public discussion. When asked why he had reversed a previous decision not to grant the shah entrance to the United States, his pithy response was "for humanitarian reasons": he was a sick man and "I took the right decision. I have no regrets about it nor apologies to make because it did help to save a man's life, and it was compatible with the principles of our country." When the press asked if the United States would assist in the investigation of serious charges against the shah, Carter declined to comment on any role the government might play in such proceedings. He said he "didn't know of any international forum within which charges have ever been brought against a deposed leader who has left his country," and he added as a gratuitous afterthought that no such forum would listen anyway, as long as Iran held the hostages. Following a meeting with the hostage families he asserted, "I am not interested in trying to resolve whether or not the Shah was a good or bad leader or the history of . . . Iran." And again, at his news conference of 13 February 1980, he was asked if he thought it proper for the United States to restore the shah to the throne in 1953. He responded, "That's ancient history, and I don't think it's appropriate or helpful for me to go into the propriety of something that happened 30 years ago." Considering that the militants, the official representatives of Iran, and the spokesmen for Khomeini were harping on the shah's sins as their major issue, Carter's response had the domestic effect of a rebuttal to the Iranians' complaint.[12]

The president was equally reluctant to entertain any discussion of American responsibility for events in Iran. Thus, Carter maintained that the embassy's fall was not America's fault: the Iranian government had given assurances that the embassy would be protected, and the changes in Iran had occurred so rapidly that "no one on Earth predicted them"; and he was uninterested in "public debate, at this time, with former secretary Kissinger about who is or who is not responsible for the events that took place in Iran" (United States Department of State January 1980c, 1–2). Intended or not, the effect of this reluctance was to nip in the bud any suggestion of American culpability for this frustrating event. It kept the target of public discussion clear: the illegal holding of American citizens.

Consonant with his aversion to questions that criticized the United States, Carter was quick to chastise anyone who dared to entertain them. When former United Nations ambassador Andrew Young suggested that to the Iranians "our protecting the Shah is about like our protecting Adolf Eichmann," National Security Adviser Zbigniew Brzezinski was sent to instruct Young graciously but clearly "to stop talking about it for the duration of the crisis" (Newsweek 1979, 23). Sen. Ted Kennedy's ill-timed December attack on admitting the shah into the United States met with disbelief and then quick condemnation from the White House. The general posture with regard to not entertaining the Iranian point of view reflects an ethnocentric bias that not only delegitimated the Iranian side of the story but also distorted the cultural differences at play in all phases of the affair. To a domestic audience ignorant of Iranian culture, an imposed American perspective as the only perspective made the Iranian actions seem all the more extreme and menacing.[13]

Perhaps the most blatant attempt to quash criticism came in response to Ramsey Clark's participation in the May 1980 Tehran meeting that castigated the United States for its interference in Iranian internal affairs. Armed with his recent ban on travel to Iran, the president vented his aggravation before the press, denounced Clark's participation, and indicated that he favored the Justice Department's proceeding with a civil suit. His exasperation was heightened when he was informed of Secretary of State Edmund Muskie's comment that the purpose of this ban was to keep Americans from traveling to dangerous places, not to punish them. Carter shot back, "I don't think Ed Muskie has any legal responsibility for determining whom to prosecute or not to prosecute." For that matter neither did the president, a point former attorney general Clark was only too willing to make. In fact, on his behalf Clark cited the Constitution, Supreme Court decisions, and Carter's own human rights posture toward the Soviet Union's repression of the rights to travel by political dissidents (Time 30

June 1980, 10). In general, however, the Carter administration was successful in minimizing discussion of Iranian complaints.

Finally, the administration did not welcome discussion of topics that could lead to public exploration of its options. Obviously, no party to hostilities wishes to reveal its retaliatory plans. But Carter was willing to insinuate his retaliatory possibilities into the public realm in ways that asked for blind acceptance of America's potential to act. For example, early in the crisis Carter informed the American people that he was sending naval forces to the Arabian Sea to prevent injury to the hostages. And when the possibility of placing the hostages on trial was raised, Carter ominously warned, "We are prepared to take action that would be quite serious in its consequences for Iran" (United States Department of State March 1980c, 31; March 1980b, 32).

On these and other occasions when the administration did not wish Iran to ignore the specter of armed intervention, the president and his staff were naturally reluctant to specify time, place, and manner of action. However, the speculative and even unrealistic character of these threats invited questions of clarification from the American press and people. The policy of publicly raising the possibility of armed intervention and then closing discussion was nothing less than a pronounced effort to keep the threat alive for the Iranians. But, trumpeted on the public stage, it kept the threat alive for the domestic audience as well. Thus on 13 April, Deputy Secretary of State Warren Christopher, appearing on *Issues and Answers*, proclaimed that the United States had military options. When asked how viable these were, since they lacked definition, Christopher responded that the government was not going to telegraph its decisions. Pressed on how the administration had any realistic military options, since the embassy walls apparently had been equipped with explosives, he answered that they had to weigh these threats carefully but would make no comment on military options (United States Department of State May 1980a, 25).

This strategy of keeping alive the possibility of armed intervention collapsed when the ill-fated rescue attempt of 25 April was aborted after mechanical failures and then pilot error resulted in the deaths of eight American servicemen. Later that day Secretary of Defense Harold Brown held a news conference at which he refused to outline the rescue plan beyond the point at which it aborted. He asked, in effect, that the American people take his word that it would have worked. The press then questioned why this act would not have increased tensions since Iranians would have been confronted and possibly killed. His response was reminiscent of Richard Nixon's on the 1970 Cambodia incursion.[14] He asserted that this was not a military action but a rescue attempt. When asked if there remained viable military options, he refused to discuss the matter, simply stating that the administration was keeping all options open. The press was incredulous. Reporters inquired how he could claim not to rule out *any* options, since the United States had just blown one. To this he merely repeated his previous position (United States Department of State June 1980b, 39–41). Two days later, on *Issues and Answers,* Brzezinski had this to say about the disastrous mission: "I believe that one of the very important lessons to be drawn from the events of the last few days, by everyone concerned, is that the United States, and the President of the United States, is prepared to do all that is necessary to obtain their release and will persist in these efforts; I repeat will persist in these efforts." The panel refused to buy this attempt to transform a disaster into a bald assertion of power and wondered whether this failure had not effectively ended any prospect for the hostages' early release. Brzezinski replied that this mission sent a very important message to Tehran: "Do not scoff at American power, do not scoff at American reach." He followed this comment with a stream of ambiguous characterizations of possibilities but refused to discuss specific military options (United States Department of State June 1980a, 47–48).

These three topics had enormous potential to redirect public attention from the plight of the fifty-two persons held hostage to matters of the nation's conduct in Iran, both before and during the hostage crisis. Had grievances against the shah, or America's responsibility for events in Iran, or alternatives to the administration's chosen options become subjects for public deliberation, public opinion might have swung in another direction, seeing the hostages as victims of misguided American policy. As long as Carter could insulate the government from criticism, then clearly America appeared as an aggrieved, innocent nation, and the hostages' role as heroic representatives of American honor was solidified. As Carter was fond of repeating, "We have done nothing for which any American need apologize" (United States Department of State December 1979b, 19).

Third, and finally, the American perception of the captives as heroes was distorted by the administration's depiction of the Iranians. Four days into the crisis Secretary Vance stated, "It is a time not for rhetoric, but for quiet, careful, and firm diplomacy" (United States Department of State December 1979c, 49). Yet American officials portrayed Iran in a manner that could serve only to sustain national outrage, maintain support for the Carter initiatives, and prevent the hostages from appearing as victims of any force except Iranian malice.

Undeniably the incident called for stern language in official public statements. It shocked no one to hear Iran depicted as violating international law and defying world opinion. It followed that the Iranians would be characterized as isolating themselves from the international community and as setting a precedent that undermined the assumed sanctuary of diplomatic missions and the diplomatic process. So much was inevitable. The tone of public discourse that Vance called for was exemplified by his own testimony before the Senate Foreign Relations Committee. In March 1980 he explained: "International condemnation of Iran and the economic measures which have raised the cost to Iran of their illegal actions are bringing home to Iranians the fact that the holding of the hostages is harmful to their interests and to the success of their revolution. But divisions within Iran have prevented progress" (United States Department of State May 1980d, 17).

However, Vance's quiet restraint was not representative of the administration's rhetoric. Daily fare for the American people characterized Iran as an "irrational opponent" in "arrogant defiance of world community." Iran was contemptuous of international law and international diplomatic structures. It continued to "flaunt [*sic*] with impunity the expressed will and law of the world community," issuing a "drum-fire of propaganda out of Tehran." Her act was an "abhorrent violation" of moral and ethical standards. Iranian officials and militants were called kidnappers, blackmailers, criminals, terrorists, international terrorists, zealots, and political and moral bankrupts. Through innuendo it was suggested that the Iranian leaders permitted the hostage crisis to drag on so as to divert their people from internal problems. Iran was depicted as a nation in chaos; it lacked cohesive leadership; its rulers were opportunists; and it was on the verge of collapse.[15] Indeed, in a remarkable exchange reflecting a prophet's zeal for predicting demise, Zbigniew Brzezinski proclaimed:

> B. The country is gradually disintegrating.
> Q. Now you have said that for a long time.
> B. Its peripheries are falling apart.
> Q. Excuse me, you've said that for a long time.
> B. Its enemies are gathering force. (United States Department
> of State June 1980a, 47–48)

The inflammatory nature of these characterizations and the repeated references to the motivations of Iranian leadership could only narrow public perceptions and subsequent public discussion. How could Americans seriously entertain any assertions of legitimate grievance from people who clearly were evil? Seething anger seemed the only appropriate response. At a time when the United States was once again put to the wall by a small nation, seething anger also was a politically useful response. Without it the country might well have lapsed into the post-Vietnam syndrome of presuming American guilt for interfering in the affairs of another nation. Then the fate of these hostages, like that of Vietnam veterans, might be perceived as America's own fault. Rather than heroic symbols of national honor, the hostages might have been seen as pitiful victims of bankrupt American diplomacy.

The Emergence of Doxa

Although we currently lack sufficient documents to determine whether the patterns I have been discussing were planned, their cumulative effects remain no less apparent.[16] There is no denying that the out-pouring of emotion and the euphoric spectacle pervading the hostages' return were indicative of the symbolic value Americans placed on the detained embassy personnel. In retrospect one might question whether "heroic" accurately describes the hostages' ordeal. But in the context of their 444-day captivity, the Carter administration's rhetoric surely encouraged the nation to perceive it as "heroic." By word and deed Carter invested these men and women with a significance reserved for heroes: important symbols of American honor and character. Further, the administration explicitly urged Americans to share in the captives' sacrifices by restrained policy and conduct. The hostages united the nation in a common bond by asserting what it stood for—even if what America stood for was expressed only by what it opposed. Supporting the hostages was thus a patriotic act evoking national identification, which befitted paying the source of such unity the homage due a hero. Moreover, since the administration suppressed alternative interpretations or consideration of related issues, perspectives and information that might have encouraged different perceptions were unavailable. Finally, the characterizations of Iranians served to strengthen domestic opinion. Administration rhetoric celebrating the captives' bravery in the face of a maniacal and malevolent foe galvanized the widespread perception of their heroism. Cast as symbolic representatives who opposed the forces of wickedness and injustice, they functioned to certify national worth. Insofar as the administration's rhetoric helped shape the public sphere of citizens and journalists whose abiding concern became the hostage-taking, its rhetoric was a source of narrow and unbalanced discourse among these participants. The evidence is plain that this discursive arena was distorted in a way that encouraged Americans to perceive their captive countrymen as heroes.

And what of the public that formed? If public expression by a people may serve as evidence of a public's emergence and of the opinions it holds, then the facts of the hostages' welcome home are an undeniable proof. A public did find itself and form an opinion. However, this opinion was significantly colored by administration attempts to craft unified public opinion. This public located itself not only in the officially provided characterizations of its mood and temper, but in the vernacular interactions among the populace evoked by officialdom's rhetoric. If anything, the administration's rhetoric was too successful at planting a seed crystal around which fragmented popular thought could solidify. These captives appeared to embody a common interest of all Americans. Carter's use of the heroism theme provided a rhetoric suited to transforming disparate groups gradually into a single body shouting abhorrence and intolerance at the events in Tehran and newfound pride in American bravery.

This vernacular expression of patriotism was no less than a public opinion, but it was an opinion of special cast. The public's image of the hostages' heroism was akin to what the ancient Greeks termed *doxa,* or opinion, which was contrasted with *episteme,* or knowledge. Moreover, it was a special type of opinion—a form of thought that typifies an unqualified state of mind.[17] The public discussion of the hostages encouraged formation of an opinion about the ethos of the hostages—an opinion that was personal and bimodal. They were *our* hostages; they represented America as a put-upon nation. Iran was a clear enemy, personified by the cartoonlike image of a Draconian cleric. Judging from the euphoria publicly displayed upon their return, one would have to conclude that this state of doxa—simplified, clarified, and polarized—was widespread.[18]

Obviously other important factors contributed to this public's bestowal of honor on the returning hostages. Media coverage certainly contributed, as did Iran's own conduct and its manner of publicizing the matter. It would be simplistic to seek the full account for Americans' response in any single doorway. My aims have been more modest: to set forth the reasonable beginnings for an account of how American officials contributed to evoking, sustaining, and managing this aspect of public opinion by constraining the public sphere in which it was a national preoccupation.

Public Opinion as Technological Constraint

The vernacular rhetoric of America's neighborhoods festooned with yellow ribbons, of lawns planted with an American flag for each day of the captivity, of billboards depicting the Ayatollah Khomeini as the bulls-eye of a target and bumper stickers deriding him as "Ayatollah Assaholah," followed by the returned hostages' reception of welcome home parades, a deluge of gifts, appearances on local and national broadcast media, and local tributes to their state of grace in the form of keys to the city and, more significantly in American male culture, lifetime passes to major league sporting events—these and more provided empirical evidence of a widespread public opinion that the hostages were heroes. Yet if, as I have argued, the character and quality of this opinion were sculpted by the rhetoric of Jimmy Carter and his administration, then an obvious question follows: How could this same public, so supportive of its president through most of this crisis, have rejected Jimmy Carter at the polls?

In the judgments of campaign brain trusters such as Robert Strauss and Patrick Caddell, the voters did so precisely because of the hostage affair (Germond and Witcover 1981, 294). Why was this so? By shifting our focus from how Carter's discourse encouraged a civil judgment to the administration's perception of public opinion and how it inflected the character of presidential rhetoric, we may gain insight into this election and the troublesome nature of understanding public opinion. Here we will be concerned with the consequences of theorizing public opinion as a technological construct rather than as a product of discourse. I intend to show how this conception by Carter's political staff resulted in ill-conceived rhetoric by the president. The contrast between discursive and technological images in this concrete case promises insight into the contribution a vernacular rhetoric model may offer to our understanding of public opinion.

In the opening discussion of this chapter, the problem of equating the data of opinion polls with public opinion pointed specifically to the dangers of instrumental rationality distorting the political process. Under the influence of an epistemology that regards human behavior as manipulable and controllable to achieve predetermined ends, the Carter administration misconceived the hostage situation as a source of opportunity to be interjected into the president's reelection campaign.

Planning the Reelection Campaign

Political observers, not to mention Carter's opponents, were quick to comment on the president's attempts to exploit the political value of the hostage situation. But more can be said than this easy generalization. Close examination of the timing and content of Iran-related statements by Carter and of public opinion data reveals an intriguing pattern. The president or his staff apparently selected items to discuss and times to discuss them by referring to popular attitudes revealed by his personal poller's data on opinions about Iran and other salient matters.

To set the president's political uses of public opinion data on the hostage affair in perspective, two observations are germane as background. First, the Carter White House was exquisitely sensitive to the symbolic value of projecting a presidential image suited to the nation's mood. Witness Carter's "plain-folks" inaugural stroll down Pennsylvania Avenue hand-in-hand with Mrs. Carter; or the initial banning of "Hail to the Chief" as too imperial and its subsequent revival after intense criticism of his administration's competence; or his attempted emulation of Franklin Roosevelt's fireside chats, embellished with the "down-home" casualness of cardigan and jeans. Politicians doubtless have been concerned with their public image since Kleon's bold declaration that he spoke for the city. However, Carter's embrace of the data provided by technological advances in polling and media techniques represented a qualitative leap in a new direction. Not only did he use technologically derived data as a guide for crafting messages, he then extended these technologically grounded images into areas of substantive decision.

For better or worse, Carter's confidence in the work of his political technologists was not capricious. This was especially true with respect to Caddell's polling data. Caddell hypothesized that when voters cast their actual ballots, they carefully weigh a variety of factors that go untapped by standard preferential questions. Through regression analysis of answers to questions employing a semantic differential, he located salient factors weighed by voters when arriving at their final judgments. He discovered, for example, that voters opposed to Carter responded differently when reminded of deeds that corresponded favorably with his positive factors. Voters switched choices along lines of thought they might follow when weighing all factors in their own final balloting. These views and their supporting data are presented in two of Caddell's memos to Jimmy Carter (reprinted as appendixes in Drew 1981, 338–439).

The significance of Caddell's polling techniques are most apparent in their relationship to voter behavior. Voters sometimes seize primary elections as opportunities to express protests. Ballots for a challenger may represent attempts to send an incumbent a message. In general elections voters appear to be more deliberate, taking stock of a candidate's personal attributes as well as policy commitments. Polling data that revealed a candidate's perceived strengths and weaknesses would therefore be most useful in devising tactics designed to encourage voters to ballot "correctly." For a sitting president, the obvious rule of thumb is to minimize protest votes by encouraging voters to think of the primary as if it were the general election.

The data from this more elaborate polling technique also permitted Caddell to make revised estimates of the point spread between candidates. The "second cuts" proved to be unnervingly accurate in telling the candidate precisely how matters stood going into the election—sometimes, as in the New York primary, forecasting an outcome opposite from that indicated by preferential polls. Caddell's polls played a significant role in Carter's use of the hostage affair because they provided the president with indexes of popular sentiment relating to the presidential race and suggested times when positive steps by the president might prove politically useful.

A second background observation concerns the strategy Carter aides had mapped for the reelection campaign prior to the embassy takeover. Hamilton Jordan, Carter's White House chief of staff, had examined strategies and their consequences in previous presidential campaigns. Among his conclusions were that incumbents erred if they did not plan for opposition and attempt to defeat opponents soundly from the outset; that incumbents erred if they ignored the advantages of incumbency for securing endorsement; and that incumbents erred if they did not campaign from the White House, using it rather than the campaign trail to present their messages. In October 1979 Carter gathered with his strategists at Camp David. Jordan's observations on incumbency were incorporated as major features of the Carter primary campaign plan. Carter would make Senator Kennedy chase him, would use incumbency to secure endorsements, and would emphasize his leadership abilities by tending to the business of the White House.[19]

As the Carter forces left Camp David, public perceptions of the president's leadership were their chief concern. Caddell's polls showed that on questions of character Carter had a decisive edge over Kennedy. And the Carter people were confident that the president's use of discretionary federal funds for well-placed and well-timed executive grants would garner the endorsements of mayors, governors, and other party regulars who were opinion leaders. But Caddell's polls also showed Kennedy with a decisive edge in leadership. Carter's problem was that he did not act in ways that appeared "presidential" (Drew 1981, 124).

Shortly thereafter the American embassy in Tehran was seized. Its importance to the campaign was recognized instantly. Elizabeth Drew reports these reactions by Carter strategists:

> One of the decisions made at the Camp David meeting was that the most important thing for the President to do to enhance his chances of renomination was to be seen as being "Presidential." One of the participants at the meeting says, "There was acceptance of the idea that Carter would win or lose based on how he was seen doing his job in the White House, far more than on what he did on the campaign trail." The following week—on November 4th, one year before Election Day—the hostages were seized in Iran. One of Carter's strategists says, "The perception of his handling of Iran and Afghanistan had more impact than anything we could have done—tripled or squared." (Drew 1981, 124)

Incumbency, especially for presidents, assuredly provides political aspirants the great advantage of opportunities to appear fit for office. They can to some extent command events and to a greater extent command the news media. Presidents can open relations with previously hostile nations, arrange and attend summits, dispense discretionary favors, initiate legislative proposals, sign bills, hold "nonpolitical" press conferences, and in it all appear most "presidential." Certainly no one should have expected Jimmy Carter to be above exploiting the unique opportunities incumbency provided. But his repeated reliance on the Iranian crisis to boost his reelection bid was less predictable.

Carter vehemently denied charges that he was playing politics with the hostage crisis. Assertions such as "I've never used the hostage issue for political purposes and never will" and "I do not make, and have not made, and will not make decisions nor announcements concerning the lives and safety of our hostages simply to derive some political benefit from them" (United States Office of the Federal Register, 1980a, 2013; 1980d, 710) were typical and often repeated. Whether this was sincerely the case may never be known, since it raises a question of motivation.[20] Nonetheless, there were political benefits to be derived from this situation, and they were not entirely fortuitous. The Carter strategists apparently believed that to reap them the president must be seen handling the crisis; conducting the nation's business would display his "presidential" attributes.[21] Of course, this conviction committed the administration to the delicate course of weaving the hostage affair into the campaign—*not as an issue but as the foundation of an image.* And it committed the president to respond less to the informed opinion of the electoral public sphere than to the image of that sphere projected by the technology of opinion polls. This latter commitment was freighted with baggage, since acts intended to create an image might actually set policy and since Iranian actions beyond Carter's control might actually undermine the campaign itself—if, for example, the Iranians' intransigence should stymie "presidential" initiatives, as that of the North Vietnamese had those of Lyndon Johnson twelve years earlier.

Appearing Presidential

Within the context of his reelection strategy, Carter addressed the electorate's concerns about the hostages at propitious moments during the campaign—that is, when the polls coincidentally showed that the Carter candidacy could use a boost. Moreover, the hostage question was addressed in several ways that fit into the overall campaign strategy I have briefly outlined. I will comment on three of these campaign tactics designed to enhance the presidential image of Jimmy Carter.

First, *Carter's operatives instantly employed the Iranian crisis as a shield to protect the president's administration from scrutiny and simultaneously as a showcase to display him in a leadership role.* Although Carter had no control over the timing of events in Tehran, a quick glance at Carter's standings in the polls suggests that the embassy seizure could not have occurred at a more opportune political moment. The opinion polls of late summer 1979 did not bode well for the president. In August the Yankelovich, Skelly, and White survey showed that among Democrats 62 percent favored Kennedy for nomination, whereas only 24 percent favored Carter. More telling, their poll revealed a dismal level of confidence in the president's ability to perform his job, with one-third to nearly one-half of the respondents expressing no confidence in his ability to deal with the economy, conduct foreign policy, appoint the right people to office, or manage domestic affairs. One month later the AP-NBC News Survey showed that only 19 percent of Americans thought Carter was doing an excellent or good job. By the end of October, as Kennedy's announcement for candidacy appeared imminent, the race for the nomination took on more realistic proportions, but Carter still trailed 39 percent to 49 percent in the Yankelovich survey ("Still Looking for a Leader" 1979; "Kennedy: Ready, Set, . . ." 1979; "Kennedy's Lead is Shrinking" 1979). At the very best, the president appeared to have a serious fight on his hands. This was especially so because the economy was in recession, with interest rates and inflation at record highs and unemployment climbing. These were Kennedy issues that placed the president in apparent jeopardy of losing an economic debate and the nomination.

The seizure of the Tehran embassy became a compelling diversion from these problems. Hostage developments were dramatically enacted on the public stage and embedded in the electorate's consciousness as an important matter, contributing to the swift swing in national concern from economic matters to diplomacy and Carter's handling of this foreign crisis. The nation's concern only intensified when the Soviet Union invaded Afghanistan in late December, thereby posing a serious threat to American oil interests in the Mideast. In terms of the campaign, the immediate issues suddenly swung in Carter's favor, and for all practical purposes Kennedy was left without salient issues to discuss.

Most important, the crisis provided a perfect excuse for Carter to remain aloof from the partisan politics of the campaign: not only from the stump speeches and the debates but also from the risky scrutiny of his whole administration that such encounters would have involved. If the press had been given the chance to report on normal campaign speeches defending his record, they could have zeroed in on matters where he was weakest. And Kennedy's remorseless hammering at Carter's poor performance in dealing with the economy and at an alleged absence of leadership would only have intensified the electorate's focus on Carter's record as the issue. As long as he could remain above the fray he would continue to appear presidential, and the issue would be whether Kennedy was fit to serve. This was precisely what the Carter forces wanted, since "fitness to serve" was not a substantive issue that challenged the Carter record but one of image, hinging on the perceived character of the candidates; and it was Kennedy's weak suit.[22]

The celebrated Rose Garden strategy was the manifestation of a decision to sustain this shield, a decision that appears to have been the result of poll data reflecting increased Carter strength as a result of the patriotic surge following the embassy's fall. Indeed, two days into the crisis, with the president trailing Kennedy in the polls, he agreed to the *Des Moines Register* debate scheduled for mid January. By 29 December, having overtaken Kennedy and with 66 percent of the electorate rating his handling of the crisis as "just right," he withdrew ("U.S. Attitudes" 1980). Martin Schram reports a senior adviser as explaining, "Things were going well for us in the polls. . . . By being president, by leading, he could do more for himself than by campaigning. . . . We had nothing to gain by Carter debating." Carter himself acknowledged as much to his staff. "Look, you guys," Jordan quotes him as saying, "if I go out to Iowa to debate Ted Kennedy, I go out there as a President and return as just another political candidate." Schram also suggested that the Iowa debate bailout was part of the larger scheme of keeping the president at home. Indeed, one Carter aide confessed that even though the president was preoccupied by the crisis he could still have campaigned through January and into February, which is when serious decisions on negotiations were being made (Schram 1980, 107; Jordan 1982, 99).

In the short run, the Rose Garden strategy worked. It compromised Kennedy's campaign options and virtually assured the renomination of Jimmy Carter as the Democratic candidate. However, the strategy had only short-term value. Early on Jody Powell recognized that criticism of Carter's handling of the crisis was inevitable, but he anticipated it would not come until the general election, and that was not his problem at the moment (Drew 1981, 37). More than this, the Rose Garden strategy created a trap. Since the president gave the hostage affair as the reason for not debating, it became all the more important that he not be seen making other political appearances. But what was he to do if the hostage situation lingered and the polls reflected impatience with him? No plans were laid for resolving this problem, and thus Carter was vulnerable to becoming became a political prisoner of sorts, a point I will revisit.

That Carter settled on the Rose Garden strategy for the political gain of appearing presidential is indicative of his flawed conception of voter opinion. The embassy seizure raised a number of serious questions, most of which went begging for answers through sheer lack of information: Who were these people demonstrating on the streets of Tehran? Who was the shah? Who were the hostages? Who were the activists? What did the shah do to make Iranians want to kill him? And, perhaps most fundamentally, there was the frustrated question of Stephen Smith, Kennedy's campaign director: "In the end, the basic question about the Iranian crisis is whether it was necessary for the Shah to be here. Obviously, there will be a rather careful examination of all that. I don't know why he's here. Do you?" (Drew 1981, 42).

Since Carter chose not to answer these questions, the primary data at the public's disposal were not about the issues but about events played out as spectacle on the world stage: Americans were being held hostage by fanatical Iranians in apparent contravention of international law; and the president was acting presidential by attending to the crisis through initiatives in the United Nations and the World Court, by levying economic sanctions, and by rallying the nation to lend support and remain temperate.

As the campaign season rolled into late winter, basic questions remained unanswered, the Americans were still held hostage, and expressions of disenchantment with the president's conduct started to mount.[23] Unable to free himself from the Rose Garden but needing to campaign, unwilling to discuss Iran as a legitimate issue of public debate and yet interjecting it into the electoral public sphere as a shield against the issue of his stewardship, Carter was encountering the long-term weakness of his appearance as presidential.

How had Carter led Americans to form their expectations of his leadership abilities? Safeguarded against the criticisms of press and opponents, *Carter used the Iranian issue as an impenetrable sanctuary from which he could speak without fear of attack and from which he could attack without fear of retaliation.* This second tactic exploiting the hostage situation made it a one-sided issue that only Carter might legitimately manage, aided by the press's insatiable desire to cover the event and its management.

Americans became familiar with Carter's presidential quality through a montage of scenes that uncritically suggested that he was a leader of stature: scenes of the president huddled with his aides or taking a lonely stroll in the Rose Garden, always looking concerned; scenes of televised epideictic moments, such as the nonlighting of the White House Christmas tree at the 1979 ceremony, that showed Carter leading the nation in its somber vigil awaiting the hostages' release;[24] scenes of Carter addressing groups of legislators or the hostage families, his remarks covered but no questions permitted; scenes from backgrounders at which the president or one of his aides would talk to the press about coming events or the president's thoughts, later dutifully reported as news from "sources close to the President"; scenes of brief presidential statements announcing another sanction or initiative designed to bring Iran to its senses, broadcast from the Oval Office and without opportunities for questions. In these ways Carter made his views known without subjecting them to interrogation, while portraying himself as presidential.

When the president did open himself to scrutiny, it was at a news conference or interview in which, inevitably, the subject of Iran was featured and the questions generally friendly. Such press events also provided convenient forums in which the president assumed the role of leader—the area of Carter's "negatives," according to Caddell's polls—by emphasizing his unique responsibilities during the crisis.[25]

Press events also were convenient forums in which to remind opponents and voters that it was unpatriotic at this time not to support Carter's actions. So, while restricting his own political activities, he called "on those who might be opposing me in the future for president to support my position as President and to provide unity for our country and for our nation in the eyes of those who might be looking for some sign of weakness or division in order to perpetuate their abuse of our hostages" (United States Department of State January 1980c, 2).

Through publicity of this sort the president used his power to command the media in ways that kept attention focused on Iran and off domestic issues. He also kept attention on himself in his leadership role, showing Americans that at least some of the time he could act presidential. Furthermore, he undermined the substantive and symbolic base of Kennedy's challenge, since in the face of a foreign crisis economic matters engendered neither enthusiasm nor interest.

When Kennedy decided to risk his own credibility as a fit leader by challenging the president's concentration on the hostages,[26] Carter castigated him as irresponsible at best, and perhaps even unpatriotic.[27] Still, Kennedy's attacks seemed to be working. As the New Hampshire primary neared, Caddell's adjusted figures indicated that the president's lead was only five points; Kennedy's campaign was gaining strength, and voters were thinking of the election as a primary, where protest votes are more likely to occur. Carter had to reach New Hampshire voters; he had to allay their fears about his action on Afghanistan and convince them that he was not hiding out, as Kennedy was charging; and he also had to undercut his opponent.

Carter found his opportunity to address these needs when he held a press conference on 13 February, his second since the embassy seizure. After using carefully chosen language to deal with negative voter perceptions on other issues, he turned to Kennedy. The senator had accused the administration of endorsing a United Nations commission on Iran only because Kennedy had urged the formation of such a body. The president used this topic as a point of departure for a general attack on Kennedy's offensive. Carter angrily denounced Kennedy for this charge that he had stolen Kennedy's foreign policy ideas. "His statements have not been true, they've not been accurate, and they've not been responsible, and they're not helping the country." And later, "This thrust of what he has said throughout the last few weeks is very damaging to our country, and to the establishment of our principles and the maintenance of them, and the achieving of our goals to keep the peace and to get our hostages released" ("Transcript of the President's News Conference" 1980).

Elizabeth Drew comments on the connection between Carter's attack and the Caddell polls: "Carter's anger was real anger, apparently, but the demonstration of it was calculated. Caddell's figures showed afterward that Kennedy's 'negatives'—questions about his credibility and dependability—went up" (1981, 135).

The unifying influence of the hostage crisis on national attitudes and its convenience as an opportunity for Carter to demonstrate his presidential stature also indicate the precarious and artificial nature of Carter's popularity during the primaries. Developments in Iran (and to some extent Afghanistan) permitted him to undermine the substantive basis of his opponent's challenge and simultaneously to deflect attention from his own record, but what was he to do if the crisis were resolved, or if the public's patience grew short, or if either Kennedy or Ronald Reagan found a political vulnerability on Iran? Clearly, as the crisis lingered its political capital diminished. Further, the press's insatiable appetite for the story threatened to sustain an impression Carter increasingly did not desire—that his management of the Iranian matter indicated how well he functioned as a leader.

The administration's decision to use Iran as Carter's exclusive domain and to exploit for political gain the media's interest and the public's emotional susceptibilities was a self-constructed trap. Consequently, even after the president quit the Rose Garden to deliver his message personally to the people, there was no effective way to remove the Iranian matter from the public sphere or to open the affair to debate, or to restrict the power he gave the press and television to keep attention focused on the incident, or to reduce the salience of video images as the basis for judging Carter's presidential stature. In the end, even the images of Carter acting presidential served as subtle reminders that as a leader he was seriously flawed, as this recollection by Robert Strauss of the Sunday before the election testifies:

> Let me tell you the final straw for me, when I almost felt like throwing it in. We finally staged it: the President flies back on Sunday morning of the hostage thing. He's got his message, he comes back from the campaign, he helicopters in to the White House, and he takes a long stroll by himself, not even with his wife with him, so he'll look dramatic. Here's this man dealing with the issue. I'll be a dirty son of a bitch if in the middle of the television screen I'm looking at, and thinking how good it's looking, out runs Brzezinski, puts his arm around him, and hands him a paper. And the two of them walk off together talking about the paper. He [Brzezinski] put the negative touch on that, a great scene, a poignant scene. So he killed that morning. The news could have been good. It turned out to be a *negative* instead of a *positive*. That's the story of the campaign there. (Germond and Witcover 1981, 14; emphasis added)[28]

Strauss's comment, in addition to its analysis of how the president's campaign of images returned to haunt him, reflects how thoroughly the Carter camp had entrenched its thinking about the public in a technological mold. Carter's public—the voters of the nation—was neither an aggregate with shared interests nor an aggregate discursively formed and identified by consensus; it was seen as a quantity assembled in bits and pieces by projecting orchestrated images before voters to excite "positive" and "negative" impressions. This mode of thinking governed the Carter campaign generally, and it even governed treatment of what had been built up as the most solemn of all issues, the problem of freeing the hostages. We can see most clearly how such thinking apparently led Carter to exploit the Iranian affair by *inserting Iran into the campaign precisely when opinion polls suggested it would be politically efficacious.*

From the beginning White House political advisers realized that galvanizing American public opinion around Iranian events worked in Carter's favor. The liabilities of three years were swept aside. Economic woes, fits and starts of foreign policy, and controversial management of his own staff and cabinet would be forgotten as each new development in the Iranian situation triggered a positive image of the president. Early developments—such as official acts of retaliation against Iran, the World Court and United Nations initiatives, the shah's departure from New York and locating a haven in Panama when Mexico denied him refuge in Cuernavaca, the ominous response when Iran threatened to place the hostages on trial—were all reflected in the public mood, as an AP-NBC News poll revealed. Over 70 percent believed Carter was doing everything in his power to release the hostages, and two-thirds opposed extraditing the shah. By the end of November he had edged ahead of Kennedy in the ABC News–Lou Harris poll for the first time, 48 percent to 46 percent (Germond and Witcover 1981, 86).

Carter displayed the hostage issue prominently in early December as he announced his candidacy for a second term. Not only did he call for unity and support during his absence from the campaign trail, but he magnified the crisis—and his leadership—by comparisons to World War II and to Abraham Lincoln. Indeed, Carter proclaimed, "At the height of the Civil War, President Abraham Lincoln said, 'I have but one task, and that is to save the Union.' Now I must devote my concerted efforts to resolving the Iranian crisis." Shortly thereafter Carter's lead over Kennedy grew to eight points in the Gallup poll. Later in December, after the shah left the United States and Iran called for trials of the hostages, Carter responded by appealing for United Nations sanctions. Yankelovich, Skelly, and White showed that his lead increased to twenty points (United States Office of the Federal Register 1979, 2194; Germond and Witcover 1981, 89). As these trends continued and the president retreated into the Rose Garden, he seemed to send out timely reminders and announce developments that coincided with the polling data on his reelection chances.

Iowa came first, scheduled for 21 January. As this test drew near, Carter called in a small group of columnists and television commentators for a backgrounder. There he in effect wrote his own news story, although under White House rules the material was not attributed to him. The Soviet Union's invasion of Afghanistan, in tandem with the Iranian crisis, had the potential to emphasize America's Middle Eastern plight and the president's leadership in framing an effective response. Haynes Johnson gives this account:

> The stories said the President was prepared to take any action, including war, to block Soviet aggression in the Mideast after the invasion of Afghanistan; that he would cancel U.S. participation in the Summer Olympic games scheduled for Moscow, and that he was planning a new, tough speech to the nation outlining a "Carter doctrine" for the Mideast. The stories were a trial ballot for Carter, and they made him appear strong just at a time when the first critical primary contests with Kennedy loomed. (Broder et al. 1980, 61)

Carter's outmaneuvering of Kennedy the day before the Iowa caucuses was less disguised. On 20 January the president appeared on *Meet the*

Press. His appearance was tantamount to inserting his leadership role into the public's consciousness in a way that could only aid his chances in the Iowa caucuses and damage Kennedy's. An internal memo written by a *Washington Post* reporter assigned to Kennedy depicts Carter's exploitation of the hostage issue this way:

> I often get the feeling that this election campaign is being run of, by, and for the TV networks, and so it was fitting that it was a TV show that perfectly crystallized Ted Kennedy's dilemma. The show was the January 20 edition of ABC's "Issues and Answers," on which Kennedy appeared only after he was turned down in an effort to worm his way onto "Meet the Press" for a joint appearance with Carter. (Must note there the utterly brazen arrogance of Carter agreeing to go on that show one day before the Iowa caucuses after he had said in writing that he would have to forego personal appearances until the Tehran hostages were freed.) Kennedy's whole campaign has been upstaged by Carter's handling of the Mideast situation, and sure enough, his appearance on "Issues and Answers" was interrupted twice by news bulletins reporting what Carter was saying at the same time on "Meet the Press." (Broder et al. 1980, 57–58)

Iowa, of course, went two to one for the president in caucuses, and his campaign was off to a strong if not decisive beginning. The next primary, New Hampshire, was in Kennedy's backyard, and the Carter people were concerned that a Kennedy rebound might reverse his faltering campaign start. As discussed earlier, when Caddell's polls indicated that these fears were justified, Carter held a news conference, attacking Kennedy's statements on Iran and thereby directing attention to Kennedy's negatives—credibility and dependability. The desired outcome, of course, was for voters to perceive Kennedy's character, not Carter's record, as the overriding concern in casting their votes.

Carter won the New Hampshire primary and a string of others in quick succession. Voters were perceiving him as the eventual winner and started to cast votes on a primary basis of "let's send him a message" rather than on a general election basis of "I want this person in office." New York's primary gave Carter such a warning. After Ambassador McHenry voted for a United Nations resolution sanctioning Israel, the Carter campaign in New York started to slip. Preferential polls showed him with a substantial lead (on the Friday before the primary the Harris polls gave Carter a twenty-seven point lead), but Caddell's figures proved the contrary. In fact, six days before the primary Carter trailed in his own poller's adjusted figures, and the bottom was dropping out of "character" as a significant issue in New Yorkers' minds. Discontent over the economy and the lack of development in Iran started to take hold, and Kennedy eventually trounced Carter 59 percent to 41 percent.

Carter was facing a similar problem in the Wisconsin primary. While the preferential polls showed a sizable Carter lead, Caddell's adjusted figures indicated that Kennedy was moving closer. Recent losses in New York and Connecticut compounded matters. Another defeat could make these look like a trend rather than exceptions. Appearances here were especially important, with the Pennsylvania primary just ahead and not looking secure for the president. In Caddell's view, "The Iranian thing was clearly a problem. . . . The President's ratings on his handling of it were declining" (Schram 1980, 113). Carter again played his Iranian card.

For some time Hamilton Jordan had been involved in secret negotiations with go-betweens approved by the Iranians.[29] They had worked out a scenario for transferring the hostages from the militants to the government, scheduled for 29 March. Despite delays, news reports raised speculation that some movement on the crisis was likely soon. On 1 April, the day of the Wisconsin primary, the president appeared before the television news cameras at 7:20 a.m., just in time to make the morning newscasts, to announce the "positive step" that President Bani-Sadr had declared the intent of the Iranian government to take control of the hostages—a report that subsequently proved false. But in the context of the Wisconsin primary, the weekend speculation and Carter's primary morning message proved significant. According to Caddell, "When it was made clear over the weekend that there was going to be some progress, that bumped the race for us. It went from a lead of 15 to 18 points to a win of almost 30 points. Wisconsin was the only state where we ever got the undecided to go for us in the end" (Salinger 1981, 114).

Carter paid a price in the long run, however, for the 1 April announcement. The press was alienated by its impression of his apparent willingness to manipulate Iranian news to gain campaign advantages. Having used the press to shape popular opinion by controlling the information released to the voters, Carter now had to contend with the license he issued the press to cover the story. As the voting public's main source of information, the press could and did adopt a more critical attitude toward Carter's handling of the crisis, presenting a less favorable view of his presidential timber than he and his staff desired. In the words of a senior adviser, "That 7 a.m. thing crossed the line. Carter no longer seemed decent and honorable, but manipulative." Then, in admission that the intent behind the Wisconsin announcement was misconceived, he observed, "Ironically, it probably had no impact—usually it takes a 24-hour gestation period for big events to have an impact on the public" (Salinger 1981, 114).

The observation on "crossing the line" was not unfounded. Shortly after Wisconsin the apparent progress toward securing the hostages' release vaporized, and voter impatience with Carter's handling of Iran began to grow. For the first time he received a negative rating on the hostage affair as a *Newsweek*-Gallup poll showed 49 percent to 40 percent disapproved ("Carter's New Tack on Iran" 1980).

Carter made a concerted effort in the Pennsylvania primary to remind voters of Kennedy's character and to keep the press's remorseless questioning of his timing of Iranian announcements from casting doubts on his own character. And at that, he only managed a near draw, actually losing the delegate count by one to Kennedy.

Although Carter was going to win the nomination, he did not have deep support. His aides warned him to end his self-imposed seclusion in the White House and go on the campaign trail lest he face grim consequences in the fall. But the Rose Garden strategy had created a lingering problem. Carter had made a point of giving his word not to campaign until the Iranian crisis was resolved. Against this backdrop Carter made his most dramatic move on Iran, the military attempt to rescue the hostages.

In the middle of April, Carter approved the rescue plan, with his people well aware of the political risks the mission involved. Germond and Witcover report Jody Powell's recollection of a prophetic conversation among the cabinet members after being briefed on the planned raid: "Somebody said on the way out, 'God, I hope to hell this works.' To which a Cabinet member replied: 'Well, if it doesn't it could be the end of the Carter presidency'" (Germond and Witcover 1981, 160).[30]

Political risks were not the only ones. The mission did not have a high probability of success without significant casualties. The Central Intelligence Agency had prepared a secret report on the prospects of the mission and presented it to CIA director Stansfield Turner on 16 March 1980. The pertinent portion of the report begins with item 6.

    6. The estimated percentage of loss among Amembassy hostages
       during each of the five major phases was:
        (a) Entry/Staging : 0%
           Assumes no loss of cover
        (b) Initial Assault : 20%
           Assumes . . . immediate loss of those under State FSR and
           FSS cover and others
        (c) Location/Identification : 25%
           Loss of State personnel before full suppression of resis-
           tance. Problem accentuated since Amembassy hostages
           not collocated.
        (d) Evacuation to RH-53s : 15%
           Assumes loss from snipers, from inside and outside
           Amembassy Compound, and AT and Apers mines.
        (e) Transfer—RH-53s to C-130s : 0%
           Assumes maintenance of site security.

7. The estimate of a loss rate of 60% for the Amembassy hostages represents the best estimate of CA & M7P Staff. (Salinger 1981, 237–38)

One can only speculate if the president would have ordered a rescue attempt that his own intelligence service predicted would result in the deaths of 60 percent of those it was attempting to liberate were he not involved in a presidential campaign apparently headed for trouble.[31] The facts remain that he did order a raid of precisely this nature under precisely these circumstances. Moreover, despite aborting the attempt because of mechanical failure and the subsequent loss of eight lives when an RH-53 and a G-130 collided, Carter gained the political support a president predictably receives in a moment of crisis. His ratings rose in the polls. Caddell explains, "People wanted the President to do something, and something happened. It's that simple. It dissipated the growing anger and pressure over the crisis. It's the one reason no one in the country cared whether Cyrus Vance was leaving [his post as secretary of state]—especially once [former senator Edmund] Muskie was chosen" (Drew 1981, 180).

But the support Caddell points to was fashioned out of the death of eight servicemen and another failure by the president to free the hostages. The popularity of the attempted rescue reflected the electorate's frustration with the futility of American diplomatic efforts. The tragedy also carried the danger that voter frustration could turn to cynicism toward Carter for his exploitation of the hostages' plight, suggesting the error of regarding the voting public as a technological concept expressed by polling data and managed through incremental adjustments of symbol and mood.[32]

Ironically, even the polling data began to reflect the futility of crafting policy in line with quantified reflections of this public. By mid March a *Time* poll showed only 14 percent optimistic about the future (versus 47 percent early in Carter's administration); 74 percent considered inflation our number one problem (versus 50 percent in January); over 50 percent thought Carter was too soft in dealing with Iran; and only 17 percent thought his handling of Afghanistan enhanced United States prestige abroad. One month later, on the very day that the aborted rescue mission was announced, an ABC-Harris survey showed Ronald Reagan now leading Carter by 42 percent to 33 percent. In February, Carter had led Reagan by 64 percent to 32 percent ("Out of the Rose Garden" 1980). Having misconceived the voting public in terms of mood and sentiment as measured by opinion surveys, Carter actually thwarted the formation of a truly *public* opinion by successfully restraining open debate of the salient issues implicit in the hostages' detention. Now this technologically imaged "public" was swinging against him.

Having failed to create a consensus on Iran, Carter now found himself trapped from doing and saying what his polls suggested was politically expedient. He had no political alternative to placing distance between himself and the hostage issue and trying to redirect the nation's attention. On 29 April, in response to a planted question at a briefing for civic leaders (Germond and Witcover 1981, 162–63), Carter offered the awkward ad lib that "none of these challenges [Iran and Afghanistan] are completely removed [*sic*], but I believe they are manageable enough now for me to leave the White House for a limited travel schedule, including some campaigning if I choose to do so" (United States Office of the Federal Register 1980e, 804).

The transparent implausibility of this remark escaped no one, including the president's advisers, who grumbled about it for weeks afterward (Jordan 1982, 284–88). However, in case anyone had not been listening closely, Kennedy was only too ready to render a verdict. "We have had a failed military intrusion into Iran. [Carter] has lost five of the last seven primaries [and state caucuses] and now he is willing to come out of the White House. I think the decision is quite clearly a political judgment" ("Out of the Rose Garden" 1980).

Nor did Carter's public treatment of Iran-related matters, once he started campaigning, engage voters in a way that might abate their suspicions. Specifically, he dropped the hostage issue. Apart from the Ramsey Clark incident, the White House initiated little if any discussion of Iran from May until September. There are very few remarks on the subject in the *Department of State Bulletin* for this period. The statements that do appear are usually those of Secretary Muskie, who all but replaced Carter as the American spokesperson on the matter. Moreover, the press cooperated by providing limited coverage during this time ("Talk of the Town" 1980). For six months Americans had been asked to think of nothing but the hostages. After the failed rescue mission left no room for bold new moves to secure their release, Americans were asked to forget them. At the very least the sudden silence spoke loudly as reinforcement to a growing public perception of Carter as incompetent. To the more contemplative observer, and perhaps the more skeptical, Carter's sudden silence on the hostage situation had the air of a strategy to manipulate the voting public by gearing events and information flow about Iran to political ends. In brief, voters sensed "they'd been had" ("Talk of the Town" 1980).

Iran resurfaced as a topic in the fall. As the election campaign broke into full stride, there was growing discussion that the president would secure the hostages' timely release just before the election (Germond and Witcover 1981, 1–22). But these discussions were not of the president's doing. Since the Clark incident Carter had commented on the Iranian situation only when asked, responding almost always with the same topoi— America's policy, national honor, and safety of the hostages; they are daily in my thoughts and prayers; the nation should not raise expectations falsely; there is no promise of early release; it would be inappropriate to comment on possible actions; shame on my opponent for interjecting the hostage matter into the campaign. Under the circumstances Carter plainly was not interested in reinitiating discussion of the hostages: any mention of contact with Iran fueled speculation that they might be returned soon and also evoked suspicion that he had used earlier discussions for political ends. Since there were no new sanctions to impose or bold rescue missions to undertake, the president was at the mercy of Iranian will to negotiate— as, quite probably, he always had been. And since there had been no public debate on the matter, Jimmy Carter became the focal point for the frustration and rage promoted in the early stages of the crisis. However cautious and however responsive his public comments now were to actual events in Tehran, his use of the crisis in the primaries had led to a widespread suspicion that administration hints at an impending resolution were calculated for political gain.

The Republicans fueled this perception by repeated mention of an "October surprise." They suspected Carter was going to stage a last-minute return of the hostages and that the emotions of this event could cost Reagan the election. They laid elaborate plans for appearances on televised news forums by former president Gerald Ford and his secretary of state, Henry Kissinger, and for speeches by Reagan to indict the president for playing politics with the hostages. To ensure that their message would be received accurately the Republicans talked incessantly about the October surprise, keeping the idea alive in the election campaign and raising the electorate's expectations that it would happen (Germond and Witcover 1981, 1–22). If it did, the Republican strategy hoped that Carter would seem to be continuing his manipulation of crisis events for political gain; if not, it would appear as another indication of Carter's ineptitude.

Nothing captured Carter's bind more clearly than the last weekend of the campaign. Trailing in the polls and almost certain to be defeated, he found the hostage issue once more thrust upon him as the Majlis, Iran's parliament, finally acted by issuing the conditions for the hostages' release. Carter hastily flew from Chicago to Washington; his arrival received wide coverage. He strode boldly from the helicopter to the White House, looking presidential and weighted with responsibility, but the earlier-cited image Robert Strauss described appeared on America's television screens. The adviser Americans saw as most deviously calculating, Zbigniew Brzezinski, rushed to Carter's side.

Later that afternoon Carter interrupted the Sunday football telecasts to announce "a significant development" that provided a "positive basis" for negotiating the hostages' release, but, he said, he would not broker a deal for his own political advantage. That evening the networks ran specials on the full year of captivity. The public arena in which Americans deliberated their presidential choice, now dialogized by dissident voices and images, was saturated with reminders of the hostage affair and of the president's failure to return these "heroes." Two days later, one year after the embassy was overthrown, the voters removed Jimmy Carter from office.

Carter's Phantom Public

The significance of Carter's technologized conception of a public and its opinions had a profound influence on the president's rhetorical choices. The foregoing analysis suggests that these choices often were ill conceived. Certainly it was a mistake to exploit the popularity of a strong, visible stand against the Iranians when the president could not control how the Iranians responded. It was no less mistaken to publicize the event and promote press coverage since there were no available means for silencing the press if the incident became protracted. It was equally ill-advised to capitalize on the populace's susceptibilities to hopeful news and willingness to rally in support of elected leaders during a crisis, since the president was powerless to transform hopeful news into crisis-ending results.

These decisions by Carter and his staff constrained and distorted the electoral arena, much as they had the public discussion of the hostages by their management of the "hero" theme. The electoral arena was narrowed and contoured through a one-sided portrayal of Jimmy Carter's presidential qualities while resolving the crisis. But it must be added that even though this arena was distorted by the president, he was considered by its inhabitants on his own terms.

Jimmy Carter went into the 1980 election campaign without a broad base of political or popular support. Regardless of the stature of his accomplishments, Carter was not particularly eloquent in his own defense and had not enjoyed significant success at presenting his stewardship in the best light. In his eyes, his lack of popular support was most tellingly portrayed in opinion polls that indicated a sizable portion of Americans thought he lacked leadership ability. Carter persistently analyzed his problem as one of *weak image,* as if failed policies or misconceived programs were not relevant to American voters. The strategy-setting Jordan report and Caddell memo— both prior to Carter's reelection bid announcement—indicate that the president did not envision a campaign of issues but a campaign of images. From the outset a hard-nosed pragmatism marked his mapping of a reelection strategy that would exploit his strengths and his opponents' weaknesses of image. There was also every indication of willingness to capitalize on the opportunities of incumbency to enhance the appearance of leadership, where Carter's image was most vulnerable.

Carter's perspective on the American voters did not project them as weighing issues but as responding to appearances: they were, in this perspective, interested in the semblance of honesty, compassion, decency, pacifism, strength, and so forth. Indeed, this is precisely the data Caddell's polls provided, an instrumentalist's technological portrayal of audience.

Cadell's approach assumed that voters are passive and impressionable. Reminded of the right qualities, each subset of the electorate would fall into line with a positive image of Carter, a negative image of his opponent, and a ballot for the president's reelection. It was as if this instrumental epistemology could not conceive of an active electorate capable of judging on the basis of conduct.

Carter's embrace of a technologized image of the electorate is no exception among contemporary politicians; that he is representative in his reliance on polling data makes his rhetoric on the Iranian matter all the more telling. The Carter camps' definition of the campaign as image making, not issue resolving, made exploitation of the hostage crisis predictable. Nothing could have been more opportune than this foreign development that diverted attention from issues to image and allowed a politician saddled with a "weak leader" image to demonstrate that he actually was a bold leader of presidential stature.

Yet, despite enjoying initial poll approval from announcements and initiatives geared to mesh with the campaign needs of caucuses and primaries, eventually Carter had to produce some tangible accomplishment. After all, the hostages were not images; they were real, and they were still incarcerated on election day. That fact undermined Carter's campaign strategy by decoupling his projected image of presidential stature from supporting deeds.

Thus, we must conclude that the technologically constructed public Carter imagined was a phantom. His strategists mistakenly believed that a public was a constellation of opinions pieced together or "constructed" by telling people first this bit, then that bit, depending upon what the polls showed they wanted to hear. But a public is not a quiescent assembly. Its intelligence, understanding, and stability are not revealed by a nose count but rather in its mutual discursive experiences of actively weighing partisan appeals that lead to a civil judgment. Although Carter's polls may have disclosed popular mood, they lacked the potential for indicating rhetorical strategies and appeals with enduring suasory potential toward that end.

Certainly other factors were at play in Carter's loss of the 1980 election. The condition of the economy, the scandals in his administration, a general swing to the political Right, and Ronald Reagan's campaigning skills contributed in large measure. But there is no denying that the hostage affair loomed throughout as an issue Carter himself defined as an important index of his presidential qualities. In retrospect one might question the wisdom of this as the litmus test of his administration, since there were accomplishments of economic, social, and diplomatic substance of which he could have boasted. And a review of the campaign rhetoric during the 1980 general election will show that Carter did point to his accomplishments. However, in the context of national concern for the hostages' return, his earlier appearance as "Jimmy One-note" served to sustain interest in and fuel public frustration over the hostage situation well past the point where it served a politically expedient end for the president. Harsh as the American public may appear for judging Carter's capacity to lead by his failures with an intractable and unreasonable foe, that test was significantly one of his own making.

Conclusion

The different responses to Carter's rhetoric on the Iranian hostage-taking—the acceptance of the hostages as heroes and the rejection of Carter as leader—tell us something important about public opinion. That Americans regarded the hostages as heroes reinforces the discursive character of public opinion. Although Jimmy Carter's words and deeds were not the only force shaping this opinion, they did play a significant role. That this opinion was not particularly well informed or balanced underscores the influence the quality of public discussion bears on the shape and quality of public opinion. That the Carter strategists seized the hostage-taking as an opportunity for the president to demonstrate his leadership and then geared messages and, apparently, hostage-related decisions to what their polls told them about voter perceptions of the president's leadership qualities indicates the vulnerability of public opinion to manipulation by those with power.

In this respect, Habermas's concluding critique in *The Structural Transformation of the Public Sphere* is informative. After arguing that the struggle between a genuinely critical publicity and one staged for purposes of manipulation remains open, Habermas describes the condition of the contemporary political public sphere, invaded by private interests and fraught with struggle between the competing tendencies of an elite attempting to make economic decisions for the masses and of the welfare state attempting to appropriate economic decisions and regulations for the general well-being. The consequence of the former is a *manufactured* public sphere in which the appearance of debate and rational choice produces what he terms "nonpublic opinion." The manufactured public sphere does not engage voters as participants in political dialogue but renders them spectators to contrived spectacles. It replaces a public opinion produced through critical publicity with what Habermas describes as "an in itself indeterminate mood-dependent inclination" of popular opinion (1989, 237). The consequence of the latter is an attempt to rationalize public opinion on models of liberalism or on institutional criteria for participation, neither of which will bear scrutiny.

Habermas's critique is especially pertinent today, when mass opinion often is portrayed as public opinion. Public opinion differs from mass opinion in structure and function in the ways that knowledge differs from behavior. Characteristically publics are theorized as engaging in the open exchange of opinions. Their members can respond directly and, depending on medium, often immediately. These open exchanges form opinions that can be translated into political, social, economic, or cultural actions.[33]

Mass opinion, by contrast, results from opposite conditions of communication. Mills's discussion in *The Power Elite* (1957, 304) identifies what Habermas (1989, 249) calls "empirically usable criteria" for defining this condition: Opinions are expressed by a few, who have access to information and to the mass media (which are the dominant media), thereby controlling the opinions that may be expressed. The mass is reduced to spectators who receive opinions presented to them and to which they are unable to respond directly, since they lack access to mass media. Moreover the translation of opinion into action is controlled by authorities, who not only organize and dominate the avenues of action but have penetrated this mass and stripped it of its power to frame autonomous action.

Certainly Carter's rhetoric of exclusivity on the Iranian matter and his reelection campaign's attempt to craft public opinion based on poll portrayals of voter moods estranged voter opinion from the structural and functional requirements to establish a public truth. By treating the voting public as a mass, Carter's reelection strategy also severed it from the political function within political institutions that public opinion serves. In fact, treating voter opinion as mass opinion detaches it from communication, since it is neither bound by principles of public discussion nor concerned with political domination. Instead, mass opinion expresses the social psychology of the group, as Habermas has observed. Concern for group members' states of mind is solely for purposes of determining how its collective psyche must be adjusted to assure compliance.

Equally, that the voters rejected Carter at the polls, in important measure because they perceived him to have failed in his management of the hostage affair, indicates that a public is more than an image. Habermas's structural analysis of the bourgeois public sphere suggests that the voting public's demise within the liberal democratic state has undermined the state's rationality. On the other hand, rhetorical analysis of the Carter campaign finds evidence in vernacular rhetoric that a public did form around the Iranian issue. If the rationality of the Carter administration was undermined for its treatment of the voters, it was not from success in bringing about their demise but that a public formed despite its best efforts to undermine its emergence.

At the same time, we must note that the failure of Carter to elicit a favorable opinion in support of his efforts to end the crisis reflects the odd conditions under which this public formed—a public responsive to the plight of fellow citizens, whose understanding came less from open debate than from the administration's characterization of events. If we find its opinion wanting, that is less the fault of the public that formed than of those who managed the discussion in a way that hampered its quality. The absence of a spirited public debate on the hostage-taking and the role played by the United States in the internal politics of Iran unquestionably hampered deep public understanding of the complex issues that lay at the heart of the hostage-taking in the first place.[34] This opinion's imperfection, nonetheless, contains a tension between a public opinion formed from a particular way of speaking and an image of public opinion as something less the product of discussion than of image management. When this public was denied the necessary conditions of public discourse that could certify the meaning of the Americans held hostage, it also was denied the means of critical publicity that might have certified the wisdom of Carter's actions. Still, its rejection of Carter underlines a public's possibilities for detecting bogus attempts to create the appearance of meeting this precondition for legitimation through a manufactured public sphere that produces the Habermasean condition of *nonpublic* opinion. As public opinion is conceptualized in terms that diminish its discursive character, or as the discourse which purports to anchor public opinion fails to provide critical publicity, the nature and function of public opinion become problematic.

The generating ideals of face-to-face democracy encourage us to think of public opinion as a product of informed citizens engaged in collective discussion from which communal consensus emerges. That ideal always has been subject to misgivings (Sagan 1991) and certainly does not travel well to describe the politics of large nation-states (Fishkin 1995). Some, like Fishkin, have argued that "we have lost social conditions that would reasonably motivate collective discussion by an informed public over a sustained period" (25). But that ideal takes its guidance from a premodern period in which the conditions of communication and decision making were different in kind from those that have prevailed at least since the Enlightenment. Moreover, the clubs of the Enlightenment, on which the model of the bourgeois public sphere as an open discursive space is based, were not necessarily bastions of reasoned consensus. They were susceptible to the vicissitudes of rivalries, fashion, and bias that have always made opinions debatable. At the same time, we adhere to an ideology born during the Enlightenment that considers public opinion as the legitimating agency for political action.

The seeming disjuncture between the vanishing presence of informed public discussion as the basis from which a reliable public opinion is formed and the reliance on public opinion to legitimate the state's actions has produced a series of calls for interventions that might produce a more enlightened body of citizen opinion on public problems. Fishkin, for example, who sees public discussion for unmotivated citizens reduced to sound bites, calls for deliberative polling in which a national random sample of citizens would be taken to the same location and immersed in the issues, with carefully prepared briefing materials and intensive discussions.

After several days of working together, they would be polled in detail. Fishkin maintains that the results would reflect "the considered judgments of the public—the views the entire country would come to if it had the same experience of behaving more like ideal citizens immersed in the issues for an extended period" (162). As Fishkin notes, this poll would be neither descriptive nor predictive of public opinion but rather prescriptive of the conclusions people would come to if they had the opportunity and motivation to examine issues closely. Dryzek, after excoriating survey research in political science for its "mismeasure" of voters, calls for reform through implementation of Q methodology, a highly sophisticated statistical method for arraying survey data, on which to base a program of discursive democratization (1990, 173–89). And Yankelovich, after indicting the culture of technological control for its embrace of instrumental rationality, urges replacing public opinion as reported by traditional polling with public judgment, a state of mind that we deduce from surveys designed to test stability, coherence, and recognition (1991, 234).

Each of these proposals posits a prescription for ideal citizens. Each of these proposals claims to redeem the discursive center of public opinion but relies on the discourse of surveys rather than of those participating in actually formed publics to deduce what their opinions might be. None has considered the alternative of examining the admittedly complex but nonetheless available dialogizing interchange between official and vernacular rhetorics that form and reflect public opinion.

Public opinion, as experienced among the quotidian, vernacular exchanges of social actors, has a self-consciously open rhetorical status. Our quotidian, vernacular exchanges on events and leaders create a measure of shared meaning that informs and constitutes society's prevailing views. The dialogizing character of public opinion's rhetorical face—civil judgment—is unlike the data of polls in that it invites identification with the public that is forming it. Polls suggest direction without narrative, whereas the rhetorical status of civil judgment joins opinion to beliefs and values that are enacted concretely in the events of public life and are thematized in the arenas of the Public Sphere.

The perceptiveness of an actively engaged public in detecting the management of the hostage affair as a ruse to keep them distracted from the issue of Carter's record carries an optimistic suggestion. Although the voting public apparently did not get beyond the bimodal image of the Iranian affair itself, it is significant that it saw Carter's use of the affair as image-projection. The voting public's awareness suggests that the voters can become actively engaged whenever they are able to penetrate the projected images of their leaders and perceive the substantive issues. At the level of issues, they are ready for informed discussion and affirmative judgments of virtuosity. This informed discussion, the vernacular rhetoric of public opinion formation, will be the concern of the next chapter.

Chapter 8

DEMOCRACY'S NARRATIVE: LIVING IN ROOSEVELT'S AMERICA

Behind the door of every contented man there ought to be someone standing with a little hammer and continually reminding him with a knock that there are unhappy people, that however happy he may be, life will sooner or later show him its claws, and trouble will come to him—illness, poverty, losses, and then no one will see or hear him, just as now he neither sees or hears others.

Anton Chekhov, *Gooseberries*

On 9 January 1940 Pearl Elder, an American citizen, wrote the following letter to the White House (Official File [OF] 2526, Box 22):[1]

> To Mr. Franklin D. Roosevelt
>
> Washington, D.C.
>
> Dear Sir and Friend.
>
> The fingers writing this letter are not just my fingers, they are the fingers of countless hundreds of other women.
>
> We are the ordinary, every day women of the United States. . . . The great mass of women whose voice, when once raised, rolls over America as thunder in the mountains.
>
> We have watched you, Sir. We have seen your efforts to help us. We have quietly listened to praise, criticism and debate concerning you, and this fact stands out in our minds as clear as the morning star. WE NEED YOU. We need your straight thinking—your pity and consideration for the weak and the helpless, your fearlessness, and most of all we need your sense of humor.
>
> Please keep on being our President. Only if you are too tired will we willingly let you go. In these troubled times we simply do not dare to lose your able statesmanship. Please don't fail us.
>
> George Washington is justly called "The Father of his Country." You, Sir, can justly be called "The Saviour of his Country."
>
> Had you not took over when you did, these United States would have seen the bloodiest revolt in the history of the World.
>
> We were jobless, our savings were in banks with closed doors, our children were in want and we were sick with desperation.

232

Then you, Sir, gathered up the tangled reins of government and saved us.

Please stay where you are for a few years longer. We are
afraid without you. The vote is a mere formality.

God Bless You Sir.

Your Sincere Friends, The plain women

By Pearl Elder, Raymond, Mississippi[2]

Ms. Elder's simple yet powerful eloquence testifies to a politics that
seems to have passed from the American scene. Americans still write the
White House to register political views, but we know our views are unlikely to receive the chief executive's personal attention, much less his personal reply. They are fated to be part of the pro-and-con tally on the issue
they address. Ms. Elder's letter shares none of these impersonal expectations. It defies reduction to a stroke in the yea column, or pushing the
key on the telephone keypad. A tally mark would miss its point and dis-
tort its meaning by forcing it through the mill of a political technology.
Writing such a letter today, while knowing that it would become merely
another datum to be tabulated, would require detachment from political reality. Ms. Elder seems neither detached nor likely to have brooked
complicity with a technologized politics. She has more to express than
her mere preference. She has insights to share, opinions to urge, personal hopes and fears to voice. She makes appeals that are specific to this
president, with comments on qualities of his person that endear him to
the women of America and make his reelection vital to the nation's survival. Her use of imagery and cadence gives immediacy to her plea and
transcendence to her cause. She has constructed a *rhetorical* document,
perhaps more stylized than most but nevertheless, by the standards of
her day, illustrative of vernacular rhetoric that rained upon the White
House. She wrote to an audience she assumed would read its contents
and be moved to respond, even as the contemporary reader is moved to
respond with questions about the political consciousness implicit in her
words.

What understanding of political relations does Ms. Elder possess that
would lead her to express them in terms of a leader's personal caring?
What encouraged such a formulation? How does she understand the
basis for political action? Why did she feel free to argue her case for
action on grounds of personal commitment? Why does she understand
political empowerment as derived from a leader but lost without him?
What had encouraged such an awareness? Such questions are not incidental to our understanding of public opinion—how it forms and gets
expressed; what it expresses; what, if anything, unifies those who share it;
and what its expression reveals of a public, including its members' self-
understanding as social actors and their relationship to their society's
model of knowledge and power.

Pearl Elder's self-awareness includes her membership in the collectivity that has captured the means of social action and used them to produce a new social order. She has internalized her active participation in a process of radical social change. Her political consciousness also is acutely aware of the fragility of her political authority, which exemplifies a more general state of mind shared by the majority of Americans who had lived through the Depression and the first two terms of Franklin Roosevelt's administration. The immediacy of urging Roosevelt's impending candidacy for a third term is symptomatic of something more monumental. Ms. Elder's letter reaffirms her awareness of a prevailing social will, with its incumbent political relations and the trajectory of their political economy to produce and sustain a particular type of society. In its own orbit her letter iterates the ongoing discursive production of society. Her voice may not speak from an institutional site, but she is exquisitely sensitive to the potential an ensemble of such voices has to influence society's course.

Throughout this book I have argued that publics are an essential source of legitimation for state and institutional action. Whether in dramatic and world-shaping ways, as occurred with the demise of communism in Central and Eastern Europe, or through mundane enactments, as occur when voters decide a local referendum, the character and quality of their validation is an outcome of complex, interacting forces. State officials do not have exclusive dominion over the resources that can forge social will; the active segments of society also have access to them, sometimes significantly so. Legitimation requires a context of shared meaning in which to interpret present actions. For example, as we saw in chapter 5, Europe's communist states held enormous power over the economic and social conditions of their citizens' lives but were unable to express the conditions of daily life or the objectives of state planning in terms that people found authorizing. Languages of national identity, which situated native meaning within cultural memory and communicated a set of social relations different from those advanced by the state, were fatally inaccessible to a foreign ideology. The party's inability to produce meaning that might link policy to tradition and heritage deprived it of the essential means for motivating social cooperation and cohesion.

Conversely, events in these nations since 1989 (in many cases since the end of World War II) indicate that publics often provide impulse for direction and guidance for action in the complex process of constituting social reality. As they are shaped by discourse, the symbolic acts of publics also may frame the discursive field in which institutional actors are themselves defined and redefined. My present concern is gaining insight into this interactive process.

In this chapter I will examine a limited and focused set of discourse: the letters written by the American public to Franklin Roosevelt offering advice on whether he should pursue a third term as president of the United States.

234

These letters form a text about hopes and fears, rights and duties, and dreams of a national future. I will examine them as a conversational text exploring the relationship between social actors and the state. We will see how the vernacular rhetoric that expresses a public opinion explores the evolving meaning of their society, the meaning of Roosevelt's America. Together they define a discursively constituted world shared by the people and a leader who is designated to decide. Moreover, their conversation may provide a vehicle for insight beyond that afforded by survey research into the dialogical possibilities between the governed and those who lead on the character of the world they inhabit.

The Election of 1940

The 1940 presidential election was unprecedented in American history.[3] For the first time voters were asked to consider a sitting president for a third term. The prohibition against a third term was not yet a constitutional amendment; it was a legacy of American political tradition, dating from the nation's founding. George Washington, urged to continue in office, declined primarily due to age. Jefferson also declined after two terms, offering more philosophical reasons in opposition. On the other hand, Jefferson had also expressed opposition to a president serving more than a single term, a principle that did not deter him from running for reelection. Andrew Jackson made a similar case, arguing in his first six annual messages to Congress for a constitutional amendment changing the presidency to a single six-year term. Congress did not follow his recommendation nor did his principles prevent him from standing for a second term. However, he declined a third term bid for reasons of age and health.

By the end of Jackson's administration, the tradition had been set that American presidents would sit for no more than two consecutive terms. Although the record of invoking the tradition appears to have rested more on partisan interest than principle, the fact remains that it provided potent rhetoric for those who opposed third terms by Ulysses S. Grant, Grover Cleveland, and Theodore Roosevelt even though it is doubtful that this caused their respective defeats. Indeed, by the time of the 1912 election the third-term tradition had been reduced to "an impotent archaism" (Stein 1943, 221). Health reasons were offered to explain why Woodrow Wilson did not seek reelection in 1920, and if Calvin Coolidge had philosophical reservations about a third term, he kept them to himself, offering only the enigmatic "I do not choose to run" as reason enough for not standing once more in 1928.

The possibility of Franklin D. Roosevelt's candidacy had been a subject of highly partisan speculation almost since his reelection in 1936.[4] By 1940 the outbreak of war in Europe strengthened these partisan views. For those opposed to a third term, recollections of World War I evoked intensified expressions of isolationism and fears that FDR was leading the nation into war. For those in favor of his candidacy, the world crisis mandated experience in the White House to preserve the country's neutrality while preparing its defenses against the Nazi threat. The electorate also was deeply concerned and divided about the direction of the economy if Roosevelt were or were not to continue in office. Opponents pointed to America's 7.7 million unemployed workers, 14.3 percent of the labor force, as a clear sign that New Deal policies had been a stopgap at best but were unable to steer the nation to full economic recovery. Moreover, New Deal programs of state intervention seemed antagonistic to the interests of industry, finance, and commerce. For supporters, the New Deal had adopted fiscal policies and provided financial and legislative relief that allowed them to achieve at least minimal economic security and inclusion in democracy's promise of economic opportunity. For these millions, the New Deal had to be preserved.

Data available on the voters in the 1940 election provide a fairly clear and well-documented picture of who was voting for whom and why. The accepted analysis argues that were it not for the fear of American involvement in World War II, FDR would not have been reelected.[5] This conclusion is based on polls taken between 1938 and 1940 concerning the general issue of the third term, and these polls do support some basic inferences about voter behavior.[6] They indicate a growing conviction that FDR would run, in direct correlation with the deteriorating situation in Europe. They show that support of a third term was in inverse relation to a person's economic means and directly related to party affiliation. They reveal that in the event of war, voters believed Roosevelt was the nation's best choice for a leader, apparently based on his experience in dealing with the European heads of state and his conduct of national policy to maintain neutrality while building the country's defenses. They also reveal that the majority of Americans did not regard the third-term issue as a major consideration when casting their ballots. In light of these data, it would be difficult to minimize the European war's influence on the American voters.

While there can be no gainsaying the force that Hitler's military invasions exerted on the electorate, reducing the 1940 campaign to the ominous threat posed by this brute reality blurs its snapshot of what Americans then understood to be at stake. These same data, for instance, also show that among those who had most benefited from the New Deal there was a strong level of support for a third term independent of the war. They show that while a third-term candidacy did not appear to have public favor until after the invasion of Poland, a substantial percentage of voters were undecided, and therefore open to persuasion, well before that event. They reveal that the election was decided during its last two weeks, when Roosevelt actively joined the campaign by delivering five major political speeches.[7] They indicate that reasons associated with the person of the president account for one-third to one-half of his votes, suggesting a personal identification between the voters and FDR—a theme that he developed in his five speeches. Significantly, they are mute on the sea change that had occurred in American society during the preceding seven years of Roosevelt's presidency. Although there is every reason to agree with the polls' focus on the threat of an impending war as the transcendent issue in the election, followed closely by the respective candidates' perceived ability to lead their nation during its moment of international crisis, for millions of Americans the more basic issue remained the meaning that threat posed to an evolving consciousness of national identity and class power. The 1940 campaign provided a context for national dialogue on the country's direction: on the type of society America had become during Roosevelt's tenure and the future Americans wished to embrace. This was a dialogue, by its very nature, about the very core of social will. One does not find this issue or plumb its dimensions as a discursive formation through scientific calibrations because it is incommensurable with scientific measurement. It is a distinctively discursive formation, embedded in narratives and revealed through rhetorical analysis.

The People's Letters and Public Opinion

It is a commonplace of American politics that Franklin Roosevelt revolutionized the ways in which presidents use mass media to communicate to and with the electorate (Boorstin 1965; Nicholas 1945). In many respects he seems to epitomize what Jeffrey Tulis (1987) has termed "the rhetorical presidency," in which the chief executive tends to make direct appeals to the people in order to evoke citizen pressure on politics. Roosevelt's "fireside chats" are perhaps the most celebrated example of his direct communication with the people (Braden and Brandenburg 1955). But he also pioneered the management of the press conference, setting ground rules for publication and attribution and showing inimitable deftness at managing the press's version of a story.[8] FDR was a careful orchestrator of what we now call photo opportunities, taking the necessary precautions to maintain the pretense that his physical impairment was less serious than it was.[9] Whether on the front page or in the film clip, he was a person in charge, often on his feet, and usually with his characteristic smile. And Roosevelt was an innovator in the uses of the White House mail as a barometer of American public opinion (Sussmann 1963, 51–86; Smith and Morris 1949, 150–70).

People wrote to Franklin and Eleanor Roosevelt. The Roosevelt White House received a staggering volume of mail that can only be described as a sea change in comparison to that of previous administrations. During his first year in office FDR's average weekly mail was tenfold greater than the heaviest depression-period mail received by Herbert Hoover.

Previous administrations had employed one person to answer the public's mail; FDR's White House quickly had to increase the staff to fifty. The average daily volume was between five thousand and eight thousand letters. Leila Sussmann estimates that the rate of mail written annually to Roosevelt during the Depression was 160 per 10,000 literate adults. This compares to rates for Lincoln during the Civil War and Wilson during World War I, the previous leaders in volume of mail received, of 44 and 47 per 10,000 literate adults respectively (Sussmann 1963, 11).

The sheer volume of the general public's correspondence indicates the average American's sense of Roosevelt's accessibility. And Roosevelt found that among their values was the insight these letters provided into public opinion. According to Louis Howe, FDR considered letters from typical Americans as his most reliable index of the public mind (1934, 22–23).[10] They were an important means for escaping Washington's isolation from the rest of the nation. People wrote about their circumstances and their concerns—the right to work, the right to organize, the right to fair wages, the policies of the New Deal, the need for extraordinary measures to preserve the family farm, the plight of the elderly and the unemployed, and a host of economic and social problems that accompanied the Depression. Some were written to offer thanks for the New Deal and personal homage to the president. Some discussed their personal problems and asked for assistance, such as a loan or a letter authorizing a public agency to grant them special consideration. Some provided surveillance of the local scene, such as local reaction to policies and proposals that might conflict with the impression created by the press. Selected letters were pulled from each day's mail for the president to read: those from individuals whose positions or relationships to the president suggested themselves and those on key issues that seemed to be particularly informative. This daily regime kept him in tune with the experienced reality of the Depression and New Deal initiatives.

This monitoring also suggests a dimension of the Roosevelt presidency that Tulis's thesis on the rhetorical presidency overlooks. Tulis (1996) argues that there is a danger in governance through direct appeals to the people rather than through persuasion aimed at Congress because such populist governance looses its tether to the constitution. Although FDR used the radio to speak directly to the people, Tulis's thesis would interpret this to mean that his messages were crafted to engage citizen susceptibilities, producing a rhetoric lacking on a principled advocacy. Roosevelt's fireside chats, however, are lessons on the possibilities of democracy when a leader addresses the masses with messages that actually have something to say. Roosevelt's monitoring of the mail enhanced his ability to engage citizens in terms that related to their problems and allowed them to understand what the government was considering to do about them. Actually talking through the issues involved citizens in the process of advancing policy decisions whose consequences they bore; this was, if anything, in the tradition of participatory democracy and a major redefinition of the meaning of America.

The pulse of the New Deal acquired a personalized beat when felt in terms of the impact of its measures in the daily lives of average people. Unlike an opinion poll, each letter provided a narrative that gave Roosevelt a feel for what people were thinking, for the language they used to express their experiences of social and economic conditions and their felt experience of legislation and public policy. Writing about the interpretive significance derived from tapping lived experiences, Samuel Lubell notes that while he was a correspondent in Washington he shared the common opinion of those in the capital that the New Deal was a mélange of ad hoc measures lacking a coherent philosophy. "When one translated its benefits down to what they meant to the families I was interviewing in 1940, the whole Roosevelt program took on a new consistency" (Lubell 1956, 59).[11]

By today's standards, Roosevelt's use of the public's correspondence may seem a primitive mode of accessing public opinion. For example, Bruce Gronbeck, commenting on the frequency of poll-related stories at a rate of one and a half a day on the front pages of the *New York Times* and the *Washington Post* during the last month of the Bush-Dukakis campaign, concludes, "When polls chart public opinion with but 5 percent error on a daily basis, they create a virtual conversation between leaders and constituencies" (1995, 36). But this is a vastly different conversation from the one between Roosevelt and letter writers. To judge his mode of tapping public sentiment by polling criteria begs the question by assuming that a survey would provide the same information, only with greater speed, volume, and accuracy. Roosevelt's behavior suggests he proceeded from a radically different and essentially rhetorical starting point. Rather than relying exclusively on polls Roosevelt acquired his sense of public opinion by monitoring the public sphere. He encouraged a vital epistolary space into being.[12] By becoming an active participant in it, he conferred on each letter the significance of an acknowledged contribution to an ongoing conversation about America's course. The general public's correspondence, in turn, provided the president a rich and valuable source of vernacular exchange from which he then extrapolated a sense of what people thought, or public opinion.[13] He then moved this epistolary dialogue to the larger public conversation he conducted with the people through his public speeches and radio addresses, drawing on it for guidance to present the politics of recovery and war in terms that addressed the fears and hopes of the American people. Finally, the president's ability to trigger an overwhelming volume of correspondence allowed him to turn mass mail, in Robert Merton's felicitous phrase, "into the functional equivalent of an episodic plebiscite" (1963, xv).

The letters from the public on the question of the third term follow this pattern and give us insight into the public mind, as FDR understood it, on whether or not the president should seek a third term. They engage him on the national conversation about the issues of the day but more fundamentally on the character of the national community and the citizen's relationship to it. Their dialogue casts fresh light on the 1940 election and is instructive on the role of vernacular rhetoric for publics: how publics form and express a public opinion, the relationship vernacular rhetoric implies among their members, and the suggestive possibilities for political discourse when vernacular rhetoric is heeded and answered.

"Public" Opinion on the Third Term

I began this chapter with a letter written by Pearl Elder urging FDR to seek a third term. By today's standards her remarks may appear quaint, even naive. But in 1940 she was representative of mainstream America. The Franklin D. Roosevelt Library (FDRL) contains massive correspondence to the president from people like Ms. Elder on the topic of the third term. In total, there are roughly twenty-four linear feet of letters, postcards, and telegrams filling seventy-two containers.[14] This volume is exclusive of letters on other topics that may have touched on the third-term issue, letters to Eleanor Roosevelt or others on this matter, and items housed in the National Archives addressed to the third term. By comparison, correspondence to the White House between 1934 and 1936 concerning the second term fills only three containers at the FDRL.

The volume of correspondence, impressive as it is, does not completely indicate the sentiment evoked by the prospect of the president leaving office. The file includes several different types of correspondence that are relevant to assessing its contents as an expression of public opinion. Among these are a considerable number of organized appeals urging FDR to seek a third term. For example, many postcards were sent in response to a "Rally Round Roosevelt" campaign organized under the signature of Anthony G. Neary. Mostly they were handwritten personal notes such as the one J. A. Goldberg wrote on 25 June 1940:

> Dear Mr. President, now, more than ever, you are needed at the head of this government. While I know that the work has been arduous and nerve racking, I sincerely hope that you will hold on for another four years. You are needed.
>
> Very Truly
J. A. Goldberg
Businessman

A typical box contains twenty postcards with similar messages. Chain letters of both local and national origin are also in the file. And it contains correspondence from organizations and groups conveying resolutions of support as far-ranging as motions adopted by national and local labor unions, such as the American Communications Association (9/5/39), the California State Legislative Board of the Brotherhood of Trainmen (2/24/38), and the Allegheny Valley Industrial Union Council (6/21/39), to the "bad news" that on 5 November 1938 the students attending the Howard Lake Public Schools voted thirty-three to seventy against a third term for the president. In addition, there are letters like that sent by Abraham Alboun on 20 September 1938 informing FDR that clubs, such as Mr. Alboun's "R-3 Clubs of America," were being formed with the aim of having one in each community. However, the majority of this correspondence consists of handwritten letters from average Americans expressing sentiments and making arguments to buttress convictions about the third-term issue. These letters are of particular interest.

I was originally curious to learn what the contents of this collection might reveal about popular sentiment being urged on the president. However, it soon became apparent that these letters communicated something more complex than a simple pro or con view on the third-term issue. They were individual attempts to influence the president's judgment. They were vernacular expressions that projected an image of political relationship between a leader and the people and, through that relationship, an understanding of social change.

Topoi of Political Relationship

The letter is a medium of direct communication. It bypasses the town meeting as the venue for directly expressing a need or sentiment and permits one to argue his own case unimpeded and without risk of public refutation. By encouraging members of the general public to write their representatives about important issues and thereby jointly apply pressure to Congress, Roosevelt reversed the normal legislative process for making the will of the people known. Perhaps the most obvious characteristic of these letters is their writers' awareness of a restructured public sphere that gave them epistolary access to the president.

The third-term correspondence to Roosevelt reveals a widespread perception by typical Americans of their relationship with him. Quite apart from the issue they address, their contents and tone express a personal attachment to the president that these writers regard as reciprocal. They offer support and advice, they volunteer local surveillance, they report the results of their personal "public opinion" polls, and they proffer schemes that are "sure bets" to gain his reelection (and reap their authors some form of personal gain in the bargain). Some attempt to cheer him with jokes, poems, and homespun campaign songs (one of which has over one hundred verses!); some ask personal favors. More than 90 percent of those who wrote did so to plead the case in favor of a third term. And the characteristic that binds them together is the poignancy with which they express their relationship to him in personal terms—how he has touched their lives and what they now expect of him for their continued security.

By tone and content these letters conducted the nation's politics with a personal rhetoric that put questions on the intimate plane of their impact on people's lives. They closed the distance between the people and their leader by addressing Roosevelt as if he were accessible to them and open to their ideas. At the same time a rhetoric of familiarity also carried the risk of distortion by overvaluing personal experience and importance in assessing the overall consequences of federal policies. The depth of these connections and their potential dangers are graphically evident in the types of appeals made to support or oppose the third term.

The letters regarding the third term reflect a public with divided views of its leader based on his perceived relationship with the common citizen. The apparent issue that evoked this outpouring of opinion about Roosevelt's reelection to a third term was the threat of war. But in addressing that matter, arguments were raised that told of a more profound concern. The transcendent issue for both sides was their respective ability to control the future and, not incidentally, the oppressive impulses they found in one another. This was a time when paranoid stances made their way into this epistolary public sphere. We may see this most plainly in the differences of emphasis that mark the two sides.

The sample of letters analyzed for topoi[15] was overwhelmingly favorable to the president, as I have already noted, and at a rate of nearly ten to one urged him to seek reelection. This division is, in part, an artifact of the letters' voluntary nature. Roosevelt's supporters who felt their interests were at risk would have had greater incentive to write than opponents who were hostile to him. FDR's own reluctance to clarify his intent undoubtedly added to the mobilizing urgency for supporters to make their sentiments known. Consequently, the collection lacks randomness across the American electorate. The letters' obvious bias notwithstanding, the patterns of reasons offered to sway the president remain indicative of what a significant cross section of citizens believed was at stake in the 1940 election.

Those who wrote in opposition to a third-term bid divide into two groups, with the majority, or roughly two-thirds, friendly in tone toward the Roosevelt presidency (see tables 8.1 and 8.2). They used topoi of praise to express admiration for FDR's accomplishments and the belief that future historians would regard him as one of America's greatest presidents. They offered advice, in the manner of one looking after a friend's best interests. They stated concern for his health and fear that the strains of another term might kill him. They eulogized his accomplishments in saving the party and aligning it with the New Deal. For the party's welfare and the continuance of its accomplishments they urged him now to step aside. They expressed regret at bearing the unwelcome news that Amer-

I. Friendly correspondents

    1. Third-term issue

        a. Pragmatic reasons (no support, dire consequences)

        b. Principle (bad precedent)

        c. Personal concern (dispensableness, personal danger)

    2. War issue

        a. National unity (will be divisive issue when unity needed)

        b. Name your successor

        c. Run for vice president

        d. Free you to mount support for England

    3. Party welfare

        a. Avoid backlash over third-term issue

        b. Another candidate will unify party

        c. Strong candidate necessary for Democrats to win

    4. Retaining power (you'll lose)

    5. Personal welfare

        a. Your health

        b. Your place in history

        c. You've earned retirement

II. Unfriendly Correspondence

    6. War issue (you're getting us into war)

    7. Policy failure (economic, military preparedness, national debt)

    8. Dangerous tolerances (Jews, Roman Catholics, Communists, Republicans)

    9. Personal dislike (unresponsive to the people, trading on family name, egomania)

    10. Third-term issue (power lust, dictatorship)

    11. No support

    12. Adverse economic effects from another term

    13. General nonsupport

Table 8.1: Appeals in Opposition to a Third-Term Bid

icans would not vote for him and that his defeat would spell disaster for all he had accomplished and for his place in history. They appealed to his sense of national unity during a time of external threat to urge that by not running again he would strengthen his hand in dealing with the Nazis. Surprisingly, however, of the 165 letters that advised him not to run, only 23 raised the war issue. Of these, 17 advanced the positive argument that national unity would be better served if he did not run, while 6 conveyed the negative judgment that he was getting us into war.

The overriding concern, however, among personal supporters who urged that he retire now was the no-third-term tradition itself. They offered several reasons to support their view, including the pragmatic consideration that he lacked sufficient support to win and the more personal observation that were he to run he would subject himself to personal danger from malcontents who might attempt assassination. Nonetheless their

Appeals	Total Writers Using	Percent of Writers Using
Third term (friendly)	95	57.58
War (friendly)	17	10.30
Party welfare	15	9.09
Retaining power	8	4.85
Personal welfare	22	13.33
War (unfriendly)	6	3.64
Policy failure	15	9.09
Dangerous tolerances	3	1.82
Personal dislike	9	5.45
Third term (unfriendly)	8	4.84
No support	5	3.03
Adverse economic effects	1	0.02
General nonsupport	3	1.82
N = 165		

Table 8.2: Frequency of Negative Appeal Usage

chief fear (79 of 95, or 83.15 percent) was the bad precedent he would set by violating the no-third-term tradition. Such a bid, they cautioned, eventually would lead to an American dictatorship.

A smaller segment of opposing letters was overtly antagonistic to FDR. They were written to register profound disagreement with his policies, the conviction that he had ruined the economy and even the country, and utter contempt for his person. They blamed him for the current international situation and for entangling the United States in Europe's war. Among these writers, fewer explicitly raised the third-term issue than did those who were friendly to the president. Their general political opposition to the Roosevelt administration doubtless suggested reasons other than the third term itself that made the prospect of another term bitter. Those who did raise this issue shared the fear of his more admiring advocates for retirement that a third term traveled the path toward dictatorship.

In the eyes of those viewing a transformed political landscape from outside Roosevelt's own base of popular support, the enormous enthusiasm for Roosevelt among the disenfranchised segments of society represented a dislocation of political values. His policies inserted the state into economic relations in a way that shifted the impulse of the national agenda from policies of long-term growth to immediate relief, from profit to security, from trickle-down to bubble-up economic measures. Were this dislocation of political values insufficient to make a distanced observer wary, Roosevelt's political style added its own disconcerting note. His restructuring of the nation's political dialogue established a different relationship between the people and the government and a different basis for conducting the nation's business. Many saw danger in his skill at activating the masses to exert influence over the government's decision-making process. For those threatened by or concerned about this shift in the model of governance, a third term carried the scent of demagoguery.

The same patterns seen through other lenses, however, reflected a very different meaning for this important election. Michael Kamen's impressive work *Mystic Chords of Memory* (1991) makes the point that tradition has not been a strong component in shaping American civic life. Until well into the nineteenth century America was busy exploring unknown territories. Unlike Europe, whose identity was tied to ancient roots, America lacked a centuries-old past. It invented its identity fresh; it defined itself with reference to the future. When tradition was invoked to legitimate social conduct, sometimes it was hooted off the stage, but just as likely tradition was altered to fit the pragmatic exigencies of the moment.

1. **Third-term issue**
   a. Washington argument irrelevant
   b. Issue irrelevant
2. **War issue**
   a. Leadership—need a strong leader now
   b. Depoliticization—nation cannot risk changing leaders now
   c. Policy—keep us out of war
3. **Political issues**
   a. Need you to keep Democrats in office
   b. Need you to keep Republicans out of office
4. **Campaign issues**
   a. Run, you'll win
   b. Results of my grassroots poll
   c. Suggestions for winning
5. **Domestic issues**
   a. Need New Deal to advance social/ economic justice
   b. Fear Republicans will dismantle all you've done
6. **FDR's public virtues**
   a. *Experience* to handle problems
   b. *Leadership* to guide us now
   c. *Humanity* to address suffering and restore dignity
   d. *Greatness:* you are our idol, you are a great man

e. *Identification* with common people
f. *Good works:* you have done so much for the nation
g. *Excellence:* you are the best man (now/ever)
h. *Exclusive power:* only you can save us
i. *Wisdom*
7. **Self-interest**
   a. We (poor, elderly, labor, etc.) are better off since you took office
   b. You are the only one who looks after our needs
8. **Personal attachment**
   a. Love you
   b. Believe in you
   c. Friend of my class (race, etc.)
   d. Don't desert us, don't fail us
   e. We're lost without you
9. **Draft issue**
   a. We need you
   b. Your patriotic duty
   c. Heed the voice of the people
   d. You have a moral duty
10. **Destiny**
    a. You are chosen by God
    b. You are chosen by fate
11. **Invocation of God's blessing**
12. **General support**
13. **Intelligence report**

Table 8.3: Appeals in Support of a Third-Term Bid

Appeals	Total Writers Using	Percent of Writers Using
Third-term issue	49	3.09
War issue	375	23.61
Political issues	19	1.20
Campaign issues	116	7.30
Domestic issues	124	7.81
FDR's public virtues	500	31.49
Self-interest	104	6.55
Personal attachment	149	9.38
Draft issue	591	37.22
Destiny	38	2.39
Invocation of God's blessing	88	5.54
General support	94	5.92
Intelligence report	15	0.94
N = 1588		

Table 8.4: Frequency of Affirmative Appeal Usage

The people's rhetoric regarding the third term is, in this sense, typically American. As intent as opponents to a third term were on raising concerns about dangers to the republic that loomed from violating tradition, those in favor of Roosevelt's reelection were equally scornful of or oblivious to tradition's weight. Nearly 62.5 percent of the sample opposed to a third term raised tradition as their specific objection. On the other side, strikingly few took the traditional prohibition seriously. Only 3.09 percent of the sample who favored Roosevelt's reelection thought it even worth raising, and then only to assure the president that concern over this tradition was irrelevant. His supporters were more focused on matters of special significance to the national welfare and their affirmation that in such perilous times Roosevelt was the only hope for America and for them personally (see tables 8.3 and 8.4).

The prospect of war was the most dominant worry of those who wrote to urge that he seek a third term. However, the manner in which this sentiment was expressed suggests their concern was related to a complex of political values that exceeded fear of international involvement. Although rare exceptions embraced war and advocated American involvement, most of Roosevelt's writers were adamant about avoiding war but ambivalent about how continued escalation of Nazi and Fascist aggression should be met. They were wrought with anxiety and conflicting interpretations of these events. For writers in 1939, and to some extent early in 1940, the war was considered a European problem best left to Europeans. Consonant with the prevailing isolationism that followed World War I, many urged that Roosevelt do everything possible to escape another entanglement. That desire was not easily translated into practice, however. Following the German invasion of Poland, FDR had sought changes in the Neutrality Act to permit sale of arms to England and France. Public opinion was divided between those who believed this inevitably would draw the United States into the conflict and those who thought it America's best hope to insure its neutrality. When England and France became further embattled and more of Europe's smaller countries fell, the letters reflected increased apprehension that little could be done to avoid conflict. As 1940 progressed, and especially after June, when France fell, letters that addressed the war issue developed appeals in terms of the nation's welfare.

These letters have a peculiarity that reflects the nation's dread of war and how that dread was to be handled. The war-issue letters fall into two groups. One set of writers addressed the likelihood of war directly but with a detached posture of political and moral principle that called for Roosevelt's reelection. To their way of thinking, the nation was in crisis and required strong leadership; to change leaders now would be risky and contrary to America's best interests. Roosevelt was the best choice because he was experienced in handling crises, was known among other world leaders, and, consequently, was in the best position to steer the country clear of war. Nearly one-quarter of the letters (23.61 percent) made direct appeals of this sort concerning the war.[16]

A second set of letters never mentioned the war, but their argument that under the circumstances Roosevelt had no alternative but to stand for reelection made clear allusion to the prospect of war. These writers, who comprise 37.22 percent of the sample, wrote in a spirit of drafting him for a third term. They developed the argument that when the country was in danger, it was every true patriot's duty to serve. It followed from this that Roosevelt now had to meet his patriotic duty and serve another term. They often acknowledged that he may be tired and in poor health, but he had an obligation to put country first. The nation he was to serve was not understood abstractly as a political entity. The appeal was framed in terms of his relationship to the people. Many letters invoked the voice of the people, wrote as its representative, informed him that he had the people's mandate, and reminded him of his moral duty to heed their call. They were emphatic to assert that they needed him and pleaded that he not abandon them now, for without him they were lost.

These writers never mentioned the war, but clearly it was on their minds, as if its presence were felt but too dreadful to name. They wrote as if America stood at the precipice facing an unnamed force that threatened to insinuate power over their lives, sever their security, and leave them uncertain of their future. They questioned their wherewithal to face alone a future made ominous because it confronted them with the paralyzing authority of a dreadful specter to contort their lives in yet unknown but nonetheless dreadful ways. And they looked to the president as the one person able to assert the counteracting redemptive authority over national life that would prepare America to resist this evil in its midst.

The personal dependence reflected in their common proclamation "We need you!" is indicative of a bond between FDR and these writers that transcended their fear of war while designating his exclusive power to deal with their current crisis. Their reliance on him cannot be separated from the national experience of the preceding seven years and what Roosevelt represented in that context.

The second most used line of argument employed by Roosevelt's supporters was an appeal to his public virtues. Nearly one-third of the sample linked the New Deal's meaning in their lives with FDR's person. Letter upon letter cited his recovery policies as the substantive basis for imploring him to continue in office. They affirmed Roosevelt as a great president because he was the first one who cared about them or about their class, or group, or people in general. He looked after their needs as no one had before. Some even referred to him as father. They grouped him with Washington and Lincoln as father of a country that had been thrice born, each time a saving moment. Some also referred to him as if he were their natural father, a person to whom they might turn for advice and guidance and on whom they could depend to make certain their material needs were met. More commonly he was revered as their friend who had been attentive to their problems and needs and who had included them in the national agenda. They affirmed their confidence in him. Whether to save the nation or to resolve their present personal problems, they were secure in his affection, and they professed their personal attachment and love for him.

Consonant with their personal attachment, Roosevelt's supporters freely offered observations on the climate of the times that mandated a third term. Surprisingly few voters were third-term advocates out of party loyalty. Although, as we saw earlier, the opinion polls showed that third-term preferences divided along party lines, the letters made scant reference to institutional affiliations. They bore allegiance to the New Deal as a social revolution to ameliorate economic and social suffering typically experienced on the basis of class; it transcended political parties. Although these writers may have regarded Republicans as the enemy, they expressed their concerns in other terms. When the Republican Party was mentioned, it was typically with reference to the New Deal and the fear that Republicans would dismantle the social programs that had been initiated during the previous seven years. Nearly 8 percent of the writers made an explicit appeal that America not forsake the revised domestic priorities Roosevelt had established.

Others who had experienced poverty and then were recipients of New Deal benefits shared the view that the New Deal would be jeopardized by FDR's retirement. Their stories have less to do with broad issues than with their own self-interests. They honored Roosevelt as the only president who had shown understanding and compassion for their distress and acted to relieve it. Their gratitude grew from a restored sense of dignity. Writers of 6.55 percent of the supporting letters, mostly poor or elderly, assured him that he alone was responsible for their economic salvation, out of gratitude they pledged their unwavering support.

For some, their economic salvation was a reaffirmation that the nation had been blessed by God, who had sent FDR as his saving agent. Historically American political rhetoric has developed the theme of the United States as exceptional; American Zion was God's new promised land. Over 5 percent of the letters echo this theme. They prayed for the president and invoked God's blessings on him and his family. They took his frequent references to America's religious faith in his speeches and fireside chats as a sign that he would succeed because he was a man of faith. Some went so far as to declare that he was foreordained, like Moses, to lead his people out of the darkness of poverty and the danger of war. In fact his leading America out of the Depression was sometimes summoned as a sign that he had been chosen to lead at a time when the nation was endangered by war. He also was forewarned of hubris. It was not his place to deny God's will; he was destined to lead, and all—including the president—must obey.

Others, less prone to attribute the nation's fate to divine intervention than to political design, stressed the urgency of Roosevelt's candidacy as the sole antidote to mounting political opposition to the New Deal. Major newspapers, such as the *New York Times* and the *Chicago Tribune,* had adopted editorial positions antagonistic to the administration. Gauging public sentiment by their stories made defeat seem inevitable. Roosevelt's partisans responded by conducting their own sampling of local opinion and conveying it to the White House. They echoed the president's frequently expressed criticism of the press for misrepresenting or distorting facts and urged him to disregard its predictions of dire consequences from a third-term bid. They suggested that if he wished to learn the true feelings of Americans, he would be better served by heeding their personal intelligence report. Such letters ran the gamut from a poll taken at Harry's barbershop to the reconnaissance report of businessmen whose work took them to different cities across the country and who wished to share what they heard in their travels. Others, more secure in their assumptions that Roosevelt had already decided to run but was biding his time for political reasons, offered opinions and suggestions on strategies they were certain would prove successful. Included in this activity was another group who engaged in local intelligence work. They wrote to inform the president of untoward comments being made by his enemies in their community.

The vast majority of those who wrote about important domestic issues and personal welfare that mandated another term did not offer sophisticated conceptual analyses of the Roosevelt administration's programs. Nonetheless their arguments exhibited an awareness that class relations were at their core. The New Deal reforms were more than its alphabet agencies; they were a politics of inclusion, predicated on economic and social justice, that had altered the relationship of poor and working class Americans with the state. These letter writers saw the New Deal as Roosevelt's legacy but lacking a national champion of stature to succeed him. He must stand, they argued, for this new politics to endure.

The undercurrent of war may have provided the impulse for many of these citizens to write, but the reasons they offered in support of their cause blended patriotic duty with moral obligation and their sense of personal dependency on the president. The appeals of personal dependence that run across the sample reflect their ascription of political authority to Roosevelt. They called on him to continue his service because he was exceptional. His public virtues inspired confidence that went beyond his attributes as a leader. He was admired and idolized for traits that combined the efficacy of political acumen and the charisma of moral virtue. He was extolled for his experience and leadership. He was admired for his humanity and good works, which were evidence that he genuinely understood common people and their aspirations and needs. They invested him with a modern form of ancient virtues: aretê and phronêsis, virtuosity and wisdom. This was no mere mortal but a great man who had the exclusive power to save them.

What are we to make of this outpouring? Consonant with American individualism, Depression-era narratives of poverty often associated it with personal integrity. Poverty had meaning as a matter of personal responsibility. Rather than raging against economic policies that had brought ruin and hardship to fully one-third or more of the country, they commonly expressed *humiliation,* an emotion of personal failure that brought shame before one's neighbors and to one's self.[17] But these letters narrate a more complex story. The loss of material means also made the economic disparity between the haves and the have-nots starkly evident and a source of social interpretation. Those with means were regarded as a vested interest attempting to keep the nation's wealth to themselves, joined in a conspiracy of privilege at the expense of those on the economic fringe. The great strides by labor to organize and win legislative protections and contractual guarantees speak directly to an awareness of the central question of social life: *who is in control?* For the poor, those with means were an enemy driven by greed. Their economic agenda for recovery was not predicated on what would produce the greatest good for the greatest number, but on what would satisfy their own avarice. For the economically secure, those without means were society's failures, driven by their fixation on class interests. They were an ignorant and misguided mob less concerned with genuine economic recovery than with asserting its will to power regardless of cost.

For both sides Franklin D. Roosevelt was the lightning rod, the Pericles or Jackson of his age, reforming American democracy to include beleaguered segments of the middle class as well as its fringes—the poor, the immigrant, and, to a limited extent, the African American—in the process. From the small entrepreneur whose business was suddenly saved by government assistance through a small business loan or the farmer whose farm was saved through federal price supports of his crop, to the elderly person whose life savings were rescued by new banking measures or the unemployed who found some form of direct financial assistance through a federal work or relief program, Roosevelt touched their lives. These were his policies; they were felt directly, and he was revered for changing the system to make it responsive to their needs. He was their leader.

Such extreme loyalty defined the public identity of Roosevelt's supporters. To an observer who may not have experienced the Depression in the same way, or who saw Roosevelt as a politician first, or who subscribed to a different political and economic creed, its sheer rabidity could be alarming. Seen through the prism of events in Europe, the fervor of Roosevelt's supporters resembled a cult of personality promoted by Roosevelt's political style. The ascription to Roosevelt of such exclusive power only intensified the fear that he posed a threat and that a third term was, as the anti-third-term writers professed, an invitation to dictatorship.

On the other hand, the awakened class consciousness suggested by the topoi informing these letters speaks to an alternative interpretation. Roosevelt's biographers tell us he was, before all else, a party man. The institutions of governance worked according to the lights of those in office. Roosevelt did his best to help his kind gain the seats of power. That he played the political game to win does not distinguish him among politicians. As his career of public utterances testifies, he was greatly respectful of representative democracy. He also was thoroughly American in his appreciation of the lobby as the fuel that made the engine run. Those who saw him as attempting to destroy democratic institutions were guilty of misreading his utter conformity to the rules of the game. What set him apart from his age was the Jacksonian spirit with which he brought the weight of public sentiment to bear on the political process of legislating. His genius lay in galvanizing the opinions of the least organized segments of society around issues that bore on their interests. He activated a public to make its views known. Although there was greater variability in this public, as in all publics, than we would find in a lobby, its members acted as a pressure group or lobby might for measures no less in their interests than the shape of gun legislation is in the interests of the National Rifle Association. Roosevelt's discourses made the common citizen's interests palpable. His speeches provided clear guidance on how to make a focused response and where to direct it. The fact that these disparate individuals happened to be poor, minorities, immigrants, and without access to institutional forums of power may have caused alarm to those who were vested, but that did not make Roosevelt a demagogue any more than Solon's resolution of class strife in ancient Athens made Solon one; it merely indicated he was rhetorically skilled.

Orchestrating social action of this sort was true to the spirit of American democracy because it returned to ordinary citizens their ultimate power and maximized citizen authority through pressure they applied on their elected representatives. In addition to their economic significance, the New Deal's measures were equally a source of empowerment that revolutionized the democratic experience for millions of Americans. Without new lands to conquer, they were returning to the pioneer spirit of their ancestors (a common ground for all) to redefine what it meant to be American.

From its inception America's identity has been mythologized. It was the "new world," a place where immigrants made a new start, where people formed communities with common beliefs and interests without fear of persecution from external powers. Its freedom and opportunities were based on the primacy of the individual. Here you were rewarded for your accomplishments rather than your affiliations. America was a beacon for optimism about a future whose bounty for talent and hard work would exceed the past's and about the opportunity for each of its members to participate and to benefit. Once America began the transformation from an agrarian society to an industrial one, that image, born in the country's infancy and nurtured during its phase of territorial expansion, was at odds with the prevailing reality for millions of its citizens.

At least as early as the end of the nineteenth century there were evident seeds of alienation from a system that had promised personal autonomy through economic security. William Jennings Bryan's campaign of 1896 waged against the gold standard as a one-sided economic imposition and the riots that accompanied the Pullman strike were signs of diminished allegiance by a significant portion of Americans to a system based on false hope. Whatever aspirations the early twentieth century may have encouraged for economic well-being as a product of hard work were drowned in a sea of despair when there was no work at all. The letters urging a third term bespeak a recovering confidence in the American dream, as destroyed and then recast during the decade of the 1930s. Collectively they contain an inchoate narrative of national identity, recast as this public of common Americans understood it—its dearness and its fragility.

As we have seen, the frequency of topoi use (table 8.3) indicates that the question of the third term, per se, was of almost no concern to these writers. Although the prospect of war weighed heavily on their minds, neither was it the dominant topic of explicit appeal. Rather, the preponderance of explicit argument focused on FDR's civic virtues and the right of the people to draft their leader (with the leader's corresponding obligation to heed the people's call). These appeals situate democratic politics on personalized (if not personal) relationships. Further, they exhibit a social will forged by their authors' experiences of the New Deal. Although coming from every section and stratum of the nation, they are organically related as a presentation of interconnected attitudes and values, themes and images that emerged in their authors' individual experiences.

Collectively they form a people's narrative on civic relations that elevate common citizens above institutional actors in shaping the state's course, a text on living in America. To flesh out the contours of this understanding we must consider the narrative on America these letters compose.

Defining America

These are politicized writers. Their differences in background and circumstance provide alternative assumptions about the meaning of America, sometimes remarkably so. But they also share confidence that Roosevelt understands their interests and that his policies and leadership will advance them. The possibility of his imminent retirement from public life confronted their world with threats beyond war. Ominous interests and policies at odds with the New Deal lurked on the political horizon.

The most basic perceived threat was economic. Capitalism is predicated on growth to sustain the accumulation of excess wealth. Accordingly, Depression-era conservatives had repudiated the active hand of a liberal administration in the economy and were fond of asserting that their primary concern was to produce the type of economic growth necessary for full employment. To those who had suffered the consequences of misplaced economic priorities, however, cries for return to the old ways were heard as upper-class lust for personal gain.

Without denying the virtues of capitalism, the laboring class was skeptical that it worked to its advantage, especially when avarice overcame justice. How, for example, was one to trust politicians, mostly Republicans, who advanced the agenda of industrialists and acted as if they were agents of special interests? Their claims to have the public interest at heart were perceived as hypocritical. D. C. Hogodone, a western farmer, found the promises of Republicans, and ousted politicians generally, to be the height of dissimulation. "Just because those who were defeated and their friends squeal like hogs they do not know what to do now after you have brought us thru. in spite of there lying and mud slinging, they tell us what they will do (but never did) never intending to do anything but back the money men." Another western farmer, C. S. Horton, shared Mr. Hogodone's sentiments and pointed to the opposition's arguments against Roosevelt's deficit spending as a case in point. "The general public is not so terribly interested in that budget balancing propaganda being spread by the Republican party," he wrote, "for we know that as long as money is considered king + the ruling factor with profits for some and increased indebtedness for others, there can be no budget balancing" (OF 2526, Box 28). Policies that forced the farmer to bring his yield to market at a depressed value were outrageous, in their view, because they doomed the farmer to economic failure. The economic system as steered by Congress and the Republicans no longer commanded blind faith. They had let these farmers down once with dire consequences, and it could happen again.

Others who shared the sentiment that the Republican party and Congress were responsible for the Depression indicated it would be difficult for them to regain the people's faith. E. J. Kruse was ready to dismiss "the Administrations of Harding, Colidge + Hover + the gang of Shyster Lawyers we send to congress." In his opinion, they were lamentably "a Barnical to American History," only proving the stupidity of the American people who flocked to their standards. Mr. Kruse was not without hope, however, because Roosevelt had shown a way to return the system to the people by circumventing Congress. "I always wondered before what was the good of a President if he was shackled by a congress but you up set that when you took our/your Troubles before the people (Radio)" (OF 2526, Box 30).

In addition to the Republican Party and elected officials who seemed to oppose the New Deal, the third-term writers were wary of other institutions and institutional leaders who called for their trust. For example, one of the nation's principal labor leaders, John L. Lewis, had engaged in bitter sniping at Roosevelt about the third term. To members of the American Federation of Labor, who had been a primary beneficiary of New Deal legislation regulating conditions in the workplace, Lewis's conduct seemed to place personal power over the common good of the rank and file. Union locals became the arenas for repudiating Lewis's position by passing resolutions of support urging FDR to seek a third term. Jesse Jackson, an Illinois miner, summarized feelings when he wrote to assure the president that "Mr. Lewis does not speak My Sentiments in regard to your coming out for a third term" (OF 2526, Box 30). At the level of the individual, the failure of America's banks visited calamity upon millions. Mrs. G. F. Hair, at the other end of the economic spectrum from the rank-and-file union member, wrote of the consequences that befell her and her husband: "We thought we had security for old age, four banks went under that Dr. Hair had stock in" (OF 2526, Box 28).

Such institutions as banks and unions had claimed society's trust and, in some cases, personal affiliation. Their members expected them to be jealous of their best interests. Instead they were perceived to break this trust. To those who suffered the consequences of an economy that had collapsed under the weight of misplaced priorities, claims that the general welfare would be advanced through returning to the old-style economics of a laissez-faire marketplace distorted reality. The third-term writers were distrustful of politicians who seemed more cynical than blind by ignoring the consequences of laissez-faire economics on their lives.

Roosevelt's writers understood the differences between themselves and those with property, money, education, and position. Their separation from a social model that made the poor, the unemployed, the elderly, and even the common laborer subservient to elite interests reflected a growing class consciousness in America. Without couching the bases for class conflict in theoretical language, their letters explicitly disengaged from the conservative rendition of a capitalist society and sought distance from managerial powers that denied them their subjectivity. Matilda Emerson expressed the general sentiment of the poor and elderly when she observed: "When i reads about what the Old Dealers say that the new Deal is a failure well i can say This much the new deal has put The poor in some kind of houses to live in the Old deal had the poor In allays with no work and no place to go both womens and children was out with no place to go they house hold was dumped Out in allays with the so called REads trying to force them back In their houses. that was the result Of the Old deal" (OF 2625, Box 22).

Her sentiments were echoed by farmer Hogodone, who assailed the audacity of politicians now attacking Roosevelt as a dictator in light of their own policies that had exercised a truly dictatorial force by suppressing the market value of the farmer's yield. In Hogodone's view, "The truth Is that before 1931 was when we had a dictatorship, there was an over supply of wheat and people starving, at 25c wheat. that was what we got for wheat hauled In." Farmer Horton, more cautionary in tone, issued a postscript no less adamant in warning against the false rhetoric of those who wished a return to the open-market conditions that had nearly ruined the economic viability of farming in the first place.

> [The] farmer not influenced by any AAA checks or W.P.A. job. wheat is worth 44c per bu to day at Custer, believe me, Mr. consumer had better watch his step or through the Gamblers-Speculators + World Conditions we producers are going to be forced out of production "or a large majority of us." Then what will Mr. Consumer eat for bread—where will it come from, + what will he pay for it, + who will make the profits.? And what chance will he have of ever sharing in a percentage of those profits. (OF2526, Box 28)

Together they indict the Republicans and those economic powers then urging a return to pre-Depression policies for their callousness toward the personal degradation individuals such as Ms. Emerson felt. Rather than a politics of inclusion, wrote William P. Hardy, the Republicans had committed felonies whose viciousness went unassailed until FDR took office. Then, after being salvaged from the self-wrought wreckage of their own greed, they showed their true colors by calling for an end to programs that now were of primary benefit to those whose economic hopes were for survival, not affluence. "You filled all their stomachs yet the GOP is so utterly selfish that the only plank they have now is a narrow one, not big enough to carry half the load you carry" (OF 2526, Box 28). John Jacob Jones considerably advanced these sentiments when he predicted that, "if the Republicans get in especially will they in all probability immediately stop all relief measures and the starving people who have no intention of meekly starving will start a revolution" (OF 2526, Box 30).

Although Mr. Jones's views are more extreme than most, they reflect a general class consciousness of being objectified by social actors who control their means of survival without regard for their individual dignity. Roosevelt's correspondents refused to be defined by the historical situation of their economic means. By distancing themselves from it, the conditions of their subjectivity were no longer given in a discursive situation in which they were a means of production but rather were created by the discourse itself, which happened to be about basic human rights.[18]

Their discourse constitutes a *narrative of opposition*. Letter after letter expressed complete distrust and utter contempt for the pieties of concern issuing from conservative ranks. The unvarnished capitalist motive was seen as economic exclusion which, in the minds of these writers, had serious political ramifications. Principal among them was the reassertion of a Hamiltonian bias to rest power with the economically vested. In many cases this bias surfaced through the transparent use of exclusion and intimidation to challenge the basic democratic principle of the vote. Obviously there was the exclusion presented by the poll tax. In southern states at this time the disparity between voting-age citizens and those registered to vote could be as large as three to one. Still, citizens such as Bentley Jackson wanted the president to know that "if You are going to Run for President again if I was Legal to vote for You I Realy would" (OF 2526, Box 29). In places where the poll tax did not serve as a legal means of exclusion, corporate powers brought their weight to bear. Some, like C.E.H., wrote to the president at what they perceived to be great personal risk: "I am only a poor hard working mother that has been forbidden at the cost of my Job not to take any part in politics" (OF 2526, Box 28).

More sophisticated conservative voices tried to mount rhetorical offensives. Since the constitutional guarantee of suffrage precluded the availability of Hamilton's arguments favoring rule by an elite, they resorted to appeals to self-interest. But, as James Boyd White (1984, 76) has observed, that type of argument requires a language in which "self" and "interest" can be defined, which posed a significant obstacle in light of an economic perspective that objectified those they were attempting to persuade. Consequently, corporate speakers had difficulty framing arguments that connected with the civic values of egalitarian relationships, as communications worker Ellen Campbell remarked. She wrote to share with the White House a notice she once received in her pay envelope directing how she should cast her ballot, and she warned that more of this tactic might be in the offing. The notice from the Telephone Engineering and Management Company of Lima, Ohio, where Mrs. Campbell worked in

1932, informed its employees that while it had no intention to dictate how they should vote, TE&M did want them to know "what effects the policies of certain candidates will have." It then proceeded to rate candidates for national, state, and local office in terms of their likely economic effect on utility companies. The lack of moral sensibility reflected by this rhetorical tactic was not lost on communications worker Campbell, however, when juxtaposed with the pay cut she had received just a few weeks earlier, down to fifteen dollars per month. "I had worked for the company thirteen years and knew quite a lot about company political work so I voted for all not listed in this letter. I cast my first vote for a Democratic President and have never been sorry" (Democratic National Committee File 112). Unable to make rational and moral sense to individuals who refused to abandon their self-identity, such discourse was read as another attempt by big business to exploit workers.

Rhetorical inconsistencies such as that to which Mrs. Campbell objected were open invitations for these narratives to debunk the sincerity of Republican political claims. For example, in spring 1940 Roosevelt had invited several Republicans to join his cabinet. This bipartisan offer was received by the Republican Party with an insistence that in return for their accepting these posts Roosevelt should declare his intent to retire. Commenting on the Republicans' attempt to corner the president, H. R. Hyndman wrote:

> This stipulation is an affront to the intelligence and patriotism of the American people. Directly after the French admit they are facing disaster on account of following military tradition and when the English give up all traditional personal freedom for the common good, the Republican Party says, in so many words, that a very small minority shall decide how many terms a President shall serve and the subject should not be decided by a majority of the people. (OF 2526, Box 28)

More direct evidence of this inferred bias was reported by wildcatter Isaac Jenkins, who had listened to a Republican speaker hold forth on the evils of Roosevelt and the lack of intelligence among his supporters. "He said it was not right for the Pick and Shovel men to be allowed to organize for they had no thinking ability at all" (OF 2526, Box 30).

Comments such as these were heard with great sensitivity by people who had acquired their own taste of active participation in the political process. As long as they had access to America's political power structure, they had the potential to influence its social structure. Conservative expressions of concern for the working class were belied by actions that shouted of their desire for an elite to rule. Florence Hall, a resident of Red Bank, New Jersey, certainly felt that way as she vented her indignance over the spectacle she encountered at a Wendell Willkie rally. She reported that it was devoted to much mudslinging but no constructive proposals and issued under banners that read "willkie the choice of the thinking man." "Of what are they thinking?" she wondered, "their pocketbooks?" She went on to offer her own reflections on the gulf that divided those who were pining for a return to the old politics from those they falsely believed had been the sole beneficiaries of the New Deal:

> I saw there several thousands of well fed and well dressed American men and women, who had come there in thousands of the worlds finest automobiles, latest models. I wondered if there were not many around me, who were concious, of the well being of these people, who had traveled miles to get there, through rich prosperous farm country, over super highways, passing school after school, built by P.W.A. whose children were enjoying better education, better opportunity, because of an administration, this man, and his party were maliciously and falsely maligning, an administration they would have us toss in the scrap heap. (OF 2526, Box 28)

As an antidote to an elitist political threat, their narratives of opposition reminded the president that the efforts of the New Deal to help the needy, while noble, were not the solution they sought. They wanted jobs, not relief, so that they might preserve their self-respect for earning what they needed. They warned against opponents of New Deal reforms who desired "to return to their old pirate methods" (OF 2526, Box 28). And as the election campaign commenced, their narratives refuted Willkie's blasts at Roosevelt's stewardship. Against the story line that depicted Roosevelt as an incipient dictator, they presented a chronicle of Roosevelt's battle with the other branches of government to achieve social justice. "He compared your administrations acomplishments with that of Mr. Hitlers," wrote Walter Hines. "But Mr. Wilkey didnt tell anyone about your seven year war with Congress. Big Business. The Supreme Court and many other individuals and groups. He didnt tell any one about the Banking law. Social Security. Stock laws. and many other fine pieces of Legislation that has come out of Washington since you have been there" (OF 2526, Box 27).

Collectively these writers indicted the American political system for abandoning its traditional dreams. Their narrative of opposition challenged the veracity of the American creed that all humans are created equal. It was not true that poor people were equal to those of means when it came to voting or to participating with an equal say in decisions affecting their destiny. While America struggled to maintain an egalitarian image, in fact it was a class-riven society in which the poor were treated as incompetents who had no business seeking partnership in the process, and in which poor were set against one another for the limited resources allocated for their share, often resulting in expressions of racism from poor whites driven by fear that they would be denied the means for survival. For these third-term writers, the Depression exposed the lived lie that power rested with the people; it rested with wealth. This realization diminished the potency of conservative America's language, power relations, and values as sources of motivation and allegiance. Republican appeals to isolationism against the threat of war, to the fear of dictatorship as the consequence of a third term, and to visions of economic recovery by return to an emphasis on profit were doomed by a collapse of meaning. They were speaking a language that failed to make sense of the world as these writers, and millions for whom they were representative, had experienced it.

Against the backdrop of disintegrating prospects to escape war, they clearly were not prepared to defend a system that had consigned them to political impotence and economic servitude. Their allegiance was to an America in which they had a redefined sense of place. At the same time that they developed a narrative of opposition, the third-term letters expressed a people's struggle to reappropriate their historicity.[19] Their authors wrote as participants in a populist movement to reclaim society's resources in order to define a new base of political power. This is most evident in their story that redefined American democracy. The Republican rhetoric tied the meaning of democracy to prosperity. The national conversation between Roosevelt and the people over the past seven years spoke a counter-rhetoric addressed to the concerns of "the common man." The consequence of appropriating the meaning of the American democracy was evident in the letter of Frances Marquis to the president. After hearing Willkie maintain that "Democracy survives only under prosperity," Marquis wrote FDR to revise his formula. "Not only is that not true, but if it were true Democracy would not be worth preserving. Only those things are truly valuable that survive adversity; that way with what has seemed complete lack of self-interest you have boldly and fearlessly instituted changes necessary to adapt our way of life to the new world around us. But never have you sacrificed even a little bit of those fundamental principles on which we stand" (OF 4040, Willkie file). Expressions such as this suggest that the experience of seven years of words and deeds that seriously entertained the concerns of "the common man" had unhinged democracy's meaning from its economic link to prosperity and rehinged it to the social link emphasized in the dialogical language of community. In addition to their consciousness of being in opposition, *the third-term writers also were engaged in projecting a model of their own self-representation.*

Society's inevitable clashes between classes and interests center on the terms of their relationships and the consequences of dominant relational patterns on knowledge and power. What counts as social knowledge entails control over the terms which ascribe meaning to actions, and what counts as social power, equally, entails the ability to act consonant with one's own interests. Social actors hold and experience knowledge and power when they are able to assert their self-identity and when their relationships to other individuals, groups, or classes do not subject them to domination. Touraine has argued that by reappropriating their historicity, social actors are able to use the resources of knowledge, acquisition, and culture to produce a model of themselves based on their own actions (1981, 59–62). Were we seeking a textbook example of his contention that societies are defined by this self-producing activity, the New Deal's breach in political meaning would qualify. The social and economic forces it set in motion produced a conversational chiasmus. While it provoked the opposition to talk about a past, the vernacular rhetoric of these writers was envisioning a future. The third-term letters to Roosevelt redefined America in terms of a common set of values on which the future could be depicted. Primary among these were their visions of a *moral America* and a *virile America.*

Moral America was dedicated to peace, patriotism, and decency. Publisher John J. Greene, who printed a small-town newspaper, wrote to define its specific features. He saw it manifested in labor relations, where both sides seek peaceful resolution of their differences and where management offers a fair wage and labor delivers a full day's work. It appeared in commerce through fairness toward competition, the public, and employees. It emerged in politics through practices that minimize waste, graft, and favoritism (OF 2526, Box 7). Rev. Wm. E. Kunz saw the matter in terms of the humanitarian changes that were introduced during the Roosevelt administration. To his mind, these had to be protected against falling "into the hands of those misguided, rapacious, reactionaries who seem to always be harking back to the 'good old days' of McKinley, Harding, Coolidge and poor Old Hoover" (OF 2526, Box 30). Moral America was a humane society in which meeting others on the plane of equality and caring for those less fortunate than oneself became social practices. Mr. and Mrs. Evan Jones felt these mattered more than balancing the budget. A moral society should have its priorities in order: feeding and clothing those in need and saving humans from the indignity of begging have greater meaning than making the wealthy wealthier (OF 2526, Box 29). Teacher Mary Jane provided a specific example when she described the effects of the New Deal on her students: "I wish you could have seen the difference in the children in my classroom—whole shoes on little feet once more, mittens on formerly mitten-less hands, bananas and milk again appearing in the scrubby lunch pails" (OF 2526, Box 30). In her view, the defining trait of a Roosevelt supporter was a broad mind and a generous heart.

At the same time that a moral society did not let those in need go under, there was also an assertion of pride in self-sufficiency. Virile America, for F. C. Hunn, was a reassertion of individual independence. He had stayed off relief, he told the president, even though he was unemployed. The virile American exhibited virtues of frugality and caution during times of plenty so as not to become dependent in times of scarcity (OF 2526, Box 28). Virile America believed that rewards were earned through personal effort, which made such efforts worthy in themselves. In this spirit, authors frequently established themselves as self-sufficient and responsible by opening their letters with a narration of identity in terms of personal accomplishments. They assumed it was important for the president to know their personal circumstances if he were to take them seriously. Willa Hurst's story is typical:

> I was born and raised in Arkansas on a farm. had to walk 3 miles to the "little old school house." and of course it was not so good, as the schools we now have. but any how we got by. there were seven of we children. but I really thank God for the way I was raised. now I am a woman nearing fifty years of age but I still have my memories of my child hood where we were taught to be good Americans and we have good red blood in our veins, not blue. (OF 2526, Box 28)

The self-sacrifice that Ms. Hurst describes was the cornerstone to making America a great country. FDR's supporters drew a distinction between those whose material possessions had come through privileges of birth or position and those whose rewards had come through personal initiative. They considered the president, despite his patrician lineage, a role model for citizenship through personal effort. The strains of office had taken a serious toll, many wrote, but Roosevelt had given of himself because the people and the nation needed him. His self-sacrifice made him the exemplar of the virile American.

These beliefs in a moral and virile America summoned a new patriotism based on devotion to country as a symbol for egalitarian politics. Roosevelt was told that he would win because he advanced the will of the people, who viewed campaigning for his reelection as "an opportunity to win, draw, or loose, to battle for justice" (OF 2526, Box 30, J. Houston). He must run again because "your guidance and your policies seem to be the only intelligent glimmer of encouragement that the spirit of the revolution can and will withstand this barbaric onslaught of counter revolution" (OF 2526, Box 30, I. Johnson). Lillian Herroit warned that this was not a historic moment of false patriotism that exacted sacrifices of hard-won gains under the guise of an emergency measure. Nor was this blind obedience to institutional figures presumed to know better how to conduct the nation's business. The new patriot must no longer be "too diffident to write or . . . too disorganized to apply pressure" (OF 2526, Box 28, Mrs. P. Hoogterp). These Americans were to act as a lobby, and they looked to the president who had "labored and fought for the best interests of all the people" (OF 2526, Box 27, A. A. Horrall) to serve in a redefined role as the representative of their interests.

Conclusion: Forgotten Publics in a Land of Strangers

Living in a democracy involves a greater degree of uncertainty than living in other forms of government. Its processual nature produces decisions that are made on the basis of deliberation, not edict. A democracy's telos is the involvement of all citizens, which places the ultimate power to chart society's course in the hands of those who may be most easily swayed by the heat of passion. Capitalist democracies are further beset by a contradiction in the basic assumption of equality. The implied equality of all citizens in political affairs is offset by the economic inequality implicit in private ownership. Although the people may reign in a democracy, the practical reality is that elites rule. Consequently there is always tension and often conflict between its reigning and ruling powers for control of society's model of itself. When these conflicts appear to threaten class interests, democracy's general optimism about neighborly conduct is compromised by decidedly antidemocratic tendencies. When the elite governs with disregard for the welfare of the masses, a democracy tends to resemble an oligarchy. When the masses turn to a charismatic leader to whom they abdicate their rule, a democracy tends to resemble a dictatorship. The letters to Roosevelt urging that he seek a third term reveal that average Americans were conscious of these conflicts and dangers. They turned to him as their best hope for sustaining a populist political agenda and for neutralizing the power advantage of the economically secure.

The letters are a manifestation of this redefined presidential role. Although many writers express their deference to the president's authority, their letters are political acts of rhetorical participation in democracy's business. Although they were without official position and lacked the opportunity to enter a realm where political appeals were subjected to public scrutiny, these writers nevertheless entered a discursive space millions of Depression-era Americans perceived as potent for making their sentiments known. Together with Roosevelt they repositioned the traditional town meeting to conduct their business through the vernacular rhetoric of personal, epistolary dialogue with the president.

The redefined presidential role is part of a restructured national politics. Certainly the powerful elites who had controlled the country for most of the late nineteenth and early twentieth centuries were still formidable in setting the national agenda. Yet the active public writing to Roosevelt perceived an ebbing of this elite's sway on the ultimate decisions that sculpted America's domestic and foreign policies. The immediacy of federal programs in the lives of these writers had raised their awareness of a personal stake in the deliberations and decisions whose impacts they felt. They were, in that sense, a prime example of Dewey's classical understanding of a public (1954, 3–36), attentive to the indirect consequences they bore of legislative decisions, aware of the state as an extension of the people, relying on communication to bring the state's actions in line with this public's interest, and even framing a sense of national commitments that might have normative force in directing legislative and administrative action. Moreover, their consciousness that their place at the table would remain vacant under the political formulas of the old guard indicates their identity as a rhetorical formation. Though it may have proclaimed its solidarity with the interests of the working class, the unemployed, the poor, and the elderly, the novelty of political empowerment that came only when domination of the old guard had been displaced led most of the third-term writers to dismiss such rhetoric as deceitful. The Republican Party spoke for established wealth, which had never before been their political friend. They certainly were not about to regard it as anything but the enemy now.

Nor were these letter writers passive supporters of the president in waging this struggle. They expressed genuine excitement about their role in shaping a new national direction. Admittedly many of these writers were poor people whose means of survival came from federally funded programs. But many also held steady jobs, some comfortably middle-class ones, whose support was no less conscious that the New Deal had changed how America was governed. The country's recovery measures were focused on the needs of small business, labor, agriculture, the unemployed, the chronically poor, and the elderly—those who were typically the last to feel the results of economic expansion and the first line of economic pinch in times of recession. Whether this reversal of conventional wisdom made sound economic sense remains a source of continuing debate even as the twentieth century wanes. But incontestably, in the view of its supporters, it expressed a commitment of greater value—to being first a humane society.

For them, a humane society acceded to the primacy of justice. A world based on justice went beyond the class struggles that were predictably a part of the period. These letters more profoundly opposed the loss of self through objectification by the economic forces that had dominated the lives of poor and working-class Americans. They also celebrated regaining their sense of self through a national community whose commitment to justice would not permit it to compromise human dignity. The primacy of justice and the inviolable status of human dignity defined the world of feeling, action, and judgment for Roosevelt's America. The letter writers were engaged in the important political work of building a grassroots consensus on national direction based on these precepts. At a time when many Americans were nearly paralyzed with fear over the prospect of war, these people— common people—appealed to Roosevelt to accept his duty and not let that consensus, and with it quite possibly the nation, die.

Each letter, then, contributes to a public opinion. The text that results from their composite story—a distinctly rhetorical expression—differs from the representation of public opinion one gets from survey research. Rather than inferences supported by statistical distributions of responses by a random sample to a poller's questions, it supports inferences on the basis of language and arguments chosen by its multiple authors to address their own concerns. Public opinion of this sort projects a possible world. The narrative of each writer's story and imagined future tends away from theory and toward a way of life, setting the tension between self-interest and civic community. Whereas the poll tells an objectivist story of instrumental relations, the composite of these public opinions tells a rhetorical story of organic relations.

Their story contained a moral Roosevelt was led to ponder. During the 1940 campaign FDR delivered only six strictly political speeches, his acceptance speech to the Democratic Convention plus five addresses to political rallies. Their contents, themselves worthy of detailed rhetorical analysis, provide evidence that he was an acute listener to the often unheard vernacular discourse whose essential rhetoricality gives voice to public opinion in a public's own terms. These speeches celebrate the newly inclusive America valorized by his correspondents and envision a future in which the experiment of the New Deal brings justice and security to every citizen. If voters were reassured by his appeals for an American future, their optimism was encouraged by the themes, examples, humor, and vision of his American narrative spoken as if he were one of them and shared their concerns.

We will never know what these speeches might have contained had Roosevelt not opened the epistolary public sphere that helped to define the rhetorical distinctiveness of his presidency, other than to note that his relationship to the American people would have been other than it was, and thus his presidency other than the one that occurred. The fact is that Roosevelt did open an epistolary public sphere, and because of that millions of Americans who theretofore had no voice in American democracy were activated to urge courses of action to protect their interests. Ironically, at the birth of the research method that has come to define the popular and press understanding of public opinion, Roosevelt opened a parallel domain in which the discursive nature of opinion might manifest itself more completely through vernacular rhetoric and, not incidentally, also might afford the types of discourse necessary to engage in representative reasoning capable of shaping the chief executive's own understanding of it.

In a time that seems removed from the pace and reach of communication today, we are tempted to dismiss the dialogue of this American public with Roosevelt as quaintly anachronistic. Easy dismissal would miss the deeper significance of this story for present realities. The general public's correspondence with Roosevelt on the third-term question indicates that narratives of vernacular rhetoric can afford a certain accuracy in gauging public opinion that otherwise is unavailable. Were leaders to hear these opinions and take them seriously, the quality of public discourse might take a positive turn. Understanding people's concerns and why they hold them holds promise for helping leaders to *communicate* with society's active members rather than *manipulating* them.

Rhetoric of this sort would have a different character than messages calculated to play on our susceptibilities. Politicians whose sole intent is to get elected, retain power, and cater to their patrons obviously have as much opportunity to misuse the insights of vernacular rhetoric as is currently the case with survey research findings. Setting self-serving ends aside, however, attending to the daily stories told by covert and often overlooked publics would open a self-generated social narrative for inspection, understanding, empathy, and response. We locate these narratives in the myriad of public spheres in which people exchange opinions about the impact of worldly conditions and public policies on families, jobs, health, neighborhoods, children, the environment, schools, and the host of problems and issues that are the common struggles they share with strangers. We capture insights from these narratives that escape polls and the formulations of decision-making elites. Listening to them teaches us about rhetorically active but overlooked publics dispersed across a land of strangers, of their causes and cries for help, of why they seek change, and of why their calls for relief so often seem beset by contradictions. These narratives might open paths to a public rhetoric that is sensitive, responsive, and humane. They might also encourage a public rhetoric that appreciates the public sphere as a place to actually talk to people about something. Listening to vernacular rhetoric provides us with a shared context for conversing; it promotes dialogue in which words matter for understanding problems and the complex relations they spawn and for addressing the contradictoriness of the human condition.

In Anton Chekhov's *Gooseberries* (1961) the character Ivan Ivanych tells his companions a story about the falsehoods we embrace because they exalt us, while we hide from life's meaner truths. His story's denouement occurs when Ivanych offers this remarkable recollection:

> I saw a happy man, one whose cherished dream had so obviously come true, who had attained his goal in life, who had got what he wanted, who was satisfied with his lot and with himself. For some reason an element of sadness had always mingled with my thoughts of human happiness, and now at the sight of a happy man I was assailed by an oppressive feeling bordering on despair. It weighed on me particularly at night. A bed was made up for me in a room next to my brother's bedroom, and I could hear that he was wakeful, and that he would get up

again and again, and go to the plate of gooseberries and eat one after another. I said to myself: how many contented, happy people there really are! What an overwhelming force they are! Look at life: the insolence and idleness of the strong, the ignorance and brutishness of the weak, horrible poverty everywhere, overcrowding, degeneration, drunkenness, hypocrisy, lying— Yet in all the houses and on all the streets there is peace and quiet; of the fifty thousand people who live in our town there is not one who would cry out, who would vent his indignation aloud. We see the people who go to market, eat by day, sleep by night, who babble nonsense, marry, grow old, good-naturedly drag their dead to the cemetery, but we do not see or hear those who suffer, and what is terrible in life goes on somewhere behind the scenes. Everything is peaceful and quiet and only mute statistics protest: so many people gone out of their minds, so many gallons of vodka drunk, so many children dead from malnutrition— And such a state of things is evidently necessary; obviously the happy man is at ease only because the unhappy ones bear their burdens in silence, and if there were not this silence, happiness would be impossible. It is a general hypnosis. Behind the door of every contented man there ought to be someone standing with a little hammer and continually reminding him with a knock that there are unhappy people, that however happy he may be, life will sooner or later show him its claws, and trouble will come to him—illness, poverty, losses, and then no one will see or hear him, just as now he neither sees or hears others. But there is no man with a hammer. The happy man lives at his ease, faintly fluttered by small daily cares, like an aspen in the wind—and all is well.

Although we might hope, with Chekhov, for the lone actor who will stand strong and straight to point us toward a righteous course, his image leads elsewhere. Most of us are like aspen. We see ourselves as reasonable people, reasonably happy and content with the way things are. We pass our lives "faintly fluttered" by daily cares, unaware of or insensitive to larger problems that are the unhappy fate of strangers who surround us. Ivan Ivanych's striking invocation moves us to wonder where we might find the hammer with sufficient weight to prod responses of understanding, caring, and action. The discourse of Roosevelt's correspondents suggests that it may be at hand, if we only take care to look and listen to appeals and exchanges of everyday life.

Looking for and listening to vernacular rhetoric may lead us to see the men and women in our society as anything but apathetic and perhaps not completely unhappy. In their responses to the world we might hear a convergence of voices that introduce us to publics that are engaged but often overlooked or forgotten because they lack a place in our institutional public spheres. Finding them will not produce easy solutions to complex problems, nor will their discovery erase competing interests and the agonistic relations they spawn. But locating them and hearing their voices can provide a basis for engaging one another in ways that make democracy something more than a theory and that assails the indifference to suffering and injustice so virulent today in public life. We may resuscitate our moribund politics by putting the hammer in the hands of those whose voices are now barely audible as whispers of discontent.[20]

Chapter 9

THE RHETORIC OF PUBLICNESS: THEORY AND METHOD

> ... almost every day I come across some piece of heartening evidence that the
> dissidents are really saying nothing other than what the vast majority of their
> fellow citizens think privately.
>
> Václav Havel, *Living in Truth*

At midcentury Hannah Arendt (1958) published her much-celebrated book *The Human Condition*. Arendt argued that the ills of the modern age were the result of losing a vital public realm in which we could form a common sense of reality and of agency for action. Her book begins with a powerful reconstruction of life in the Golden Age of Athens, with a life divided between polis and oikos captured by her felicitous expression as the vita activa. For these Athenians, the bios politikos of the polis provided the arena in which they might distinguish themselves from the crowd by establishing their identity through publicly esteemed words and deeds. The oikos, by contrast, offered a retreat from the agon of politics to the private pleasures of the family, intimacy, and the pursuit of economic well-being. In Arendt's rendition this distinction between public and private was fundamental to Athenian understanding of the good life. They were reciprocal parts of a full existence; each would be incomplete without the richness offered by the other.

Arendt posited the public/private distinction at the outset of *The Human Condition* to contextualize her analysis of the modern era's disorientation. The division between public and private was essential for getting beyond preoccupation over the narrowly economic concerns with survival and moving forward to a society of individual worth and responsibility. The public/private distinction created the conditions of possibility for a world of agency in which individuals might act rather than merely behave. In this respect she set herself apart from most of Western thought in which intellectuals and scholars, finding little to recommend a realm wherein an ignorant citizenry convulsed with emotion made public decisions, have urged retreat from the hurly-burly of the polis. By removing themselves from the distractions of politics, humankind would be free to pursue a life of reflection, or the *vita contemplativa*. Arendt, however, found flight from this world mystifying in that it represented turning from the very untidy circumstances of public life that provide our basis for understanding the human condition. The public realm, she argued, is the locus of words and deeds by which humans established their truths. If, under the tyranny of technology and industry, the modern era had displaced this world of action and agency with one marked by the aggregate of behavior and the concomitant loss of agency, the blame lay in the erosion of the public/private division. Only public acts, whose virtuosity was witnessed by the community's members, could establish human realities and permit common acts in pursuit of the public good.

Arendt's argument is worth noting because the uncertain boundary between public and private life is one that resonates deeply and consequentially through American social, political, and economic relations. For example, twenty years ago Richard Sennett (1978) posited that we have lost our sense of publicness and with it the difference between our public and private roles. The consequence, he argued, has been the steady migration of privacy into the public realm, accompanied by inappropriate expectations for interactions with strangers and, in Sennett's view, a distorted politics. In the mid 1980s Robert Bellah and his associates (1985) found that Americans generally regarded their private lives as more meaningful than their public ones and had mastery of several well-developed vocabularies, such as those of religion and therapy, to express what those meanings were. Yet a large number of the middle Americans they interviewed expressed a desire for a richer life than the one they were leading. On the other hand, their expressed commitment to the importance of community lacked a vocabulary to express their concerns with sophistication. Bellah and his associates wondered if that might account, in part, for why Americans neither sought nor found personal enrichment in their public lives. More recently the rise of new social movements and cultural politics has marked a shift from concentration on material conditions of oppression to issues of identity oppression and formation (Laraña, Johnson, and Gusfield, 1994). The rhetoric of new social movements often makes interests, meanings, and the demands of rhetorical situations the products of negotiations about interpersonal behaviors we commonly associate with private life. Finally, we need look no farther than American politics and its preoccupation with a sitting president's sex life or the general outpouring of grief over the death of Princess Diana for indications of the public/private distinction's labile nature.

Evidence of this sort suggests that our understanding of publicness is not as well formed nor the boundaries between the public and private realms as rigid as those Arendt valorized in the opening sections of *The Human Condition*. In large measure Arendt thought these were the consequences of replacing a political with a social model of human relations, of moving from concern with the arête of individual virtuosity to a Rousseauian *volonté générale*. But it was this part of her analysis that exposed her to serious criticisms. Jürgen Habermas (1977), for example, found her exclusion of the economy from the public sphere problematic, while Seyla Benhabib (1992) considered the political/social distinction untenable because it excluded the primary struggle of the modern era over issues of justice, which is often the struggle to make an issue public.

More generally, critical and social analysis seems predisposed to reject the public/private distinction (Robbins, 1993; Phillips, 1996). Objections to classical distinctions between public and private, such as Arendt's, prompt arguing as if the distinction itself is invalid. Despite the seemingly unstable public/private boundary, we nonetheless need a model of a public sphere that accommodates public issues, publics, and the publicness of public life as something not identical with our private, intimate existence. This is another way of stating that the idea of the public sphere is both contested and essential for a model of social, political, and economic life in pluralistic societies. This study has attempted to address this conceptual need.

Theoretical Considerations

The central concepts of this study—publics, public spheres, and public opinion—arose with the shift from civic virtue to civil society as the model of social and political organization. Consonant with emerging conditions of expanding trade relations with foreign countries, the lessening hold of the absolute monarchy on the reins of governance, and a developing understanding of the individual as an autonomous moral agent new ideas about economy, public opinion, and moral conduct introduced three means by which society expressed its own identity apart from the state and, moreover, established *self-regulating* domains independent of governments for social coordination. Importantly for political relations, the arenas for public opinion formation were different from those of the polis in which the same persons populated both the agora and ekklesia. The concept of civil society introduced a new arena independent of the government, existing between it and the family. The discursive spaces of government were no longer the only domain in which social will could be articulated and executed. Now there was a public sphere in which a public could form its own opinion that might challenge the state's primacy in setting social purposes and that might expect its understanding to bear weight on what the state did.

Our attention is still directed to civil society as the locus of opinion formation. In principle, it functions as society's arena of self-regulation, with the opinions that form there asserting authority to guide the state. Whether civil society is colonized by the state and power elites, as Habermas depicts in his rendition of late capitalism, or remains open to the possibility of its own self-regulation is itself subject to the rhetorical possibilities and performances it can sustain. In less theoretical terms, and accepting the precondition of free speech, whether or not civil society embraces and lives in truth is fundamentally dependent on whether or not its members are informed and attentive to the truth.

My concerns in this study have been to outline a framework for thinking about publics, public spheres, and public opinion in a way that does not presuppose they are distorted. I have taken my lead from the liberal democratic tradition of political thought which theorizes each of these concepts in close connection to discourse. My attempt has been to reconsider each of these terms using discourse, specifically the rhetorical character of discourse, as its starting point. The academic study of rhetoric has a long tradition of critical inquiry into institutional political discourse, as it is performed by officials and political parties. Sustaining and broadening rhetoric's place in the critical discussion of political relations is not only relevant but essential because it offers a rich theory and critical apparatus specifically addressed to the suasory character and consequences of the symbolic choices on which political relations rest. It goes beyond the general postmodern insight that "discourse is all" to offer specific analysis of how discourse actually induces social cooperation.

As the preceding case studies demonstrate, when we conceptualize publics in rhetorical terms they are locatable as that portion of society actively engaged by issues. They are activated both by the discourse of leaders or the media and among themselves, making the wisdom with which they exercise their judging function contingent upon the character and quality of the rhetorical engagements they share. These studies suggest that publics are more than ideal; they are concrete emergences whose contours form through the materiality of the rhetoric to which they are attending and who make themselves evident through the materiality of their own vernacular modes of rhetoric. The case studies suggest that we may recover our political relations as more than a sham of manipulation by the elites of wealth, power, and technical knowledge so much in evidence today as "in control" of our public life, at least as we experience them as members of publics. Others have sought a similar recuperation; however, what distinguishes the framework developed here is its insistence on regarding publics, public spheres, and public opinion as discursive phenomena whose characters are definitively rhetorical.

Publics, public spheres, and public opinion are the basic terms of a modern democracy. They reference assumptions about freedom of assembly and expression on which we base our social and political lives. We could not imagine a democracy, or life as a free people, were we denied these rights or if the views emerging from their exercise were inconsequential in influencing decisions that affect our lives. Yet much that we experience in a modern, complex society indicates that these assumptions are precariously close to being negated. Modern democracies are seldom marked by high levels of political participation; issues typically are controlled by organized and often well-financed special-interest groups; and legislation often reflects the interests of the most effective lobby rather than those of the people. Although these patterns of political life suggest that publics with a sense of civic community are moribund, other patterns suggesting high civic engagement often go unnoticed because we overlook the actual discursive practices that reflect attention to and a point of view toward public problems.

The problem of "the moribund public," as Dewey (1954) put it, during the early part of the twentieth century was one of too much information and too little social cohesion to permit informed and active participation in the discussion of public problems. At the turn of the next century the problem of "the moribund public" has taken a more sinister turn through colonization of our public spheres and technologizing of public opinion by elites of knowledge, wealth, and position. Equally, as assumptions that take the socially inscribed practices of the majority as the norm by which everyone and everything else is judged, voices on the margins tend to be excluded from deliberations shaping the world they must inhabit. Whether the terms of public discussion have been placed beyond the range of the average person or the terms for participation have been set in a way that excludes vast segments of society from participating in the discussion, discourse becomes a fatality. The practical consequence of these tendencies has been a lessening of public participation in political processes and encouragement of individualism's continuing march away from publicness and toward the sanctuary of private goals and pleasures (Cloud 1998).

The price of living in a democracy is that the people have a say in decisions made on their behalf. Democracy raises the possibility that informed and reasoned discussion among the governed will shape the politics and policies under which they live. This poses a dilemma of sorts. The reality of democratic life is that if everybody participates, then we must contend with a segment of participants who may not read newspapers or understand the complex nature of public problems, or who are guided by narrow self-interest, or who, without counterbalancing participation in thorough and reasoned discussion of the issues, are vulnerable to the lure of political ads. Speeches and essays, plays, films, and television programs addressed to and reflective of the people open the possibility that the majority who reigns will form around appeals that are not entirely based on reason, that admit and even encourage emotional considerations as valid in public deliberations, that are advanced by partisans who are unabashedly biased in their analysis and advocacy, and that surface in arenas outside the mainstream of public discussion. They open the possibility that engaged voices will be overlooked or their views excluded from consideration because the only arenas in which their dissident appeals can be expressed freely and taken seriously are the subaltern arenas of counterpublic spheres.

At its best, a democracy's rhetoric is untidy by Enlightenment standards of reason. Consequently some thinkers, such as Habermas, who have been the staunchest champions of discourse as democracy's anchoring concept have found the strategic impulses of rhetoric problematic. But excluding rhetorical processes from our assessment of democracy's ongoing conversation also excludes the agency by which democratic decisions are reached. Before we can rehabilitate public life, we first must understand the way actually occurring discourse shapes it. Otherwise whatever critique we advance or remedy we propose is entirely analytic, producing conclusions that follow logically from a priori assumptions about the rational/ideological standards for "valid" assent but that lack an empirical referent in the actual discursive method that members of publics employ.

The foundations of publics, public spheres, and public opinions reside in the rhetorical transactions of a society. To dismiss these transactions as flawed is to dismiss the means by which society posits the order of its own representaions. Equally, to propose radical revision to society's ongoing albeit flawed self-ordering activity in order to approximate a theoretical ideal is to embark on a quixotic adventure. Society's understanding of its own historical environment and its options for responding to it are rhetorical inventions, developed in and through the ways in which we discuss the issues that engage us. The resources of shared identity provide our storehouse of significant symbols on which our rhetorical practices draw. They make it possible for individuals who are quite literally strangers to share in a public discussion conducted over distributed space, in which they may actually conceive of themselves as belonging to an autonomous, civic community.

This does not mean that anything goes or that a rhetoric untethered from actual events is as persuasive as one firmly tethered to them. Rather, it means that our understanding of reality is a function of how we talk and write about it. We compose narratives and make arguments using specific language and highlighting certain assumptions about our reference world. In the hands of the powerful this insight has led to a degenerate rhetoric more concerned with manipulation of emotion than with decisions based on reasoned appeals. Narratives certainly may be constructed more for popular consumption than rhetorical invention of social possibilities. As the mythic themes of American exceptionalism frequently demonstrate, they may even possess the power to pacify the general public into spectatorship. But, as the rhetorics of ethnic identity in Central and Eastern Europe, of the body in the Meese Commission report, of national honor in the Iranian hostage situation, and of the meaning of America constructed by FDR's letter writers show, shared narratives that signify terms of relationship and opposition also may solidify a public around its internal impulse to action on an unbounded world.

The rhetorical understanding of publicness emerging from these cases is inherently deliberative. Although political leaders may attempt to define publicness as an epideictic celebration of the present fixated by its alignment with the past, publics that move from spectatorship to active consideration of issues exhibit their publicness with a forward-looking concern for constructing the future from an interpretation of the present. The dialogical achievement of their civil judgments requires a viable civil society in which difference is recognized as inherent to relationships of mutual dependency.

As the vernacular and official rhetoric of much of Central and Eastern Europe makes evident, relationships of mutual dependency become dysfunctional without a shared reference world. A world of mutual dependencies must accommodate alternative historicities each seeking traction on a common problem. Accommodating difference cannot occur without collaboration. Associative networks of civil society prepare us for this task, involving us with strangers and teaching us to communicate with difference. A world of mutual dependencies requires publics able to form and express informed opinion and leaders able to grasp social dialogue as a valuable source for understanding public opinion. As we saw in the case of Bosnia and the Iranian hostage affair, sustaining this set of rhetorical relationships can be fragile. But the politics of FDR exemplifies its possibility when the vernacular exchanges of the people are taken seriously. We should be mindful, in this regard, that FDR's politics included active encouragment to the emergence of a public shere whose permeable borders invited citizens to join a national dialogue with their neighbors and leaders on the problems and choices of a nation in distress.

Accommodating alternative historicities does not mean there will be consensus. Certainly Roosevelt's letter writers and the Republicans they opposed had very different understandings of America, as did partisans of New Democracy and Pasok of Greece, but they were able to contextualize their differences in a larger frame of shared allegiances that kept their differences from assuming the more deadly forms manifested in the former Yugoslavia. Perhaps it would go without saying that civil society, and a fortiori its reticulate public spheres, is intensely interactive were it not for the tendency of the social sciences to explore these concepts almost exclusively in terms of their structural and functional character while ignoring communication processes, save in the idealized philosophical formulation provided by Jürgen Habermas. Once we focus on the type of discourse that permeates civil society, we cannot escape the conclusion that the overall Public Sphere and each specific sphere within it are defined by their rhetorical conditions—the conditions of possibility for individuals to make arguments and appeals that are intended, in principle, to produce cooperation within conditions of difference and interdependence. For this reason a rhetorical theory of publicness is necessarily normative. As a rhetorical domain it presupposes that those who participate are capable of understanding and responding to rhetorically salient meanings and will be afforded the opportunity to do so.

The rhetorical norms of publicness set forth the antecedent conditions on which the character and quality of any given public sphere depend. They provide the criteria for assessing the quality of agreements reached in a public sphere, recognizing that what passes as *good reasons* may not always satisfy the Kantian norms of critical rationality but that critical rationality is but one form of reasonableness and not necessarily the one best suited as normative for deliberative discussions. Civil judgments are tied to particular issues considered by particular publics. The rhetorical norms of publicness offer criteria for assessing the defining conditions of any public sphere in relationship to the possibilities of rhetoric to actually function as a method for dealing with issues or as a mode of manipulation to create the appearance of public opinion and legitimating assent to official action.

Methodological Considerations

Contrary to the prevailing idealized views that seem mired in characterizations of these relations as distorted, I have argued that we may recover them as more than a sham of manipulation by powerful elites. Others have sought a similar recuperation; however, what distinguishes the approach I have taken is its insistence on considering publics, public spheres, and public opinion in terms of their rhetoricality.Rather than indicting the weaknesses and failures of "the public," "the public sphere," and public opinion and then proposing a radical revision of political relations as a solution, I have sought to explore these dimensions of public and political life in terms of their concrete manifestation in the ongoing social conversation on society's direction and the relationship this bears to the rhetorical environment in which they are situated. This has involved adopting an *empirical attitude* toward the ways publics, public spheres, and public opinion are manifested.

By *empirical* I mean that the framework draws its inferences about publics, public spheres, and public opinion from actual social practices of discourse. In this sense it is grounded in the strongest sense of rhetoric, a Ciceronian sense, in which there are no a priori assumptions about what is real or true, and finds these inferences instead in what among expressible ideas and feelings can gain assent among the interacting parties (see Buckley 1970; Hauser 1979; and McKeon 1957). The evidentiary requirements of the framework, therefore, ultimately are tied to statements social actors advance on public problems. Evidence includes not only what can be said but what is proscribed; not only formal statements of officials, leaders, and spokespersons or of institutional voices, such as the press, but vernacular exchanges among the actively engaged segment of society; not only institutional forums but counter- and preinstitutional public spheres where those who are not privy to official sites or are marginalized engage as publics and counterpublics in society's multilogue on issues that impact their lives.

I do not mean to suggest that this framework is empirical in the narrowly technical sense of that term as understood within the social sciences, although its import is wedded to the general concern for evidence shared among the social sciences. It signifies more the *attitude* of an investigator who, cognizant of the *intentional fallacy*, determines to go beyond the critic's own sensibilities to the text and inquire into how those who appropriated it responded. He or she exhibits awareness, for example, that knowing Upton Sinclair wrote *The Jungle* with the socialist intent of impressing upon its readers the evils of capitalism must be balanced against how actual readers appropriated the book. In the United States, at least, its contemporary readers regarded *The Jungle* as an exposé of sanitation conditions in the meatpacking industry. Rather than fomenting revolution, as Sinclair had hoped, it inspired political agitation supporting passage of the Pure Food and Drug Act. The rhetoric of Sinclair's text stretched beyond his intentions and beyond the understanding of any given critic. How citizens read his novel, found it intersecting meaningfully with their experiences, and appropriated it through their own critical responses raise an empirical question that bears on the interpretation and criticism of the text.

The framework thus borrows from the tradition of rhetorical criticism, which is attentive to texts as statements designed to evoke specific responses. But it differs from some aspects of rhetorical criticism as it is currently practiced. Recent rhetorical criticism has come to focus intensely on texts. Sometimes this focus is manifested in specific theories of texts, such as reader response theory in literary studies, that privilege the construction of meaning a specific critic finds in the text. More generally it is displayed through the critical strategy of *close reading* that explores the *internal* dynamics of the text without necessarily taking account of specific external considerations that may have borne upon its meaning and its rhetorical force.

The ways we use symbols undeniably invite meanings, and the interpretation of texts from a rhetorical concern with how they induce social cooperation contributes to our understanding of the consequences of language use in shaping our political, social, and cultural relations. Close reading of a text is essential to understanding and criticizing its rhetorical character. The relationship of ideas and emotions embedded in the rhetor's use of language is elementary for understanding the way the text invites the listener/reader/viewer to experience and respond to a boundless world open to interpretation and reconstruction. At the same time, the meanings a critic finds in a text are not necessarily those found by its consumers. The empirical attitude of asking whether there is evidence of symbolic exchange indicating that a segment of society was actively engaged by a public problem, participated in a sphere of discourse in which the problem was explored, and formed a prevailing opinion about it requires going beyond the critic's reading of the discourse to inquire about how citizens who were addressed and addressing one another read it. It requires challenging our understanding of *text* as a performance by a specific writer, speaker, filmmaker, or other author. The text, in this framework, is the dialogue, and because it is often scattered and inchoate in its form, its interactive nature requires reconstituting by the investigator. One must piece together the morass of disparate discursive evidence that indicates how statements were understood, discussed, supported, and responded to by those who were actively engaged by an issue.

Paying greater attention to how actual participants in rhetorical exchange entered into dialogue with persuasive attempts directed to them invokes a classical understanding of rhetoric as discourse for use. Although restricting rhetoric to a specific genre is no longer in intellectual favor, the general enterprise of investigating the rhetoricality of communication cannot escape a distinguishing concern for how people use symbols to address some other. Discovering how those others remake and make use of messages is essential for understanding the rhetoricality of any and every public dialogue that seeks to escape privileging the voices of those with ready access to the podium or the mass media and to include the range of voices that contest issues. An empirical attitude in rhetorical studies seeks to determine how the range of participants in these transactions actually appropriated messages, the uses they made of them, and the roles these transactions played in constituting a human world. Without advancing causal claims, inspecting the actual dialogizing responses to formal and informal appeals advanced on public issues offers insight into how discourse shapes our world.

This rhetorical framework's empirical attitude also borrows from but stands in a different relation to discourse than critical theory. It shares critical theory's telos, as represented by the rhetorical norms it postulates about a well-functioning discursive arena. But its norms are derived from discursive practices rather than the rational and ideological norms that apply to a search for a transcendental truth with emancipatory power. They are centered in the discursive practices of agents who transact their business in a boundless world of contingencies and pluralism. Rhetorical transactions always take place among specific partners engaged in a collective process of sense-making within an indeterminate situation. The contingencies and multiple possibilities for resolution of an unbounded human world are constant reminders of Aristotle's observation that rhetoric's telos is judgment of and for the given case. Rhetoric's truths are not transcendental; they have validity only for the specific participants in the specific situation who acceded to specific appeals addressed to their specific concerns, needs, and interests. Its contexts are pragmatic, involving commitments to practical actions that grow from interpretations of reality.

Judgments of this sort are not captured by rationalistic canons. They are arational in their specificity to the given case, their open consideration of who is making the appeal, emotional responses to the circumstances, persons and consequences under discussion, and reliance on the inter-subjective meanings negotiated by particular dialogical partners. An empirical attitude toward rhetoric is sensitive to these as conditions of a nonobjective *humanitas;* its rhetoric yields judgments that are perishable.

Although Habermasean ideal speech conditions provide procedural guidelines consistent with the assumptions of participatory democratic practices, they also impose a seductive vision of rationality for assessing public judgments that themselves are not necessarily best made following these criteria. The empirical attitude asks what reasonable men and women deliberating about the contingencies confronting their community regard as good reasons for judging and acting as they do. Whether and to what extent a public sphere exhibits border crossings, its public's sense of a capacity to act, contextualized language, opportunities to make believable appearances before strangers, and tolerance of diverse perspectives and interests are empirical questions related to the character of the rhetorical environment for and performance of public dialogue. Answering them permits an assessment of a public sphere's scope and its impact on the publics and public opinions that form within it.

The empirical attitude of rhetoric also shares concerns of but stands apart from the empiricism of opinion polls. It shares the concern of survey research to locate the responses people have to circumstances that call for their judgment. Insofar as public judgment legitimates public action, knowing the opinions of those who are affected by them is fundamental to gauging the course of society. Equally, in this regard, the framework developed in this study and polling share a concern with the direction and weight of public opinion as empirical determinations relevant to an understanding of public life.

On the other hand, the argument of this study has been for widening the scope of what counts as evidence for public opinion. This requires reorienting our understanding of opinion in a way that is sensitive to its discursive nature. Thus, I have argued for the efficacy of a revived appreciation for public opinion's rhetorical antecedents. By inferring public opinion from the actual concerns and positions articulated in social exchange, such as those of Roosevelt's letter writers or of Greek voters, I have tried to display how inspection of vernacular rhetoric discloses differences and offers rich insights into a public's beliefs beyond those available from polls.

There is a reversal of priority in beginning the search for what people think with an empirical question about their own expressions rather than those of the poller or the interested owner of the poll. Expressions of affiliation and dissent take many forms. Each contributes to the fabric of social dialogue in which opinions are forged and expressed. There is, perhaps, greater fidelity to fact in an empirical attitude that seeks to determine what those who were interested thought and how they expressed those thoughts in formal and vernacular ways. Leveling opinion by assuming that everyone has one and everyone's counts equally may satisfy the protocols of randomness necessary for scientific validity but does not necessarily inform us of what engaged citizens believe or why they believe it.

To learn what a public thinks, we first must monitor the social conversation within a reticulate public sphere to ascertain who is speaking to whom about what. And if we wish to get beyond the apparent volatility of opinion as reflected in the radical mood swings reported by opinion polls, we must locate the categories of assertion and response used by engaged members of society. Their rhetorical exchanges provide more than data; their narratives of common meaning, web of associations, and historicity each reveal the reference world of meaning they are coconstructing and provide the context for understanding their specific judgments.

The world of contingencies is untidy, fraught with unpredictability, and open to manipulation. Public opinions are not always reasonable, public spheres do not always operate democratically, and publics often are unenlightened. But whether and why they act in distorted or enlightened ways are questions we can address only if we first tend to the empirical considerations of how actual people interacted on the questions that matter to them. Such understanding obligates the critic to reengage with the rhetorical characters of publics, public spheres, and public opinion as they actually manifest themselves. Tending to these rhetorical considerations obligates the critic further to go beyond the text of formal discourse and beyond a critical reading of the text to discover how it was understood and responded to by those who were paying attention and responding to what was being communicated. This is especially necessary if we wish to understand more fully the way in which discourse is related to the quality of public judgment.

That relationship is not an incidental concern. Democracies have a fundamental need for informed publics to legitimate public policies and public actions. Yet we seem to have lost faith in our publics' ability to exercise competent judgment. We live at a time when the types of problems confronting a technologically complex and culturally diverse society seem to outstrip the average citizen's capacity to comprehend them, much less to arrive at an informed opinion on their resolution. Additionally, complex societies have experienced a proliferation of roles on a scale that defies shared understanding of role expectations and produces a problem of trust (Seligman 1997). Since at least the 1920s, when the critiques of Lippmann and Dewey raised these concerns, theorists and commentators have treated the concept of "the public" as problematic.

This loss of faith in a public to form a competent judgment mirrors the problem of modernity, which has translated its Cartesian legacy of the disengaged self into the disengaged reason of instrumentalism.

In response, most commentators have argued, in the tradition of Lippmann's elite press corps of issue specialists and Dewey's pyramidal great community of multileveled public discussion, that the malaise and/or mass behavior of a public in eclipse require radical intervention. Seventy-five years and countless proposals later there does not seem to be much change in the behavior of publics or lack of confidence in public opinion than existed after the end of World War I. The reason may lie in the character of democracy and the nature of civil society. Such proposals as Barber's (1984) reforms to insure "strong democracy," Yankelovich's (1991) agenda to arrive at the rational consensus of "public judgment," Dryzek's (1990) advocacy of Q-methodology to measure public opinion, or Fishkin's (1995) design for citizen retreats to produce "deliberative polling" aspire to an ideal form of discussion leading to public opinions that can pass tests of rationality. But valorizing an ideal form of discourse that seldom, if ever, has materialized as normative for free and democratic societies fails to regard society's discursive practices on their own terms. Rather than giving credence to discourse as it actually occurs in existing democracies and asking what these very social practices of formal and vernacular exchange may tell us about our public life—about the conditions of discourse that pervade the reticulate Public Sphere, the publics and counterpublics that actually form, and the rhetorical processes by which they form and raise awareness of prevailing opinion—they seek a sanitized form of rationality itself divorced from the untidy realities of democratic political relations.

These approaches, in my view, are fatally flawed by smuggling in a confusion between theoretical and empirical levels of analysis. While it is the case, as Hume observed, that government rests on opinion, the empirical reality of how that opinion is established bears no necessary relationship to the idealized discursive practices implicit in liberal democratic theory's projected rationalizing function. In fact, the founding theorists of liberal democratic thought were acutely aware that bias, partisanship, and self-interest colored public discussion. Locke (1959) and Hume (1888) both observed that fancy replaced conviction in guiding public opinion. In fact, their accounts are missing any declaration of faith in the ensemble of well-informed and responsible parties, highly educated and skilled at deliberation, who are capable of weighing arguments and arriving at reasoned judgment about public affairs and who then critique state action on that basis. The empirical reality of the public opinion process Locke and Hume observed had more to do with interests than achieving rational consensus.

The human tendency toward advancing interests was not viewed as necessarily evil, as Albert O. Hirschman's celebrated study *The Passions and the Interests* (1997) shows. Enlightenment thinkers who were propounding the theory of civil society as a new concept of social organization—thinkers such as Giambattista Vico, Montesquieu, and Adam Smith—regarded humans as less than wholly rational, as driven by passions which, if left unchecked, might do irreparable social harm. In the view of French and Scottish Enlightenment thinkers, the pursuit of interests served as a check against more violent passions because, in the context of civil society, it encouraged cooperative exchange of ideas and goods to accomplish group and class goals.

Hirschman's history of the changes that occurred in European understanding of human motivation between the sixteenth and eighteenth centuries is intended to establish the evolving argument for capitalism. But his discussion makes clear that the emerging recognition of interests as serving a positive end went beyond an economic concern with taming unbridled avarice to include the entire compass of social relations. His study reminds us that people have interests in line with their group affiliations and class. Interests influence values, beliefs, and actions, and within civil society's web of associations they are not necessarily debasing. They often compete, but endemic difference defines a world that calls for an alternative measure of public conduct to the Greek preoccupation with glory and an alternative standard for judgment to a neo-Kantian adherence to transcendent truth.

Our post-Nietzschean awareness of the contingency of all has become the only orientation we have. It connects us back to the pre-Socratic rejection of metaphysics by the Elder Sophists, who maintained that the human world evolved in relation to the quality of public argument. The indeterminateness of our humanly made world, as was true of theirs, accentuates the inherently unpredictable character of political action within a framework that is never entirely manageable or reliable. Studying the rhetoric of publicness can make a valuable contribution to our understanding of the fragile hopes and perilous dangers that flow from open possibilities. In this study I have attempted to show how its focus on the actual discursive practices of leaders and citizens, borne of real-world experiences and susceptible to mischief as well as capable of understanding and courage, can help us to better understand how publics, public spheres, and public opinion form and function. Studying the rhetoric of publicness keeps us empirically rooted in society's ever-present need to secure cooperation. In a world defined by awareness of the contingency of all, we cannot hope to secure cooperation without a language and reasons for acting that are perceived to accommodate the interests of others and instill mutual confidence that partners will act in ways that bear out the rhetorical performance of words in the performance of future deeds. The validity of public judgment itself is contingent on these rhetorical practices. Understanding them and acquiring skill at them are basic for our participation in a democracy and for living in freedom in a human world that, despite its nonobjectivity and perishability, is boundless and always a construction of human choice.

Appendix I
CHRONOLOGY OF HOSTAGE DEVELOPMENTS

The following chronology is based on articles appearing in the *Department of State Bulletin*, January 1980 through February 1981.

22 Oct. 1979	The deposed shah of Iran, Mohammed Reza Pahlavi, enters the United States for medical treatment.
4 Nov.	Iranian students seize U.S. embassy in Tehran and hold one hundred hostages (sixty-five Americans), protesting that the deposed shah be returned to Iran to stand trial.
5 Nov.	Press Secretary Jody Powell says the U.S. will not return the shah. He is here for medical treatment. He indicates U.S. desire to negotiate a settlement with Iran.
6 Nov.	Prime Minister Bazargan's provisional government dissolves, yielding power to the Islamic authority of Ayatollah Ruhollah Khomeini and his secret Revolutionary Council. Former attorney general Ramsey Clark and William Miller, U.S. Senate Committee senior staff official, leave Washington carrying a message from the president to Iranian officials.
7 Nov.	Khomeini rejects talks with Clark and Miller.
8 Nov.	President Carter postpones Canada visit until 1980.
9 Nov.	U.S. suspends deliveries of about $30 million in military equipment and spare parts to Iran.
10 Nov.	Carter directs Attorney General Civiletti to deport any Iranian student who is in the U.S. illegally. Abolhassan Bani-Sadr becomes Iran's acting foreign minister and reaffirms Iran's demand that the U.S. return the shah.
12 Nov.	Carter orders suspension of purchase of Iranian oil by U.S. Iran announces it is cutting petroleum shipments to the U.S.
13 Nov.	American naval vessels start maneuvers in the Arabian Sea. Iran charges U.S. with threatening war.
14 Nov.	Bani-Sadr announces Iran will withdraw its funds from

American banks. Carter acts to block all official Iranian assets in the U.S.

16 Nov. Iranian militants threaten hostages if the shah is allowed to go anywhere but to Iran.

17 Nov. Khomeini orders the militants to release all women and blacks among the hostages.

18 Nov. Khomeini declares hostages face being tried as spies.

19 Nov. Three of the hostages—two black marines and one white secretary—are released.

20 Nov. Ten more Americans are freed. U.S. suggests to Iran that it might resort to military force if the remaining hostages are not freed. Carter orders a second naval task force into the Indian Ocean.

21 Nov. Militants warn that all hostages will die and the embassy will be blown up if the U.S. attacks.

25 Nov. U.N. Security Council session is called by Secretary General Waldheim because Iran fails to respond to an appeal to release U.S. hostages. It is only the second time in nineteen years that a secretary general has requested such a meeting.

27 Nov. Hospital officials announce that the shah is able to leave the hospital and return to Mexico within the week.

28 Nov. Bani-Sadr is dismissed as Iran's acting foreign minister. Sadigh Ghotbzadeh is named in his place.

29 Nov. U.S. initiates action against Iran in the International Court of Justice.

Mexico announces it will not renew visa for the shah.

30 Nov. Carter postpones six-state political tour because of Iranian crisis.

1 Dec. U.N. Security Council begins debate on the hostage affair.

2 Dec. Carter gives shah temporary sanctuary at Lackland Air Force Base Hospital in San Antonio, Texas.

12 Dec. U.S. orders expulsion of 183 Iranian diplomats in retaliation for continued detention of the hostages. They must leave in five days.

15 Dec. International Court of Justice orders Iran to immediately release all hostages. Shah leaves U.S. for residence in Panama.

16 Dec.	President Carter proclaims 18 December National Unity Day to demonstrate support for the hostages.
18 Dec.	Carter administration reports it is seriously considering "nonviolent" military action if hostages are put on trial.
21 Dec.	Carter decides to ask U.N. Security Council to impose economic sanctions against Iran.
27 Dec.	The Soviet Union invades Afghanistan.
1 Jan. 1980	Waldheim arrives in Tehran to seek negotiations for release of the hostages.
3 Jan.	Khomeini refuses to meet with Waldheim.
8 Jan.	U.S. wins approval from other major industrial countries on new financial sanctions against Iran.
13 Jan.	Security Council votes 13 to 2 (USSR and East Germany) on a draft resolution calling for economic sanctions against Iran.
14 Jan.	The Revolutionary Council orders all U.S. news correspondents to leave Iran because of their "biased reporting."
15 Jan.	U.S. files its memorial with the World Court on the merits of the U.S.-Iran hostage case.
25 Jan.	Bani-Sadr wins Iran's first presidential election.
29 Jan.	Six U.S. embassy employees who had been hiding in the Canadian embassy escape from Iran.
6 Feb.	U.S. delays imposing formal economic sanctions against Iran to avoid upsetting possible chances for settling the crisis.
13 Feb.	Carter approves of an international commission of inquiry into Iran's grievances.
14 Feb.	Bani-Sadr states that hostages could be freed within forty-eight hours if Carter agrees to conditions approved by Khomeini.
20 Feb.	At Iran's request, U.N. inquiry commission delays trip to Tehran for three days.
23 Feb.	Commission arrives in Tehran, but Khomeini issues a statement saying the fate of the hostages should be decided by the new parliament to be elected March/April.
10 Mar.	Commission of inquiry departs Iran after failing to see the hostages.

23 Mar.	Shah departs Panama for Egypt.
25 Mar.	Ayatollah Mohammed Beheshti, leader of the Islamic Republican Party, announces he favors holding trials for those accused of espionage if the shah is not returned to Iran to stand trial.
30 Mar.	U.S. and its Western allies are said to make major efforts to pressure Iran to take steps to release hostages.
31 Mar.	U.S. gives Iran until 1 April to announce steps to remove hostages from militants' control or face new U.S. economic and political retaliations.
1 Apr.	Bani-Sadr offers to take custody of the hostages if the U.S. agrees to a truce in its "War of Words" and in its economic and political pressures on Iran. Carter, regarding this as a "positive development," defers plans to impose new sanctions against Iran.
2 Apr.	Carter publicly pledges silence to Iran about hostages as long as progress is being made to resolve the crisis.
7 Apr.	Khomeini rules that hostages must remain in hands of the militants. U.S. breaks diplomatic relations with Iran and imposes a formal embargo on U.S. exports.
13 Apr.	Eight Common Market countries announce they would withdraw their ambassadors temporarily from Iran in protest against the holding of U.S. hostages.
18 Apr.	Carter orders new economic sanctions against Iran and indicates that if Iran does not release the hostages, military action will be the next step.
20 Apr.	Public notice is issued restricting the use of U.S. passports for travel to, in, or through Iran.
21 Apr.	Secretary of State Cyrus Vance submits a letter of resignation to Carter stating that he could not support the president's decision to attempt a rescue mission of the hostages in Iran.
22 Apr.	Common Market foreign ministers vote unanimously to impose full economic sanctions against Iran on 17 May unless "decisive progress" is made in freeing the hostages.
25 Apr.	A mission to rescue the hostages is aborted by President Carter because of equipment failures.
28 Apr.	Carter accepts Vance's resignation.
29 Apr.	Sen. Edmund S. Muskie is named to succeed Vance.

24 May	International Court of Justice rules that Iran must immediately release all U.S. Hostages.
2 June	Despite Carter's ban on travel to Iran, Ramsey Clark leads a ten-member group to an Iranian-sponsored conference on U.S. "intervention in Iran."
10 July	Khomeini orders the release of hostage Richard Queen, for reasons of health.
20 July	Majlis, Iran's parliament, takes over legislative power from the Revolutionary Council.
22 July	Bani-Sadr takes formal oath of office as Iranian president.
27 July	Shah dies in Cairo.
10 Aug.	Muskie says U.S. is considering new diplomatic initiatives for the release of the hostages.
12 Sept.	Khomeini sets four conditions on which the hostages are to be released.
18 Sept.	Carter rules out an apology to Iran as a prerequisite to releasing the hostages.
19 Sept.	Air and ground battles break out between Iran and Iraq.
16 Oct.	Prime Minister Rajai leaves Tehran for New York to attend a U.N. Security Council meeting on the Iran-Iraq war.
18 Oct.	Rajai says a decision on the release of the hostages is "not far away."
20 Oct.	Carter says he will lift U.S. sanctions against Iran if the hostages are freed.
31 Oct.	Despite numerous delays by Majlis, administration officials appear optimistic that Iranian authorities seem to have committed themselves to releasing the hostages.
2 Nov.	Majlis sets first official release terms.
3 Nov.	Militants turn jurisdiction of hostages over to the Iranian government but not the hostages themselves.
5 Nov.	Carter administration officials suggest that the president will agree to conditions if Iranian authorities accept a "narrow interpretation" of the Iranian parliament's demands.
10 Nov.	Deputy Secretary of State Christopher begins U.S. negotiations with Algerian intermediaries.
20 Nov.	The U.S. confirms that it has accepted in principle the four conditions "as a basis for resolution of the crisis."

18 Dec.	Iran's new terms for release of the hostages are delivered to Algerian intermediaries.
20 Dec.	U.S. views Iran's conditions as unacceptable.
30 Dec.	U.S. gives Algerians a "reformulation" of American proposals.
8 Jan. 1981	President-elect Reagan states he could honor any agreement with Iran made by President Carter but also says he reserves the right to draw up new proposals if the crisis is not settled by 20 Jan.
18 Jan.	U.S. and Iran sign final documents agreeing on central issues and issue a final declaration for release of the hostages.
20 Jan.	After 444 days in captivity, hostages are freed.

Appendix II
CHRONOLOGY OF
THE 1980 CAMPAIGN*

Fall 1979   Poll data on President Carter's standing with the voters
Democratic preference for presidential nominee
(*GOI* No. 172)

	Carter	Kennedy	Undecided
28 Sept.–1 Oct.	27%	59%	14%
12–15 Oct.	30	60	10
2–5 Nov.	31	54	15

Carter approval rating

	Approve	Disapprove	No Opinion
12–15 Oct.	31%	55%	14%

4 Nov.   Iranian students seize U.S. embassy in Tehran

7 Nov.   Senator Kennedy announces his candidacy.

16–19 Nov.   Democratic preference for presidential nominee
(*GOI* No. 172)

Carter	Kennedy	Undecided
36%	55%	9%

Carter approval rating

Approve	Disapprove	No Opinion
38%	49%	13%

4 Dec. President Carter announces his candidacy.

7–10 Dec.   Democratic preference for presidential nominee
(*GOI* No. 173)

Carter	Kennedy	Undecided
46%	42%	12%

Carter approval rating

Approve	Disapprove	No Opinion
75%	16%	9%

Carter handling of Iranian situation

Approve	Disapprove	No Opinion
76%	16%	8%

*Poll data are from The Gallup Poll (1980, 1981) and The Gallup Index (1980, 1981

28 Dec.   Carter cancels *Des Moines Register* debate scheduled for
               early January.

1–4 Jan. 1980 Carter approval rating (*GP* 1981)

	Approve	Disapprove	No Opinion
	56%	33%	11%

4–7 Jan.   Carter handling of Iranian situation (*GP* 1981)

	Approve	Disapprove	No Opinion
	61%	30%	9%

               Democratic preference for presidential nominee
               (*GOI* No. 175)

	Carter	Kennedy	Undecided
	51%	37%	12%

21 Jan.   Iowa caucuses, won by Carter.

23 Jan.   Carter delivers State of the Union Address.

25–28 Jan.   Democratic preference for presidential nominee
               (*GOI* No. 175)

	Carter	Kennedy	Undecided
	63%	24%	13%

28 Jan.   Kennedy delivers campaign address at Georgetown,
               attacking Carter's foreign policy.

1–4 Feb.   Carter approval rating (*GP* 1981)

	Approve	Disapprove	No Opinion
	55%	36%	9%

               Democratic preference for presidential nominee
               (*GOI* No. 175)

	Carter	Kennedy	Undecided
	61%	32%	7%

12 Feb.   Kennedy delivers campaign address at Harvard, sus-
               taining his attack on Carter's foreign policy.

13 Feb.   Carter holds a press conference, using it to refute
               Kennedy's attacks.

26 Feb.   Carter wins New Hampshire primary.

29 Feb.–3 Mar.   Carter approval rating (*GP* 1981)

Approve	*Disapprove*	*No Opinion*
52%	37%	11%

Carter handling of Iranian situation (*GP* 1981)

Approve	*Disapprove*	*No Opinion*
58%	35%	9%

7–10 Mar.   Carter approval rating (*GP* 1981)

Approve	*Disapprove*	*No Opinion*
43%	45%	12%

18 Mar.   Carter wins Illinois primary.

25 Mar.   Kennedy wins New York primary.

28–31 Mar.   Carter approval rating (*GP* 1981)

Approve	*Disapprove*	*No Opinion*
39%	51%	10%

Carter handling of Iranian situation (*GP* 1981)

Approve	*Disapprove*	*No Opinion*
40%	50%	10%

1 Apr.   Carter makes early morning announcement of "positive developments." He wins Wisconsin primary.

11–14 Apr.   Carter approval rating (*GP* 1981)

Approve	*Disapprove*	*No Opinion*
40%	50%	10%

25 Apr.   Rescue mission to free the hostages fails.

25–27 Apr.   Carter handling of Iranian situation (*GP* 1981)

Approve	*Disapprove*	*No Opinion*
46%	42%	12%

2–5 May   Carter approval rating (*GP* 1981)

Approve	*Disapprove*	*No Opinion*
43%	47%	10%

16–19 May   Carter approval rating (*GP* 1981)

Approve	*Disapprove*	*No Opinion*
38%	51%	11%

30 May–2 June   Carter approval rating (*GP* 1981)

	Approve	*Disapprove*	*No Opinion*
	38%	52%	11%

3 June   Final primary date.

13–16 June   Carter falls behind Reagan in presidential trial heat polls for first time.

	Carter	*Reagan*	*Other*	*Undecided*
	43%	44%	6%	7%

14–17 July   Republican National Convention, Ronald Reagan nominated.

1–4 Aug.   Poll shows Democrats favor Carter's releasing of pledged delegates to Democratic National Convention to vote for whomever they please (*GP* 1981).

	Yes	*No*	*Don't know*
	54%	36%	10%

11–14 Aug.   Democratic National Convention, Jimmy Carter nominated.

4 Nov.   General election, won by Reagan.

20 Jan.   1981 Inauguration Day.

NOTES

Chapter 1: The Public Voice of Vernacular Rhetoric

1. There is disagreement over whether the sophists who first taught the art of making public arguments actually called it "rhetoric," though clearly they were offering tutelage in its practice. See J. Poulakos (1983, 1990) and Schiappa (1990a, 1990b).

2. In order to preserve with accuracy the understanding of a public domain that was exclusively male I use masculine references in this and subsequent sections that discuss classical antiquity. Other than in the context of classical antiquity or when referring to a particular person, my use of feminine or masculine personal pronouns is random.

3. Aristotle introduces the three genres at *Rhetoric* I.3, which are then discussed in relation to *idia*, or material topics, specific to each genre and used to develop their special enthymemes.

4. For a discussion of the political and moral implications of the economic thinking at the inception of Enlightenment theorizing of civil society, see Hirschman (1977).

5. For a more promising assessment of citizen awareness of public issues, see Barber (1984), Fishkin (1995), and Yankelovich (1991).

6. The internet possesses enormous potential to become a significant discursive arena within civil society. Certainly the proliferation of interest-based chat groups is suggestive in this regard. My point here reflects the significant material limitation posed by the requirement of having access first to a computer and then to the internet. Its potential notwithstanding, the internet currently is a venue limited to those with basic computer skills plus institutional support or personal means often beyond those of the average individual.

7. A good illustration of how these vernacular exchanges radiate out can be found in Lynn Stearney's (1992) study of a feminist newsletter, *Notes from the First Year*, written to record memorable discussions and ideas shared among a small group of women in New York who met regularly. These women shared the newsletter with friends, who shared it with their friends, and so forth, until it acquired a broad readership and became a point of reference in the feminist counterpublic sphere.

Chapter 2: Discourse, Rhetorical Discourse, and the Public Sphere

1. Emotivism is a philosophical position concerned with the status of evaluative terms, such as *good*. It emerged in the early middle period of the twentieth century and was influenced by the criteria for knowledge set forth by the positivists, although its roots are traceable to Humean skepticism of the eighteenth century. Emotivism maintains that the language of moral discourse is qualitatively different from the language of signification. Since it has no indicative function, it cannot be verified. By the same token, neither can we specify the conditions under which a

claim advanced with moral language can be falsified. Instead, such language functions as a self-report by communicating one's attitude and has meaning only insofar as it is understood as such. See Ayer (1936), Edwards (1955), Hare (1964), and Stevenson (1944) for reasonable samples of its iterations.

2. See Speier (1950) for a synoptic discussion of the history of public opinion's modern political meaning.

3. A sampling of these criticisms can be found in Calhoun 1992; and Robbins 1993.

4. In this respect, Habermas distinguishes his model of discourse from Michel Foucault's. Foucault emphasizes the hegemonic status of discourse to form rules of exclusion constituting the authority of those who may speak it over the "other" who is constituted as subject by being denied a voice (1972). Habermas (1992, 429) observes, "Those who participate in the discourse do not share a common language with the protesting other." A Foucauldean model conceptualizes the dominant culture as devaluing the counterculture of the common people, forcing them to move and communicate in an alien world of knowledge and power that constitutes their "otherness." Habermas insists that the bourgeois public articulates its publicness differently in discourses that provide room for common ground with other publics and that can alter self-constitution. "From the very beginning," he maintains, "the universalistic discourses of the bourgeois public sphere were based on self-referential premises; because they differ from Foucauldean discourses by virtue of their potential for self-transformation." For this reason he holds that his model, though simplistic at points in its original formulation, envisions a political process whose core remains open to revision. These exclusions raise important points about historical infringements on civil rights, but they are themselves themes that give additional insights into how communicative action provides a normative model for society.

5. Farrell (1993) has explored this problem in some detail and offers a modification to Habermas's idealized model that would make it more receptive to rhetorical discourse. Farrell's modification is basic to his argument for a normative rhetorical culture. My concern here is rather with the basic rhetoricality of the public sphere, which is distorted by fundamental assumptions Habermas makes about communication.

6. See Landes (1988, 69–70) for an illustrative discussion of how Rousseau enacted the eighteenth-century ideal of "the public" as an egalitarian body of free and equal human beings that excluded women under the ideology of motherhood.

7. In line with French sociologist Alain Touraine's actionist sociology (1977, 1981), which views society as a field of action rather than an already existing set of systems, Rodger points to the discursive activity of "new social movements" as constituting these preinstitutional public spheres. They are brought into being by social movements in which participants negotiate new normative standards and provide a new framework for experience (211–12). Touraine distinguishes social from political movements. Social movements are concerned with constituting their identity by communicating and sharing an alternative set of values and priorities to those of the dominant society. They become political movements when they confront the power structure to effect change, thereby moving onto the institutional level for resolving public problems (Touraine 1981, part 1, chaps. 5 and 6).

8. Here I am using a cognitive conception of emotions in which emotions are understood as judgment about the projection of a condition or state of being that follows from a specified set of circumstances. I take this to be the conception of emotions Aristotle finds appropriate to the art of rhetoric in book 2 of the *Rhetoric*. This idea is developed in Fortenbaugh (1975). Also see Hauser (1986, 107–19) and Solomon (1976) for further elaboration on a cognitive model of emotions.

9. For a discussion of "good reasons" as a basis for reasonableness, see Ehninger (1968), Fisher (1978, 1980), Gottlieb (1968), and Wallece (1963).

10. The distinction between dialectical and rhetorical modes of discourse, including the differences in the types of questions they address, was established in Greek antiquity, most notably in the writings of Aristotle's *Analytics, Topics,* and *Rhetoric*. The assignment of general questions to dialectic and particular questions to rhetoric corresponds to their respective ends: dialectic being concerned with criticism and rhetoric with public judgment. This distinction, especially as it relates to the present discussion, is treated in great depth and with considerable scholarly erudition in Farrell (1993, 14–50).

11. The "tu quoque" argument was developed by William Bartley III (1962, 88–175) as a form of redact *ad absurdum* to undermine the standard of universalizable rational norms. In response to the rejection of a claim as irrational, one asks for the rational defense of the relevant criterion invoked. Then the defense must be justified and the justifications justified until the point is reached where the call for justification can only be responded to with a claim that it is a basic axiom incapable of more basic justification. At this point the irrationalist responds "*tu quoque,*" indicating that at the point where no further justification is possible, the rationalist is guilty of begging the question and equally as irrational as the irrationalist.

Chapter 3: Civic Conversation and the Reticulate Public Sphere

1. See, in this regard, the literature on rhetoric's epistemic function. The interested reader will find a convenient overview in Richard A. Cherwitz, ed., *Rhetoric and Philosophy* (1990).

2. I am indebted to Joseph Flay for calling this distinction to my attention.

3. Habermas maintains that to recover the *we,* a process of reaching consensus must ensue. If a new consensus must be forged, then so must a new we. His commitment to rational consensus leads him to search for an overarching we-perspective from which to construct it. The condition of rationality conceptualizes discursive spaces as nested domains with we-perspectives embedded in other, overarching we-perspectives. At this point Habermas's theory of communicative action comes into play as the embodiment of rationality in the life-world. Habermas does not assume an external rational norm but ties rationality to the process of repairing ruptures in the we-perspective. Habermas's model searches for reason within the horizon of acceptable common properties. From this follows the ideal process of reaching understanding motivated solely by reason. However, at this point we encounter the problems with Habermas's principle of disinterest, criterion of communicative rationality, and model of ideal speech vis-à-vis diversity discussed in chapter 2. Charles Taylor (1991, 28–29) points out that for overarching perspectives to embrace other, in extremis ones assumes the availability of a common set of reasons that all can embrace to reestablish consensus. This leads Taylor to wonder what will justify adherence to consensual norms outside one's own value

system. "As an actor I can always ask the question why I should actually proceed according to a particular norm, namely rationality. Why should this be a norm I cannot deny? This is a question which one can only answer, to use my own terminology, with 'strong valuations'" (Taylor 1991, 29).

4. Kathleen Domenig called to my attention this characterization, which she discusses further in her doctoral dissertation (1995).

5. Farrell (1993) has developed this point in greater detail. See his chapter 5 for a discussion of the consequences that result in Habermas's theory of communicative action from an overemphasis on illocution while ignoring perlocution.

Chapter 4: Reading Public Opinion from Vernacular Rhetoric

1. See Robert Nisbet (1975) for a representative projection of Lowell's position into the context of late-twentieth-century challenges to liberal democratic theory.

2. This tradition received its impetus in the studies of the 1940 election by Lazarsfeld and his group (Lazarsfeld, Berelsen & Gaudet 1968). Its development from then until now has resulted in highly sophisticated techniques of survey measurement. What these measures mean, however, is a matter of considerable dispute, even within the polling community. See Bourdieu (1979), Dryzek (1990), Ginsberg (1986), Habermas (1989), Herbst (1993), Noelle-Neumann (1993), Popkin (1991), and D. Taylor (1986) for a sample of this range.

3. I am distinguishing public opinion from mass opinion (Mills 1963) and popular opinion (Nisbet 1975).

4. McGee (1975) and McGee and Martin (1983) offer an insightful analysis of the problem of reifying *the public.*

5. This I take to be the point of the feminist critique of Habermas's model (1989) of the bourgeois public sphere. A convenient survey of feminist critiques of Habermas's position may be found in Calhoun (1992), especially in chapters by Seyla Benhabib, Nancy Fraser, and Mary Ryan.

6. For Aristotle, the arts of pure reflection and contemplation, such as physics, produce theoria, or theoretical knowledge; those of correct conduct, such as ethics and politics, of which rhetoric is a branch, result in praxis that reflects practical knowledge or phronêsis; while arts of poeisis, such as poetics, require mastery of the technê that produces them, or productive knowledge. One must be cautious, however, not to draw these distinctions too rigidly with respect to Aristotle's thinking on rhetoric. Rhetoric has the hybrid status of being a technê; a *dynamis,* or power; and a praxis. When one masters the art, one masters the technê, or principles for finding or discovering arguments. To actually construct them is a dynamis. In this respect rhetoric has a shared dimension with poeisis. The concrete manifestations of rhetorical technê and dynamis through actual appeals is a praxis. The technical aspects of Aristotle's distinction are elaborated in a variety of places. See especially Farrell (1993, 51–100), Grimaldi (1980, 349–56), Kennedy (Aristotle 1991, 12–13), McKeon (1973, xxvi–xli; 1971, 44–63), and Olson (1976, 186–99). The distinction between *Erklaren* and *Verstehen,* or explanation and understanding, was introduced by the German historian Johann Droysen in the nineteenth century in order to distinguish between the concerns of science to account for natural phenomena and those of interpretive disciplines to explain the subject matter within their respective domains. For a discussion of explanation and understanding, see von Wright (1971).

7. Common sense, Arendt tells us, is the anchor for personal reflection in our public lives: "It is by virtue of common sense that the other sense perceptions are known to disclose reality and are not merely felt as irritations of our nerves or resistance sensations of our bodies." She further implies that representative thinking is essential to the active life when she identifies the political debilitation that follows from common sense's decline: "A noticeable decrease in common sense in any given community and a noticeable increase in superstition and gullibility are therefore almost infallible signs of alienation from the world" (1958, 208–9).

8. The literature on rhetoric's epistemic character is vast and complicated. For a cross section of positions, see Brummett (1976), Cherwitz (1990), Cherwitz and Hikens (1986), Farrell (1976), Gregg (1984), and Scott (1967). My use here is aligned with that of Farrell.

9. My interpretation of the role of phronêsis differs from that developed by Farrell. Farrell's extension of practical wisdom to audiences goes beyond what I believe Aristotle's distinction between phronêsis and understanding warrants. However, we are in agreement insofar as the understanding Aristotle requires of the judges necessitates that they be able to participate in a process of practical reasoning in which wisdom is distinguished from cleverness and the activity of deliberation is aimed at making prudent choices. See Farrell (1993, 72–83).

10. The problem of assuming the native's point of view is discussed in greater detail and with attention to issues beyond the scope of this project by Bourdieu (1990).

11. See Richard McKeon (1957, 1969, and 1971). McKeon's conception of rhetoric as a method that transcends a priori reasoning is explored in Hauser and Cushman (1973).

Chapter 5: Narrative, Cultural Memory, and the Appropriation of Historicity

1. The concept of social practice has a number of traditions. Among those relevant to my use are MacIntyre (1984, chap. 14), Gadamer (1981, 69–138), and C. Taylor (1985, 91–115). See also Bourdieu (1990).

2. One can point to traditional or primitive societies of the past which would not be active in this sense. At the end of the twentieth century, however, conditions of global economy, electronic information transfer, and ease of transportation have rendered the pristine status of aboriginal societies highly questionable.

3. The speeches referred to in this section are found in John Paul II (1979), *Return to Poland*.

4. The church's stewardship of Polish national life and its leadership in challenging the state during periods of external domination made the church a site of signification for rhetorically salient meanings. As Poland's counterpublic sphere, the church's discourse fused Polish religious and political sentiments. As a result Poles thought and spoke of their political situation with religious imagery. For example, one of the more significant of these bonds in Polish literature and tradition depicts Poland as the Jesus Christ of nations. This theme was developed especially during the period of partition in the works of Poland's great Romantic poets, who were urging active resistance to reclaim their right to a place on Europe's map. In the secular realm messianism portrays Poland as Jesus crucified, the messiah leading to another realm through death in this realm. Certainly Poland's

tragedies during partition, World War II, and the communist period helped to reinforce this self-perception and also kept the nation hopeful that one day a secular messiah would offer resurrection from political and social morbidity by leading them to freedom. Poland also has seen itself in messianic terms in the religious sphere as a savior nation. These depictions portray Poland as the eastern outpost of Western Christianity destined to be a beacon of Christian belief for all nations. These obviously are beliefs coupled to the role of the Church in national life. However, messianism was also an important reason Poland survived as a national entity. Messianism has been a particularly robust source of faith that Poles would overcome temporal circumstances that should have depleted their powers to resist. Polish national culture makes such religiously based beliefs reasonable loci for secular sustenance and identity.

5. These and other symbols that were significant statements of protest during the period of the late 1970s and early 1980s are discussed by Weschler (1982). Weschler's excellent discussion, on which I have relied heavily, makes clear the rhetorical function graphic art may play in social movements.

6. The pope's arrival, his official greeting at Belvedere Palace, and his open-air masses in Warsaw's Victory Square and at Auschwitz received national television coverage. All other appearances received only local coverage. Television news reporting was limited to ten minutes each evening. Television shots were restricted to the pope and clergy in attendance. Crowd shots were prohibited. Polish press restrictions were even more limited. See "Pope John Paul II in Poland" (1979, 234–36). By contrast, see the account in chapter 4 of Greek television coverage of political rallies during the 1985 national election campaign.

7. Kazimierz Brandys, who is not a practicing Catholic, reports the enthusiasm of other non-Catholics to the pope's sermons and wonders about the rhetorical qualities contributing to this phenomenon. He writes:

> I've been doing some hard thinking about just how to define the unusual style of John Paul II's sermons, what makes them so out of the ordinary? The absence of both priestly and worldly rhetoric? I don't know. Yes, the Pope used simple words. It's often said that the truth is simple. I would add that the truth is also known. Known by people and so familiar that he seems to be speaking their thoughts. The Pope expressed the thoughts of those great crowds of Poles, the thoughts and memories that had been falsified; he spoke to them out of their own experience and expressed their own much-abused truth. Their best truth, I would say. These are dark years; this is an age of evil prophets. Using the words of a good prophet, the Pope gave people access to what is brightest in them and of which they had been aware from time immemorial. He cleansed them of everything that had been rendered opaque and stony by years of adversity and falsehood, preaching ideas that the Church in Poland had not always expressed with such ardent conviction. And perhaps that is the source of the riveting individuality of

John Paul II's style. It's as if with his words he had pointed to a locked door and then had flung it open, letting in the light. The words he spoke at Auschwitz about the Jewish people, the stress he keeps placing on tolerance for other religions and rites, the section of his homily that was devoted to the Russians. . . . Had the Church spoken like that when I was at school and in the university, how much less poison I would have imbibed. (1983, 86)

8. The reader interested in accounts of the relationship of John Paul's visit to the formation of solidarity should consult Bingen (1984), Cywinski in "Pope John Paul II in Poland" (1979), Stehle (1982), Szczypiorski (1982), J. Taylor (1981), Tomsky (1979), and Weschler (1982).

9. A confessional society is one in which a significant attribute, such as religion, must be declared publicly because it has public significance for employment, eligibility for public office, and so forth.

10. Dobrica Cosic, then a writer and member of the Serbian Academy of Arts and Sciences, was a dissident agitating for Serbian unity. He and a circle of writers collaborated on a statement calling for the political unification of all Serbs, which Milosevic then adopted as his broad platform (Kovacic 1994). See also *Unfinished Peace* (1996, 25–26).

11. I am indebted to Susan Whalen for calling this distinction to my attention.

12. The alienation of most Poles from the Communist Party was not shared by Yugoslavians. The party had greater legitimacy there because it had fought on the side of the partisans, who resisted the Nazis in World War II. It also built legitimation through opposition to Stalin.

13. The political problems associated with a rhetoric of difference are not confined to ethnic clashes, such as those of the former Yugoslavia. Closer to home, issues of "political correctness," or, more commonly, new social movements of identity have exerted a strong influence on the climate for political dialogue, making it difficult to address issues that involve identity without invoking personal attacks and moral judgments. See Elshtain (1995); Laraña, Johnson, and Gusfield (1994); and Hauser and Whalen (1997).

Chapter 6: Reshaping Publics and Public Spheres

1. The tenderloin districts of most large urban centers and the discourses they both engage and inspire exemplify this point.

2. The Moral Majority was a fundamentalist Christian movement in the mid 1980s spearheaded by the Reverend Jerry Falwell which sought to advance a political agenda based on traditional Christian values and in opposition to significant social legislation of the preceding two decades. Its most visible adherents were the fundamentalist Christian preachers whose televised services were popular during this period.

3. The phrase "common sense" is an interesting rhetorical choice. Whether consciously aware of the eighteenth-century philosophical school of common sense, its use of the phrase hearkens to that era. The Scottish thinker Thomas Reid (1710–1796) had developed a systematic treatment of axiomat-

ic principles, or commonsense axioms, that defied proof but which, he argued, every person knew to be true and accepted as true in daily life. His argument was intended to refute the empirical skepticism of David Hume's (1711–1776) philosophy. Reid's views were the basis for his contemporary George Campbell's discussion of moral reasoning in his *Philosophy of Rhetoric* (1776). Campbell's treatise emphasized the persuasive power of natural description. Campbell shared with many of his contemporaries the assumption that a verbal portraiture associated with commonsense axioms in a manner that compelled the listener or reader to draw the desired conclusion (Hauser 1972). Here the commission seems to be invoking a similar psychology of argument since it proceeds to build its case by bringing the scene before the reader, apparently confident that "common sense" will impel drawing a single and unequivocal conclusion.

4. Apparently some commissioners regarded the quasi-forensic character of their public hearings to entail the same protection privileges sometimes invoked by congressional bodies; they did not consider them as public spheres subject to the norm of openness.

5. Sennett (1994) develops this theme of body heat as a recognized dimension of the Athenian rhetorical experience through a compelling analysis of Xenophon's *Hellenika*. Athenian commanders had left some of their sailors to drown during the battle at Arginoussai in 406 B.C. The ensuing trial for cowardice is particularly suited to his point on the consequences of passions aroused through rhetoric since the citizens lurched back and forth for two days over how the commanders should be tried, then whether they were innocent or guilty, and finally over remorse at having rendered a guilty verdict. After the generals were executed, the *dikasteria* changed their minds and sought retribution against the accusers, whom they charged with deception for having persuaded them to return the guilty verdict. The drama of Sennett's illustration notwithstanding, he overlooks the countless acts of more orderly, albeit passionate deliberation that were also part of the Athenian experience and that were set forth in the extant speeches of Isocrates, Demosthenes, and the Attic orators.

Chapter 7: Technologizing Public Opinion

1. See Herbst (1993), Noelle-Neumann (1993), and Speier (1950) for overviews of the concept "public opinion."

2. For an insightful analysis, along with internal memorandums providing insider thinking on the nature and use of poll data for political purposes, see Drew (1981). Also see Jamieson's (1992) discussion of the specific uses to which polling data can be put in mounting media campaigns to manipulate the electorate.

3. For a discussion of the manifestation of objectivism in several intellectual traditions, see Bernstein (1978, 1983). The consequences of this shift are partially explored in the more general and withering critique to which objectivism is still being subjected. The general position that scientific reasoning is under the aegis of a universal logic of scientific inquiry is seriously attacked in the works of Bartley (1962), Feyerabend (1965, 1970), Kuhn (1970), Lakatos (1968), MacIntyre (1984), McMullin (1974), and Weimer (1979), to name a few. As Kuhn's work shows, the outcomes of rival research paradigms cannot be reduced to a common set of objective standards.

4. Yankelovich (1991) makes exactly this argument in his attempt to repair the damage inflicted by the critique of the objectivist assumptions of public opinion polls. However, his argument is predicated on the assumption that the deficiencies of polls are not epistemological but methodological. It is a problem of time and money, not of the mismatch between theory and phenomenon.

5. There were suggestions that the welcome was a form of catharsis. The whole nation had been held hostage. Thus there was the need to celebrate the release of 220 million Americans. A milder version held that the celebration was a way of demarcating the end of a state of emergency. The welcome was a collective sigh of relief. Others claimed that it allowed a clean cut between capture and return. Americans lacked such a break in the wars in Korea and Vietnam, as both actions merely trickled off. Some believed that Americans needed heroes; the captives satisfied this need. And there were psychologists who viewed the nation's euphoria as a form of overcompensation; it arose from a need to hide a collective sense of humiliation. These and other hypotheses were discussed in national television and newsweekly commentaries and interviews immediately prior to and following the hostages' release.

6. Despite Hamilton Jordan's claim that from the start it was not possible to reduce the glare of public attention on the hostage affair, the administration adopted a volatile rhetorical posture in attacking Iran publicly, as his own account illustrates (Jordan 1982, 55–56). But see also Jordan's remarks a few pages earlier (44–45) and Cyrus Vance (1983, 380).

7. The "Rose Garden Strategy" refers to an incumbent president not campaigning for reelection on the excuse that his duties as president are too demanding. If successful, it relieves the incumbent from defending his record on the hustings, where press and opponents will critically scrutinize his claims. It also creates the appearance that as president he is above partisan politics that accompany campaigning. Finally, it forces the opponents to chase about trying to create issues, which does not appear presidential. In the 1976 campaign Gerald Ford attempted to use this strategy until Ronald Reagan scored impressive primary victories. In 1980 Jimmy Carter was more successful. Senator Kennedy kept harping on the fact that Carter would not debate the issues and was hiding in the Rose Garden. Obviously Kennedy believed he could not get his issues to solidify unless he successfully forced Carter to campaign publicly. Equally obviously, from a political standpoint Carter had no incentive to leave the Rose Garden as long as he was winning primaries and caucuses.

8. Here and throughout this chapter it is important to bear in mind the multiple roles of the press. Obviously the press serves as a conduit of information between institutional representatives (in this case the Carter administration) and the reading, listening, and viewing audience. But equally obviously the press can (and in this case did) serve as an active agent, shaping public perceptions through choices of what to cover and how to present the issues. Further, the press can act as the general public's agent and representative when it questions officials and probes beneath the surface of events to reveal information salient to framing sound opinion. Finally, the press can provide the critic with an indication of public opinion by reflecting concerns being voiced in the community.

The publics of a mass society, but especially the voting public, receive their information on public affairs largely through the mass media. Hence, the reporting of this affair cannot be divorced from the analysis of Carter's rhetoric. With each piece of evidence examined, important critical distinctions must be drawn in terms of the press's function. Since my interest is with Carter's rhetoric as a force molding public opinion, I have concentrated on administration statements that would have received press coverage. The reader will note, however, that I have relied extensively on government records, not press reports, for evidentiary sources of what was actually said. Later in this chapter, when the role of the press as a source of opinion formation or as the voting public's agent and representative is raised, I have attempted to be clear on how that role was linked as a source of opportunity or limitation to the administration's rhetoric. Of significance here, the administration did not discourage press coverage in the early going.

9. The concept of *condensation* as a use of language to distort perceptions is discussed in Marcuse (1964). See especially chapter 4, "The Closing of the Universe of Discourse." Condensation refers to a linguistic style in which the syntax of an utterance pushes ideas together in a way that leaves no "space" for qualifications, contrast, differences, explanation—in short, for *meaning*—to develop. Marcuse identifies this style particularly with the discourse of bureaucracies in mass Western societies.

10. A sampling of these comments by Carter and administration spokespersons can be found in the United States *Department of State Bulletin* (*DSOB*) (December 1979a, 50; January 1980a, 49; January 1980b, 51; and March 1980a, 33).

11. The patriotic responses to Carter's pleas for conservation of oil and for his imposed embargo on Iranian oil—like the general linking of the hostages and energy—were not fortuitous. Rosalyn Carter reports asking with disbelief whether the United States was still using Iranian oil. "I don't know anybody in the United States that wants to use Iranian oil," she reports telling the president. A few days later the oil embargo was imposed (R. Carter 1984, 311). And Jordan reports that the president said about the tough talk to the AFL-CIO, "You know, I've got to give expression to the anger of the American people. I guarantee that if I asked the people of Plains what I should do, every last one of them would say 'Bomb Iran!' I've got to keep a lid on their emotions. If they perceive me as firm and tough in voicing their rage, maybe we'll be able to control this thing" (Jordan 1982, 57). Whether or not Carter's assessment of his impact on defusing emotions is correct, the fact remains that he was clearly making a link to patriotism by connecting the hostages to energy policies.

12. Carter's reluctance to discuss past American involvement in Iran was not completely without concern for his own part in supporting the deposed shah's regime. Indeed, the diplomatic corps received with raised brows his Tehran toast to the shah on 31 December 1977. He lavishly proclaimed: "Iran, because of the great leadership of the Shah, is an island of stability in one of the more troubled areas of the world. This is a great tribute to you, Your Majesty, and to your leadership and to the respect and the admiration and love which your people give you." Then, "The cause of human rights is one that also is shared deeply by our people and by the leaders of our two nations." Finally, "We have no other nation on earth who is closer to us in planning for our mutual military security. We have no other nation with whom we have closer consultation on regional problems that concern us both. And there is no leader with whom I have a deeper sense of personal gratitude and personal friendship" (qtd. in Salinger 1981, 4–5). In light of Carter's human rights policy and the shah's notoriety as a repressive monarch, the presi-

dent's words could have encouraged some sympathy for the militants' claim of American culpability in the shah's practices.

13. See Higgins (1984, 132–45) for a summary of important cultural differences that were at play in the negotiation process with Iran and the Carter administration's reluctance to engage experts on these differences to aid them in interpreting the other side.

14. See United States *DSOB* (11 May 1970) for a text of Nixon's remarks on American involvement in Cambodia. A critical analysis of this speech can be found in Gregg and Hauser (1973, 167–81).

15. See, for example, *Time* (19 November 1979, 26); United States *DOSB* (February 1980d, 55; February 1980c, 53; March 1980b, 32; March 1980a, 33; March 1980c, 30–31; and May 1980c, 4).

16. Despite books written by the major administrative players, the intent behind public statements remains ambiguous. As one would expect, the beleaguered Carter principals wrote defensively about a press out to get them and in a manner that cast glowingly on their own "nonpolitical" motivations at every step along the hostage affair trail. As we will see in the next section of this chapter, other observers of the Carter White House held a different view. Regardless of intent, however, the point here has to do with public rhetoric that galvanizes common perceptions and, eventually, a public opinion. In addition to memoirs by Rosalyn Carter, Hamilton Jordan, and Cyrus Vance cited above, see Brzezinski (1983), J. Carter (1982), and Powell (1984).

17. *Episteme* is the ancient Greek term for knowledge. In Greek philosophy it is contrasted with *dionoia,* which refers to informed opinion, and *doxa,* which refers to uneducated opinion lacking in the supports of evidence, reasoning, or qualification. See Havelock (1967, 251, n. 1).

18. However, see "Letters" in *Time* (16 and 23 February 1981) for some statements questioning the "heroism" of the Tehran hostages.

19. Discussions of the Carter strategy going into the 1980 campaign may be found in Broder et al. (1980), Drew (1981), and Germond and Witcover (1981).

20. Despite protests to the contrary, intersecting public management of the affair with Carter's reelection bid was a continuing preoccupation. Especially illuminating in this regard is Jordan's *Crisis* (1982), which is peppered throughout with calculations on the impact the hostages' detention was having on the presidential campaign (see pp. 45, 55, 65, 98–99, and 285 for a random sampling of such reflections).

21. See Caddell's "Memorandum I" (qtd. in Drew 1981, 388–409 passim).

22. Edward Kennedy was particularly vulnerable to questions of character on at least two counts. His marriage to Joan Kennedy was subject to press scrutiny when the couple separated. Joan Kennedy had publicly acknowledged that she had an alcohol dependency, for which she received treatment. She was also disenchanted with the rigors of campaigning, and her statements of independence, such as living apart from her husband to pursue an advanced degree, suggested she did not find the spousal demands of marriage to a public figure of Kennedy's stature conducive to her personal growth. Speculations about the senator's unsettled marital status were constantly fueled by the specter of the Mary Jo Kopeckne drowning. Kopeckne, a campaign worker for the slain Robert Kennedy, was alone with Senator Kennedy on the evening of 18 July 1969 when he drove off a narrow

bridge on Martha's Vineyard. The midnight incident received considerable public attention at the time and for years afterward. Throughout the 1980 campaign references to "judgment" were taken as code to remind voters that in the Chappaquiddick incident Kennedy seemed to panic under pressure. Beyond this, there remained unanswered questions and ugly speculations about Kennedy's relationship to Kopeckne, his state of sobriety on the night of the accident, his intentions upon departing with Kopeckne, the implausibility of his making a wrong turn accidentally, and his motivations in leaving the scene of the accident.

On another plane, Kennedy was suspect as trading on his brothers' reputations without meriting his leadership role through strength of ideas or performance. A most damaging blow to his campaign came when, in a CBS interview with television correspondent Roger Mudd, he was unable to explain why he wanted to be president. The Mudd interview left the impression that Kennedy wanted the nation's highest office but did not have a program of leadership to enact. The Mudd interview is discussed in greater detail in Germond and Witcover (1981, 48–78).

23. See, for example, "Interview with the President: Question-and-Answer Session with Reporters from Westinghouse Broadcasting Company" (United States, Office of the Federal Register 1980b, *Weekly Compilation of Presidential Documents* [*WCPD*], 733) and "Interview with the President: Question-and-Answer Session with Reporters from Pennsylvania" (United States 1980c, *WCPD*, 744–45). See also *Time* (18 February 1980, 24; 17 March 1980, 14.

24. Contrary to custom, when Carter activated the switch for the lights on the national Christmas tree, only the star at the top was illuminated as a symbol of hope for the hostages' swift and safe return.

25. See "Interview with the President: Question-and-Answer Session with Reporters from Westinghouse" (United States, Office of the Federal Register 1980b, *WCPD*, 733).

26. See *New York Times* (29 January 1980, A12; 13 February 1980, A18).

27. One of the more regrettable flaps in the primaries occurred when Vice President Mondale suggested that Kennedy's remarks on Iran were geared more to serve his own purposes than the welfare of the nation. The implied questioning of Kennedy's patriotism infuriated the senator and is indicative of the exclusiveness with which Carter viewed his right to speak on the hostage question. See Germond and Witcover (1981, 142–43).

28. The authors add: "Strauss was convinced that Brzezinski was a political albatross, and he had repeated arguments with Carter about permitting the national security adviser to appear on network interview shows. Finally, Strauss persuaded Caddell to test Brzezinski's public standing in a poll. Caddell dragged his feet until Strauss threatened to cut off campaign payments to him. Finally he made the test and reported that Brzezinski, according to Strauss, 'set new records in five states, and his best negative was 68 percent negative.' Strauss dutifully—and gleefully—reported the results to Carter, with Caddell present to back him up."

29. Jordan's role in the negotiations with Iran is discussed in detail in Salinger (1981) and in his own *Crisis* (1982).

30. Powell's version (1984, 228) has him saying to Secretary of Defense Brown, "Mr. Secretary, the President is going to go with this thing, I can sense it. If we can bring our people out of there, it will do more good for this country than anything

that has happened in twenty years." Brown replies, "Yes, and if we fail, that will be the end of the Carter presidency."

31. See Brzezinski (18 April 1982, 28ff.) for an account of how the president arrived at his decision to attempt the rescue. A more comprehensive analysis, based on a collation of all available data, can be found in Ryan (1985). Ryan has this to say in review of the planning process: "In sum, the actors included a president anxious to avoid 'wanton killings'; a national security advisor pushing for rescue; a cautious secretary of state who opposed the mission; a defense secretary whose role remains vague; senior military officers under pressure to organize a complicated operation on an ad hoc basis in the shortest possible time; and a commando officer whose recommendation for more helicopters was denied, a decision that augured ill for the mission" (Ryan 1985, 61–62).

32. Jody Powell expressed the precise source of this danger when he explained: "One of the reasons that [attacks on] the Rose Garden strategy . . . had not cut very much was that they weren't particularly credible . . . I think most people judged up to that point that the President had a considerable amount of logic on his side, but in fact it wouldn't be credible anymore because [after the aborted rescue attempt] it wasn't true anymore" (qtd. in Germond and Witcover 1981, 162).

33. Although Habermas maintains that these translations require institutional guarantees, that does not appear to be an empirical necessity, as the 1989 wave of bloodless revolutions in Eastern Europe exemplifies. In fact, effective action took place in Eastern Europe against the opposition of prevailing institutional authority, confirming Mills's observation that publics tend to be autonomous; they shield themselves from penetration by authoritative institutions (1957, 303–4).

34. See Said, "Inside Islam" (January 1981, 25–32) for a discussion of Americans' distorted awareness of causes behind the affair. American susceptibility to a rhetoric of "heroes" is suggested by Harden (7 February 1982, B1).

Chapter 8: Democracy's Narrative

1. Unless otherwise indicated, all letters cited are found in the Franklin D. Roosevelt Library (FDRL). Citations are given in the text. OF refers to the Official File; DNC refers to the Democratic National Committee file; PPF refers to the President's Personal File.

2. In each case where I have quoted from the letters introduced as evidence in this chapter, I have retained the spelling and grammar of the original to provide the reader with a reminder of the power and elegance of expression that is less dependent on formal education than conviction born of a righteous cause.

3. See Boller (1984, 250–58), Burke (1971, 350–84), Lydgate (1944, 98–115), Parmet and Hecht (1968), Robinson (1955, 247–65), Roseboom (1957, 460–76), and Rosenman (1952, 222–55) for representative discussions of the 1940 campaign.

4. For a sample of such views see Donahoe (1965), Hamby (1976), Jones (1974), and Weisbord (1966).

5. Elmer Roper offers a typical analysis of polling data to support the conclusion that, were it not for the war, Roosevelt would have been defeated in the 1940 election (1957, 36–40). At best, however, this argument makes a moot point. Were it not for the war, the third term issue likely would not have been tested. Although some advance the thesis that FDR was unable to relinquish the reins

of power for fear that Congress (and his successor) would undo the New Deal and, therefore, that he was aided fortuitously by the war in his plans to retain office, this lacks factual basis. The preponderance of evidence suggests the opposite—that FDR was actively contemplating retirement and the role of elder statesman that Americans accord their former presidents. He had signed a contract with *Collier's* magazine to write a political column (at a salary of $75,000 per year, equal to his income as president). The Roosevelt Library was under way, and he was urging Sam Rosenman, his longtime chief speech writer, to relocate to Hyde Park so he could assist him with the writing projects that a president who had guided the nation through its darkest economic hours would undertake. Moreover, he was openly indicating to his staff and friends his full expectation that he would be in retirement after his second term expired. There is good reason to believe that were it not for the war, the issue would not have been tested. The point is moot in a second sense. The conclusion that Roosevelt would have been defeated were it not for the war is based on polling data. But polling data, especially the data from this period when survey research was still in its infancy, can be extremely deceiving. Off-year elections, for example, often have the party out of power gaining added strength in Congress, which political pundits interpret as a sign of public dissatisfaction—a way of sending the administration a message. On the other hand, once a presidential election campaign is joined, the American electorate also shows a marked reluctance to "send messages," tending to consider their own interests in terms of the actual choices they must live with for the next four years. Although polls taken in 1938 and 1939 indicate a majority stating they would not vote for Mr. Roosevelt for a third term, the spread was slight and a significant percentage remained undecided. One can only assert that there is no certainty how a third-term bid would have been resolved, especially when Roosevelt's formidable prowess as a campaigner is taken into consideration.

6. For polls related to the 1940 election see Cantril (1951), Gallup (1972), Lazarsfeld (1968), and Roper (1957).

7. This finding is in direct contradiction to the view of Joseph Barnes, who believes "the campaign itself was relatively unimportant, serving only to confirm already committed voters to speed up changes in voting habits which had begun before the speeches started" (1952, 211).

8. See Brandt (1939), Cornwell (1959, 1965), Pollard (1959), Ragland (1962), and White (1979) for representative discussions of Roosevelt and the press. FDR was the first president to name a former journalist, Stephen Early, as his press secretary, an act much appreciated by the press. For the first time White House information was being released with an understanding of the constraints of deadline and copy to which reporters must conform. He also was a trendsetter for ongoing press dialogue through the sheer frequency of his press conferences. Finally, he opened his first press conference with the announcement that, despite warnings of its impossibility, he proposed to abolish the format of written questions adopted by his Republican predecessors in order to permit spontaneity to return to the president's interactions with the press.

This cheery picture should not distract us from FDR's efforts to control the press. One finds, for example, exchanges of memorandums within the White House addressing how to deal with the Scripps-Howard chain's "distortions" of the administration's defense policies (FDRL PSF 147, Early folder, 28 May 1940), or the 16 August 1940 memo to Early showing that the president responded with pique at the characterizations of and proposals for his administration appearing in the *New York Times*. Accompanying the memo is Roosevelt's draft of a letter to the editor of the *Times* for the signature of another (FDRL PPF 675, *New York Times* folder 1938–1941).

9. Ward (1989, 600ff.) describes the management of the scene at the Eastport railroad station when Roosevelt, newly stricken with infantile paralysis, was taken back to New York. Through deft handling of the press corps by Roosevelt's long-time adviser, Louis Howe, and fortunate timing the press arrived just as the train was leaving the station. Roosevelt was glimpsed through the window of his car "smiling and smoking in apparent comfort." Ward's book, in general, provides an excellent treatment of the personal battle FDR waged to resume public life in spite of his infirmity and to shield the extent of his impairment from the public.

10. The stock Roosevelt placed on correspondence from the public was not unmindful of polling data. He was in frequent touch with the emerging leaders of the new social science of opinion polling—Hadley Cantril, George Gallup, and Elmer Roper—to learn of their findings and discuss their meaning. Richard Steele (1974) makes the point that when Roosevelt did use polls, it was not to learn about an undifferentiated public opinion but to learn of specific publics and groups on specific issues, especially to learn of obstacles to courses of action on which he had already decided. On the other hand, Howe's comment and Roosevelt's practice suggest that although he was an avid consumer of polls, he was not captive to them and found information gleaned from the vernacular rhetoric of the public's correspondence to have greater value for gauging public opinion.

11. Lubell goes on to discuss the strains on lower-income families in which heads of households lost their jobs, some never to regain full-time employment. Robbed of self-respect and lacking material goods, the New Deal often eased these family strains. Whether the administration actually did have a coherent philosophy is still debated. But writers from the public media narrated its program as if it did.

12. The result, quite obviously, was a mode of sampling public concerns and public understanding on a scale theretofore unknown. Roosevelt often knew more about the American people's thinking on an issue than almost any other participant in the political process. When opportunity presented itself, he apparently delighted in using this information as the basis for cornering a much needed vote or keeping a potentially troublesome representative in line. One can imagine the unnerving experience of being summoned to the White House where, upon being ushered into the Oval Office, the conversation might begin with the concerns of Mrs. McGillicudhy—one's own constituent—whose views on a measure now before you were better known to the president than to oneself.

13. Inferring public opinion from letters written to the president has its obvious shortcomings. Those who hold a strong view on an issue obviously have greater motivation to write than those who do not. Therefore, the representativeness of the opinions inferred from letters can be challenged. On the other hand, the same objection can be raised about any mode of discourse as an evidentiary base for inferring public opinion, since motivation plays a key role in willingness to share an opinion with others. Moreover, this objection overlooks the relation between the openness and responsiveness of a public sphere and the type of communication it invites and receives. The massive increase of letters to the president

during FDR's administration and his own encouragement of these letters are not unlinked. Insofar as citizens saw letter writing as a mode of communication that might influence policy, this epistolary public sphere became an arena of opinion exchange across the broad spectrum of American political views and provides a valid source of discursive information for extrapolating public opinion.

14. In the summer of 1986 and spring of 1992 I examined the Official File (OF 2526) at the FDRL containing the public's correspondence to the president on the topic of the third term. This is an "Alpha" file organized by year in which the correspondence was received. There are fifty-nine containers of public correspondence in this file. In addition, I examined the Democratic National Committee File (DNC) for the 1940 election. In addition to personally composed or locally produced campaign literature forwarded by the correspondents, often in hopes that their work would be adopted for the election campaign, the file also includes thirteen containers of public correspondence to the president on the third-term issue. It is difficult to know precisely how many letters there are in these collections combined. Although each box can hold up to eight hundred sheets of paper, onionskin responses are attached to most, and the contents include postcards, stationary of different weights, and multiple-page letters. However, the twelve containers of letters included in the sample described below contain 1,773 letters, suggesting a collection size of approximately 11,000 letters, exclusive of postcards.

To make apparent the often tacit understandings of political relationship and social change expressed in these letters, I systematically inspected the contents of the Official File and the Democratic National Committee File containing letters from the public on the third-term issue. A sample of twelve boxes, representing approximately 20 percent of the letters received, was analyzed for types of appeals. First, the letters were coded for their appeals in support or opposition to a third term for Roosevelt. The specific appeals offered by the first 250 writers were recorded. These responses were examined for patterns of likeness, on which a taxonomy of the writers' topoi was established. The remaining letters in my sample of 1,773 letters were coded within this taxonomy. Letters often contained multiple appeals to support the authors' advocacy, so that the total number of arguments recorded exceeds the number of letters coded. After this sample was coded, additional boxes from both the Official File and the DNC File, equal to 50 percent of the total collection, were examined. Letters that illustrated the narrative quality of these appeals, both pro and con, were selected for more detailed analysis. There were 103 letters selected for this sample.

15. Topoi are lines of reasoning used to develop an argument. The theory of topoi was developed by Aristotle in his *Topica* and later in his *Rhetoric* and became an important part of Roman rhetorical treatises, such as Cicero's *De Inventione* and Quintilian's *Institutio Oratoria*, from which it was passed forward in the Western tradition. It remains a part of contemporary rhetorical thought, as is exemplified by Perelman and Olbrechts-Tyteca (1969) and McKeon (1987).

16. Sussmann (1963, 105) claims that these letters discussed the war very little in comparison with the New Deal. I believe her claim oversimplifies their contents. Nearly one-quarter of the letters in my sample made direct reference to the war. Another third of the sample made arguments that clearly had fear of impending war in mind. The references to the war are vague, as she claims, in this latter group. Moreover, while the New Deal is the primary concern of these writers, as I will

demonstrate, the fears of its loss are linked by many writers to the dangers of military engagement with fascism.

17. A convenient collection of Depression-era correspondence to the White House, in which this sentiment will be found, is in McElvaine (1983); see also Turkel (1970).

18. The attitude of these writers is akin to what philosopher Paul Ricoeur has called "distanciation," discussed in chapter 5. As opposed to participatory belonging, the individual experiences an alienating distancing of the subject from oneself caused by the objectification imposed by some power structure. Distanciation, as Ricoeur explains its function, occurs in part as the subject rejects the terms by which an external power imposes a self-understanding. See Ricoeur (1981, 131–44).

19. For a discussion of historicity, see chapter 5. See also Gadamer (1975), Ricoeur (1981, 274–96), and Touraine (1977).

20. I wish to acknowledge Lloyd Bitzer, my mentor and friend, who urged me to incorporate the voices of the letter writers in this case study and suggested a form for doing so. The analysis of this chapter is an outgrowth of that conversation.

BIBLIOGRAPHY

Achen, Christopher H. 1983. "Toward Theories of Data: The State of Political Methodology." In *Political Science: The State of the Discipline*, edited by Ada W. Finifter, 69–93. Washington, D.C.: American Political Science Association.

"An Issue of Consent." 1986, 9 June. *Los Angeles Times* Sec. Z, p. 4.

". . . And Unto Poland, What Is God's." 1991, 25 May. *Economist* 341: 51–52.

Andric, Ivo. 1959. *The Bridge on the Drina* [1945]. Trans. Lovett F. Edwards. New York: Macmillan.

Arendt, Hannah. 1958. *The Human Condition*. Chicago: University of Chicago Press.

———. 1965. *On Revolution*. New York: Viking.

———. 1968. *Men in Dark Times*. New York: Harcourt, Brace & World.

———. 1971. "Thinking and Moral Considerations." *Social Research* 38: 417–46.

———. 1977. *Between Past and Future* [1968]. Baltimore, Md.: Penguin.

Aristotle. 1941. *Nichomachean Ethics. The Basic Works of Aristotle*. Ed. Richard McKeon. Trans. W. D. Ross. New York: Random House.

———. 1991. *Aristotle, On Rhetoric*. Trans. George A. Kennedy. New York: Oxford University Press.

Arnold, Carroll. 1968. "Oral Rhetoric, Rhetoric, and Literature." *Philosophy and Rhetoric* 1: 191–210.

Aronowitz, Stanley. 1988. *Science as Power: Discourse and Ideology in Modern Society*. Minneapolis: University of Minnesota Press.

Ash, Timothy Garton. 1988, 13 October. "The Opposition." *New York Review of Books* 35: 3–6.

———. 1990, 15 February. "Eastern Europe: The Year of Truth." *New York Review of Books* 37: 17–22.

———. 1995, 13 July. "Central Europe: The Present Past." *New York Review of Books* 42: 21–23.

Ayer, Alfred Jules. n.d. *Language, Truth and Logic* [1936]. New York: Dover.

Baker, John F. 1986, 11 July. "An American Dilemma." *Publishers Weekly* 233: 31.

Bakhtin, M. M. 1981. *The Dialogic Imagination: Four Essays*. Ed. Michael Holquist. Trans. Caryl Emerson and Michael Holquist. Austin: University of Texas Press.

Ballenger, Bruce. 1997. "Methods of Memory: On Native American Storytelling." *College English* 59: 789–800.

Barber, Benjamin. 1984. *Strong Democracy: Participatory Politics for a New Age*. Berkeley: University of California Press.

Barnes, Joseph. 1952. *Willkie: The Events He was Part of—The Ideas He Fought For*. New York: Simon.

Bartley, William Warren III. 1962. *The Retreat to Commitment*. New York: Knopf.

Bateson, Gregory. 1972. *Steps to an Ecology of Mind*. New York: Ballantine.

Baudrillard, Jean. 1994. *Simulacra and Simulation* [1981]. Trans. Sheila Glaser. Ann Arbor: University of Michigan Press.

Beiner, Ronald. 1982. *Hannah Arendt: Lectures on Kant's Political Philosophy*. Chicago: University of Chicago Press.

Bibliography

Bellah, Robert, et al. 1985. *Habits of the Heart: Individualism and Commitment in American Life.* Berkeley: University of California Press.

Benhabib, Seyla. 1986. *Critique, Norm, and Utopia: A Study of the Foundations of Critical Theory.* New York: Columbia University Press.

———. 1992. "Models of Public Space: Hannah Arendt, the Liberal Tradition, and Jürgen Habermas." In *Habermas and the Public Sphere,* edited by Craig Calhoun, 73–98. Cambridge: MIT Press.

Benjamin, Walter. 1969. "The Storyteller: Reflections on the Works of Nikolas Leskov." In *Illuminations,* edited by Walter Benjamin, translated by Harry Zohn, 83–109. New York: Schocken.

Bennets, Leslie. 1980, 13 February. "Kennedy Lashes out at President, Charging Passivity and Pessimism." *New York Times* p. A18.

"Bergman Affair: Still a Tangle." 1979, 26 November. *Newsweek* 94: 20–23.

Bernstein, Richard J. 1978. *The Restructuring of Social and Political Theory.* Philadelphia: University of Pennsylvania Press.

———. 1983. *Beyond Objectivism and Relativism.* Philadelphia: University of Pennsylvania Press.

Bingen, Dieter. 1984. "The Catholic Church as a Political Actor." In *Polish Politics,* edited by Jack Bielasiak and Maurice D. Simon, 212–40. New York: Praeger.

Bitzer, Lloyd F. 1968. "The Rhetorical Situation." *Philosophy and Rhetoric* 1: 1–14.

———. 1978. "Rhetoric and Public Knowledge." In *Rhetoric, Philosophy and Literature: An Exploration,* edited by Don M. Burks, 67–95. West Lafayette, Ind.: Purdue University Press.

Black, Edwin. 1965. "Frame of Reference in Rhetoric and Fiction." In *Rhetoric and Poetic,* edited by Donald C. Bryant, 26–35. Iowa City: University of Iowa Press.

"Blackmailing the U.S." 1979,19 November. *Time* 114: 14–26.

Block, Robert. 1993, 18 November. "Killers." *New York Review of Books* 40: 9–10.

Blumer, Herbert. 1966. "The Mass, The Public, and Public Opinion." In *Reader in Public Opinion,* edited by Bernard Berelson and Morris Janowitz, 43–50. New York: Free Press.

Boas, George. 1969. *Vox Populi: Essays in the History of an Idea.* Baltimore, Md.: Johns Hopkins University Press.

Bob, Murray L. 1986, 15 October. "The Right Questions About Obscenity: An Alternative to the Meese Commission Report." *Library Journal* 111: 39–41.

Bodnar, John. 1992. *Remaking America: Public Memory, Commemoration, and Patriotism in the Twentieth Century.* Princeton, N.J.: Princeton University Press.

Boller, Paul F. Jr. 1984. *Presidential Campaigns.* New York: Oxford University Press.

Boorstin, Daniel. 1965. "Selling the President to the People." In *The President: Roles and Powers,* edited by David E. Haight and Larry D. Johnston, 264–74. Chicago: Rand McNally.

Bourdieu, Pierre. 1979. "Public Opinion Does Not Exist." In *Communication and Class Struggle,* edited by Armand Mattelart and Seth Siegelaub, 124–30. New York: Bagnolet.

———. 1990. *The Logic of Practice.* Stanford, Calif.: Stanford University Press.

Bowers, John, et al. 1993. *The Rhetoric of Agitation and Control.* 2d ed. Prospect Heights, Ill.: Waveland.

Braden, Waldo, and Earnest Brandenburg. 1955. "Roosevelt's Fireside Chats." *Speech Monographs* 22: 290–302.

Brandt, Raymond Press. 1939. "The President's Press Conference." *Survey Graphic* 28: 446–49.

Brandys, Kazimierz. 1983. *A Warsaw Diary: 1979–1981.* Trans. Richard Lourie. New York: Random House.

Broder, David, et al. 1980. *The Pursuit of the Presidency 1980.* Ed. Richard Harwood. New York: Putnam's.

Browne, Stephen H. 1995. "Reading, Rhetoric, and the Texture of Public Memory." *Quarterly Journal of Speech* 81: 237–49.

Brummett, Barry. 1976. "Some Implications of 'Process' or 'Intersubjectivity': Postmodern Rhetoric. *Philosophy and Rhetoric* 9: 21–51.

Bruner, Jerome. 1987. "Life as Narrative." *Social Research* 54: 11–32.

Brzezinski, Zbigniew. 1980, 18 April. "The Failed Mission: The Inside Account of the Attempt to Free the Hostages in Iran." *New York Times Magazine* pp. 28–31, 61–62, 64, 69, 79.

———. 1983. *Power and Principle: Memoirs of the National Security Advisers, 1977–1981.* New York: Farrar.

Buckley, Michael J. S. J. 1970. "Philosophic Method in Cicero." *Journal of the History of Philosophy* 8: 143–54.

Burke, Kenneth. 1968. *Language as Symbolic Action.* Berkeley: University of California Press.

———. 1969. *A Rhetoric of Motives* [1950]. Berkeley: University of California Press.

———. 1973. *The Philosophy of Literary Form.* 3d ed. Berkeley: University of California Press.

Burke, Robert E. 1971. "Election of 1940." In *The Coming to Power: Critical Presidential Elections in American History,* edited by Arthur M. Schlesinger Jr., 350–84. New York: Chelsea House.

Calhoun, Craig, ed. 1992. *Habermas and the Public Sphere.* Cambridge: MIT Press.

Campbell, George. 1963. *The Philosophy of Rhetoric* [1776]. Ed. Lloyd F. Bitzer. Carbondale: Southern Illinois University Press.

Campbell, Karlyn Kohrs, and Kathleen Hall Jamieson, eds. 1978. *Form and Genre: Shaping Rhetorical Action.* Annandale, Va.: Speech Communication Association.

Cantril, Hadley, ed. 1951. *Public Opinion, 1935–1946.* Princeton: Princeton University Press.

Carson, Rachel. 1987. *Silent Spring* [1962]. Boston: Houghton Mifflin.

Carter, Jimmy. 1982. *Keeping Faith: Memoirs of a President.* New York: Bantam.

Carter, Rosalyn. 1984. *First Lady from Plains.* Boston: Houghton Mifflin.

"Carter's New Tack on Iran." 1980, 21 April. *Newsweek* 95: 32–41.

Charland, Maurice. 1987. "Constitutive Rhetoric: The Case of the *Peuple Québécois.*" *Quarterly Journal of Speech* 73: 133–50.

Chekhov, Anton. 1961. "Gooseberries." In *Twelve Short Stories,* edited by Marvin Magalander and Edmond L. Volpe, 76–85. New York: Macmillan.

Cherwitz, Richard A., ed. 1990. *Rhetoric and Philosophy.* Hillsdale, N.J.: Erlbaum.

Cherwitz, Richard A., and James W. Hikens. 1986. *Communication and Knowledge: An Investigation in Rhetorical Epistemology.* Columbia: University of South Carolina Press.

Clark, Donald Lemen. 1957. *Rhetoric in Greco-Roman Education.* New York: Columbia University Press.

Clark, Henry. 1986, 9 June. "Don't Turn Back the Clock on Reality by Fighting Playboy." *Los Angeles Times*, p. II5.

Clausen, Aage. 1968. "Response Validity: Vote Report." *Public Opinion Quarterly* 32: 588–606.

"Clerics Sign Antismut Statement." 1986, 2 August. *Washington Post* p. C7.

Cloud, Dana L. 1994. "The Materiality of Discourse as Oxymoron: A Challenge to Critical Rhetoric." *Western Journal of Communication* 58: 141–63.

———. 1998. *Control and Consolation in American Culture and Politics*. Thousand Oaks, Calif.: Sage.

Cohen, Jean L., and Andrew Arato. 1992. *Civil Society and Political Theory*. Cambridge: MIT Press.

Connor, W. Robert. 1971. *The New Politicians of Fifth-Century Athens*. Princeton, N.J.: Princeton University Press.

Cooper, Martha. 1983. "The Implications of Foucault's Archeological Theory of Discourse for Contemporary Rhetorical Theory and Criticism." Diss., Pennsylvania State University.

Cornwell, Elmer E. 1959. "The Presidential Press Conference: A Study in Institutionalization." *Journalism Quarterly* 36: 370–89.

———. 1965. Presidential Leadership of Public Opinion. Bloomington: Indiana University Press.

Danforth, Kenneth C. 1990. "Yugoslavia: A House Much Divided." *National Geographic* 178: 93–123.

Danielian, Lucig H. 1992. "Communication and the New Social Movements: Armenia and the NKAO's Struggle for Unification." In *Political Communication: Engineering Visions of Order in the Socialist World,* edited by Sarah S. King and Donald P. Cushman, 89–116. Albany: SUNY Press.

Democratic National Committee File. 1938–1940. "Miscellaneous Letters and Replies." Hyde Park, N.Y.: Franklin D. Roosevelt Library.

Denitch, Bogdan. 1989. "Yugoslavia: The Limits of Reform." *Dissent* 36: 78–85.

Dewey, John. 1954. *The Public and its Problems* [1927]. Chicago: Swallow Press.

Dizdarevic, Zlatko. 1994, 10 April. "Sarajevo's 700 Days." *New York Times Magazine,* pp. 34–41, 64–69, 78.

Dodd, Lawrence C. 1994. "Political Learning and Political Change: Understanding Development Across Time." In *The Dynamics of American Politics,* edited by Lawrence C. Dodd and Calvin Jillson, 331–64. Boulder, Colo.: Westview Press.

Domenig, Kathleen. 1995. "The Rushdie Crisis in the United States: A Rhetorical Analysis of Contemporary Publics and the Mass Media." Diss., Pennsylvania State University.

Donahoe, Bernard F. 1965. *Private Plans and Public Dangers*. Notre Dame, Ind.: Notre Dame University Press.

Donnerstein, Edward. 1986, August. "Research Misused." *Playboy* 33: 42.

Downs, Donald. 1989. *The New Politics of Pornography*. Chicago: University of Chicago Press.

Drakulic, Slavenka. 1993, May. "Zagreb: A Letter to My Daughter." *Harper's* 286: 13–16.

Drew, Elizabeth. 1981. *Portrait of an Election*. New York: Simon and Schuster.

Dryzek, John S. 1990. *Discursive Democracy: Politics, Policy, and Political Science*. New York: Cambridge University Press.

Duggan, Lisa. 1985, 1 September. "The Dubious Porn War Alliance." *Washington Post*, p. C1, C4.

Eagleton, Terry. 1984. *The Function of Criticism: From the Spectator to Post-Structuralism.* London: Verso.

Eberly, Rosa. 1993. "Andrea Dworkin's Mercy: Pain, Ad Personam, and Silence in the 'War Zone.'" *Pre/Text* 14: 273–304.

———. 1994. "Novel Controversies: Public Discussions of Censorship and Social Change." Diss., Pennsylvania State University.

———. 1995, March. "From Readers to Publics." Paper presented at CCCC Convention, Washington, D.C.

Edelman, Murray J. 1988. *Constructing the Political Spectacle.* Chicago: University of Chicago Press.

Edwards, Paul. 1955. *The Logic of Moral Discourse.* New York: Free Press.

Ehninger, Douglas. 1968. "Validity as Moral Obligation." *Southern Speech Journal* 33: 215–22.

Ehninger, Douglas, and Gerard A. Hauser. 1984. "Communication of Values." In *Handbook of Rhetorical and Communication Theory,* edited by C. C. Arnold and J. W. Bowers, 720–48. Boston: Allyn and Bacon.

Elshtain, Jean Bethke. 1995. *Democracy on Trial.* New York: Basic.

"The Fading of the Red." 1994, 15 January. *Economist* 344: 56.

Eley, Geoff. 1992. "Nations, Publics, and Political Cultures: Placing Habermas in the Nineteenth Century." In *Habermas and the Public Sphere,* edited by Craig Calhoun, 289–339. Cambridge: MIT Press.

Farrell, Thomas B. 1976. "Knowledge, Consensus, and Rhetorical Theory." *Quarterly Journal of Speech* 62: 1–14.

———. 1993. *Norms of Rhetorical Culture.* New Haven, Conn.: Yale University Press.

Feyerabend, Paul K. 1965. "Problems of Empiricism." In *Beyond the Edge of Certainty,* edited by Robert G. Colodny, 145–260. Englewood Cliffs, N.J.: Prentice-Hall.

———. 1970. "Against Method." *Minnesota Studies for the Philosophy of Science* 4: 17–130.

Fielding, Ian. 1995. "Examining an Argument by Cause: The Weak Link Between Pornography and Violence in the Attorney General's Commission on Pornography Final Report." In *Warranting Assent: Case Studies in Argument Evaluation,* edited by Edward Schiappa, 239–56. Albany, N.Y.: SUNY Press.

Fields, Howard. 1986, 30 May. "Two on Meese Panel Dissent from Report's Conclusion." *Publishers Weekly* 233: 14.

Finley, M. I. 1962. "The Athenian Demagogues." *Past and Present* 21: 3–24.

Fisher, Walter R. 1978. "Toward a Logic of Good Reasons." *Quarterly Journal of Speech* 64: 376–84.

———. 1980. "Rationality and the Logic of Good Reasons." *Philosophy and Rhetoric* 13: 122–25.

———. 1987. *Human Communication as Narration: Toward a Philosophy of Reason, Value, and Action.* Columbia: University of South Carolina Press.

Fishkin, James. 1995. *The Voice of the People.* New Haven, Conn.: Yale University Press.

"Flip-Flops and Zigzags." 1980, 12 May. *Time* 115: 31.

Fortenbaugh, W. W. 1975. *Aristotle on Emotion.* New York: Barnes.

Foucault, Michel. 1972. *The Archeology of Knowledge.* Trans. A. M. Sheridan Smith. New York: Harper.

Bibliography

—————. 1980. *The History of Sexuality*. Vol. I [1976]. Trans. Robert Hurley. New York: Vintage.

Fraser, Nancy. 1990. "Rethinking the Public Sphere: A Contribution to the Critique of Actually Existing Democracy." *Social Text* 25/26: 56–80.

Gadamer, Hans-Georg. 1975. *Truth and Method*. New York: Seabury Press.

—————. 1981. *Reason in the Age of Science*. Trans. F. G. Lawrence. Cambridge: MIT Press.

Gallup, George H. 1972. *The Gallup Poll 1935–1971*. Vol I. New York: Random House.

—————. 1980. *The Gallup Poll: Public Opinion 1979*. Wilmington, Del.: Scholarly Resources.

—————. 1981. *The Gallup Poll: Public Opinion 1980*. Wilmington, Del.: Scholarly Resources.

The Gallup Opinion Index. November 1979–May 1980. Nos. 172–77. Princeton: Gallup Poll International.

Galtung, Johan. 1980. "Poland, August-September, 1980: Is a Socialist Revolution Under State Capitalism Possible?" *Journal of Peace Research* 17: 281–90.

Germond, Jack W., and Jules Witcover. 1981. *Blue Smoke and Mirrors*. New York: Viking.

Giddens, Anthony. 1984. *The Constitution of Society*. Berkeley: University of California Press.

Ginsberg, Benjamin. 1986. *The Captive Public*. New York: Basic.

Glenny, Misha. 1992. *The Fall of Yugoslavia: The Third Balkan War*. London: Penguin.

Glover, T. R. 1935. *The Ancient World*. Baltimore, Md.: Penguin.

Goleman, Daniel. 1986, 17 May. "Researchers Dispute Pornography Report on its Use of Data." *New York Times*, pp. A1, A35.

Goodnight, G. Thomas. 1982. "The Personal, Technical, and Public Spheres of Argument: A Speculative Inquiry into the Art of Public Deliberation." *Journal of the American Forensic Association* 18: 214–27.

Gottlieb, Gidon. 1968. *The Logic of Choice*. New York: Macmillan.

Graham, George J. Jr., and William C. Havard Jr. 1984. "The Language of the Statesman: Philosophy and Rhetoric in Contemporary Politics." In *Sophia and Praxis: The Boundaries of Politics*, edited by J. M. Porter, 73–92. Chatham, N.J.: Chatham House.

Gramsci, Antonio. 1971. *Selections from the Prison Notebooks of Antonio Gramsci*. Ed. and trans. Quintin Hoare and Geoffrey Nowell Smith. New York: International Publishers.

Green, Michelle, 1986, 30 June. "The Shame of America." *People* 25: 28–33.

Gregg, Richard B. 1984. *Symbolic Inducement and Knowing: A Study in the Foundations of Rhetoric*. Columbia: University of South Carolina Press.

Gregg, Richard B., and Gerard A. Hauser. 1973. "Richard Nixon's April 30, 1970 Address on Cambodia: The 'Ceremony' of Confrontation." *Speech Monographs* 40: 167–81.

Grimaldi, William M. A., S.J. 1980. *Aristotle, Rhetoric I: A Commentary*. New York: Fordham University Press.

Gronbeck, Bruce. 1995. "The Presidency in the Age of Secondary Orality." In *Beyond the Rhetorical Presidency*, edited by Martin J. Medhurst, 30–49. College Station: Texas A&M University Press.

Grove, Lloyd. 1986, 7 June. "Descent into the World of Porn." *Washington Post*, pp. D1, D8–9.

Gusfield, Joseph. 1981. *The Culture of Public Problems: Drinking-Driving and the Symbolic Order.* Chicago: University of Chicago Press.

Gutman, Roy. 1993. *A Witness to Genocide.* New York: Macmillan.

Gwertzman, Bernard. 1980, 30 January. "Six U.S. Diplomats Hidden by Canada, Leave Iran Safely." *New York Times* pp. A1, A12.

Habermas, Jürgen. 1970a. "On Systematically Distorted Communication." *Inquiry* 13: 205–18.

———. 1970b. "Towards a Theory of Communicative Competence." *Inquiry* 13: 360–75.

———. 1971a. *Knowledge and Human Interests.* Trans. Jeremy J. Shapiro. Boston: Beacon.

———. 1971b. *Toward a Rational Society.* Trans. Jeremy J. Shapiro. Boston: Beacon.

———. 1974. "The Public Sphere." *New German Critique* 3: 49–55.

———. 1975. *Legitimation Crisis.* Trans. Thomas McCarthy. Boston: Beacon.

———. 1977. "Hannah Arendt's Communications Concept of Power." *Social Research* 44: 3–24.

———. 1979. *Communication and the Evolution of Society.* Trans. Thomas McCarthy. Boston: Beacon.

———. 1984–1987. *The Theory of Communication Action.* 2 vols. Trans. Thomas McCarthy. Boston: Beacon.

———. 1989. *The Structural Transformation of the Public Sphere.* Trans. Thomas Burger with the assistance of Frederick Lawrence. Cambridge: MIT Press.

———. 1992. "Further Reflections on the Public Sphere." In *Habermas and the Public Sphere*, edited by Craig Calhoun, 421–61. Cambridge: MIT Press.

———. 1994, 24 March. "'More Humility, Fewer Illusions'—A Talk between Adam Michnik and Jürgen Habermas." *New York Review of Books* 41: 24–29.

Hall, John A. 1995. "In Search of a Civil Society." In *Civil Society: Theory, History, Comparison*, edited by John A. Hall, 1–31. Cambridge, U.K.: Polity.

Hamby, Alonzo L. 1976. *The Imperial Years: The United States Since 1939.* New York: Weybright and Talley.

Harden, Blaine. 1982, 7 February. "The Impresario of Heroism." *Washington Post*, p. B1.

Hare, R. M. 1964. *The Language of Morals* [1952]. New York: Oxford University Press.

Hariman, Robert. 1995. *Political Style: The Artistry of Power.* Chicago: University of Chicago Press.

Hauser, Gerard A. 1972. "Empiricism, Description, and the New Rhetoric." *Philosophy and Rhetoric* 5: 24–44.

———. 1979. "Searching for a Bright Tomorrow: Graduate Education in Rhetoric During the 1980's." *Communication Education* 28: 259–70.

———. 1985. "Common Sense in the Public Sphere: A Rhetorical Grounding for Publics." *Informatologia Yugoslavica* 17: 67–75.

———. 1986. *Introduction to Rhetorical Theory.* New York: Harper.

———. 1987. "Features of the Public Sphere." *Critical Studies in Mass Communication* 4: 437–41.

———. 1989a. "Administrative Rhetoric and Public Opinion: Discussing the

Iranian Hostages in the Public Sphere." In *American Rhetoric: Context and Criticism*, edited by Thomas W. Benson, 323–83. Carbondale: Southern Illinois University Press.

———. 1989b. "'The Course of the Avalanche Depends on the Stones Over Which it Rolls': Arguments from the Underground." In *Spheres of Argument*, edited by Bruce E. Gronbeck, 530–36. Annandale, Va.: Speech Communication Association.

Hauser, Gerard A., and Carole Blair. 1982. "Rhetorical Antecedents to the Public." *Pre/Text* 3: 139–67.

Hauser, Gerard A., and Donald P. Cushman. 1973. "McKeon's Philosophy of Communication: The Architectonic and Interdisciplinary Arts." *Philosophy and Rhetoric* 6: 211–34.

Hauser, Gerard A., and Susan A. Whalen. 1997. "New Rhetoric and New Social Movements." In *Emerging Theories of Human Communication*, edited by Donald Cushman and Branislav Kovacic, 115–40. Albany, N.Y.: SUNY Press.

Havel, Václav. 1987. *Living in Truth*. London: Farber and Farber.

———. 1993, 18 November. "How Europe Could Fail" [9 October 1993]. *New York Review of Books* 40: 3.

Havelock, Eric A. 1957. *The Liberal Temper in Greek Politics*. New Haven, Conn.: Yale University Press.

———. 1967. *Preface to Plato*. New York: Grosset & Dunlop.

Hefner, Christie. 1987, January–February. "Meese Commission: Sex, Violence, and Censorship." *Humanist* 48: 25–29, 46.

Hefner, Hugh. 1986, January. "Sexual McCarthyism." *Playboy* 33: 58–59.

Herbst, Susan. 1993. *Numbered Voices: How Opinion Polling Has Shaped American Politics*. Chicago: University of Chicago Press.

Hertzberg, Hendrik. 1986, 14/21 July. "Big Boobs." *New Republic* 207: 21–24.

Hiaasen, Carl. 1986, December. "Commentary." *Playboy* 33: 53.

Higgins, Patricia J. 1984. "Anthropologists and Issues of Public Concern: The Iranian Crisis." *Human Organization* 43: 132–45.

Hirschman, Albert O. 1977. *The Passions and the Interests: Political Arguments for Capitalism before Its Triumph*. Princeton, N.J.: Princeton University Press.

Howe, Louis. 1934, June. "The President's Mailbag." *American Magazine* 117: 220–23, 118–20.

Howell, Wilber S. 1961. *Logic and Rhetoric in England, 1500–1700*. New York: Russell & Russell.

———. 1965. *Introduction. The Rhetoric of Alcuin & Charlemagne*. New York: Russell & Russell. 3–64.

———. 1966. "Renaissance Rhetoric and Modern Rhetoric: A Study in Change." In *The Rhetorical Idiom*, edited by Donald C. Bryant, 53–70. Ithaca, N.Y.: Cornell University Press.

Hume, David. 1888. *A Treatise of Human Nature* [1739]. Ed. L. A. Selby-Bigge. Oxford: Clarendon.

Hyde, Michael J. 1981, November. "Rethinking the 'Public': Deconstructing an Ideograph." Paper presented at *SCA Convention*. Anaheim, Calif.

Ignatieff, Michael. 1993a, 13 May. "The Balkan Tragedy." *New York Review of Books* 40: 3–5.

———. 1993b. *Blood and Belonging: Journeys into the New Nationalism*. New York: Farrar, Straus and Giroux.

————. 1994, 21 April. "Homage to Bosnia." *New York Review of Books* 41: 3–4, 6.

Jamieson, Kathleen Hall. 1992. *Dirty Politics, Deception, and Democracy.* New York: Oxford University Press.

John Paul II. 1979. *Return to Poland: The Collected Speeches of John Paul II.* Trans. L'Osservatore Romano and William Collins Sons. New York: Collins.

Johnson, Hank. 1994. "New Social Movements and Old Regional Nationalisms." In *New Social Movements: From Ideology to Identity,* edited by Enrique Laraña, Hank Johnson, and Joseph R. Gusfield, 267–86. Philadelphia: Temple University Press.

Johnstone, Henry W. 1982. "Bilaterality in Argument." In *Advances in Argumentation,* edited by J. R. Cox and C. A. Willard, 95–102. Carbondale: Southern Illinois University Press.

Jones, Alfred Haworth. 1974. *Roosevelt's Image Brokers: Poets, Playwrights, and the Use of the Lincoln Symbol.* Port Washington, N.Y.: Kennikat Press.

Jordan, Hamilton. 1982. *Crisis: The Last Year of the Carter Presidency.* New York: Putnam's.

Kamen, Michael G. 1991. *Mystic Chords of Memory: The Transformation of Tradition in American Culture.* New York: Knopf.

Katriel, Tamar. 1994. "Sites of Memory: Discourses of the Past in Israeli Pioneering Settlement Museums." *Quarterly Journal of Speech* 80: 1–20.

"Kennedy: Ready, Set, . . ." 1979, 24 September. *Time* 114: 14–17.

"Kennedy's Lead is Shrinking." 1979, 12 November. *Time* 114: 22–23.

Key, V. O. 1961. *Public Opinion and American Democracy.* New York: Knopf.

Kinsley, Michael. 1986, 12 June. "Apostle of Violence." *Washington Post,* p. A25.

Korbonski, Andrzy. 1983. "Dissent in Poland, 1956–76." In *Dissent in Eastern Europe,* edited by Jane Leftwich Curry, 25–47. New York: Praeger.

Kovacic, Branislav. 1994, 27 June. Personal interview.

Kovacic, Branislav, and Bozidar Travica. 1992. "Yugoslavia: Ethnic Dramas Without Denouement." In *Political Communication: Engineering Visions of Order in the Socialist World,* edited by Donald P. Cushman and Sarah S. King, 59–88. Albany: SUNY Press.

Kuhn, Thomas S. 1970. *The Structure of Scientific Revolutions.* 2d ed. Chicago: University of Chicago Press.

Kundera, Milan. 1981. *The Book of Laughter and Forgetting.* Trans. M. H. Heim. Baltimore, Md.: Penguin Books.

Kurtz, Howard. 1986, 10 July. "Attorney General's Panel Says Some Porn Causes Sexual Violence." *Washington Post,* pp. A1, A8.

Laber, Jeri. 1992, 23 April. "Witch Hunt in Prague." *New York Review of Books* 39: 5–6.

————. 1993, 25 March. "Bosnia: Questions About Rape." *New York Review of Books* 40: 3–4, 6.

Lakatos, Imre. 1968. "II—Criticism and the Methodology of Scientific Research Programmes." *Proceedings of the Aristotelian Society* 69: 149–86.

Landes, Joan. 1988. *Women in the Public Sphere in the Age of the French Revolution.* Ithaca, N.Y.: Cornell University Press.

————. 1992. "Jürgen Habermas, The Structural Transformation of the Public Sphere: A Feminist Inquiry." *Praxis International* 12: 106–27.

Laraña, Enrique, Hank Johnson, and Joseph R. Gusfield, eds. 1994. *New Social Movements.* Philadelphia: Temple University Press.

Lasch, Christopher. 1978. *The Culture of Narcissism.* New York: W. W. Norton.

————. 1995. *The Revolt of the Elites.* New York: W. W. Norton.

Lazarsfeld, Paul F., Bernard Berelsen, and Hazel Gaudet. 1968. *The People's Choice: How the Voter Makes Up His Mind in a Presidential Election* [1944]. 3d ed. New York: Columbia University Press.

Leff, Michael. 1995, March. "Hermeneutical Rhetoric and the Construction of Community." Paper presented at CCCC Convention. Washington, D.C.

"Letters." 1981a, 16 February. *Time:* 4–5.

"Letters." 1981b, 23 February. *Time:* 5–8.

"Letters." 1992, May. *Harper's* 284: 4–7, 72–78.

Link, Perry. 1989, 29 June. "The Chinese Intellectuals and the Revolt." *New York Review of Books* 36: 38–41.

Lippmann, Walter. 1949. *Public Opinion* [1922]. New York: Free Press.

Lipton, Morris S. 1986, 18 July. "No, the Evidence Against Porn is Shoddy." *Los Angeles Times,* sec. 2, p. 5.

Lizhi, Fang. 1989, 2 February. "China's Despair and China's Hope." *New York Review of Books* 36: 3–4.

Locke, John. 1959. *An Essay Concerning Human Understanding* [1689–1691]. 2 vols. New York: Dover.

Loraux, Nicole. 1986. *The Invention of Athens: The Funeral Oration in the Classical City.* Trans. Alan Sheridan. Cambridge: Harvard University Press.

Lord, Albert B. 1971. *The Singer of Tales.* New York: Atheneum.

Lowell, A. Lawrence. 1913. *Public Opinion and Popular Government.* New York: Longmans Green.

Lubell, Samuel. 1956. *The Future of American Politics.* 2d ed. New York: Doubleday.

Lydgate, William A. 1944. *What Our People Think.* New York: Thomas Y. Crowell.

Lyotard, Jean-François. 1984. *The Postmodern Condition: A Report on Knowledge.* Trans. Geoff Bennington and Brian Massumi. Minneapolis: University of Minnesota Press.

MacIntyre, Alasdair. 1984. *After Virtue.* 2d ed. Notre Dame, Ind.: University of Notre Dame Press.

Mailloux, Steven. 1989. *Rhetorical Power.* Ithaca, N.Y.: Cornell University Press.

Malcolm, Noel. 1993. *Bosnia: A Short History.* New York: Macmillan.

Mann, Judy. 1986, 23 July. "Censorship's Nose in the Text." *Washington Post* p. 33.

Marcuse, Herbert. 1964. *One Dimensional Man.* Boston: Beacon.

McDaniel, Ann. 1986, 21 July. "A Salvo in the Porn War." *Newsweek* 120: 18.

McElvaine, Robert S. ed. 1983. *Down & Out in the Great Depression: Letters from the Forgotten Man.* Chapel Hill: University of North Carolina Press.

McGee, Michael Calvin. 1975. "In Search of 'The People': A Rhetorical Alternative." *Quarterly Journal of Speech* 65: 235–49.

————. 1977. "The Fall of Wellington: A Case Study of the Relationship Between Theory, Practice, and Rhetoric in History." *Quarterly Journal of Speech* 63: 28–42.

McGee, Michael Calvin, and Martha Anne Martin. 1983. "Public Knowledge and Ideological Argumentation." *Communication Monographs* 50: 47–65.

McKeon, Richard. 1942. "Rhetoric in the Middle Ages." *Speculum: A Journal of Medieval Studies* 17:1–32.

————. 1956. "Dialectic and Political Thought and Action." *Ethics* 65: 1–33.

————. 1957. "Communication, Truth, and Society." *Ethics* 67: 89–99.

———. 1969. "Discourse, Demonstration, Verification, Justification." In *Legique et Analyse* 11: 37–55.

———. 1971. "The Uses of Rhetoric in a Technological Age: Architectonic Productive Arts." In *The Prospect of Rhetoric*, edited by Lloyd F. Bitzer and Edwin Black, 44–63. Englewood Cliffs, N.J.: Prentice-Hall.

———. 1973. *Introduction to Aristotle.* 2d ed. Chicago: University of Chicago Press.

———. 1987. *Rhetoric: Essays in Invention and Discovery.* Ed. Mark Backman. Woodbridge, Conn.: Oxbow Press.

McMullin, Ernan. 1974. "Two Faces of Science." *Review of Metaphysics* 27: 655–76.

Meadwell, Hudson. 1995. "Post-Marxism, No Friend of Civility." In *Civil Society: Theory, History, Comparison*, edited by John A. Hall, 183–99. Cambridge: Polity.

Merrick, Frank. 1980, 30 June. "At the Bridge of Sighs." *Time* 115: 10–11.

Merton, Robert K. 1963. "Introduction." In *Dear FDR: A Study of Political Letter-Writing*, by Leila Sussmann, v–xxv. Totowa, N.J.: Bedminster Press.

Mianowicz, Tomasz. 1989. "Polish Pope, Polish Church and Polish State." *Survey* 30: 131–54.

Michnik, Adam. 1981. "What We Want To Do and What We Can Do." *Telos* 47: 66–77.

———. 1985. *Letters form Prison.* Trans. Maya Latynski. Berkeley: University of California Press.

———. 1993, 10 June. "An Embarrassing Anniversary." *New York Review of Books* 40: 19–21.

Miller v. *California.* 1973. 413 US 15.

Mills, C. Wright. 1957. *The Power Elite.* New York: Oxford University Press.

———. 1963. *Power, Politics, and People.* Ed. Irving Horowitz. New York: Oxford University Press.

Negt, Oskar, and Alexander Kluge. 1967. "The Proletarian Public Sphere." In *Communication and Class Struggle*, vol. 2, edited by Armand Mattelart and Seth Siegelaub, 92–94. New York: Bangolet.

Nelson, Milo. 1986, September. "Meese's Peep Show." *Wilson Library Bulletin* 60: 4.

Nicholas, H. G. 1945. "Roosevelt and Public Opinion." *Fortnightly* 157: 303–8.

Nisbet, Robert. 1975. "Public Opinion versus Popular Opinion." *Public Interest* 41: 166–92.

Noelle-Neumann, Elisabeth. 1989. "Advances in Spiral of Silence Research." *KEIO Communication Review* 10: 3–49.

———. 1993. *The Spiral of Silence: Public Opinion—Our Social Skin.* 2d ed. Chicago: University of Chicago Press.

Norr, Henry. 1982. "Poland and the Logic of Solidarity." *Survey* 26: 184–91.

Nussbaum, Martha C. 1986. *The Fragility of Goodness.* New York: Cambridge University Press.

Official File 2526. 1938–1940. "Third Term." Hyde Park, N.Y.: Franklin D. Roosevelt Library.

Official File 4040. 1940. "Wendel Willkie, October 1940." Hyde Park, N.Y.: Franklin D. Roosevelt Library.

Olson, Elder. 1976. *On Value Judgment in the Arts and Other Essays.* Chicago: University of Chicago Press.

"Out of the Rose Garden." 1980, 12 May. *Time* 115: 31.

Palczewski, Catherine. 1995. "Survivor Testimony in the Pornography Controversy: Assessing Credibility in the Minneapolis Hearings and the Attorney General's Report." In *Warranting Assent: Case Studies in Argument Evaluation* ed. by Edward Schiappa, 257–81. Albany, N.Y.: SUNY Press.

Park, Robert E. 1940. "News as a Form of Knowledge: A Chapter in the Sociology of Knowledge." *American Journal of Sociology* 45: 669–86.

Parmet, Herbert A., and Marie B. Hecht. 1968. *Never Again: A President Runs for a Third Term.* New York: Macmillan.

Pelczynski, Z. A. 1988. "Solidarity and the Rebirth of Civil Society." In *Civil Society and the State,* edited by John Keane. London: Verso.

Perelman, Ch., and L. Olbrechts-Tyteca. 1969. *The New Rhetoric* [1957]. Trans. John Wilkinson and Purcell Weaver. Notre Dame, Ind.: Notre Dame University Press.

Peterson, Merrill D. 1994. *Lincoln in American Memory.* New York: Oxford University Press.

Petrovic, Bishop Petar II (Njegos). 1986. *The Mountain Wreath.* Trans. Vasa D. Mihailovich. Irvine, Calif.: Charles Schlacks, Jr.

Phillips, Kendall R. 1996. "The Spaces of Public Dissension: Reconsidering the Public Sphere." *Communication Monographs* 63: 231–48.

Piven, Frances Fox, and Richard A. Cloward. 1988. *Why Americans Don't Vote.* New York: Pantheon Books.

Plato. 1961. *Protagoras.* Trans. W. K. C. Guthrie. In *The Collected Dialogues of Plato,* edited by Edith Hamilton and Huntington Cairns. New York: Pantheon.

Pollard, James E. Summer. 1959. "The White House News Conference as a Channel of Communication." *Public Opinion Quarterly* 23: 663–78.

The Pope in Poland. 1979. Munich: Radio Free Europe Research.

"Pope John Paul II in Poland." 1979. *Survey* 24: 230–36.

Popkin, Samuel. 1991. *The Reasoning Voter: Communication and Persuasion in Presidential Campaigns.* Chicago: University of Chicago Press.

Poulakos, John. 1983. "Toward a Sophistic Definition of Rhetoric." *Philosophy and Rhetoric* 16: 35–48.

———. 1990. "Interpreting Sophistical Rhetoric: A Response to Schiappa." *Philosophy and Rhetoric* 23: 218–28.

Poulakos, Takis. 1990. "Historiographies of the Tradition of Rhetoric: A Brief History of Classical Funeral Orations." *Western Journal of Speech Communication* 54: 172–88.

Powell, Jody. 1984. *The Other Side of the Story.* New York: William Morrow.

President's Personal File 675. 1938–1941. *New York Times* folder. Hyde Park, N.Y.: Franklin D. Roosevelt Library.

President's Select File 147. 1940. Early folder, 28 May. Hyde Park, N.Y.: Franklin D. Roosevelt Library.

Quinn, Krystal. 1986, 7 August. "Ex-Bunny Leads Antipornography Rally." *Washington Post,* p. C4.

Ragland, James. 1962. "Merchandisers of the First Amendment: Freedom and Responsibility of the Press in the Age of Roosevelt, 1933–40." *Georgia Review* 16: 366–91.

Rangel, Jesus. 1986, 26 July. "Church Leaders Make a Target of Pornography." *New York Times,* p. A31.

Reeves, Richard. 1995, 27 March. "The Polls Are Clinton's One Real Constituency." *Boulder Daily Camera,* p. C3.

"Report on the State of the Republic." 1980. *Survey* 25: 3–18.

Richards, I. A. 1965. *The Philosophy of Rhetoric* [1936]. New York: Oxford University Press.

Ricoeur, Paul. 1981. *Hermeneutics and the Human Sciences*. Ed. and trans. John B. Thompson. Cambridge: Cambridge University Press.

———. 1990. *Time and Narrative*. Vol 3. Chicago: University of Chicago Press.

Riesman, D., et al. 1961. *The Lonely Crowd*. New Haven, Conn.: Yale University Press.

Robbins, Bruce, ed. 1993. *The Phantom Public Sphere*. Minneapolis: University of Minnesota Press.

Robinson, Edgar Eugene. 1955. *The Roosevelt Leadership 1933–1945*. Philadelphia: Lippincott.

Rodger, John J. 1985. "On the Degeneration of the Public Sphere." *Political Studies* 33: 203–17.

Roper, Elmer. 1957. *You and Your Leaders: Their Actions and Your Reactions, 1936–1956*. New York: William Morrow and Company.

Roseboom, Eugene H. 1957. *A History of Presidential Elections*. New York: Macmillan.

Rosenman, Samuel I. 1952. *Working with Roosevelt*. New York: Harper.

Roth v. United States. 1957. 354 US 476.

Rousseau, Jean Jacques. 1986. *The First and Second Discourses*. Trans. and ed. Victor Gourevitch. New York: Harper.

Ryan, Mary. 1992. "Gender and Public Access: Women's Politics in Nineteenth-Century America." In *Habermas and the Public Sphere*, edited by Craig Calhoun, 259–88. Cambridge: MIT Press.

Ryan, Paul B. 1985. *The Iranian Rescue Mission: Why It Failed*. Annapolis, Md.: Naval Institute Press.

Sagan, Eli. 1991. *The Honey and the Hemlock*. New York: Basic.

Said, Edward W. 1981, January. "Inside Islam." *Harper's* 280: 25–32.

Salinger, Pierre. 1981. *America Held Hostage*. Garden City, N.Y.: Doubleday.

Scammell, Michael. 1990a. "The New Yugoslavia." *New York Review of Books* 37: 12, 37–42.

———. 1990b. "Yugoslavia: The Awakening." *New York Review of Books* 37: 11, 42–47.

Scheer, Robert. 1986a, 1 May. "Commission Founders on Limits to Sex." *Los Angeles Times*, pp. A1, A24.

———. 1986b, August. "Inside the Meese Commission." *Playboy* 33: 60–61, 157–67.

Schiappa, Edward. 1990a. "History and Neo Sophistic Criticism: A Reply to Poulakos." *Philosophy and Rhetoric* 23: 307–15.

———. 1990b. "Neo Sophistic Rhetorical Criticism or the Historical Reconstruction of Sophistic Doctrines?" *Philosophy and Rhetoric* 23: 192–217.

Schram, Martin. 1980. "Carter." In *Pursuit of the Presidency 1980*, edited by Richard Harwood, 83–120. New York: G. Press/Putnam's Sons.

Schudson, Michael. 1992. "Was There Ever a Public Sphere? If So, When? Reflections on the American Case." In *Habermas and the Public Sphere*, edited by Craig Calhoun, 143–63. Cambridge: MIT Press.

Scott, Robert L. 1967. "On Viewing Rhetoric as Epistemic." *Central States Speech Journal* 18: 9–17.

Seligman, Adam. 1992. *The Idea of Civil Society*. New York: Free Press.

———. 1995. "Animadversions upon Civil Society and Civic Virtue in the Last

Decade of the Twentieth Century." In *Civil Society: Theory, History, Comparison*, edited by John A. Hall, 200–223. Cambridge: Polity.

———. 1997. *The Problem of Trust*. Princeton, N.J.: Princeton University Press.

Sells, Michael A. 1996. *The Bridge Betrayed: Religion and Genocide in Bosnia*. Berkeley: University of California Press.

Sennett, Richard. 1978. *The Fall of Public Man*. New York: Vintage.

———. 1980. *Authority*. New York: Knopf.

———. 1994. *Flesh and Stone: The Body and the City in Western Civilization*. New York: Norton.

Sharbutt, Jay. 1986, 30 May. "Mahoney's Porn Attack Zero's in on Cable TV." *Los Angeles Times*, pp. V1, V14.

Shenon, Philip. 1986a, 18 May. "A Second Opinion on Pornography's Impact." *New York Times*, p. E8.

———. 1986b, 20 May. "Playboy and Booksellers Suing Playboy Panel." *New York Times*, p. A24.

Sidey, Hugh. 1980, 18 February. "Refuge in the Rose Garden." *Time* 115: 24.

Smith, Adam. 1969. *The Theory of Moral Sentiments* [1790]. 6th ed. Indianapolis: Liberty Classics.

Smith, Ira T., and Joe Alex Morris. 1949. *"Dear Mr. President . . ."* The Story of Fifty Years in the White House Mail Room. New York: Julian Messner.

Smith, Jack. 1986, 29 May. "Pornography and Censorship: The Argument Rages on, 25 Years after 'Tropic of Cancer.'" *Los Angeles Times* p. V1.

Solomon, Robert C. 1976. *The Passions*. Garden City, N.Y.: Anchor Press.

Speier, Hans. 1950. "Historical Development of Public Opinion." *American Journal of Sociology* 55: 376–88.

Stearney, Lynn. 1992. "Private Expression in the Public Sphere: The Rhetoric of Contemporary Feminism and Its Implications for an Understanding of Public Discourse in Rhetorical Theory and Criticism." Diss., Pennsylvania State University.

Stengel, Richard. 1986, 21 July. "Sex Busters." *Time* 121: 12–22.

Stehle, Hansjakob. 1982. "Church and Pope in the Polish Crisis." *World Today* 38: 139–47.

Stein, Charles W. 1943. *The Third Term Tradition: Its Rise and Collapse in American Politics*. New York: Columbia University Press.

Stevenson, Charles L. 1944. *Ethics and Language*. New Haven, Conn.: Yale University Press.

Stewart, Susan. 1991. *Crimes of Writing*. New York: Oxford University Press.

"Still Looking for a Leader." 1979, 10 September. *Time* 114: 10–11.

Stump, Eleonore. 1978. *Introduction. Boethius's De topicis differentiis*. Ithaca, N.Y.: Cornell University Press.

Sussmann, Leila A. 1963. *Dear FDR: A Study of Political Letter-Writing*. Totowa, N.J.: Bedminster Press.

Szczypiorski, Andrzej. 1982. *The Polish Ordeal: The View from Within*. Trans. Celina Wieniewska. London: Croom Helm.

Taylor, Charles. 1971. "Interpretation and the Sciences of Man." *Review of Metaphysics* 25: 3–51.

———. 1985. "Social Theory as a Practice." In *Charles Taylor, Philosophy and the Human Sciences: Philosophical Papers*, vol. 2, 91–115. Cambridge: Cambridge University Press.

————. 1991. "Language and Society." In *Communicative Action,* edited by Axel Honneth and Hans Joas. Cambridge: MIT Press.

————. 1995. *Philosophical Arguments.* Cambridge: Harvard University Press.

Taylor, D. Garth. 1986. *Public Opinion and Collective Action: The Boston School Desegregation Conflict.* Chicago: University of Chicago Press.

Taylor, John. 1981. *Five Months with Solidarity.* London: Wildwood House.

Thackaberry, Jennifer. 1997. "Discursive Border Crossings and Charitable Organizations' Resistance to Co-optation in Welfare Reform." National Communication Association, Chicago.

"Talk of the Town." 1980, 12 May. *New Yorker* 56: 31–36.

"Talk of the Town." 1980, 2 June. *New Yorker* 56: 29–33.

Thucydides. 1951. *The Peloponesian War.* Trans. John H. Finley Jr. New York: Random House.

Tisdale, Sallie. 1992, February. "Talk Dirty to Me: A Woman's Taste for Pornography." *Harper's* 284: 37–46.

————. 1994. *Talk Dirty to Me: An Intimate Philosophy of Sex.* New York: Bantam.

Tomsky, Alexander. 1979. "John Paul II in Poland: Pilgrim of the Holy Spirit." *Religion in Communist Lands* 7: 160–65.

Touraine, Alain. 1977. *The Self-Production of Society.* Trans. Derek Coltman. Chicago: University of Chicago Press.

————. 1981. *The Voice and the Eye: An Analysis of Social Movements.* Trans. Alan Duff. Cambridge: Cambridge University Press.

————. 1988. *Return of the Actor.* Trans. M. Godzich. Minneapolis: University of Minnesota Press.

"Transcript of the President's New Conference on Foreign and Domestic Matters." 1980, 19 February. *New York Times* p. A16.

Tulis, Jeffrey. 1987. *The Rhetorical Presidency.* Princeton, N.J.: Princeton University Press.

————. 1996. "Revising the Rhetorical Presidency." In *Beyond the Rhetorical Presidency,* edited by Martin J. Medhurst, 3–14. College Station: Texas A&M University Press.

Turkel, Studs. 1970. *Hard Times: An Oral History of the Great Depression.* New York: Random House.

Turowicz, Jerzy. 1973. "The Changing Catholicism in Poland." In *Gierek's Poland,* edited by Adam Bromke and John W. Strong, 151–57. New York: Praeger.

"U.S. Attitudes: Unity and Strength." 1980, 7 January. *Time* 115: 18.

Unfinished Peace: Report of the International Commission on the Balkans. 1996. Foreword by Leo Tindemans. Washington, D.C.: Carnegie Endowment for International Peace.

United States. Department of Justice. 1986. *Final Report of the Attorney General's Commission on Pornography.* Washington, D.C.

United States. Department of State. 1970, 11 May. "A Report on Progress in Viet-Nam. Address by President Nixon." In *Department of State Bulletin* [*DOSB*] 62: 601–4.

————. 1979a, December. "President's Announcement, November 12, 1979." *DOSB* 79: 50.

————. 1979b, December. "Remarks at the Thirteenth Constitutional Convention of the AFL-CIO, in Washington, D.C. on November 15, 1979." *DOSB* 79: 18–20.

———. 1979c, December. "Secretary's Statement, November 8, 1979." *DOSB* 79: 49.

———. 1980a, January. "Ambassador McHenry, November 27, 1979" [remarks to the UN Security Council]. *DOSB* 80: 49–50.

———. 1980b, January. "Ambassador McHenry, December 1, 1979" [remarks to the UN Security Council]. *DOSB* 80: 50–51.

———. 1980c, January. "News Conference of November 28." *DOSB* 80: 1–4.

———. 1980d, February. "State of the Union Address" [23 January 1980]. *DOSB* 80: A–C.

———. 1980e, February. "U.S. Seeks Sanctions Against Iran." [remarks to reporters assembled in the White House Briefing Room, 21 December 1980]. *DOSB* 80: 53.

———. 1980f, February. "Vice President Mondale, December 5, 1979" [remarks made to reporters assembled in the White House Briefing Room]. *DOSB* 80: 55.

———. 1980g, March. "Hostages in Iran" [remarks by the president at a White House briefing for members of Congress, 8 January 1980]. *DOSB* 80: 33–35.

———. 1980h, March. "Interview for NBC News" [7 January 1980]. *DOSB* 80: 32.

———. 1980i, March. "Meet the Press Interview" [20 January 1980]. *DOSB* 80: 29–31.

———. 1980j, May. "Deputy Secretary Christopher Interviewed on 'Issues and Answers'" [13 April 1980]. *DOSB* 80: 25–28.

———. 1980k, May. "News Conference of April 17." *DOSB* 80: 8–11.

———. 1980l, May. "U.S. Course in a Changing World" [remarks to the American Society of Newspaper Editors in Washington, D.C. on 10 April 1980]. *DOSB* 80: 3–8.

———. 1980m, May. "U.S. Foreign Policy: Our Broader Strategy" [statement before the Senate Foreign Relations Committee, 27 March 1980]. *DOSB* 80: 16–25.

———. 1980n, June. "National Security Adviser Brzezinski Interviewed on 'Issues and Answers'" [27 April 1980]. *DOSB* 80: 47–49.

———. 1980o, June. "Secretary Brown's News Conference, April 25, 1980 [12:15 P.M.]." *DOSB* 80: 39–42.

United States. Office of the Federal Register. 1979. "1980 Democratic Presidential Nomination: The President's Remarks Concerning His Candidacy and Campaign Plans. December 2, 1979." *Weekly Compilation of Presidential Documents* [*WCPD*] 15: 2194.

———. 1980a. "Flint Michigan: Interview with Joe Straud and Remer Tyson of the Detroit Free Press, October 1, 1980." *WCPD* 16: 2013.

———. 1980b. "Interview with the President: Question-and-Answer Session with Reporters from Pennsylvania." *WCPD* 16: 744–45.

———. 1980c. "Interview with the President: Question-and-Answer Session with Reporters from Westinghouse Broadcasting Company." *WCPD* 16: 733.

———. 1980d. "The President's News Conference of April 17, 1980." *WCPD* 16: 744–45.

———. 1980e. "White House Briefing for Civic and Community Leaders: Remarks and a Question-and Answer Session. April 10, 1980." *WCPD* 16: 804.

Vance, Carole S. 1986, 2/9 August. "The Meese Commission on the Road." *Nation* 255: 65, 76–82.

Vance, Cyrus. 1983. *Hard Choices.* New York: Simon and Schuster.

von Wright, G. H. 1971. *Explanation and Understanding.* Ithaca, N.Y.: Cornell University Press.

Wald, Matthew. 1986, 16 June. "'Adult' Magazines Lose Sales as 8,000 Stores Forbid Them." *New York Times,* pp. A1, A14.

Wallace, Carl. 1963. "The Substance of Rhetoric: Good Reasons." *Quarterly Journal of Speech* 49: 239–49.

Ward, Geoffrey C. 1989. *A First-Class Temperament: The Emergence of Franklin Roosevelt.* New York: Harper.

Weaver, Richard. 1953. *The Ethics of Rhetoric.* Chicago: Henry Regnery.

———. 1964. *Visions of Order: The Cultural Analysis of Our Time.* Baton Rouge: Louisiana State University Press.

Weber, Max. 1968. "Bureaucracy." In *Economy and Society,* edited by Guenther Roth and Claus Wittich, 956–1005. New York: Bedminster.

Weimer, Walter B. 1979. *Notes on the Methodology of Scientific Research.* Hillsdale, N.J.: Lawrence Erlbaum.

Weisbord, Marvin. 1966. *Campaigning for President: A New Look at the Road to the White House.* New York: Washington Square Press.

Wells, Susan. 1996. *Sweet Reason: Rhetoric and the Discourses of Modernity.* Chicago: University of Chicago Press.

Weschler, Lawrence. 1982. *The Passion of Poland: From Solidarity Through the State of War.* New York: Pantheon

White, Graham J. 1979. *FDR and the Press.* Chicago: University of Chicago Press.

White, James Boyd. 1984. *When Words Lose their Meaning.* Chicago: University of Chicago Press.

Wichelns, Herbert. 1958. "Literary Criticism of Oratory." In *The Rhetorical Idiom,* edited by Donald C. Bryant, 5–42. Ithaca, N.Y.: Cornell University Press.

Wines, Michael, and Jay Sharbutt. 1986, 10 July. "Critics See Report as a Reflection of Rising Intolerance." *Los Angeles Times,* pp. I1, I15.

Yankelovich, Daniel. 1991. *Coming to Public Judgment: Making Democracy Work in Complex World.* Syracuse, N.Y.: Syracuse University Press.

Zyskind, Harold. 1968. "A Case Study in Philosophical Rhetoric: Theodore Roosevelt." *Philosophy and Rhetoric* 1: 228–54.

INDEX